BRAGGING RIGHTS

A Season Inside the

Football's Toughest
Conference

BRAGGING RIGHTS

A Season Inside the

SEC

Football's Toughest
Conference

Richard Ernsberger, Jr.

M. Evans and Company, Inc.
New York

M. Evans and Company, Inc.
216 East 49th Street
New York, New York 10017

Library of Congress Cataloging-in-Publication Data

Ernsberger, Richard.
    Bragging rights : a season inside the SEC, football's toughest conference
/ by Richard Ernsberger
      p. cm.
    ISBN 0-87131-926-8
    1. Southeastern Conference. 2. Football—Southern States. I. Title.
GV958.5.S59 E75 2000
796.332'63'0975—dc21   00-058717

Book design by Rik Lain Schell

Printed in the United States of America

9 8 7 6 5 4 3 2 1

For Betsy and Alex

CONTENTS

ROUGHNECKS AND ROMANCE:

An Introduction to the SEC

It was *good* to be back in the South. After twelve years in New York City and two years in Tokyo with *Newsweek* magazine, during which time I wrote mostly esoteric foreign news stories, I was getting back to my roots—major-college southern football. I'd decided to write a book about Southeastern Conference (SEC) football—specifically, the 1999 season, which promised, like all SEC seasons, to be both wild and unpredictable, with a dozen roughneck teams and millions of fanatical fans, galvanized by another quest for supremacy in America's toughest conference.

The South is a region that I love, and had nearly forgotten. It's a place where you can still find people named Thurl, Longstreet, and Lurleen (George Wallace's wife); where people drawwwl and drink whiskey (happily); where men still work on carburetors and (occasionally) women wrestle alligators; where you can buy crickets for three cents each out of a box in the back room of a Macon gas station (a wrong turn on the way to Athens, and don't ask about the *Deliverance* character who was tending to the crickets); where they grow Vidalia onions, okra, and cotton; where Spanish moss grows on live oaks; where you can drink sweetened tea and eat grits, not to mention indulge a hankering for succulent barbecue at a thousand and one places with names like Dreamland and Sonny's; where you can still see billboards extolling naked dancers (WE BARE ALL) and historical fellowship (SONS OF CONFEDERATE VETERANS, JOIN NOW!); where bible-thumping Baptist preachers still holler at the damned (with righteous indignation); where magnolia trees and stately Greek revival mansions grace the landscape; where pawnshops and trailer homes (price: $20,000) are *respectable*; where you can still hear *country* songs, with *country* lyrics: "Got a six-pack and a bottle of wine, gotta be bent to have a good time." Where the plangent voice of Patsy Cline and the gutsy blues of Johnny Cash still rise blessedly out of the gloaming as you cruise into Memphis on a moonlit Friday night.

And while the South has changed dramatically in recent years—acquired a more prosperous sheen thanks partly to foreign manufacturers like Daimler-

Chrysler and BMW, which have plopped several major plants in the region—you can still find plenty of classic ne'er-do-wells. You know, folks who get "likkered up"—and then, if they're lucky, find somebody with whom to "get nekkid." One often follows the other.

The South is a place with few pretensions and, still, plenty of rough-hewn individuals—good ol' boys who are lots more into huntin' and fishin' than watching MTV. When I lived in the athletic dorm at the University of Tennessee in the late 1970s, I knew guys who would chew tobacco, dip Skoal, smoke a cigarette, and drink a beer—all at the same time. And the gals can be tough, too. You *don't* go into a gas station "quick mart" in Ocala, Florida, as I did early one morning, and ask for a fresh pot of coffee and some half-and-half to go with it. If you do, a middle-aged female cashier with an unfortunate face—who's chain-smoking Virginia Slims at 8:00 in the morning—will shoot you a suspicious "You ain't funny, are ya?" glance. You decide you don't want to displease this grizzled woman, who's probably got man troubles and just came off another long, boozy night. "Uh," you stutter, "that icky, muck-on-the-bottom-of-the-pot coffee will be just fine—and I'd forgotten how much I enjoy powdered cream."

The South is a place where people don't have a fetish about their "career"; where peccadilloes are plentiful and human frailties (mostly) forgiven. It's a place with one of the funniest words in the world—Arkadelphia. Say it out loud. It's a place known to anybody who's read Eudora Welty and William Faulkner, whose lovely old home is nestled a short distance from the University of Mississippi campus. In the South, men still throw empty Bud cans on the highway (I saw it), and women still make chicken salad and chase men.

And lest I go on too long, it's also a place where damn near everybody—governors, cooks, barmaids, and lawyers—cares deeply and truly about college football.

College football matters in the South. It has for more than 100 years. In 1891 Charles Herty, a twenty-four-year-old chemistry professor at the University of Georgia, introduced the game of football to his alma mater. Herty had become fascinated with the game as a graduate student at Johns Hopkins. One day Herty walked across an old campus field where Georgia students participated in unorganized recreation. The field was bordered by Moore College on one side, New College on the other; the university chapel was situated on one of the corners. Herty was remembered as carrying a Walter Camp rule book that day for a new style of rugby know as "football." Herty persuaded some students to take up the game he had seen in the East, and he helped prepare a field on the quadrangle that would soon be named Herty Field. A few months later, a great tradition was born: Georgia and Mercer College played the first football game in the deep South.

While studying at Johns Hopkins, Herty had made friends with a man named George Petrie. He later became a faculty member at Auburn—and that university's first football coach. Through their friendship, Herty and Petrie arranged a football game between Georgia and Auburn. On February 20, 1892, the two teams met in Atlanta's Piedmont Park. It was the start of the South's oldest rivalry. Auburn beat Georgia, 10-0. The sport caught on in a hurry—and fed into the region's primal instincts. Writer W. J. Cash described "the southern pioneer [who] began to exhibit a kind of mounting exultancy, which issued in a tendency to frisk and cavort, to posture, to play the slashing hell of a fellow—a notable expansion of the ego testifying at once to his rising individualism and the burgeoning of the romantic and hedonistic spirit." Many southern "slashing hell fellows" would play football, and the fans would latch onto its spirit.

The Southeastern Conference (SEC) began play a few decades later, in 1933. There were thirteen teams originally, and ten of those universities are still SEC members: Auburn, Alabama, Florida, Georgia, Mississippi, Mississippi State, Kentucky, Louisiana State, Tennessee, and Vanderbilt. Georgia Tech, Tulane, and Swanee dropped out, and in 1992 two new schools joined: Arkansas and South Carolina. At that time, the twelve-team conference was divided into divisions—East and West. The winners of each division play annually in Atlanta for the SEC championship.

How much do southerners care about football? Not long after Bill Curry took over as coach at the University of Alabama in 1989, his wife got a call from the couple's Methodist minister in Atlanta. The minister, Bill Floyd, asked Mrs. Curry how the couple was faring. "Well," she replied, "you know football is a religion down here." "Oh, no," said Floyd, "it's much more important than that."

How true. In the SEC, the football traditions are old and deeply cherished. In fact, college football is one of the few things which, in a sense, divides the South. When the time comes to tee up the pigskin, the South stops being a region and reverts to earlier times: it becomes a collection of hugely competitive states, each with an overweening pride in its major-college football team. Autumn Saturdays are reserved for feuding—for trash-talking and a settling of grievances as twenty-two young men throw themselves at one another on verdant fields—in Oxford and Knoxville, Gainesville and Tuscaloosa, Auburn and Athens, Baton Rouge, Lexington, and Starkville.

Football games? They're atavistic, primal fights—two-men-in-a-steel-cage survival tests—and, as some would joke, those are just the fans. At issue: who's got the toughest and most talented group of athletes, who can claim bragging rights in a sport that falls just behind God and family on the region's priority list. "College football touches people here," says Charles Wilson, who heads the Center for the Study of Southern Culture at Ole Miss. "It's very much tied up with our value system."

BRAGGING RIGHTS

"Ten minutes till Alabama-Tennessee," proclaims the public address man at Bryant-Denny Stadium in Tuscaloosa. If you are in any way associated with either of those states, either of those universities, that simple utterance—signifying that the annual blood match is about to commence—will send chills down your spine. If you've ever spent Saturday night in the Swamp, a raucous bandbox that's home to Steve Spurrier's Florida Gators, you will need no further tutoring on the shibboleths of major-college southern football. It is nothing but intense.

SEC football is Georgia fans collectively woofing like, well, dogs. (Georgia has got some of the best expressions in college football: the Bulldog defense is expected to "hunker down," the players wear "silver britches," and when things are going well, the fans yell: "Go, you hairy dogs!") SEC football is the Louisiana State University (LSU) band playing "Tiger Rag" and making a four-corner salute to a Cajun crowd stoked up on crayfish and bourbon; it's the Auburn Plainsmen and their Toomer's Corner tradition (the students "roll" trees outside Toomer's drug store after every home victory); it's the soft strains of Dixie (toned down in recent years) wafting over a Mississippi Saturday night.

Football matters in the South. It matters whether Tennessee can whip Alabama—or vice versa; whether Georgia can beat Florida; whether LSU can topple Ole Miss; whether Auburn can wax South Carolina—not in the cosmic scheme of things, of course, but very deeply in the practical sense. "In the SEC, every Saturday game is like the Super Bowl," says Jesse Palmer, a Canadian-born quarterback for the University of Florida. The psyche of states, the self-esteem of alums and students, and the economic well-being of the modest burghers in these quaint, gritty college towns all hang in the balance on game days. "Football has a life of its own down here," says SEC Commissioner Roy Kramer.

"Energy and Passion"

The demand for tickets to SEC games is overwhelming. At the more successful schools, such as Florida, Tennessee, Alabama, Auburn, and Georgia, fans must contribute roughly $2,000 to their university's athletic department just to be *eligible* to buy two season tickets. And those seats will be in the end zone. "The energy and passion in the SEC is pretty amazing," says Florida Athletic Director Jeremy Foley, who was raised in New Hampshire and went to Hobart College. In mid-April, when football tickets go on sale at the University of Florida, it's nearly impossible to get a telephone call into the school's athletic department. For some reason, its phone system is tangled up with the ticket office. The lines are always busy. South Carolina was the SEC's worst team in 1998, with a 1-10 record. Never very strong in football, the Gamecocks have won only one bowl game in the school's history. Against such a dreary backdrop, one might expect that South Carolinians would be indifferent to their football program. Who wouldn't be after years of mediocrity or worse? They are not. South Carolina has one of the biggest stadiums in America, seating 85,000, and it is filled for every home game. Despite being a conference doormat, South Carolina's total annual attendance ranks in the top ten nationally. The Gamecocks have 55,000 season ticket holders! LSU has been fairly awful for years. No matter: they're adding 11,000 seats to their stadium. Tennessee once drew 70,000 fans to its *spring intrasquad* game.

No SEC team ever gives up the quest for football glory. South Carolina hired Lou Holtz to breathe life into its football program. Holtz, who seems to be a cross between Woody Allen and Elmer Gantry, is one of the best-ever coaches in college football. To get him, South Carolina is paying Holtz about $600,000 annually, and that doesn't include his house, which the university bought for him. The Gamecocks got away cheap: this past year, LSU hired Nick Saban, the former Michigan State coach, to save its faltering football team. His pay package totals $1 million a year. It's hard to imagine that happening at Indiana or Iowa State.

Most college football fans are content to attend a game—to get out of the house on a Saturday afternoon. They enjoy the weather, the food, the color, the pageantry—and it's nice if the old school wins one. Southern fans are a *little* more serious. Oh, they like the fall foliage, the tailgating, hanging out with friends. Southern fans don't merely watch games—they suffer through them until the outcome is clear. There is too much at stake, sadly—too much bone-deep state and personal pride—for it to be otherwise. You soldier through the games— adrenaline surging, household furniture flying (for those watching on TV).

Southerners like to win—er, they almost *have* to win. SEC fans demand victories, and when they come, they remember them as others might remember a family wedding or a graduation. Big victories are chewed over for months, relished for years. Most SEC fans aren't even graduates of the schools to which they are so devoted. No matter: they are state residents following a tradition that goes back for generations. It is not uncommon for individual fans—nongraduates, no less—to bequeath large portions of their estates to their beloved football program. When I was in Alabama, I saw a wedding picture in a Birmingham newspaper: the bride is wearing white, the groom has an Alabama cap on his head. *That's* how much they care about football in Alabama. "There is a lot of state pride at work," says James Lindy Davis, a Birmingham resident who publishes a popular annual SEC football preview magazine named *Lindy's*. He tailors his magazine's cover photographs to individual states. All *Lindy's* magazines sold in Florida, for example, have a Florida player on the cover; all of his Louisiana copies have an LSU player on the cover, and so on. "You have to do that," he says. "Florida fans love the SEC, but they won't buy a magazine with a Georgia player on the front."

College football grew in the South for a simple reason: there wasn't much else to do for many years. Professional sports were late coming to the South, and in their absence college football and stock-car racing flourished. Until recently, the Atlanta Falcons and the New Orleans Saints were the only two pro football teams in the region. In the pre- and postwar years, college fans would listen to games on the radio—if they had one. Many people would walk miles from their rural homes into town, or to a relative's house, to listen.

"They've Got Bigger Butts"

And the SEC has had some wonderful radio announcers. Larry Munson has been broadcasting Georgia football games for thirty-three years. A Minnesota native, Munson's got a voice like a dump truck. He makes no attempt to be objective: he's a Bulldog announcer and a Bulldog fan—a "homer." But his humorous, old-school style is often a joy for listeners. Describing an opponent's powerful offensive line a few years back, he said: "They've just got bigger butts up front than we do." Describing an opponent's potent offense, which was racking up points against the home team, he said: "It's like they've got a big stick, and they just keeping beating us over the head with it."

Tennessee's longtime broadcaster, John Ward, retired last year after describing the Vols' national championship victory in the Fiesta Bowl. Like Munson, Ward had a very distinctive style, which he honed during thirty years behind the microphone. He coined some expressions that every Vol fan knows by heart. One example: ". . . Peerless Price DIVES for the end zone . . ." Pause. "Did he get in?" Pause. Then comes Ward's guttural, signature line: "GIVE . . . HIM . . . SIX . . . Touchdown Tennessee!" Ward is revered in Tennessee, and he perhaps thought of himself as an athlete of sorts. He was fond of walking around the Tennessee athletic complex with a rolled-up towel around his neck.

Every SEC fan has his (or her) hero—that one player who represents all that is great and good about the state football team, whose achievements are frozen in time. For Georgia, it is Herschel Walker—as pure and as powerful a college football player as ever was. He beat Tennessee almost by himself the first time he ever set foot on the field, as a freshman. Late in the game, Walker bowled over Tennessee defensive back Jim Bates (who would later have a long professional career with the Dallas Cowboys) and rumbled into the end zone to give the Dawgs (as Georgia fans refer to themselves) the win. At Auburn, Bo Jackson will always be the standard-bearer. He, like Walker, won the Heisman Trophy. At Tennessee, Peyton Manning was revered for his talent and humility; at Florida, quarterback Danny Wuerffel helped Spurrier claim his national championship; at Alabama—well, they've had more than a few great players.

Specific plays live on in the collective memory. Ask a Georgia fan about the dramatic 1980 win over Florida—made famous by a 79-yard touchdown pass from quarterback Buck Belue to Lindsay Scott in the waning moments of the game—and he might very well get teary-eyed. On a Georgia Web site, one fan recently recalled being in the Jacksonville, Florida, stadium when Scott scored that touchdown. His dominant memory is of gold-hued whiskey flying through the air as fans suddenly lurched out of their seats and threw their arms in the air as the play unfolded. It *was* a big play, paving the way for Georgia's national championship. Whiskey is something that southern football fans enjoy with their games. At the annual Georgia-Florida clash, fans sneak it into the stadium in Ziploc bags—which are easy to stash in pockets, socks, and purses.

Alabama fans get nostalgic at the mere mention of "The Goal Line Stand" or any number of other storied moments in the history of the Crimson Tide. For the initiated, The Goal Line Stand needs no elaboration. For everybody else, it is the Alabama defense, led by linebacker Barry Krauss, stopping a Penn State running back just short of the goal line in the 1978 Sugar Bowl. The play won the game for Alabama, and with it the national championship.

Thanks to Daniel Moore, that play is etched in the collective memory of all Bama fans. Moore is a painter in Birmingham who's grown wealthy commemorating great moments in Alabama football. Moore produced an oil painting showing Krauss and the Alabama defense holding back Penn State in that '78 Sugar Bowl. He titled the painting "The Goal Line Stand." Moore then, wisely, produced prints. He's since sold thousands of prints of "The Goal Line Stand," many of which are elaborately framed and hang like Picassos in living rooms, restaurants, and hotel meeting rooms all over Alabama.

Moore's the college football equivalent of Norman Rockwell. (Picture a massive painting of young boy asleep on a couch in front of a roaring fire, a football in his arms; a Bama jersey draped over an easy chair.) No dummy, he has painted numerous other winning moments in Bama's football history, which have titles such as "The Kick" and "The Interception." Hard-core fans—which means just about everybody in Alabama who's not affiliated with archrival Auburn—snatch them up. A typical Moore print costs about $2,000. He reckons he's sold about 60,000 Alabama prints over the last twenty years. It is no exaggeration to say that his prints are part of Alabama's cultural heritage.

Losses do not get talked about much in the SEC. Fans bristle when the unthinkable happens, take a defeat to heart. It sticks in the craw. No good-natured, "wait-'til-next-year" bonhomie in this neck of the woods, nosiree.

That's for the Western Athletic Conference or the Pacific Ten, by damn. When Tennessee lost a crucial game to Georgia in 1972—a game the Vols seemed to have well in hand—Tennessee fans fell into a very foul mood. On the way out of Neyland Stadium, home of the Vols, a Georgia fan let loose a joyous "Go Dawgs!" Her timing was bad: she was promptly punched in the face by an irate individual whom witnesses could not identify, although he was said to be wearing bright orange clothes.

The Georgia fan may have been bruised after that '72 Tennessee game, but Vol Coach Bill Battle was humiliated. On the Sunday morning after that loss, he was awakened at home by the sound of heavy wheels and grinding gears: somebody had hired a moving van and sent it to his house. It was cruel but prescient. Tennessee soon fired Battle. He had taken the job at age twenty-eight, if you can believe it. But Battle's inexperience—and the competition— soon caught up with him. He now runs a successful Atlanta-based sports merchandise licensing company.

The SEC is special for many reasons. But at the top of the list is this: it is a ferociously competitive football conference. Nearly every school in the conference has a winning tradition, and everyone strives mightily to maintain it. If Ole Miss expands its stadium, Mississippi State boosters will call a hurried meeting and start raising money to do the same. If Auburn renovates its weight room, be assured that Alabama won't be far behind. If Kentucky adds luxury boxes, all other SEC schools will quickly follow. Everybody seeks the slightest competitive advantage. Those found are quickly emulated. The biggest computer at the University of Tennessee is used by the football team to run its million-dollar video system. (See chapter 14.) Alabama's football players live in swanky apartments, with queen-size beds. Alabama doesn't care *that* much about the comforts of its athletes: the queen-size beds are a *recruiting advantage*. (Read more about recruiting in chapter 10.)

A Secret Weapon

Maybe it all started with Harold "War Eagle" Ketron. In the early 1900s, Ketron came out of the north Georgia mountains to become one of Georgia's most notorious football stars. When the ball was snapped, Ketron would spit tobacco juice in his opponent's eye and then make the tackle. Spitting tobacco was his secret weapon. Nowadays, Georgia is still looking for advantages in the rough-and-tumble SEC. Eager to win the conference title (Georgia has not won it since 1982), Georgia Coach Jim Donnan has been pulling out all the stops. Having lost to Tennessee nine straight years, Donnan started raiding the Vols' coaching staff for talent. He first hired away Rodney Garner—considered the best recruiter in the South—and then a year later lured Kevin Ramsey, Tennessee's defensive back coach, to Athens to be his defensive coordinator. A year after hiring Ramsey, Donnan fired him and brought in Gary Gibbs, formerly the head coach at Oklahoma, to run the defense. (Ramsey was livid about the way Donnan handled his demotion. He confronted the head coach in his office; the two men had a heated argument and reportedly scuffled.) For teams on the lower or middle rungs of the SEC ladder, sitting still is not an option. "Football is important in the SEC, and the standards are high," says Georgia Athletic Director (and former coach) Vince Dooley. "We can be ranked fourteenth in the nation but still be in third in the SEC East Division. It's a tough conference."

Football fans in Ohio, Pennsylvania, and Michigan would disagree, but it's hard to dispute the opinion that, top to bottom, year in and year out, the SEC plays the best football in the land. Seven SEC schools have won national championships. Three SEC teams won the national title in the 1990s (Alabama in 1992, Florida in 1996, and Tennessee in 1998). SEC teams win more bowl games, and more out-of-conference contests, than any other conference. There are lots of great college football players around the country, but the SEC arguably has more than anybody. In the year-2000 NFL draft, forty-one SEC players were picked by the pros—the best conference showing to date. The Big Ten Conference came next with thirty-six. Good players attract attention: for the last eighteen years, the SEC has led the nation in total attendance. More than 5.5 million fans watched SEC games, in person, last year. That's an average of more than 70,000 per game. Nearly every conference game, at every stadium, was a sell-out.

Here is a league that has produced some of the brightest lights in the football firmament: Joe Namath, John Hannah, Dwight Stephenson, Kenny Stabler, Herschel Walker, Bo Jackson, Doug Atkins, Johnnie Majors, Archie Manning, Fran Tarkenton, Peyton Manning, Emmitt Smith, Wilber Marshall, Jack Youngblood, Lee Roy Jordan, Cornelius Bennett, Reggie White, Stanley Morgan, Pat Sullivan, Terry Beasley, Tracy Rocker, Danny Wuerffel, Billy Cannon, Steve Spurrier, and Terrell Davis—to name a handful of its stars.

Legendary coaches? There have been a few, starting with Paul "Bear" Bryant, who won six national championships and more college football games than anybody (though Joe Paterno and Bobby "Aw Shucks" Bowden could soon overtake him). Nobody could motivate young men quite like Bryant. For old timers, the image of him leaning against a goal post before every game, dragging on a cigarette, is indelible. His craggy face seldom showed much except his tough Arkansas roots. "He was a crusty fucker," says Jimmy Bryan, a retired sportswriter for the *Birmingham News*. "When he first got to town, if you asked him a stupid question, Bryant would say: 'I don't answer shit like that.' He came to Alabama and made it number one." Shug Jordan (1951–1975) was a true southern gentleman who built the formidable Auburn program; John Vaught (1947–1970) led Ole Miss to six SEC titles in the 1950s and 1960s. General Robert Neyland, an innovative, tough-minded West Point grad, is synonymous with Tennessee football. He was a master of the single-wing offense. Between 1926 and 1952, he won 173 games, lost 31. Wallace Wade (1922–1930) was the other great coach at Alabama; Wally Butts (1939–1960) and Vince Dooley (1964–1988) won all ten of Georgia's SEC titles; Charlie McClendon (1962–1979) coached LSU longer than anybody. Those are a few of the men who created the SEC mystique.

In the South, as elsewhere, college football is a high-stakes, high-pressure business. Revenues from the football programs have become vitally important—so much so that practically every school in the conference has recently expanded its stadium and added scores of luxury boxes for well-heeled boosters. Nowadays, football revenues fund the lion's share of all athletic department operations—including scholarships for women's sports. Partly for that reason, SEC football programs function almost like autonomous kingdoms. They are big, rich private corporations—nearly separate from the universities themselves. That has made it difficult for the universities to harness their ambitions. While some university administrators are in thrall to the football program, others have fought mostly losing battles to reign in overzealous boosters or coaches who've cut ethical corners to keep the football team on the fast track.

The business side of the sport is repugnant to a few people. When I asked Janet McNair Cook, a middle-aged woman who works at a Holiday Inn in Athens, Georgia, if she was a football fan, she frowned. "I don't care for it," she said. "This is a big football town, but I don't understand why old men want to pay thousands of dollars to sit in glass boxes four stories high and watch twenty-year-olds run around on a field below."

Auburn President William Muse has threatened to resign because a powerful booster, Montgomery banker Bobby Lowder, controls the university's board of directors and has a disturbing tendency to meddle in the football program. Other presidents *have* resigned, tired of standing in the shadow of the football program. According to Vanderbilt Chancellor Joe B. Wyatt, the average SEC president holds his office for just over four years. The turnover rate is high, he suggests, because some presidents resent the outsize influence of the football programs. Andy Kozar was an All-America football player for Tennessee in the 1950s. He later worked as a longtime assistant to the UT president. He's been on both sides of the fence. Sitting in his isolated office in the bowels of a UT academic building, where he now writes books, Kozar describes the dominance of football over academics as "crazy." He adds: "Football is bigger than the university now—it's the tail that wags the dog. That wasn't the case when we played."

Downgrade Football?

In the late 1980s former Alabama President Joab Thomas created a huge stir when he challenged the primacy of the school's football program. Thomas, who has a Ph.D. from Harvard, declared that he wanted to boost Alabama's academic reputation—so that people around the country would not perceive the university as merely a football school. If necessary to accomplish that goal, he said, less emphasis should be placed on the sport. A noble thought, but one certain to create big waves in Tuscaloosa. Larry White, the dour Alabama sports information director, could barely disguise his disgust with Thomas as he told me the story.

Upgrade academics? Downgrade football at Alabama? That's like telling Romans to downgrade Catholicism. It was a hanging offense. College football *is* Alabama. Like their neighbors in Louisiana and Mississippi, Alabama residents were stigmatized for decades for their sundry cultural sins. They were poor, uneducated, and racist. Cheering for the Bear, watching him pile up SEC rings and national championships, was about the only thing they could feel good about in the 1960s and 1970s. "Alabama may rank low among U.S. states in education or income, but we can be number one in football," says Clyde Bolton, a longtime sportswriter for the *Birmingham News*. "It's something Alabamans take pride in: watch out, or we'll beat your ass." Adds Paul Finebaum, a radio talk-show host and columnist for the *Birmingham Post Herald*: "People here study Alabama football. They know who the third-team players are on the depth chart."

When it became clear that he was not a football loyalist, Thomas soon found himself a pariah. He was vilified by Bryant loyalists, who Thomas branded the "Bryant mafia"— a hardline faction that views Crimson Tide football like the Vatican views St. Peter's. In 1988, Thomas resigned.

Bill Curry was Alabama's football coach when Thomas was UA's president, and he had problems of his own. Curry had a successful three-year stint with the Crimson Tide between 1987 and 1989. He won 26 games and lost 10. But he resigned after the 1989 season an unhappy man. It was an odd decision, given that his team had just gone 10-2 and won the Sugar Bowl. But Curry, who was close to president Thomas and former Athletic Director Steve Sloan, had become acutely uncomfortable at Bama. There were three problems. The first was that Curry was, like Thomas and Sloan, a guy who stressed academics within the football program. The second was that Curry was considered an outsider by many Alabama fans. He had played and coached at Georgia Tech, and he had no affiliation with Bear Bryant. He was not one of "Bear's boys." That made him suspect in the eyes of many Alabama folks. Curry remembers being picked up at the Montgomery (Alabama) airport by Mae Martin Tyson, the feisty daughter of Bryant, shortly after he was hired. She wasted no time speaking her mind. "It broke my heart when they didn't hire one of Pappa's boys," Mae Martin told Curry, "but you're our coach and I'm going to support you."

Curry's third problem was that he couldn't beat Auburn. He lost to the Tigers three straight times. That's a no-no in Tuscaloosa. After the third Auburn loss, somebody threw a brick through his office window. There were death threats. Alabama won the SEC that year, and Athletic Director Hootie Ingram offered to extend Curry's contract. But Curry says it was "drastically different" from the one he already had: "It was unacceptable." He resigned. Curry was so spooked by the experience that he accepted a job as coach at Kentucky—which is best known for its basketball.

While he deplores the monomaniacal attitude of the UA athletic department about football, Curry will tell you that coaching the Crimson Tide was a "terrific privilege." He says: "You can put that crimson jersey on anybody—he may not be a great athlete—and he will play his heart out. He becomes somebody else on Saturday. You can work the team harder than the norm, and nobody will quit. A kid can't quit and go home to Dothan and say to his dad, 'I just quit the Crimson Tide.'" Bear Bryant hated quitters. Football matters in the South.

A Pressure Caldron

SEC coaches are small-town guys. They come from Winchester, Tennessee; Opp, Alabama; and Camden, Arkansas. They come from working-class backgrounds—and bring a working-class ethic to their jobs. It's a good thing, because coaching in the SEC is a pressure caldron. The head man must recruit talented young players out of high school, raise money, entertain alumni, perform charitable work, graduate his players.

And win football games. You think your job is tough? Try managing eighty-five scholarship athletes between the ages of eighteen and twenty-two. Many come from single-family homes and tough urban neighborhoods; some are indifferent students, accustomed to being lauded not for their classwork but for their athletic skills. For coping with all this pressure, SEC coaches are very well paid. The average pay package for an SEC head coach is getting close to $1 million annually. Steve Spurrier, at Florida, has a $2-million package; Phillip Fulmer of Tennessee makes more than $1 million a year. For that kind of money, favorable results are expected. "At Tennessee," says Fulmer, "the fans expect us to win all our games, all the time. That's not realistic, but just the way it is."

Amid all the hullabaloo, keeping the players focused on their schoolwork is tough. To do it, each SEC athletic department employs a small army of support personnel—tutors, counselors, academic advisers—whose job is to keep kids on the straight-and-narrow by promoting "life skills"—the new buzzword in college athletics. Their first goal, though not explicitly stated, is to make sure the players retain their athletic eligibility—and, if possible, stay on track to receive a degree. Players are given personality, career, and IQ tests to gauge their proficiencies. Poor learners are tutored extensively—both individually and in groups. Players with drug, alcohol, anger-management, or family problems receive counseling. As the football programs have grown, so have these "student-life" centers for scholarship athletes. Kentucky, Florida, and Tennessee have all recently built, or are building, new multimillion-dollar facilities.

The power of the athletic departments has created some tensions. In fact, Tennessee last year was rocked by accusations, by one of the school's English professors, that the UT athletic department had manipulated grades to keep some student-athletes eligible to play football. The professor, Linda Bensel-Meyers, also charged that the athletic tutoring program was subject to corruption because it was run by the athletic department—a sure conflict of interest. Tennessee investigated itself and declared itself clean—the school said there were no NCAA violations. But let's be candid. The notion that tutors, at all major colleges, haven't occasionally crossed the line between helping students do work and doing a bit of work for them is laughable. It's gone on for years. Every major university in America employs scores of people, spends millions of dollars—*specifically* to help *tug* academically weak student-athletes through the system. That *is* the system. Nobody should feign surprise if it comes to light that some kids have recieved a little more help than appropriate.

College football has long had a reputation for being "dirty." The charge: that players are exploited for their athletic ability and then tossed aside after three or four years, without much of an education or a degree. Recently, former Auburn star James Brooks was arrested for failure to make child support payments. When Brooks appeared before a judge to defend himself, he explained that he had no money for child-support payments because he couldn't hold a job. And the reason he couldn't hold a job? His explanation was a shocker: he was illiterate. Brooks had graduated from high school, spent four years at Auburn—during which time he became the school's third leading all-time rusher—and yet he could not read or write. He'd essentially been granted a free pass through Auburn because he could tote the football. Auburn, embarrassed by the incident, has offered to re-educate Brooks. Stories like that have given major-college football a black eye.

For all the excitement and drama it offers, college football will never be confused with mother's milk. It's got a lot of baggage, let's say, and there's no question that the big programs care about it a little *too* much. But neither is it the devil's handmaiden in a helmet and shoulder pads. Over the years, there have been plenty of ethical lapses and NCAA rules violations by coaches, boosters, and players. And, of course, a small percentage of kids get into trouble: they don't go to class, they smoke pot, they pilfer phone cards, they burglarize apartments, they accept money from agents.

And yet, there is no doubt that college programs today, including SEC schools, are striving to eradicate the notion that they are "football factories." Under pressure to win, SEC schools still recruit too many weak students to play football. But the number of so-called problem players has been slowly declining.

The NCAA has helped by toughening entrance and eligibility requirements in recent years. It has also mandated that all schools reduce their practice time and ensure that athletes are making "satisfactory progress" toward graduation. Those changes, combined with ever-growing academic support structures, are starting to add credibility to the "student" side of the term "student-athlete." "There is no question that academic success has become more and more a priority, and it should be," says Jeremy Foley, the Florida athletic director. "Our [football] graduation rates are as high as or a little bit higher than the entire student body. So in that sense, we feel good."

What is interesting about college athletics is how conflicted the NCAA itself is about academics and enrollment. The organization wants to improve academic performance, but at the same time it is reluctant to impose standards that are too stringent. And, indeed, the NCAA has now decided to close down its Clearinghouse program, which reviewed the high school transcripts of all incoming freshman football players. The Clearinghouse was controversial, and slow, but its review process did help bolster eligibility standards. Now its review function will be taken over by high schools themselves, which might be an invitation to trouble. Will high school counselors and principals be courageous enough to tell their star athletes, and their parents, that they don't meet eligibility requirements?

On the Road

My reporting started last May, when I drove down from Tampa, Florida, to Gainesville to interview University of Florida Football Coach Steve Spurrier. Gator fans affectionately call him "The Head Ball Coach." Gator foes decry his "evil genius." The book ends in Atlanta, Georgia (pronounced JAW-ja), on the cusp of the millennium, when Florida and Alabama battled for the last SEC championship of the century.

Much happened in between. Georgia Coach Jim Donnan accused me of stealing plays while I was watching his team practice. I watched Tennessee slug it out with its two archrivals, Alabama and Florida. I hunkered down with the Georgia Bulldogs when they visited Ole Miss; took a pregame stroll through the Grove, where gentile Mississippi fans greet friends and eat marvelous food as part of southern football's best social tradition. I talked with Gerry DiNardo just after he was fired at LSU; interviewed two SEC presidents, several coaches, and numerous players before, during, and after the 1999 season. Among them: Florida's Jesse Palmer and Travis Taylor; Alabama's Shaun Alexander; Tennessee's Raynoch Thompson. With the help of reporting associates, I got a taste of two classic games: Auburn versus Alabama, and Georgia versus Florida. I made two trips to Tuscaloosa, two to Gainesville, wandered through Athens and Oxford, spent a few days in Knoxville and Baton Rouge. I met with two quirky SEC boosters, who were once friends but are now enemies (see chapter 6). I ventured into Memphis—the Macau of southern sports—to track the controversial recruitment of Albert Means, one of the South's best high school players.

On my first night in Tuscaloosa, I met a former player for the University of Alabama at an on-campus pub. He was middle-aged but still as sturdy as an oak tree. One would not expect less from a guy who played for the Bear and won a national championship. When I was eating dinner, he sidled up beside me at the bar and began guzzling iced tea. After each long swallow, he'd run his tongue over his lips, lean back on his stool, and then explain why Alabama football had become such a "hellacious mess." He began most sentences by saying: "Now, I *will tell* you this . . ." or "Ima be truthful with ya. . . ." I listened—attentively—to this confident, loquacious, sincere man. Should trouble break out in the restaurant, I thought, he would happily round up the miscreants and hustle them out the door. Like all Bama fans, he was troubled by the Crimson Tide's recent spiral into mediocrity. And yet, *I'll be truthful with you*, there was a firmness in his voice as he outlined the problems. One got the impression that, one way or another, they *would be fixed*.

Entering the 1999 season, Alabama football was on shaky ground. In 1997 the Crimson Tide had posted a rare losing record. There was improvement the following year (7-4), but by Bama standards it was unacceptable. The team was waxed by Virginia Tech in the Music City Bowl. The talent level had fallen off in recent years—the result of NCAA sanctions. Tennessee had beaten Alabama four straight years. In 1997 Mike DuBose—a squat former star linebacker—was hired to replace the retiring Gene Stallings. DuBose did not at first inspire confidence. He seemed out of his element, over his head; a guy learning on the job. He needed to turn things around, and quickly, or he'd surely be trundled to the front of the Bear Bryant Museum—an impressive granite facility—and there guillotined in front of an angry mob.

Winning football games was only one of DuBose's problems. Just before the 1999 season started, it was revealed that he'd been having a long affair with his secretary. Worse, the woman was threatening to file a sexual harassment lawsuit against the university. DuBose at first denied the rumors, lying publicly in a Bill Clinton–like performance. When the truth emerged—one month before the season was to start—the university found itself in a tricky situation. Should the administration fire DuBose and risk throwing the football program into chaos? Or should the university keep him as coach and open itself to charges that its ethical credibility had been sacrificed on the altar of football?

The answer came from President Theodore Sorenson and Athletic Director Bob Bockrath: DuBose would keep his job, but be severely punished. The university gave the secretary $350,000 to settle her lawsuit—but the money would be deducted from DuBose's salary over time. In addition, two years were lopped off his contract, and he was put on probation. Alabama fans largely supported the decision. The consensus was that the team was poised to rally in 1999—and that was the first priority. The collective attitude was, "Let's play the season and see how we fare. If the team plays poorly, *then* we'll fire DuBose." On an Alabama Web site, a self-described preacher weighed in on the issue: DuBose had made a mistake, committed a sin, wrote the minister—but he deserved the prayers of the faithful because without him, who would rebuild Alabama football?

DuBose was in a spot—but he's not one to shrink from a challenge. Here is a man who wore Lee Roy Jordan's number (a high honor at Bama) and once made twenty tackles in a game against Tennessee. As Bama's coach, he had upgraded the talent level. As he told me, "We've got a chance to be a better football team. We're more intense—young, but hungry." Alabama's goal was to play its usual solid defense and, above all, to add some wrinkles to an offense that had been one-dimensional for years. Mind you, that one dimension in 1999 would be formidable: running back Shaun Alexander was a "hoss"— arguably the SEC's best offensive player. DuBose would certainly try to ride his thoroughbred. At stake was Alabama's good name—and his own.

Soon after my first Tuscaloosa visit, I visited the president of Auburn University, William Muse. He kicked me out of his office. Muse had agreed to talk to me about the Auburn football program, and we did. But shortly into the interview, I violated an Auburn University taboo, apparently: I asked Muse about Bobby Lowder, the powerful Auburn banker-booster who is a lightning rod for controversy. Muse got red in the face when I brought up Lowder's name; he stammered for a moment or two, then politely ushered me out of his office. He wouldn't talk about Lowder, or anything else for that matter. It was a real *60 Minutes* moment.

The Auburn Taboo

The last few years have been tough in the state of Alabama. While Alabama was struggling to win games, Auburn was rocked by a string of problems. Terry Bowden, Auburn's coach and the son of Bobby Bowden, quit midway through the 1998 season. Bowden had fashioned two tremendous years in 1993 and 1994, winning 20 games and losing only 1. But the program was on probation—and after the auspicious start, there was only one way to go. In the late 1990s, the program steadily lost altitude. Auburn's talent pool dried up, and there were numerous player problems. Bowden fell out of favor with Lowder and other Auburn mandarins. Fearing he would be fired at season's end, Bowden quit. There was chaos on the pretty brick Auburn campus. Only in sports can getting fired, or even quitting, be so lucrative. Bowden got a $650,000 settlement package from Auburn.

To replace Bowden, Auburn Athletic Director David Housel wanted to hire Bill Oliver, the team's defensive coordinator. Housel may have expressed that intention to Oliver. But Bobby Lowder had other ideas; he liked Tommy Tuberville, the head coach at Ole Miss. Tuberville had done a good job in Oxford, but had only been there four years. When rumors surfaced that he might run off to Auburn, Mississippi folks got nervous. They naturally didn't want to lose a talented coach. Tuberville moved quickly to allay any fears. He assured the Mississippi chancellor that he was not interested in the Auburn job. He also reaffirmed publicly his allegiance to Oxford, saying: "They'll have to carry me out of here in a pine box." It meant nothing: two days after making that melodramatic statement, he accepted the job at Auburn. Tuberville is, in fact, a good fit for Auburn. Like all football coaches, Tuberville wants very much to win. An Arkansas native who once managed a catfish restaurant, Tuberville pulled scholarships from six Auburn players deemed of little athletic value to the team. Tuberville was legally within his bounds—athletic grants are renewed annually—but the action was ethically questionable. It's one way that programs stretch rules (or traditions) to gain competitive advantage.

Things were much different in Knoxville as the 1999 season approached. Tennessee was riding high from its national championship and perfect 13-0 season. Vol Coach Phillip Fulmer had strengthened Tennessee since taking over in 1993. But until the Vols whipped Florida State in Tempe, Arizona, to cap an undefeated 1998 season, there were still plenty of people who doubted the Vols. With good reason: the Vols had had a good football program for a long time, but also had a well-deserved bridesmaid reputation. They played poorly in big games, often losing to archrivals Alabama and Florida. The 1998 national title, Tennessee's first since 1951, validated Fulmer. Could the Vols repeat as national champs in 1999? It was certainly a possibility. The Vols were top-heavy with talent—seven guys would later be drafted in the first two rounds of the 2000 NFL draft—and more experienced than the year before. But, as always, Steve Spurrier stood in Fulmer's way.

Spurrier needed no validation heading into the last year of the millennium. His pass-happy teams had dominated the SEC for most of the decade—won five SEC titles and set a passel of scoring records. The Florida coach has a reputation for being cocky, but he's really a bit enigmatic. He seems to like keeping every-one (his team, the media, Florida fans, maybe even himself) a little off balance. "He's got a peculiar side," says Finebaum of the *Birmingham Post Herald*. "Most coaches get hung up on the opposition. He's only concerned about his offense." Spurrier is often cocksure when there are question marks about his team. And then, when the Gators are rolling along, he is quick to fret about team weak-nesses. His 1998 squad was a showcase team, featuring talented defensive player Jevon Kearse. But the Gators lost a heartbreaker to Tennessee, lost also to Florida State, and fell out of the title hunt. After the season, it was learned that three Florida players—among them Kearse—had accepted money from an agent during the season. The revelation didn't affect the program—all three had either decided to turn pro or had used up all of their college eligibility. But it was embarrassing, and Spurrier was so angered by the news he banished the three former Gator players from the Florida campus.

Spurrier was excited about the 1999 team. It would be young and eager to learn. The coach seemed pleased that the stars were gone, and with them the egos that can disrupt the fragile harmony of a football team. And there was no shortage of talent—especially on offense. The only question, seemingly, was how the Gators would fare in *their* two biggest games—against Tennessee and Florida State. Spurrier enjoys playing head games with his rivals. When I left him in August, he rolled a verbal grenade at Fulmer and Tennessee. "You tell Coach Fulmer that the Swamp is going to be loud this year," he said. "As loud as it's *ever* been." He was not joking. I did, in fact, pass that message along to Fulmer in a phone conversation just before the season. The silence at the end of the line was deafening.

That was the status of four of the SEC's high-profile teams as the 1999 sea-son drew near. And what of the others? Georgia, the perennial number-three team in the SEC's Eastern Division, was determined once again to break free of the chains thrown around it by Florida and Tennessee. How can it when its division foes, the Gators and Vols, are two of the best teams in America? Asked before the season why Georgia played such a soft nonconference schedule, Coach Jim Donnan made a clever allusion to the strength of the SEC. "It would be tough to play eleven what we call 'Ben Hurs,'" he said. "They're epic games." Mississippi was ready to rally behind its new head coach, David Cutcliffe, the former offensive coordinator at Tennessee. Kentucky would be entertaining—throw the ball sixty times a game and hope for the best. South Carolina, which had won a single game in 1998, was pitiable. Before the season, Lou Holtz joked about his team's lack of depth: "We wouldn't be allowed on Noah's Ark," he said, "because we don't have two of everything."

Mississippi State was one of the favorites to win the Western conference. The Bulldogs were returning a stout defense and their typically massive group of offensive linemen, who must surely be majoring in Burger King. (Cheap shot!) Vanderbilt, the SEC's intellectual citadel, had not had a winning season since 1982. But, in another example of just how competitive the conference is, the Commodores might have the very best coach in the league. Woody Widenhofer coached the Pittsburgh Steelers' "steel curtain" defense in its prime, and his tough Vandy defense was certain to scare opponents. But would the brainiacs score any points? At LSU, Gerry DiNardo, who'd made a name for himself at Vandy, was girding for a make-or-break season. Yeah, the crayfish and whiskey are fun—but what dey gonna do about the bad mojo in Baton Rouge?

Fathers and Sons

How did I come to undertake this (crazy) project? Simple: I am a journalist, a writer for *Newsweek* magazine, and I like college football. My father, a native of Mansfield, Ohio, was an SEC football player. In the early 1950s, Dick Ernsberger was a 6-foot, 160-pound fullback for the University of Tennessee. My dad's Mansfield high school team was stout, and with the help of his high school coach he earned a scholarship to UT. In those days the Vols had a coach who would become a collegiate legend. General Robert Neyland (pronounced Knee-Land) was a soldier (by way of West Point), a disciplinarian, and, above all, a winner. Like others, Neyland believed that defense and field position were of paramount importance. Like other coaches of that time, he was happy to punt the ball twenty to twenty-five times a game, if by doing so he could gradually gain an advantage in field position. He invented tear-away jerseys. On the few occasions when he lost, Neyland would remark: "We were met and defeated by superior forces."

Tennessee's football prowess dates back to the 1930s, when if you didn't leave the field with a broken nose and your arm in a sling, you hadn't really played. It wasn't until 1951 that Neyland and the Vols finally claimed a national championship. My dad was on that team. Playing for Neyland was the most formative experience in his life. He still speaks of the man with reverence, as a former Green Bay Packer would speak of Vince Lombardi. When I was a kid, Dad would often show my brothers and me his UT football annuals, which were chock full of pictures of the Vols in action. In those days they wore thin plastic helmets with no facemasks, and not a lot of padding. The yearbooks showed lots of perfectly executed plays with precision blocking—a Neyland trademark.

In my Dad's day, teams recruited scores of new players every year—upwards of 100. There were no scholarship limitations. But practices were brutal. Half the freshmen would quit or be run off (for lacking spirit, talent, or toughness) before fall camp was two weeks old. Lying in bed, my dad would hear the fearful leaving for home in the middle of the night, dragging their suitcases along the hallways in the stadium. (That's where the players lived in the 1950s.)

Dad regaled us with stories about playing in the Cotton and Sugar Bowls. And he talked often—still does—about his stellar teammates—among them, Doug Atkins (a dominant defensive end), Hank Lauricella (an All-America tailback), and Andy Kozar, a big, gifted fullback. Tough and stoic, my father would often rap me gently on the head with his big, heavy UT letterman's ring if I wasn't paying attention. I'm sure there are a few knots still underneath my hair today.

Tradition follows from parent to child. In 1970, when I was fifteen, Dad and I drove to Knoxville from our home in Richmond, Virginia, to watch Tennessee play. It was my first game. The trip took eight hours—down the western border of the commonwealth and into northeast Tennessee—but it passed quickly. Knoxville is a modest (population 100,000), gritty southern city. But to me, on that cool autumn weekend, it was the promised land. I knew very little about the town, but a great deal about Tennessee football—many of my adolescent yearnings were wrapped up in crazy imaginings about the team.

With darkness approaching, we crossed the Tennessee River and there, looming in the distance, was Neyland Stadium. I was mesmerized by the site—especially the glowing orange-and-white letters sitting atop one end of the structure. Visible for miles, they spelled VOLS. It was thrilling! The next day we joined 85,000 other fans in the stadium to watch the Vols thump Kentucky. The Vols had a very good team that year—one of their best ever, in fact—led by quarterback Bobby Scott, linebackers Steve Kiner and Jack Reynolds, and defensive backs Bobby Majors, Tim Priest, and Conrad Graham. I remember being almost overwhelmed by a riot of sound and color—the Pride of the Southland Marching Band, the nonstop cheering, the . . . ORANGE. I will not argue with anyone who calls it garish, or even ugly. On a football Saturday in Knoxville, you'd be hard-pressed to find a single Vol fan who isn't wearing some orange-colored article of clothing. And yet, in what is surely a testimony to

An Introduction to the SEC

American ingenuity, no two people will be wearing the same thing. You can see 10,000 orange UT shirts, for example—but they'll all have a different design. Go figure.

I, too, went to Tennessee, but on a baseball scholarship. Football was my favorite sport—I always loved the physicality of the game—but I wasn't nearly big enough to play it in college. The first game I saw as a student in 1973 was against Auburn. It was played in a torrential downpour, and I sat in the stands until the very end—soaked but happy because the Vols had won. Later that year, I got into a heated argument with another baseball player. We went outside Gibbs Hall, the athletic dorm, to settle the dispute. A fight seemed imminent—one that I wasn't likely to win since the other guy was bigger and a former Golden Gloves boxer. Then came a savior: Mickey Marvin, a huge offensive tackle (who later went on to play for the Oakland Raiders for at least a decade) came storming outside, angry about all the hollering. He practically picked me up off the ground with his left hand and dropped me back inside the dorm. I never did thank him properly.

There are a few people I can thank now, however, for their help with this book. Norm Carlson, the sports information director (SID) at the University of Florida, was most helpful and gracious from the beginning to the end of this project. So was Bud Ford, the media man at Tennessee. Rod Williamson, the SID at Vanderbilt, was likewise most cooperative—and informative. Thanks, too, to Larry White at the University of Alabama and Herb Vincent at LSU. Herb did what I was sure could not be done: he got me an interview with Gerry DiNardo two days after the LSU coach had lost his job. At Tennessee, Pat Pryor, Phillip Fulmer's secretary, and Gerald Harrison were generous with assistance. Thanks to Jerry Brown for his warm hospitality in Tuscaloosa, Alabama. Jerry is as close to Alabama football as one can get—he lives in the shadow of Bryant-Denny Stadium. Dotty and Briggs Smith, of Batesville, Mississippi, hosted me for a wonderful weekend at Ole Miss, during which I ate shrimp grits. They're tasty. My biggest regret is that I was unable to write a chapter about the Grove, as I'd planned. I simply did not have the time. My thanks to two SEC journalism students who pitched in with some reporting for me: Caty Houston at Auburn and Erin Boyd McClam at Georgia. Thanks to Paul Davis, a journalist and publisher in Auburn, Alabama. He provided me with much useful information—and helped me get back into my rental car after I'd locked the keys inside. And finally, thanks to the many, many people who offered me their wit and wisdom about Southeastern Conference football. It was a joy to listen.

ONE

ROCKY TOP

August 16, 1999, Knoxville, Tennessee

It's a fine August morning in northeast Tennessee. It will be sizzling later in the day—over 100 degrees—but at 7:00 A.M. the air is cool, the Bermuda grass is damp, and it's time to practice football. Some eighty young University of Tennessee football players are gathered, ironically, on the outfield of the UT baseball field for the first of what will be two practices this day—sandwiched around at least two team meetings and one or two hours of tape watching. They take college football very seriously in the southeastern United States, in Knoxville, at the University of Tennessee, and in August. No lazy, hazy days of summer for this group. The season starts in two weeks—and the Tennessee Vols must be ready to defend their national championship. On September 4, the Vols will play their first game against Wyoming.

But that's ahead of us. There is much to be done, first, on the practice field. Because "full-contact scrimmages" have not yet begun, the Vols players are wearing black shorts, shoulder pads, white practice helmets (with names scrawled across the front on orange tape), and orange-and-white jerseys. Phil Fulmer, a burly former Tennessee player turned state hero after leading the Vols to a record 13-0 record last year, supervises the proceedings. Fulmer seldom wears anything but Tennessee colors, and this morning he's got on a Vol cap and white T-shirt—and, as is his habit, he is twirling a whistle. He is joined by nine assistant coaches, most of them middle-aged veterans who are collectively paid about $1 million annually in salaries, or roughly $100,000 per man. That doesn't include bonuses for bowl games or winning the SEC title. Their job is to transform nervous kids (not far removed from their parents and high school) into tough, dependable men with mettle enough to best Florida, Alabama, and Georgia in the pressure-packed weeks ahead.

The practice is off-limits to all except a few members of the press, although on this morning there is a special visitor: Casey Clausen, a highly-regarded quarterback prospect from California, has arrived with his father to watch the Vols work out. They've been in Knoxville before. Clausen is strongly interested in playing for Tennessee, and the Vol coaches hope to secure his commitment on this visit. "College football doesn't get any bigger than Tennessee," Clausen would say a couple of weeks later, after pledging his services to the Vols. Like a visiting dignitary, the teenager is ushered out to the center of the practice field to meet with Fulmer and Vol offensive coordinator Randy Sanders.

The Vols line up in military-like rows and stretch their muscles for a few minutes. Whistles pierce the air along with the barking voice of a strength coach who is directing the calisthenics: "Right leg, c'mon now, guys, stretch it out! . . . Left leg!" A klaxon sounds and the Vols all jog over to the sideline, where receiver coach Pat Washington is waiting to impart to the team the "winning edge" thought for the day. Pointing behind him, down the field, Washington shouts: "Go to the whistle and keep blocking your guy and don't look back!" He is explaining that receivers should keep blocking, and moving downfield, until the whistle stops the play. He doesn't want the receivers easing up too soon—looking behind them to see how the play has evolved—when they should be hunting for somebody to block. "Go thataway!" Washington hollers, pointing away from him. "Not thisaway," pointing toward the players. Everybody seems to get the message.

The klaxon sounds again, and the Vols quickly break up into position units: quarterbacks and receivers, linebackers, defensive linemen, offensive linemen, defensive backs. Each unit is supervised by an assistant coach who puts his charges through various drills aimed at improving agility and football techniques. The drills are quick, crisp, and animated. Quarterbacks Tee Martin, Joey Mathews, and A. J. Suggs practice handoffs to the tailbacks and fullbacks. Jamal Lewis, Tennessee's all-star-caliber tailback who injured a knee last year, seems to be moving well. He and Travis Henry, a human bulldozer, will be counted on heavily this year for the Vols.

Later, the quarterbacks practice their passing with the receivers. They throw five-yard "out" patterns toward the sidelines, over-the-middle slants, curls and hitches. The quarterbacks drop back three steps from the center and then throw. After that they practice their deeper five-step "drops"—typically the prelude to a long downfield pass. Football players follow the same path to good performance as violin players with their eye on Carnegie Hall—practice, practice, practice. Martin—Tennessee's charismatic quaterback—looks in mid-season form, rifling tight spirals to Cedrick Wilson, Donte Stallworth,

Eric Parker, and other nimble-footed Tennessee flankers. Clausen, strapping and stone-faced, watches the action.

Across the field, Vol defenders are honing their attack tactics. Defensive backs practice so-called corner-blitzes—which require them to dart around the offensive flank and sack the quarterback. This morning the quarterback is a big, helmeted plastic dummy with two arms. One of the arms is holding a real football. A defensive back breaks from the line of scrimmage, rushes the "QB," and knocks the ball loose with his arm. "Ball! ball! ball!" the player shouts when the pigskin tumbles to the ground. It's a clarion call to his defensive teammates that a fumble has occurred. (Don't try it at home; neighborhood dogs will come running.)

Nearby, John Chavis, the Tennessee defensive coordinator, is tutoring eight linebackers on how to "read and react" to offensive plays—and then get to the ball. Chavis, who was a walk-on defensive lineman at Tennessee in the late 1970s, has been a Tennessee coach for seventeen years. A Vol assistant describes Chavis, affectionately, as a "psycho. He's got a defensive mentality." Chavis was named the Vol defensive coordinator in 1995, after serving as the team's linebacker coach. He was not very popular with Vol fans at first, especially after his defense was torched a couple of years by high-scoring Florida. But Chavis has grown into the job, and he's now considered a star on the Tennessee coaching staff. He'd be the first to admit that he's benefited from a major influx of defensive talent in recent years.

Chavis hails from the "tough love" school of coaching: on the field, he is very demanding; off the field, he's sensitive to his players' needs. Short and stocky, with close-cropped dark hair and a mustache, he looks like an army sergeant. And he can act like one, too. On this morning, he is working closely with Dominique Stevenson, the heir apparent to Al Wilson at middle linebacker. Tennessee's outside linebackers, Eric Westmoreland and Raynoch Thompson, are both experienced and talented. Stevenson, raw and untested, will be counted on to anchor the middle. If he falters, so will the Tennessee defense.

Chavis is teaching Stevenson and the other linebackers what he calls "key progression"—which essentially is a series of physical clues from offensive players that foretell where the ball is going. The quicker a linebacker can recognize offensive cues, the quicker he can "read" a play and move himself into position to make a tackle. Good linebackers read plays accurately in, at most, a second. "Key progression is very important and the basis of everything that a linebacker does," says Chavis. "It starts with the initial movement of the fullback [or the back nearest the ball] and it takes us to the 'near' guard [the offensive guard nearest the linebacker] and then, lastly, to the blocking scheme." When a linebacker ascertains what the fullback and guard are doing, he can often deduce where the ball is going.

Rocky Top

As a skeletal seven-man offensive unit approaches the line of scrimmage, Chavis starts yelling out instructions to his linebackers in the specialized argot of football. Two things are immediately apparent: football is a much more complex game than most people realize, and Chavis is intense. "Get your base-point read!" he shouts. "Middle linebacker, get on the edge of the guard. . . . If he's blocking, then I'm pulling the trigger. . . . When the tackle is zoning off, then you *know* it's not going to be a cutback [run]. . . . Be eight-gap conscious. . . . Hug that tight end, Dominique. . . . If they're trying to rub the guard back on me, you gotta be right here . . . scrape the tight end . . . bust the A gap. . . . Two plays we're going to see on this thing: iso on the will [an isolation on the weak-side linebacker] and counter back to the strong side [the running back takes a step in one direction then takes the football and runs the opposite way]." Here Chavis gets even more animated and his voice rises: "As *soon* as I read base point, guys, I KNOW RIGHT NOW IT'S COUNTER, and I'm going to plug back and go. I gotta see that *right away, right away, right away!*"

Listen to Chavis for a few minutes and you'll want to don pads and helmet and go tackle somebody. After a play, Chavis calls in a new group of linebackers with the command: "On the hop, on the hop." That means move quickly. There is a lot to learn: Tennessee's defensive playbook is about 100 pages thick. The Vols have twenty-two different defensive "fronts," and eighteen different "cover packages" for linebackers and defensive backs, which go by names such as "Bear," "Cobra," "Eagle," "Delta," "Slide," and "Tiger."

Stevenson is not having a good morning, apparently. Whether he is moving lackadaisically or struggling to make his reads is not clear. But Chavis is displeased. He brusquely waves the inexperienced linebacker off the practice field. "I don't want you out here until you get your head into practice," he tells Stevenson. The linebacker stalks over to the sideline and throws his helmet into the turf. A young trainer is waiting to cool his nerves with a water hose. Soon, the klaxon sounds again and the players break into new groups to start a new set of drills. During a two-hour practice, the team will run through between fifteen and twenty brief workout periods—most lasting fewer than ten minutes. Some are designed to improve individual skills, others are "team" periods where offensive and defensive units will practice against one another. During those, the coaches are often hollering, "Ones!" or "Twos up." First-team players are "ones," while second-teamers are "twos."

Afterwards, Chavis elaborates on his coaching philosophy and his relationship with the players. "You need to get their attention from time to time," he says, alluding to his stern reaction to Stevenson's lackluster practice. "The players know I'm going to coach with some tempo—that's how I feel it should be done." Coaching college kids requires a "fine balance," says Chavis. "You got to push 'em, be demanding—but you got to be positive with 'em, too—put your arms around 'em and hug 'em and let 'em know that you care about them. And it's got to be sincere. You're not going to fool young people; they know when you're not sincere."

The most important thing to consider about the players, he adds, is that "they're just young guys. And there is lots of pressure on them. The recruiting process adds to it. Everybody tells them about the opportunities to play, and everybody is expecting them to play, and the media writes about a kid being a potential starter. That creates a lot of pressure on kids making the transition from high school to college. For some of them, this is a whole new world. Some are away from Mom and Dad for the first time. I'm very sensitive to that, and want to help them make the transition. But at the same time, I want to push them hard enough to reach their goals on the football team."

While Chavis works the linebackers, offensive line coach Mike Barry is explaining to a group of hulking blockers the nuances of pulling out from a three-point stance and searching for a linebacker to destroy. "Hut," and the ball is snapped: suddenly, Fred Weary, a 6'4", 300-pound right guard straightens up and begins rumbling from the right side of the line toward the left. His dark eyes scan the defense and fix on a target. Weary has spotted a linebacker. His next job is to knock him into the next county. But since there is no serious contact this morning, he merely gives the victim a low-impact "thwack" with his pads. The whistle sounds, the play stops. Sizing up Weary, I am thankful that I'm not a linebacker.

Soon, the offensive line is practicing various blocking drills—"8 gap, 3 power, 42 power." I've no idea what they mean, except generally a tailback will get the ball and everyone will try to blow his man off the line of scrimmage. Curiously, Clausen's father, dressed in a lightweight floral shirt, khaki pants, and loafers (*no socks, very California*), has spent most of the morning watching Barry and the Tennessee offensive line. He spends a lot of time chatting with a UT graduate assistant coach. Big-time football programs like Tennessee rely on a small army of graduate assistants, trainers, strength coaches, and others to tend to the immediate needs of the football team. Behind the scenes, another 100 or so personnel—the ticket managers, grounds crew, equipment men, video cameramen, NCAA compliance staff, academic support staff, marketing personnel, and secretaries grease the wheels of an operation that brings in nearly $40 million annually—and provides the lion's share of funding for all athletic scholarships at Tennessee. And Tennessee has one of the five biggest athletic budgets in the country.

During an offense-versus-defense period, Fulmer strolls over to scrutinize the offensive line. The Vol coach hitches up his shorts (he does that a lot) and puts his hands on his hips. Earlier in his career, Fulmer was a highly regarded offensive line coach himself. After a play or two, Fulmer has spotted something. He tells the blockers that they're bunched up too tightly along the line of scrimmage. That could make it easier for opposing defensive ends to rip around the outside and sack the Vol quarterback. Toby Champion, a guard, and tackle Reggie Coleman nod their heads. The offense huddles, and Fulmer hitches up his pants.

Jake Vest, a former writer for the *Orlando Sentinel*, grew up outside of Knoxville—down the river from Neyland Stadium, in what he's called "the poor direction, out toward the rock quarries, dairy farms, and tobacco patches." Here is what he wrote a few years back about Tennessee football:

> On a crisp mid-October Saturday, you could climb a hill and, if the wind was just right, you could hear the rich people booing Bear Bryant and the Tide. I spent a lot of time climbing those hills and listening. Football was the second favorite sport out in the greater Forks of the River Metropolitan area—right behind squirrel hunting, which you didn't need a ticket to do. Sometimes the squirrel hunters would carry transistor radios so they could listen to John Ward, the Voice of the Vols, calling the shots for that other sport. If Tennessee was driving for a score, there would be a general cease-fire. Now that is devotion. Anything that gets a a Tennessean's mind off hunting is something special. If it was a particularly big game, even the dogs would stop barking. They knew Ward's voice, and they could tell when he was getting serious, a fact that may seem like a stretch to some, but you've got to remember, we had some mighty good dogs. Out in my part of the woods, an affection for the Big Orange was something you took early in life and held onto.
>
> One of my first memories is of sitting on the front porch in a swing with my grandfather—that's Pappaw in East Tennessean—listening on the radio to Tennessee play Ole Miss. That was back in the days when the fore-ward pass was considered an alternative lifestyle, something you did if you weren't man enough to play real football, and both teams rushed about 300 times for about 150 yards. Every time Ole Miss would gain a step, Pappaw would cuss and spit tobacco juice. By halftime, the side yard looked like an oil spill. What's most remarkable about this is that I don't think Pappaw had any notion of what a football game was. It wasn't mentioned in the Bible, so he had no reason to ever read about it; and he sure had never attended a game. He had no idea what the Mississippians were doing. But he knew they were doing it to "us." And he was against it.

The Neyland-Thompson Sports Center is the epicenter of Tennessee football. Walk inside, and you are greeted by drawings (not especially good) of Tennessee's fifty-two All Americans going back a century. There is a massive portrait of General Robert Neyland, the great Vol pre-war coach, in his classic pose—kneeling on the sideline in woolen coat and hat. There are a half-dozen trophy cases holding the winning hardware from many of the twenty-two bowl games the Vols have won (the third highest total in college football history)—Sugar Bowls, Cotton Bowls, Citrus Bowls, Liberty Bowls, Bluebonnet Bowls, Gator Bowls, Fiesta Bowls, and more (the Vols have never won the Rose Bowl). A new case displays both the Associated Press and Grantland Rice National Chamionship Trophies for the 1998–1999 season—the latter a crystal football. Only Alabama and Southern Cal have more bowl victories than Tennessee.

Inside the adjacent indoor practice complex, large team portraits of Tennessee's SEC-winning teams hang from the walls. The Vols have won the SEC thirteen times, second only to Alabama's twenty-one. There is also a timeline of Tennessee football, dating back to 1896. One learns that in 1939, the Vols were undefeated and *unscored on*. In ten games, they gave up zero points—and yet were second in the voting for national champion! That is tough luck. The Vols have had many illustrious players, but perhaps none more talented or more fascinating than Herman Hickman, who was an All-America guard in 1931. Hickman was one of the founders of *Sports Illustrated* magazine, and when the Vol great passed away in 1958, at age forty-six, *SI* paid him a tribute. Hickman was known, wrote *Sports Illustrated*, "as the jolly fat man with a great fund of stories; as the jolly fat man who incongruously drawled Shakespeare, Thackeray, Goethe, Robert W. Service, and his own rhythmic jingles in practically the same breath. [But] the jolly fat man with the enormous appetite for good food and drink and tobacco and late hours was not the whole picture by any means. Hickman was a very serious fellow indeed, and behind the grin and twinkling eyes, he was thinking earnest thoughts about the subject he considered the most important in the world: college football." Hickman had his name on the "nine points of survival"—a critique of college football written in 1956. He wrote poetry. Grantland Rice, the brilliant sportswriter of that era, mentioned Hickman in his wonderful memoir, *The Tumult and the Shouting*.

Today's players are not *quite* the same. They do not write poetry or quote Thackeray outside of class. In fact, many do not enter college with much of an academic orientation at all. It's a sad commentary on our country, frankly. Many of the kids who play big-time SEC football nowadays come from difficult backgrounds. Many are from single-parent homes. But nearly all of the players are good kids, of strong character.

Tennessee quarterback Tee Martin was raised on the mean streets of Mobile, Alabama, by his great-grandmother. Growing up, he saw half a dozen friends and acquaintances die violently. And yet Martin is completely unflappable on and off the field. His teammates joke that he's so cool under pressure that he doesn't perspire. "That's just the way I am," Martin told Chris Low of the (Nashville) *Tennessean* newspaper. "I'm not extreme about anything—religion, money, school, or football. I guess I'm not crazy about anything. Some of the struggles I've been through, it makes you feel blessed to be where you are. I've grown up so much personally, and that's helped me to be a better football player." At 6'3", 225 pounds, Martin looks like a linebacker but runs like a tail-back. Though not as polished a passer as his predecessor, Peyton Manning, Martin had not lost a game and led the Vols to the national title. What could he do for an encore?

Two other Tennessee stars, linebacker Raynoch Thompson and offensive guard Cosey Coleman, grew up in the same New Orleans housing project. Coleman's father and three of his brothers served time in prison. His brother Jerome died in a New Orleans prison two years ago. But Coleman seems to have the personality of a preacher, albeit one who's 6'5" and weighs 320 pounds. He enjoys talking on the street to UT fans, and signing autographs. He respects authority—perhaps because he's the youngest (by fifteen years) of six sons. His mother, Olivea, moved Cosey and the family to Clarkston, Georgia, to get away from "fast-moving" New Orleans. There, she worked odd jobs to support the family—as a cashier at the Dollar General store, and a cook at Denny's and Big Greg's Barbecue.

"We've had our ups and downs," Cosey told John Adams of the *Knoxville News Sentinel*. "It kind of toughened me up, watching [my brothers'] lives, watching the wrong turns. Watching them make mistakes taught me what to look for." In a word, he learned. When Cosey was sixteen, he managed a fast-food restaurant. As a senior at Southwest Dekalb High School, he was an All-America football player *and* earned a 3.49 grade-point average. Barry calls Coleman a "good athlete with great feet. When you stamp out an offensive lineman, he's what you want." (You may think that big arms and legs, and overall strength, are the most important assets for an offensive lineman. They're vital, of course, but never underestimate the feet. A lineman who can't move is not a very good lineman.)

The Bionic Man

Like life, football can be tough. Billy Ratliff, a Vol defensive lineman from Magnolia, Mississippi, would tell you that. Mike Rollo, Tennessee's head trainer, calls Ratliff "the bionic man." It is an apt description for the often-injured but resilient Ratliff. Before even starting his senior year at UT, the 280-pound Ratliff had suffered enough injuries to merit a mention in medical textbooks. He's had knee surgery three times (once in high school, twice at UT), had a titanium rod inserted into his tibia (a leg bone) to relieve a stress fracture, and suffered a neck injury as a college sophomore that Rollo called "very frightening. We thought it would end his career." It turned out to be a neck contusion (bruise), and as Rollo notes with near-amazement: "He's still out there playing, and doing very well."

Ratliff was the hero of Tennessee's 1998 win over Arkansas, when he recovered a fumble with less than two minutes in the game and the Vols seemingly headed for defeat. Tennessee then drove for the game-winning touchdown. Ratliff was a sure-fire NFL prospect as a freshman. He had the requisite heft to play defensive line—and he was cat-quick besides. He possessed what coaches love—a strong "motor"—meaning he played hard on every play. Heading into his senior season, Ratliff's NFL prospects had disappeared. "He'd never pass an NFL physical," says Rollo. But Ratliff has kept on playing. "He's had many opportunities to walk away from the game and not play anymore," says Rollo. "The knees in particular create a lot of pain for him. Billy will probably be looking at joint or knee replacement at an earlier age than normal for football players," possibly in his thirties. "He could have quit many times, but he hasn't. Why? Not because there are millions of dollars waiting for him, but because he loves to play the game. His body has told him, time after time, 'Don't do this to me.' But he keeps doing it. Why? Because he loves the game."

As Rollo is quick to note, "There are dozens and dozens of people behind the scenes, making a football program happen. But you rarely hear about them. I don't think many people have any concept of the support staff behind Tennessee football. It doesn't just happen on Saturday." He sounds slightly miffed!

Rollo, forty-five, has been at UT for twenty-eight years—four as a student and then twenty-four with the training staff. He now supervises twenty-two people—five full-timers (four certified physical trainers and one physical therapist) and the rest student trainers and graduate assistants, all of whom minister to some 550 athletes in all sports (including the cheerleaders). In addition, UT has two primary team physicians—a general practitioner and an orthopedist (Dr. Floyd Youmans, who has been with UT for more than thirty years). With a squad size that can reach 100 some weeks, football gets the lion's share of the medical staff's sttention. The physical therapist is a brand-new addition to the medical team, says Rollo. "I think over the next eight to ten years, you'll see more physical therapists involved in college programs. More people are becoming combination physical therapists–athletic trainers. That is a trend, and we want to get in on the front of the curve."

August two-a-days are the busiest time of the year for Rollo. For two weeks he's typically in the training room at 5:30 in the morning and doesn't leave until 10:00 at night. "Once we get through this," he says, "the rest of the year seems easy." Around dawn, the spacious UT training area is rehab central: about twenty-five football players are getting one kind of treatment or another; another twenty-five are getting taped. Prior to football games, the entire training staff is used to tape ankles. Nearly all football players get their ankles taped, and Rollo says they are creatures of habit: they always want the same person to tape them. "They don't like change, and ball games are not a good time to change tapers."

Tennessee's training budget amounts to about $700,000 annually. Rollo says the university tries to ensure that its equipment is leading-edge. Inside the medical rooms, there are seven whirlpools (an old standby) plus a variety of machines that essentially produce either heat or cold—electrical-stimulation machines, combination stimulation/ultrasound machines, diothermic machines (which produce high-frequency radio waves and convert them into heat). There is also an underwater treadmill, which Rollo calls "our single most critical piece of equipment. We've always believed strongly in aquatic rehabilitation."

And what are the most common injuries in football? As expected, knee problems are most common ("The knee, always the knee," said Vince Lombardi), followed by ankles and shoulders. "Shoulder problems can be the most difficult to diagnose and fix," says the Vol head trainer. But there has been much progress over the years in dealing with knee injuries. A torn anterior cruciate ligament used to be a devastating, career-ending injury, says Rollo. Not anymore. Now, athletes can be functional again in six to eight months. "Some people say you can do it in three or four months, but you're really talking about a year with the initial recovery and subtle post-surgery issues like inflammation. The ACL is not a major [hurdle] now; it's a detour for a short period of time."

"TV Arms"

When Eric Westmoreland came to UT in 1996, he weighed 198 pounds. He'd played safety in high school. As a freshman football player for the Vols, he could bench press 250 pounds. Three years later, entering his junior season, Westmoreland was a changed man: he'd boosted his weight by 34 pounds, to 232. But the extra pounds didn't slow him down. In fact, according to John Stucky, UT's strength and fitness director, Westmoreland "runs faster, jumps higher, and moves faster than when he got here." And Westmoreland is stronger; he can now bench press more than 400 pounds. All of this has helped him become Tennessee's starting left linebacker for the last two years—and one of the best tacklers in the SEC.

Taking 198-pound "weaklings" and turning them into 232-pound linebackers is Stucky's job. He's considered one of the best strength and fitness coaches in college football. Just outside his cramped office, adjacent to the Tennessee weight room, is a counter with bowls of bananas. There is also a poster with the headline: MEN OF STEEL. It shows a half-dozen UT football players standing together—shirts off, biceps bursting. They look like what they are—weightlifters.

Stucky does *not* look like a weightlifter. At age fifty-two, he's more cerebral than buff. He speaks in a low, raspy voice. When I met him, there were boxes of creatine (a muscle builder) on his desk. "There is nothing wrong with using a supplement that adds to the creatine level in muscle," Stucky told me. He and three full-time assistants, along with a half-dozen graduate assistants, physically train UT's football players.

"There is an ideal size and weight for every athlete," says Stucky, and his job is to help every athlete reach those markers. The process typically takes years. While some freshmen come into a college football program fit, strong, and ready to play, they are exceptions. Stucky says some newcomers arrive, "and they've eaten themselves into oblivion. They're huge. This game is still very much about speed, and being overweight can inhibit speed." He called Tennessee's 1999 class—which included highly regarded line prospects Albert Haynesworth and Terriea Smalls—"A little robust, but a talented bunch." In Stucky's view, "very few" freshmen are ready to compete in the SEC. "They've got to work their way into it." That means lifting weights regularly, running frequently, and eating properly. "We'll sit down with a player and outline everything he needs to do," says the strength coach. "The players are told continuously what they should be eating." I infer from that comment that they sometimes don't.

In August, which is a heavy practice month, football players don't spend too much time lifting weights. With two practices a day in hot weather, any more physical exertion would be detrimental to the body. Or as Stucky puts it: "You can't beat a dead horse. The players will do a minimal amount of work to make sure their neck and shoulders feel good." While all the muscle groups are important to football, Stucky says that neck and shoulder strength is "crucial," adding: "Between your armpits and your earlobes, you'd better be Superman. If you don't have anything else to do, go work on your shoulders and neck."

Winter and summer months are best for weightlifting, and during those off-season periods the players may spend one to two hours in the weight room four times a week. The players are always supervised, and weightlifting programs are tailored to positions. The eight-week winter workout is especially important. That's when, says Stucky, players build a "physical foundation" for the year ahead. During the spring and fall, the lifting schedule is reduced by half. "You don't want to make them too tired to practice or to play well. You want to avoid fatigue injuries." Players concentrate on three lifting techniques: pulling (which are Olympic-type moves like "snatches" and "jerks"), squatting (for the legs), and pressing (to develop the upper body and achieve what Stucky calls "TV arms").

Rocky Top

Hips and legs are important, because they power running and jumping. But if you talk to Stucky very long, you'll realize that every muscle group is important to football. In Stucky's view, the 1998 Tennessee team had two surpassing qualities. "It was the most unselfish group of players I've ever seen. They didn't care who got the glory. It was a special group." It was, also, "quite a physical ball club, and we expect to be that way again this year."

On the wall of the UT weight room, lifters are categorized by their strength. "Studs" are the strongest, followed by "stallions" and "stags." Darwin Walker, a defensive tackle, was Tennessee's strongest player. Heading into the 1999 season, he could squat 605 pounds, bench press 505. Quarterback Tee Martin could bench press 385 pounds; Jamal Lewis, 465. Those weren't the only numbers on the wall. The strength coaches not only monitor every player's body weight, they also measure everyone's triceps, abdomen, thighs. Body fat measurements are taken. In a word, fat is bad; the lower the fat-percentage number, the better. Unsurprisingly, smaller skill-position players have a much lower percentage of body fat than those "mansters" (part man, part monster) who work the line. Last year Teddy Gaines, a defensive back, had a body fat percentage of 4.2 percent; receiver Eric Parker, 5.9 percent. The goals of Vol linemen were listed conspicuously:

	Weight Now	Weight Goal	Body Fat %	Goal
Chad Clifton	336 pounds	325	23.4	19–20
Cosey Coleman	332 pounds	320	24.0	19–20
Reggie Coleman	330 pounds	315	27.2	19–22
Fred Weary	304 pounds	300	25.2	19–20
Toby Champion			26.9	19–21

In the afternoon, the Vols were put through a rigorous practice in 101-degree heat. Actually, the team has a little device that can measure the temperature inside a football helmet. It came up with a reading of 111 degrees. Former Vol quarterbacks Bobby Scott, Heath Shuler, and Jeff Francis were on hand to watch the proceedings. Shuler, looking tan and wearing black, had had his NFL career ended prematurely by a foot injury. He's now an aspiring real estate magnate in Knoxville. Francis is a sideline reporter for the Vol radio network. The parents of Mark Jones, a Vol signee from Pennsylvania, are also looking on.

After an hour of heavy sweating, the team takes a break. Will Overton, a hardworking defensive end, is one of the first to visit the refreshment table. He (and everyone else) grabs a couple of orange slices and a Gatorade, and takes a seat under a big party tent. When practice resumes, the first-string Tennessee defense gathers on the field and starts jumping up and down together, in what seems a tribal dance. Deon Grant, the team's All-SEC free safety, leads a chant: "We're ready! We're ready! We're ready!" We'd all soon find out if that was the case.

Wandering out on the UT campus, I see Neyland Stadium, which holds about 107,000 people on Saturdays. Some 70,000 of those fans own season tickets—and almost never give them up. Soon, work will commence on seventy-two new "skyboxes," to be added to the forty-two luxury boxes Tennessee already has. The new boxes, each with sixteen seats, will run from end zone to end zone, along three levels, on the east side of the massive stadium. They will cost about $20 million to build—paid for by the Tennessee athletic department. But after completion the boxes will be a substantial moneymaker for the athletic department. The university expects to earn $500,000 to $800,000 annually from the seventy-two boxes. To even qualify for one, a fan must make a $25,000 donation to the UT athletic department. Tickets themselves will cost an additional $55 each. For that, the box holders get a great view of the field and downtown Knoxville—plus free food on game day. The school has already received about 200 requests. "That athletic program is good," smiled Tennessee Lt. Governor John Wilder after the state approved construction of the boxes. "Entertainment pays well."

Not far from the athletic complex, in the music building, Tennessee band members are themselves practicing. A brass instrument is sounding a few very familiar notes. It's a plaintive, solo version of "Rocky Top," the Vols' jaunty victory song, which will be played endlessly throughout the season. The lyrics are amusing:

> Wish that I were on Ole Rocky Top,
> Down in the Tennessee hills.
> Ain't no smoggy smoke on Rocky Top,
> Ain't no telephone bills.
> Once I met a girl on Rocky Top,
> Half bear, the other half cat—
> Wild as a mink but sweet as soda pop.
> I still dream about that.
>
> Rocky Top, you'll always be, home sweet home to me;
> Good Ole Rocky Top, Rocky Top Tennessee.

In a couple of weeks, Neyland Stadium will be chock full of enthralled fans—all but about 10,000 (the opponent's fans) wearing bright orange colors. For them, watching a Tennessee game is a profound experience, an old and dearly held ritual. The Vol Navy, a flotilla of more than 200 boats, will dock beside the stadium, on the mellow Tennessee River. Ken McMillan, who owns a UT merchandise store on Cumberland Avenue, better known as "the Strip," remembers meeting a family last year from South Fulton, Tennessee, in the far northwest corner of the state, who got up at 4:00 A.M. on a Saturday morning and set off by car for Knoxville. They arrived at 1:00 P.M. to watch the UT game, which started at 7:00 P.M. McMillan sensed that the family was a little out of place, and they were: it was their first visit to Knoxville—and their first opportunity to see the Vols play. "Where are you staying?" McMillan asked them. "Nowhere," said the father. "We're gonna drive back home after the game." As McMillan explains, for that couple, and tens of thousands of state residents like them, getting tickets to a Tennessee game is the equivalent of an opera fan cadging seats to a Pavarotti performance at the Metropolitan Opera. "It is amazing what people will do to come to a game here," says McMillan. "But it's worth it on Monday morning. You can say to your friends and to jealous neighbors, 'You should have been in Knoxville this weekend!' It places you higher in the social pecking order."

A couple of hours before kickoff, the Tennessee team will make a short walk from the athletic complex to the stadium locker room. Thousands of fans will line the route. Young men, wide-eyed children, even a blue-haired older lady or two will holler and reach out, hoping to shake the hand of John Henderson, Bernard Jackson, Willie Miles, David Martin, or *any* Vol player. It doesn't matter who. And then, moments away from the start of the game, Tennessee's Pride of the Southland marching band will form a massive T on the field. Before leaving the locker room, fully padded and ready for battle, every Vol will pass under and touch a map of the State of Tennessee. Each player will also take a quick glance at these words: "I will give my all for Tennessee today." The team will then charge out onto the field, through the band-made T. Smokey, a bluetick coon hound and the Vol mascot, will howl and take up his position on the sideline. The cheerleaders will perform athletic feats of their own to pump up the crowd—needlessly. At kickoff, everyone in the entire stadium—and probably in the entire state—will be on their feet, twittering with joyful anxiety. In the press box, Vol radio announcer Bob Kessling will utter the words that herald every game, and have for many years: "It's football time . . . in Tennessee!"

TWO

IMPRESSIONS: GROWING UP WITH TRAVIS TAYLOR

When they're in action, making tackles and scoring touchdowns, college football players seem like . . . men. On the field, Travis Taylor is a man. Florida's flashy flanker explodes off the line of scrimmage, cuts on a dime, breaks free of a defender, catches a pass softly with his hands—and then streaks down the field. He embarrassed Syracuse's defensive backs in the 1998 Orange Bowl, scoring two touchdowns and winning the game's most valuable player award. But talk to Taylor off the field, when he's not wearing his helmet, and the reality smacks you pretty plainly: he is *young*. College players are *young*. It is sometimes easy to forget that amid all the hoopla that goes with college football. Heading into his junior season with the Gators, Taylor was twenty years old and wearing braces. With his metallic smile, wide eyes, and happy disposition, he seemed an innocent. He *was* an innocent.

And yet, it was equally clear that Taylor was growing up *quickly*—as both an individual and an athlete. Though barely three years into college, he was married and had a baby. (Kevin McKinnon was the only other married player on the Gator team.) Taylor's wife, Rashadah, had given birth to a girl, Tionna, earlier in the year. She was pregnant when they got married. What is it like, I asked Taylor, being a college student and a father? "It's great," he said. "It's a joy, really, to have a child. She brings so much joy to me and my wife." The Taylors were living in an off-campus apartment in Gainesville with Rashadah's mother, who had come down from Georgia to help with the baby. Student-athletes in Taylor's circumstances—married, a father, and playing football—must mature in a hurry.

Taylor seemed very mature—and as happy as a dog with two tails. He said that marriage and fatherhood had been good for him. "It puts everything in my life in perspective," he said, "knowing what I have to do and what I can't

3 6

do. It puts my priorities in the right order." Before getting married, Taylor suggests, his life was a little too loose, too carefree—especially when it came to doing classwork. In short, he goofed off, and his grades suffered. "Going from high school to college is a big jump," he says. "Being on your own, nobody telling you what to do, it takes a while to adjust. You've got to learn to be responsible for yourself."

Taylor's dad, Cornelius, a forty-four-year-old paper mill worker in Camden County, Georgia, was a skeptic when his oldest child—Taylor has five younger sisters—told him he was getting married. "I tried to tell him he was too young," said Cornelius. "And I said, 'How are you going to take care of your baby?' And he said, 'Daddy, we got a plan.' That's what he wanted to do, so I stuck by him." I don't know what the plan entailed, precisely, but it was working. Before his son's marriage, said Cornelius, "Travis was doing just enough to get by academically. Now, his grades are much better—he's got a 2.6 or 2.7 grade point average. He's impressed my wife and me. And he's happy. He's started taking things more seriously."

Having established himself as a budding SEC star in 1998, Taylor was gearing up for a stellar junior season. As most major-college players do now, he spent the summer of 1999 on campus with his teammates, lifting weights, attending classes, and playing football with his friends. There is no off-season for players; the summer is pretty much business as usual—it's just a little hotter in Gainesville.

Four days a week in July and August, Taylor was up every morning at 5:45 A.M. "Most of the time my wife has to kick me out of bed," he laughed. He and his teammates are required to be at the practice field at 6:30 A.M. for an hour of full-bore conditioning. The sessions are mandatory and supervised by the strength coaches. Taylor dons a shoulder harness and pulls a heavy sled—a training technique designed to improve leg drive and explosiveness. After that, he will either run two miles around the track or run twenty to twenty-five 100-yard dashes. (Let me repeat that for the couch potatoes: *twenty to twenty-five 100-yard dashes*.) For good measure, he hops on the Stairmaster for a 300-step climb. Finished, he hops in his TransAm and drives home. "I take a shower and go right back to sleep—it's like I never got up," he says.

Three days a week, he and the other Florida receivers join with QBs Doug Johnson and Jesse Palmer for a little pitch and catch. The receivers practice their route-running (against defensive backs) and hone their timing with the quarterbacks. "The summer's a time for everybody to get better," says Taylor. It's also a time to either catch up or stay ahead of class work. Taylor took ten hours (four classes) in the summer of 1999—algebra, interpersonal communications, and two marketing courses. "It will help lighten the load in the fall," he says. A sports management major, he had just completed a fairly heavy, sixteen-credit spring session—architectural history, entomology, speech, tech writing, and basketball.

Taylor was lucky to get to the University of Florida. He was lucky to have a forward-thinking father, and lucky to have an uncle who lives in Jacksonville. The combination helped Taylor break out—academically and athletically— from his rather obscure hometown in Kingsland, Georgia. When he was a junior in high school, he transferred from Georgia to a school in Jacksonville, Florida, which raised his sports profile and his test scores. By doing so, he not only earned a football scholarship, but earned one to Florida—where his receiving skills were showcased in one of college football's premier passing attacks.

According to his father, "Travis has been a good athlete since he was eight years old. But where we lived he didn't get much recognition." Taylor attended Camden County High School. It was a good place, with good athletes, but according to Travis, "they just weren't getting into college. I don't know what it was." Cornelius began to fret. His son was blooming athletically but wasn't a great student, and Camden athletes had a history of doing poorly on standardized tests. "The athletes could never could pass the SAT," says Cornelius. He feared his son would suffer the same fate. Travis needed help from tutors, he said, but Camden lacked the money to hire them.

Cornelius mulled over the idea of sending Travis to live with his brother, Leonard, in Jacksonville. There, he could attend a bigger, more prosperous school. Cornelius and Travis talked, and his junior year Travis agreed to go. Camden County officials were not so enthusiastic. They tried to block Taylor's transfer to Jacksonville, arguing that the family hadn't moved to Florida and hence was just "school shopping." Cornelius hired a lawyer, and the case went to court. Cornelius testified, and four days later, a Georgia judge ruled in his favor. "I didn't have any animosity against Camden," says Cornelius, "but I had to do what I thought was best for Travis at the time."

With the approval of the Florida High School Association, Taylor enrolled at Ribault High School in Jacksonville and moved in with his uncle. Travis adjusted to his new home quickly. He and Leonard's son became friends, and Leonard taught him "a lot of good things about life and growing up." Cornelius Taylor did not find the transition so breezy. Sending a son away— even a short distance to live with your brother—is no easy thing. He was in emotional pain. "It was hard on me to let him go as a teenager—real rough," says Cornelius. "Me and Travis is real close. We communicate real good. It was harder on me than him."

It was a wise decision. Ribault is a relatively young AAA public school in Jacksonville with, Cornelius claims, good football coaches and plenty of programs to help kids prep for college. "They had it all," he says. "It is very academic." Travis joined the football team, as both a defensive back and wide receiver, but he was late getting started at Ribault, and by the time he got his uniform on the season was half over. He played in four games and turned a few heads, but was by no means a star. The next year was different. Though he only caught thirty-six passes for 800 yards as a senior at Ribault, Travis's athleticism was apparent. "It's what he does after the ball—he causes so much trouble—that got him attention," says his father. "He was the best receiver in Jacksonville."

Recruiters had noticed. Georgia Tech had spotted Travis early—when he was fifteen—and was recruiting him to play cornerback. Florida and Florida State started calling. Steve Spurrier told Travis that he'd play receiver at Florida. Travis visited Georgia Tech, which is in Atlanta and only a two-and-a-half-hour drive from Kingsland. (Gainesville is farther away.) When he got back he talked with his dad. "He hadn't decided which position he wanted to play in college," says Cornelius. "I told him to make a decision, and do what was best for him. I didn't want him going to Georgia Tech because it was close to me, because I wasn't going to be playing." Without even seeing the school, Travis committed to Florida. He was one of five receivers that Florida signed in 1997, and according to Steve Spurrier, Jr., who coached with his dad in Gainesville before moving to Oklahoma, "Travis was the lowest-rated of the bunch." No matter. As Cornelius says, it was a "good decision"—made better by the fact that Travis passed his standardized tests. He got a 980 on his SAT, and a 17 on his ACT.

"Most Definitely"

Ask Travis a question, and you're certain to hear these words as a preface to nearly all of his affirmative answers: "Most definitely. . . ." Does he like playing for the Gators? "Most definitely. . . ." Did he enjoy living with his uncle? "Oh, most definitely." Are the quarterbacks ready to go? "Most definitely. . . ." He calls Spurrier a "genius," adding, "He can make up plays on the spot and they can go for touchdowns." Is Spurrier hard to play for? Here he does not say "Most definitely." (I was not trying to trick him!) "No, not really," he says. "If you go out there and do what you're supposed to do, you don't have any problems with him." And what are you supposed to do as a Florida receiver? "He emphasizes running good routes. If you run good routes, you will play for Florida. And catch the ball! Those are the two things he stresses most."

Taylor says Florida doesn't run many pass plays in a game—maybe twelve to fifteen—and he claims to have mastered the Florida offense two games into his freshman year. He typically played flanker, meaning he was lined up off the line of scrimmage, "but in this offense it doesn't matter if you're on or off the ball." He said most of the pressure is on the quarterbacks. "A quarterback has a lot to do in this offense. Coach Spurrier is real hard on Jesse [Palmer], Doug

[Johnson], and the rest of these guys; he's real hard on them. But they make my job so much easier. We can just run routes and the ball is there."

Florida has turned out several star receivers in recent years, some of whom are playing in the pros. Travis credits them, along with Florida's quarterback, with aiding his development. During the summer, he worked out with Jacquez Green, Willie Jackson, Ike Hilliard, and Reidel Anthony—three of whom are in the NFL. "Those guys taught me a lot over the summer in Gainesville," says Travis. Like what? "They tell you simple things, like getting on top of a defensive back [before making a cut]—little things that make you so much better." Travis said that all but Green were at the 1998 Orange Bowl, "so I had to show them something."

Taylor is a natural receiver—fast, strong, and fluid. He's got excellent hands, and runs a 4.4-second forty-yard dash. When we spoke he could bench press 225 pounds sixteen times—impressive for a rising junior wide receiver. Running after the catch is, he says, "the most positive aspect of my game." I asked Steve Spurrier, Jr. to name Taylor's best qualities. "Ahhh, you name it. He's the definition of a good receiver. He's tall, he's fast, he's strong, he's got very good hands. He's grown and matured over the last year. He knows now what it takes to be a good college receiver."

Still, Taylor is quick to point out that there is a surplus of receiving talent at Florida. "Reche Caldwell, Darrell Jackson, Brian Haugabrook, John Capel— who's one of the fastest guys in the nation. We've got a lot of guys who can step up and play well." He said the team's goal was to "get back where we were and win the SEC championship. We've lost it the last two years and that's unlike the University of Florida." (Make it three.) "We have so many weapons on offense; we want to put up fifty points a game and blow out teams. That's our mentality."

What irony. In 1999, Florida's passing game sputtered badly all year. It was so bad that Spurrier was forced to run the ball to win games. Against Georgia, a game they won, Florida had ZERO passing yards in the second half. The Gators got to the SEC championship game, but with a rusty Palmer at quarterback, the passing game was so out of synch they could barely complete a pass. Alabama whipped the Gators, 34-7. It was an off year for Travis, too. He suffered a severe ankle sprain against Tennessee and missed three games. He caught thirty-four passes during the regular season, scoring six touchdowns. He was hardly noticeable in the SEC championship game, but bounced back with a huge game in the Citrus Bowl against Michigan State. In what would be his final college game, Taylor caught eleven passes for 156 yards.

I chided him last January about the SEC championship game. "Was that Florida I was watching?" I asked. "I don't know who it was," he responded, sitting at his family home in Georgia. "It wasn't the Gators. It was disappointing the way the offense finished the year. We couldn't get anything going." He said Florida's passing woes last year "were a team thing—just not executing. We had good plans, we had good practices but when we got to the game we could-n't duplicate them." He said that Spurrier was "disappointed—he didn't know what to do. He was scared to throw it. He didn't have confidence in the offense this year." Mark down those words: you may never hear them again.

Injuries certainly weakened Florida's offense last year. Taylor, the team's go-to receiver, missed the middle part of the season. And in the last half of the season, quarterback Doug Johnson developed arm problems. They were the key cogs in Florida's pass attack. Taylor said that as the season moved on, Johnson started getting "down," adding: "He wasn't saying much in practice. His arm was always hurting." Johnson's arm problems became so bad he couldn't play in the SEC championship game. He took two cortisone shots, tried to play in the second half, but could barely throw the ball. "It was bad," said Taylor. Palmer replaced him, but was ineffective against Alabama. That wasn't surprising, because he'd hardly played all year. "He wasn't used to game situations," said Taylor. "They are a dif-ferent speed than practices. That's really what he was lacking."

There were rumors that Florida was hobbled by in-fighting. Taylor down-played the rumors. "We had some situations, but everybody fought through them and tried to stay together. There was no finger pointing. I think we had a good attitude for most of the year. Everybody stood together as a team. We're a young team and are going to have some problems. But there was no dissension."

During the season, I'd asked Taylor what sort of career he envisioned for him-self. He didn't hesitate. "I'd like to be a sports agent." I was surprised by the answer for two reasons. First, while there are plenty of reputable agents around, there are also too many sleazy ones—and they have been a scourge at Florida. Second, Taylor seemed too innocent for that occupation. But perhaps that is the point. Taylor—a rising star but still a kid—had already been getting calls from agents, who typically push kids to sign service contracts with them, turn pro, take the money. Taylor suggested to me that he was not ready to turn pro.

His dad—though pointing out that Travis "doesn't associate with agents"—said something different. "Yes, he will consider it. He'll have to talk to the coaches. If things work out, he might come out early." He mentioned that Travis wanted and needed to get his degree—"that's the most important thing." Of course, degrees are *never* the most important thing when weighed against mul-timillion dollar contracts. And when the player has a wife and child to support, money takes on even added importance. Though things didn't work out terribly well for Taylor and his Gator teammates in 1999, they worked out well enough. He's in the NFL. He was drafted in the first round by the Baltimore Ravens—the tenth player taken. Taylor will become a millionaire. He'll have an agent working for *him*, not the other way around. Will he remain the same innocent, likable guy I got to know briefly last year? One can only hope so, but he's run-ning with a different crowd these days, and his braces will soon be gone.

THREE

IMPRESSIONS: STRAPPING IT DOWN WITH RAYNOCH THOMPSON

Raynoch Thompson likes to hit people—on the football field. Tennessee's All-America linebacker, named "knock-knock" by Vols fans, fit the classic definition of a headhunter: he didn't just tackle runners; he launched his 6'3", 225-pound body at opponents like a human missile. That was mostly bad for running backs, and sometimes bad for Thompson. His sophomore year, he suffered a bruised kidney early in the season. The coaches wanted to rest him for a couple of games, but according to Tennessee defensive coordinator John Chavis, "he didn't like that at all." He kept playing. Two weeks later, in a game against Georgia, he broke his nose. He didn't bother to tell the coaches or trainers. Then, said Chavis, "we noticed in practice that every time he had contact, he got a nosebleed. He didn't want to get it checked out because he thought he'd miss a game." Later in the year he suffered a concussion and blurred vision. No matter. Thompson continued not only to hold down his outside linebacker position, but to terrorize opposing offenses with his reckless style.

Indeed, Thompson seemed to develop his own signature tackle: He'd wallop an opposing running back, slowly pull himself up off the ground, wobble around in a daze for a few moments, then regain his senses just in time for the next play. "He's a warrior," says Mike Rollo, the Tennessee trainer. In 1998, his junior year, Thompson led Tennessee with ninety-five tackles and made first-team All–Southeastern Conference. He was overshadowed by the fiery Al Wilson, an All American, but was never hard to spot careening around on the football field. Says Thompson: "I just go out and react in the blink of an eye."

College football players are officially called "student-athletes." There are some who manifest that Greek-sounding ideal, who manage to major in engineering or accounting and also play stand-out football on Saturday. Tennessee defensive tackle Darwin Walker was an engineering major and outstanding player. Peyton Manning was a star on and off the field. But truth be told, they are exceptions. If you look at the starting lineups of top SEC schools, many of the players might better be described as "athlete-students." That's not to say that they don't study, don't care about school, or don't make good grades—but simply that it's hard for many major-college starters to care about classwork in *quite the same way* that they care about football.

As Thompson himself says, there are "distractions." There are the rigors of practice—football is almost a seven-days-a-week job for these kids. There is the hoopla—media coverage, marching bands, 100,000 cheering fans—none of which the players get when they turn in English papers. There is, too, the lure of professional money—a powerful itch that grows stronger in the best players as they matriculate. And beneath all the hype, there is the reality that many of the best players come from hardscrabble backgrounds and are not conditioned to study. Move down the depth chart, to second and third teamers: that's where you'll find the more serious students.

Meet Raynoch Thompson, talk to him, and you come quickly to realize: here, folks, is an athlete. Thompson has the body of a leopard—lean and muscular. The guy *looks* like an outside linebacker. When we spoke, in the Tennessee athletic complex, Thompson was wearing gray sweatpants, an orange Tennessee football sweatshirt, athletic shoes. He had a nylon skullcap on his head—and over that a Michigan hat. (He was a fan of the Fab Five—a stellar group of basketball players at Michigan—a few years back.) Each ear was adorned with a smallish diamond (or zirconium) stud. A large silver cross hung around his neck. Thompson seemed the slightest bit leery of being interviewed at first, but his personality warms as he settles into a conversation. He's not a jovial backslapper, but like most top players he's come to understand the needs of the press. He's got close-cropped hair, a bright smile, and urban eyes. He speaks in a subdued voice. He chuckles frequently—sometimes mockingly. One senses a personality that has been softened, refined, by four years in college and the discipline of playing football. It could very easily have been otherwise.

Thompson grew up in the St. Bernard housing project in New Orleans, one of a rough city's roughest enclaves. For the youngest of three boys, it was a Hobbesian nightmare—crime, drugs, violence. Thompson doesn't volunteer much information about his background—but doesn't really have to. "It was tough," he says. "My dad was never there for us. My mom and grandmother raised me, and they did a good job. They're both number one in my world." He's got two older brothers. The oldest, he says, is "incarcerated." He refuses to say why. "I'd rather not discuss it. It's tough." Thompson talks to his imprisoned brother, and visits him occasionally. Thompson says his family thought that the middle son would be the sports star in the family. He, too, was a football player, and heavily recruited. But he, too, "got into trouble" and didn't go to college. "It all faltered for him," says Thompson, "growing up in the wrong atmosphere." But he "got clean," and he now works in New Orleans.

A Clumsy Boy

Thompson could have tumbled into the thicket of crime and drugs that smothers many poor neighborhoods. But his mother made what may have been a lifesaving decision. She pulled Thompson out of a public high school after his freshman year and sent him to St. Augustine, a big, all-boys Catholic school about four miles from his home. While attending St. Augustine, Thompson lived with his grandmother in a nursing home. He slept on a couch in the living room. That's where Tennessee's coaches found him when they recruited him.

Thompson called St. Augustine "a good experience for me," he says, adding: "I think I needed to go there. It's a different school; they care for you outside of what you do in the classroom. They try to expand your horizons, get you to push yourself." His grades at St. Augustine were average, but his football tackling skills proved superior. Thompson said he was "clumsy" as a boy. If so, that trait had long since disappeared by the time he was an upperclassman at St. Augustine. He played safety at first, then moved to outside linebacker. He was light for a linebacker—weighed less than 200 pounds—but he could run and was fearless. He had more than 100 tackles and fifteen sacks as a high school senior, and was dubbed by *SuperPrep* magazine an All American. That was enough to attract college recruiters.

Thompson's favorite schools were Notre Dame and Miami. And he was courted heavily by all the SEC big boys. "Growing up, I wasn't a big Tennessee fan. I liked Miami, but they were having troubles at the time and I didn't want to get caught up in that. I came here (to Knoxville) and had a good visit. I enjoyed everything. The game atmosphere here on a Saturday is just different from anywhere else. It's orange-fever everywhere. And everybody sticks by one another; it's like a family." Having played in the SEC, he has become a staunch advocate for the league. "Just look at the last few years," he says. "We won the national, Florida won the national; each year we have a team competing for the national title. Look at the top twenty-five polls the last few years: we have six or seven ranked teams. That's outstanding."

Raynoch Thompson

Thompson didn't make a qualifying score on his standardized ACT test as a high school senior, so he was forced to sit out his freshman year. He spent most of this time at Gibbs Hall, the former athletic dormitory that now houses both athletes and regular students. He got homesick. "It was a hard first year. I was far away from home, and not used to this environment. Having to sit out that first year was disappointing, but I got a lot under my belt." Missing the excitement of Saturday games was excruciating. "I was depressed because I couldn't be out there with the team. I didn't want to go to games; it would have made me sick. I stayed in my dormitory room and sometimes watched the games on TV. Sometimes I didn't even turn on the channel." But he adjusted. "Now, looking back, that year without football was the best thing for me."

"Tremendous Instincts"

John Chavis, the Tennessee defensive coordinator and linebacker guru, has been good for Thompson, too. The two are close. "He's tough on the practice field," says the Vol linebacker of Chavis, "but I've learned a whole lot from him. He's given my knowledge of the game a big boost over the last couple of years. People always talk of Tennessee's legacy of great linebackers, but they're not looking at who is at the helm, and that's Coach Chavis. To me, it's almost like he invented the game [a chuckle]. He knows his stuff, and that's why I admire him." For his part, Chavis has lauded Thompson for his "tremendous instincts" on a football field. "Anyone who has seen him play the last two years knows what he has meant to our defense."

What of Thompson, the student? He seemed ambivalent about school. He was majoring in child and family studies, and going into this senior year he sported a 2.3 grade point average. "It could be higher," he acknowledged, "and I'm going to work hard at it and get it up this year," though he admitted that doing that during football season would be a challenge. Like most SEC football players, he'd spent the summer on campus, working out and taking a couple of classes (two urban-studies courses and a health class). He said he was on track to graduate—and professed a desire to earn a graduate business degree some day. So he likes school? "It's all right," he says with a chuckle that can be interpreted to mean "not really." "I wouldn't say that I like it, but it's something you need to do to succeed in life." Thompson was girding for a career in the NFL, but what would he do, I asked, if he couldn't play football? "Ummm. Various things, but I don't really know right now. I'm just letting my mind contemplate the options."

Thompson said that his campus life was low-key. He lived in a "quiet" off-campus apartment complex with John Henderson, a defensive tackle. There weren't many other athletes around. "I just go back and forth to class, then to practice. I ride in with John and go about my day." Afterwards, he relaxes with friends, watches TV, "just try to get off my feet [another chuckle]." He talked to his mom on the phone two or three times a week. He liked all the guys on the team, he said—and suggested that the camaraderie on the Vols was a key reason why they won the national championship the year before. "We bond on and off the field. That's why we jell."

I ask about the cross. It was given to Thompson by a close family friend. "It's just a symbol of Jesus Christ. I used to pray with a rosary. I'm really not Catholic, but [praying] is something I picked up during my three years at Catholic school. I don't go to church a lot, but I always pray. It's become a habit with me. Even when we take a rest during practice, I might say a little prayer."

Did he consider himself a role model for younger kids? No. "The parents of kids are the ones who should be role models. The first people a kid should look up to is his parents. If they're doing the right thing, the kid will, too, and follow in their footsteps." It is a wise answer from a twenty-two-year-old from the projects, who grew up without a father's love and advice, *without* a male role model.

Heading into the 1999 season, Thompson said he had only one goal: to win another national championship. He had had reconstructive surgery on his left ankle a few months before. As always, he pronounced himself good to go. He was so eager for the football season to begin, he told one reporter, "I can't sleep at night. All I think about is football." Asked to describe the 1999 team's attitude, he said: "We're eager to go out there and repeat [the national title]. I'm more hungry this year than last year. I ain't gonna say we're cocky, just confident—a cool confidence." Could the defense play well without the leadership of middle linebacker Al Wilson, who'd graduated and turned pro? "I think we can. Al will be tough to replace. He's authentic, and what he gave to the game was emotion. He'd jump down your neck if you weren't playing up to par. A lot of the players respected Al because he said what was on his mind. We don't have a duplicate. But we'll put somebody in there who can get the job done." Thompson likes to woof at opponents on the field, but as he himself acknowledged, he's not the type to holler or scream at teammates. "I like to go about my business on and off the field, and show the younger guys how to get the job done."

As it turned out, of course, Tennessee didn't quite get it done in 1999. The team didn't fulfill its lofty expectations last year—but Thompson had a solid year. He again led the team in tackles, with ninety-four in twelve games, despite having a double-hernia operation midway through the season. He missed one game. The defense played well most of the year, and Wilson's replacement, Dominique Stevenson, was solid. But Wilson's warrior-spirit was sorely missed. The defense played lackadaisically in a couple of key games that the Vols lost—against Florida and Arkansas. The latter defeat knocked Tennessee out of the title picture.

But Thompson was characteristically tough. He took barely a week off after the hernia surgery and returned in time to play Alabama. Six days before the game, he couldn't even walk. Along with Eric Westmoreland, who had an exceptional game, Thompson helped keep Bama's star back, Shaun Alexander, in check—and the Vols beat their rival. Thompson was asked frequently about Alexander before and after that game, and while he paid the talented Bama back his dues, he always made a point of saying that tackling Tennessee's backs—Jamal Lewis and Travis Henry—was tougher. He is not one to pay homage to anybody who doesn't wear orange.

Last April Thompson was drafted in the second round by the Arizona Cardinals. He was the forty-first college player picked in the draft. He did not graduate from Tennessee. The distractions obviously proved a little too much for him. Before strolling out of the meeting room, Thompson chuckled again and said this about the season in front of him—his last as a college player: "You got to strap it down, buckle up, and go, 'cuz this program [another chuckle] doesn't settle for anything but the best." And with that, Raynoch Thompson was off to do what he does best—play linebacker.

FOUR

THE HEAD BALL COACH: STEVE SPURRIER

Blindfolded, with his back to the wall, with his hands tied behind him, Steve Spurrier would still be a two-point favorite at his own execution.
                              —*Atlanta Journal*, 1966, after Spurrier kicked
                              the game-winning field goal against Auburn

It's the autumn of 1966, and Florida and Auburn have locked horns in an important SEC football game. Thanks largely to the play of quarterback Steve Spurrier, an All American, the Gators are undefeated after six games and ranked eighth in the country. Auburn has a middling team that will end the season with a losing record. But in this game, played in Gainesville, Florida, they are giving the Gators a fight. With under a minute to play, the score is tied at 24. Scores of press people are watching the game—among them, Joe Durso of the *New York Times*. It was the first time the venerable *Times* (New York's old, gray lady) had ever ventured into Gainesville to watch a college football game. Durso and other writers are there to watch Spurrier, who is a contender for the Heisman Trophy. The ballots had gone out only days before.

There is a lot on the line. A tie with Auburn would taint the Gator season—and with the clock winding down, that seems a likely outcome. A poor performance by Spurrier would ruin his Heisman bid. But, of course, Spurrier does not have a poor performance—quite the opposite, in fact. He plays the game of his life. He passes for 259 yards—a number that seems ordinary today, but was large in the 1960s, when running the ball was the rule. Spurrier is Florida's punter, too, and a good one: against Auburn that day, he averages forty-seven yards a kick.

But there would be more fireworks from the confident Florida quarterback. With less than two minutes to play, Florida has the football on the Auburn 30-yard line. It is fourth down. The Gators call a time out. Coach Ray Graves and his coaches huddle on the sidelines and decide to kick a field goal. It seems a prudent decision: Wayne Barfield, the Florida kicker, is one of the best in the nation. But while Graves has his arm around Barfield, preparing to send him into the game, Spurrier is out on the field pulling on his own kicking shoe! There is a murmur in the crowd. Graves tries to send Barfield into the game—but, amazingly, Spurrier waves the kicker back to the sideline, tells Barfield not to enter the game! "I had no idea what Steve was going to do," recalls Graves. Spurrier, of course, did: *he is going to kick the field goal himself.*

According to Graves, Spurrier had told his teammates at breakfast that morning that he'd dreamed of kicking the winning field goal against Auburn. Spurrier liked to kick—he'd practiced kicking a lot as a kid. Earlier in the year, he had a Florida trainer make him a kicking shoe, and he would often boot a few balls after practice, mostly for fun. He'd kicked once in a game that year—making a meaningless end-of-game field goal against Northwestern. This kick was different. It had enormous implications—for him and the team.

The whistle blows, Florida settles into its FG-kick formation, the ball is snapped. With all eyes riveted on him, Spurrier swings his right leg and sends the ball aloft. It carries end over end, in a low but straight arc, toward the goal posts. Viewed from the stands, the ball doesn't seem likely to reach its destination—but it does, barely tumbling over the crossbar. GOOD! The crowd erupts. Game over: Florida wins, 27-24. It is a crowning moment for Spurrier—who has passed well, punted marvelously—and, oh by the way, kicked the game-winning field goal. Largely because of that performance, Spurrier wins the Heisman Trophy.

After the game, Spurrier trots up to Graves and explains why he had defied him. "I know you wanted Wayne to kick it, but I thought it was a little long for him," Spurrier tells Graves. "I told Steve, 'It was a little long for you, too!'" recalls the coach with a chuckle. "The ball made it over by a foot."

The story is legend in Gainesville, and for good reason: kicking that field goal was the archetypal Spurrier moment—a window on the man. First, it amply illustrates Spurrier's redoubtable self-confidence: how many players would have the gall, the *cojones*, to override their coach and try such a thing? Only Spurrier. How easy it might have been to duck-hook the ball and lose the game ignominiously. Then there was the kick itself—which was captured by a photographer. It is black-and-white testimony to Spurrier's drive for perfection. His old-style kicking technique is flawless: the head is down, eyes are fixed on the ball, the right leg is stiff, the ankle is locked. Mark Mosley, the former straight-ahead kicker for the Washington Redskins, did not have better form. (I wanted to ask Barfield about that game, but nobody at the University of Florida knows where he is. I wouldn't be surprised if he is still fuming.)

Spurrier could not have thought much about the consequences of missing the kick, or he wouldn't have tried it in the first place. He doesn't fret much about anything and does not take too many things very seriously, including himself. Ask him a question—about a coaching decision, his disciplinary philosophy, his SEC rivals, his golf game—and he typically responds with a Gallic shrug: "*Naaaa*, that don't bother me." Or: "*Aaaaah*, I'm a *decent* golfer."

Let's move ahead sixteen years. . . .

In the fall of 1992, Steve Spurrier is standing on the Florida practice field. He's now the Gator football coach, and he's putting the team through a spirited practice. In addition to being Florida's head man, Spurrier was at that time—and remains—the team's offensive coordinator and quarterback coach. (Spurrier is proud of the many hats he wears, and seldom misses an opportunity to remind visitors of his multiple duties with the football program.) On this distant autumn day, Spurrier is scrutinizing the offense as it runs goal-line "skeleton drills" against the Gator defense. He does not like what he sees. Florida has three scholarship quarterbacks on the field, and they are all struggling—making bad defensive reads, throwing errant passes, just bumbling around.

Twenty-six young men have played quarterback at Florida, for Steve Spurrier, over the last decade, and if there is one thing they will all tell you— and quickly—it is that you DO NOT BUMBLE: not for one game, not for one half, not for one offensive series, not for one play, not for one play *in practice!* Bumble around as Spurrier's QB and you'll soon find yourself stumbling to the sidelines, with some Spurrier insult rattling around in your head. And soon thereafter, perhaps, if you don't have the mettle of a Nepalese sherpa, your confidence and your college football career could be in tatters.

But back to this 1992 practice: Spurrier is irritated with his sputtering offense. The starting quarterback, Shane Mathews, is bumbling. Spurrier complains and inserts the second stringer—Terry Dean. More bumbling. He puts in the third quarterback, Antwan Chiles, and he, too, is ineffective. *More bumbling!* Exasperated, Spurrier looks around and there are no more QBs . . . except for Michel Cohen. *Little* Michel Cohen, who was 5'9" and weighed 175 pounds—in pads. Mike Cohen wasn't even a regular player. He was a "walk-on," meaning that he wasn't talented enough to earn a scholarship, but still wanted so badly to play football for Florida that he spent four years running the scout team. The scout team, composed mostly of scrubs, tries to replicate the opponent's offense or defense every week. More generally, scout teamers get their heads handed to them every day in exchange for the privilege of wearing a uniform on Saturdays.

On this day, as it happens, Cohen is not feeling well. He had earned a scholarship his senior year for his dedication to the Florida program, but that hadn't changed his status with the team. He remained a bottom dweller on the depth chart. But now, his offense struggling, Steve Spurrier is looking for *somebody* to take command—if only for a play or two. Somebody who understands what he wants, somebody who will *stop the bumbling*—make the right decisions and get the darn team in the end zone. He turns toward Mike Cohen, looks at Mike Cohen, and then says these four words that still haunt Mike Cohen: "Can *you* do it?"

Mike Cohen wanted nothing more than to "do it" for Coach Spurrier. He was a Florida native, lived for Gator football. There was a time Cohen would have done anything for the chance to run the Florida offense. But after a few years on the squad, reality had long since set in. Cohen's talents were modest. He was not going to play QB for Florida, and he knew it. He had a better chance of spending a weekend with a randy, buxom cheerleader than barking out signals for the best offensive coach in the land.

And yet . . . and yet, here was Dame Fortune throwing him a small bouquet! Or was it a grenade? Steve Spurrier is hard on quarterbacks. He's a perfectionist who does not suffer fools gladly. Screw up, and Spurrier will yank you out of the lineup faster than you can say, "Uh, I messed that one up, Coach." Withering sarcasm typically follows. In this way he has reduced more than a few cocksure studs to quivering Milquetoasts.

Cohen had seen it happen. And now, with his great opportunity at hand, his athletic moment of truth, fear began to course through his veins. He wanted so badly to "do it," to defy the capricious Gods who dole out athletic talent to some, withhold it from others. But deep in the back of Cohen's mind, roaming around like a malevolent beast, was . . . the fear. The fear of humiliation. Every quarterback who has played for Spurrier has known that fear.

"*Can you do it?*" asks Spurrier. Cohen pauses, for what seemed a lifetime, and then splutters: "I . . . can . . . try." Oh, the horror. It's a meek response—absolutely the wrong thing to say to a former Heisman Trophy quarterback and ten-year pro—a man who'd ignored his coach and kicked a game-winning field goal when he was a player. Imagine an army private responding to an order from General George Patton, "Uh, I guess I can try to march up that hill, sir."

Cohen knew it was the wrong response the very millisecond the words escaped from his mouth. Spurrier flashes a look of scorn at Cohen, and replies: "I can *try*, too"—and he picks another QB. And *that* was *that*. After nearly four years of playing a foot soldier in the Gator army, Michel Cohen's big chance had gone *poof*. It's been nine years since that moment, but Cohen said recently the memory was still strong. After practice that day, he kicked himself for his diffidence. "What was I thinking?" He asked that question of himself then, and he asks it now. Cohen was one of the most obscure guys ever to play football for Spurrier, but his college career was not a total cipher. He's in the record book, however slightly. He got on the field for one game his senior year, and he even attempted a pass—the only pass he ever attempted for Spurrier. It was incomplete.

Chris Harry, a writer for the *Orlando Sentinel*, recently interviewed twenty-six QBs who have played for Spurrier, and as the *Sentinel* put it, "lived to tell about it." It is fascinating reading. The former quarterbacks sound a bit like World War II veterans recalling the Normandy invasion. There are psychological scars. Nearly all assert that Spurrier was a masterful teacher, taught them far more about playing quarterback than they would have learned anywhere else—and terrorized them with his criticism. No QB felt Spurrier's sting quite like Terry Dean. He was Florida's quarterback in 1993 and 1994. Dean was the most valuble player in the 1993 SEC championship game, and played almost flawlessly in the Sugar Bowl, leading Florida to a 41-7 trouncing of West Virginia. Dean's performance in the first half of the 1994 season was just as impressive. Dean threw *seven* touchdown passes in the first game. Under his guidance, the Gators were rolling along—undefeated after six games and ranked number one in the nation.

But somewhere along the way, Dean's confidence began to ebb. Florida whipped LSU, but Dean did not play well. Spurrier sat him down to watch the videotape of that game—and made him explain aloud every one of his mistakes. Worse, Spurrier threatened Dean: "If you play bad again, I'm putting Danny [Wuerffel] in." Dean, who was already feeling shaky under the baleful gaze of Spurrier, would soon crack. "I just had no confidence after that." In the next game, against Auburn, Dean threw four interceptions, and Spurrier made good on his threat: he benched Dean and put Wuerffel in the game. The Gators lost the game and with it their number one ranking. Dean's college career was effectively over.

Dean later blamed Spurrier for destroying his self-confidence—a comment to which many former Florida quarterbacks can relate. Spurrier is sensitive to the Dean situation, but also unapologetic: "Terry had a wonderful career here," Spurrier told Harry. "Oh, I may have jumped on him a little strong . . . but I wasn't trying to destroy his self-confidence, though I guess he felt like I did. He didn't play the way he'd been coached. He quit doing his steps. Quit his head positioning. Didn't throw where he was supposed to. I told him, 'You can't do it that way, or else I'm going to put somebody else in.'"

Replacing Dean with Wuerffel may not have been right—but it sure was a damn good call: Wuerffel turned out to be one of the best college quarterbacks ever, leading the Gators to the 1996 National Championship and winning the Heisman Trophy. He threw 114 touchdown passes in his career (the second highest total in collegiate history). Ironically, Spurrier strayed from his Darwinian keep-everybody-on-their-toes philosophy in 1999—and it probably cost him the SEC title.

Wuerffel, for all his success, had a few Spurrier moments of his own. He remembers playing against Auburn in 1995. Within the first three minutes of the game, Auburn returned a fumble for a touchdown, then picked off a

Wuerffel pass that set up a field goal. When Wuerffel, who is deeply religious, jogged to the sideline after throwing the interception, a livid Spurrier was waiting for him. "Are you trying to lose the [expletive deleted] game all by yourself?" the coach screamed. "All by yourself?" Wuerffel termed the tirade "constructive criticism."

Some players shrug off the screaming. Jesse Palmer, the current Florida quarterback, acknowledges that Spurrier can be tough. But, he asserts, the education is worth the suffering. "You want to be challenged," he says. "You don't want a layover. You want the coach to push you and tell you what you're doing wrong. That's the way it should be. You're getting taught by the best so that you can be the best." Kyle Morris (1987–1990) summed up everyone's feelings when he said simply: "Spurrier demands perfection."

Pepper Rodgers tells a third Spurrier story. Rodgers, who is sixty-eight, knows Spurrier as well as anyone. Rodgers was an assistant coach at Florida when Spurrier was the team's QB. Years later, Spurrier was an assistant coach at Georgia Tech when Rodgers was the head coach. Still later, the two men were rival coaches in the renegade U.S. Football League. Rodgers coached the Memphis Showboats, Spurrier the Tampa Bay Bandits. It was Spurrier's first head coaching job.

In 1984, the Spurrier-coached Bandits traveled to Memphis to play the Showboats. During practice the week before the game, Rodgers told his players: "Spurrier does not like to fall behind in a game. When it happens, he tries to catch up fast. Let's try to score first, then onside kick and score again. It will drive Steve crazy." Well, the Showboats did just that: scored first, then tried an onside kick. It worked; the Showboats recovered the football and, soon after, scored again. They won the game. Afterwards, recalls Rodgers, "I knew Steve would plot his revenge."

How true. A few weeks later, the Showboats played the Bandits in Tampa. Just before the game, Rodgers spotted Spurrier's son, Steve Jr., standing on the sidelines. He was a ball boy. Rodgers said hello, and little Steve looked up at him. "My dad has a surprise for you," the kid said ominously. A lightbulb went off in Rodgers' head: "I'm thinking, he's going to try an onside kick!" Sure enough, that's exactly what the Bandits did to start the game—and they recovered the football. The Bandits scored. Awaiting the kickoff, Rodgers again found himself standing next to Steve Spurrier, Jr. "My dad's got another surprise for you," said the boy. Another onside kick! The ball ricocheted off the head of a Showboat player, and the Bandits recovered again. "They tried it twice in a row, and got both," says Rodgers, laughing at the memory.

There is a point to the story, aside from the friendly gamesmanship between Rodgers and Spurrier. As Rodgers makes clear, Spurrier is ultracompetitive—he hates to lose. But, he adds, "what's scary about Steve is that he's not afraid to fail. He takes chances." Indeed, Spurrier is a risk-taker, happy to try new formations, new plays, new players, even, to get what he wants: a win. Rodgers has coached two Heisman Trophy winners: Spurrier, who won the award in 1966, and Gary Beban, who won it in 1967. "If Gary were an airline pilot," says Rodgers, "he'd be the captain of a 747. He is controlled." (And is now president of the real estate giant Coldwell Banker.) "Spurrier, on the other hand, would be a seat-of-the-pants guy, flying by superior instinct. I always knew that Steve would be a real good football coach, because he had a real good football mind." Spurrier coached in the USFL for three years, posting records of 11-7 (1983), 14-4, and 10-8, before the league folded.

"He Sees More"

Steve Spurrier is one of the most intriguing guys in sports. For one thing, he's got the cachet that comes from being a winner. In high school he was All-State in three sports (football, basketball, and baseball.) In college, the first pass he threw (a screen) resulted in a touchdown. As coach at Florida, he won four straight SEC championships, and one national title, in ten years. He was the SEC Coach of the Year five times in the 1990s. That's a pretty strong performance. He's a high-profile coach at a high-profile school. He's got a $2-million annual pay package—the highest in college football. And why not: only one team (Florida State) won more games than Florida in the 1990s. Oh, there are other big-name coaches with outstanding career records. But nobody quite invites scrutiny for his personality and coaching style like Spurrier.

To Florida fans, he is "The Head Ball Coach"—the 1960s throwback for whom offensive football is little more than a game of "pitch and catch"; a guy who will jaw a bit with the "media boys" and tell it like it is. He's the man with the caustic sense of humor—nearly always on the mark. (It was Spurrier who, after hearing that a group of FSU players had accepted free athletic gear as gifts from an agent, dubbed his Tallahassee rival Free Shoes University. It was Spurrier who named Florida's field "the Swamp.") He's a man who, in the heat of battle, can conceive a play, scream it in from the sidelines, and then watch with satisfaction as his Gator QB hurls another thunderbolt at a befuddled opponent. Joe Paterno has called Spurrier "smart, innovative, and quick," adding: "He does as good a job on game day as anybody who's ever coached. He has the great ability to improvise." Carl Franks, Spurrier's longtime assistant and now head coach at Duke University, says that Spurrier's NFL playing experience helps him as a coach. Spurrier spent a decade in the NFL—including nine years as John Brodie's backup with the San Francisco 49ers, watching games from the spot where he now stands every Saturday. He learned a lot. "Steve can see more from the sidelines than a lot of guys," says Franks.

This Spurrier is emotional during games. He jabs the air with his arm after a Florida touchdown, cocks his body on key plays, contorts his face, waves his quarterback over to the sidelines frantically. "He is excited every day about everything," says Bob Stoops, who was the Florida defensive coordinator in the late 1990s before becoming the head coach at Oklahoma. "His confidence in big games is amazing. Some people get tied up with them, or caught up in the moment, but he has a lot of fun." When Spurrier hired Stoops, he asked the new man: "Bobby, I know you're a heckuva defensive coach in tight situations or games. But what I want to know is, can you coach with a big lead?"

Spurrier is a devoted family man who refuses to be consumed by the demands of his job. When not coaching, he's apt to be playing golf—his second passion. "He's got a five handicap from the back tees, and he plays the ball down," says Norm Carlson, Florida's sports information director. When Spurrier first got to Gainesville, he was viewed skeptically by some as a "country club coach" because he didn't work fifteen hours a day. But a string of SEC championships soon proved that working well is more important than working long.

Outside of Gainesville, few people realize how loyal he is to his alma mater. Spurrier gave his Heisman trophy to the school rather than keep it for himself, prompting New York's Downtown Athletic Club to start making two bronze sculptures every year, one for the winner and one for his college. According to Richard Trapp, who played receiver for Florida in the late 1960s, Spurrier has led fundraising efforts for former Gators with problems. Spurrier insisted that his Florida playing number (11) be taken out of retirement. He pays for a hotel room for Graves when his former coach comes to town to watch a game. Though often brash, Spurrier values humility. One of his favorite expressions is: "We're not as high and mighty as we think we are."

Evil Genius?

But there is another Spurrier, and he does not conjure up such a wonderful image. He's the Florida coach as perceived by the fans at the other ten schools in the SEC. To them, Spurrier's a fierce, face-pulling "evil genius." They call him Steve Superior, because he seems cocky. This black-hatted Spurrier wins a lot, true, but is peevish and very hard to please. Watch him on the sideline—wearing (oddly) his trademark tennis visor and vest: he frowns, he winces, he throws down his play chart in disgust.

This Spurrier chews up quarterbacks if they don't perform to his exacting standards. And he can be a poor sport, complaining after games that his offense did not purr like a Porsche—even when the scoreboard reads FLORIDA

35, KENTUCKY 7. This Spurrier seems not clever but mean-spirited. He enjoys taking verbal potshots at his rivals, perhaps taking his favorite book, Sun Tzu's *The Art of War* a little too seriously. (It was Spurrier who said, famously, that "you can't spell Citrus [as in the bowl game for the SEC's *second* place team] without a U and a T.") This Spurrier finds it painful to bestow praise on an opponent. He said last year after losing to Florida State: "I don't think they're as good as they used to be. But then, neither are we." (FSU went on to win the national championship.)

This Spurrier practically drowns in his own perfectionism. We return to Michel Cohen. In the early 1990s, when he was a junior, Florida was beating Akron 59-0. With the game nearly over, Spurrier inserted Cohen to run out the clock. But Cohen and the other scrubs could not get organized in the huddle. With the play clock running out, Cohen feared that the officials would call a delay-of-game penalty. Not wanting to incur Spurrier's wrath, he called a time out. There were ten seconds left in the game. Poor Michel. Calling the time out infuriated Spurrier—so much so that, as Cohen said later, "he benched me." Spurrier pulled his fourth-string QB for screwing up with ten seconds left in the game, holding a 59-0 lead.

"How Much They Payin' You?"

This Spurrier can also be tetchy with the media. Harry, a University of Florida beat reporter for the *Orlando Sentinel*, incurred Spurrier's wrath in 1996. In the weeks leading up to the Tennessee game, he was commissioned by the *Knoxville News Sentinel* (the enemy newspaper) to write some analytical articles about the Florida team. It was an unusual arrangement, and Harry says he accepted it to earn some extra money. The articles didn't go over too well in Gainesville, to say the least. The *Gainesville Sun*, the local newspaper, called them "too revealing." And when Spurrier found out, he went ballistic. First, he had Carlson call Harry and read him the riot act. Then Spurrier got on the horn himself. "How much they payin' you?" he asked Harry. The writer's response: "Not enough to put up with all this. . . ." Spurrier: "Tennessee didn't have to send a spy down here, they've got you!" Says Harry: "He fingered me as a bad guy. I got death threats."

Until then, Spurrier had allowed Florida's beat writers to watch practices—but Harry's *News Sentinel* articles prompted the coach to close practices the week before the Tennessee game. "He said he wanted to teach [the media] a lesson," says Harry. Florida beat Tennessee, and the following week Spurrier opened his practices again. The coach saw Harry at a practice, and put his arm around the sportswriter. Harry thought Spurrier was going to make amends for closing practice and calling him a traitor. Instead, the coach said: "You *still* shouldn't have done it."

Harry has played golf with Spurrier, and like Florida's quarterbacks, (barely) lived to talk about it. "I never want to do it again," he says. "He puts so much pressure on you—everything is U.S.G.A. (United States Golf Association) rules." Harry says that on one hole he used a tee to mark his ball on the green. "Testing the green, Chrissy," said the acerbic coach. "That's normally a two-stroke penalty, but we're going to cut you some slack. Don't do it again." According to Harry, on one occasion Spurrier made Robbie Andreu, a sportswriter for the *Gainesville Sun*, hit six tee shots on one hole. Andreu kept whacking the ball out of bounds. After hitting his sixth shot, Andreu checked the flight of the ball and said, "I think that one's in." Replied the Florida coach: "Well, we're going to drive out there and take a look, and if it's OB [out of bounds] we're going to drive back and reload." As Harry says, "He takes golf real seriously. If you get an 18, it goes on the scorecard."

Listen to Spurrier talk to the press, and you'll get a quick sense of his enigmatic personality. He can be clever, entertaining, and petulant—all in the same chat. Here he is after a practice last year, speaking in his trademark staccato style—bursts of short sentences, hopping quickly from one topic to the next, a kind of verbal shorthand that reminds me of former president George Bush, who like Spurrier spends a lot of time speaking to the media. Spurrier walks up to a smallish group of sportswriters and begins.

> *Spurrier*: "Pretty good day, pretty good day. A lot of reps. A lot of guys getting a lot of action . . . staying healthy. Weather was beautiful, and looking forward to three more days of practice. . . . Earnest [Graham], Robert [Gillespie], Chuck Marks—the running backs are doing fine. . . . Receivers are getting better, quarterbacks are doing fine. . . . Everybody's trying. . . . A good attitude on this team . . . . The defense is doing a lot of good things, hustling around. It was a productive practice today, I think."
>
> A reporter asks why a Florida player, Cooper Carlisle, was not at practice.
>
> *Spurrier*: "Carlisle had class. [Thadeus] Bullard had class. Turk Wells had class. You know, this isn't a football factory. This is academia. We never had that problem at Duke—never had one player miss practice because of class. We can't juggle practice around all the players. We lose a game because they miss a practice, well, that's just the way life be's, right? They [the fans] think there is no way a guy would miss practice. During the season, quarterbacks and running backs miss practice. . . . They give tests here at 5 P.M. Five o'clock on Tuesdays and Wednesdays, on a regular basis. . . . At Duke, they're out of class by 1:30, but here they give certain classes in the afternoon—and if the players can fit football in, they fit football in. A lot of people don't know that, but they need to. They've been doing that for the ten years I've been here.

Reporter: "Is it frustrating?"

Spurrier: "No. That's just the way it is. I don't tell them how to run the university, and they don't tell me who plays quarterback. We've got a good working relationship."

A reporter asks if he has a sense of the team's potential.

Spurrier: "Naaa. It's too early. But this team has a good attitude. I think this team may play a little harder than most of our teams because we don't have star players. We don't have any pre-season All Americans, I don't think, and very few All Conference, probably. Maybe a couple. Travis Taylor is probably our biggest star right now . . . the most valuable player in the Orange Bowl. He's a big-timer; he's got a wonderful attitude, practices well. Sometimes that's good.

"Doug [Johnson] will start. He ended the season number one, and that's the way we'll go into this year. He had a good Orange Bowl working [before getting hurt]. He's going to be a senior, and we're going to give him the opportunity. . . . But if the other guy, Jesse, is better, then he'll play. It's like anything else: if the left guard goes down, the next guard steps up. The split end goes bad, the next one plays. . . . I'm not like those pro guys; they give a guy $25 million and say 'He's our guy.' They don't have to earn it. . . . We believe in earning your way around here . . . every day, week, month . . . keep earning your way."

Before leaving the group, Spurrier says: "You guys let me know if Alabama or Georgia or Tennessee players miss practice for class. Give me a call on that. . . ." And with that little closing jab, Spurrier concludes his spiel.

Throw it all together and you get—well, let the horseback psychologists interpret Spurrier's psyche. What you get, essentially, is a complicated man and damn good football coach. He's the only coach in SEC history to lead a squad to six straight ten-win seasons. Here is a guy who took Duke's talent (which is almost an oxymoron) and, in 1988, beat Tennessee. Spurrier coached Duke for two years before taking over at Florida, winning a share of the Atlantic Coast Conference (ACC) title in 1989. "That was a big confidence boost for me," Spurrier has said. It was the first time since 1962 that Duke had won the ACC.

That was an accomplishment—and a harbinger of what he would do when he got to Florida, his alma mater, which has lots more money, lots more fans, and lots more good athletes than Duke. Indeed, Spurrier's true strength may be getting more out of middling or merely above-average talent that most other coaches. When Spurrier got to Gainesville, Shane Matthews was buried on the depth chart, the fourth- or fifth-string QB. Spurrier pulled him out of obscurity, polished his skills, and soon Matthews led Florida to its first SEC title. He was twice the SEC's most valuable player. That is one of Spurrier's proudest achievements. Another is Danny Wuerffel.

Spurrier took over at Florida in 1990, after turning down a few pro offers, and immediately turned the SEC on its head. The SEC had long been a tough-guy's conference, built in the image of Bear Bryant, Vince Dooley, Shug Jordan, and Pat Dye. They were hard-nosed coaches who liked to run the ball. Even in the 1960s, when Spurrier was at Florida, the Gators typically ran the halfback on first down, ran a draw on second down, and then, if necessary, threw on third down. "We didn't really throw the ball until we got behind or it was tied," he recalls.

Spurrier does not have that conservative mindset—quite the opposite, in fact. "When I got to Florida," he says, "there were no really good passing teams in the conference. Vandy was about the only one—they could throw the ball some years, but they didn't have the talent or defense to win any championships. The word was, you gotta play defense and run the ball to win SEC championships. That's what Auburn and Alabama did, and most people believed it." Spurrier did not, of course. He was himself a passer—a guy who liked to chuck the rock. Says the coach: "I thought, 'Hey, why not just throw the ball on first down?' It's within the rules."

And so the Gators did. They passed often, and they passed well, blitzing SEC opponents with what came to be called the "Fun-and-Gun" attack. Suddenly, Florida was piling up points and clobbering opponents accustomed to defending the run. Rival teams were damn near helpless. With the exception of Alabama a few years, most SEC teams did not have enough talented defensive backs to cope with Spurrier's precision passing schemes. It was all very quick in coming: Florida won the SEC title in Spurrier's first year—but was denied the official championship because the school was on NCAA probation for an infraction that had occurred in 1986. Spurrier still seethes about the injustice. "In their wisdom, the NCAA decided to penalize the 1990 team and say, 'You are not eligible to be the champion because, four years earlier, a coach [Galen Hall] supposedly made a $360 child support payment for a player. That's how smart the NCAA is."

No matter: Spurrier got Florida its first official conference title the next year, in 1991. The Gators finished 7-0 in the SEC and 10-2 overall. That began a seven-year stretch during which the Gators completely dominated a very strong, and very proud, football conference. Humbled, his SEC rivals now place great emphasis on recruiting defensive backs, and in recent years they have succeeded in slowing down the Gator scoring machine. Florida has not won the SEC title in three years.

B.S. and A.S.

To understand how dramatically Spurrier has transformed the Florida football program, one must turn to a Florida media guide. (When Spurrier was a player, in the 1960s, the media guide was a thin brochure. Nowadays, it's 350 pages thick and costs tens of thousands of dollars for the athletic association to produce.) One page in the 1998 edition neatly summarizes Florida's success B.S. (before Spurrier) and A.S. (after Spurrier).

It is eye-opening. Simply put, Florida was a football lightweight before Spurrier arrived in Gainesville, and it's been a heavyweight program since. The 1990s were Florida's coming-out party. Indeed, before Spurrier, Florida had *never* won an official SEC championship—and had twice been sanctioned for rules violations by the NCAA. After Spurrier, the Gators won four straight, and five in the 1990s. (Only Spurrier and the legendary Bear Bryant have won four straight SEC titles.) In the eighty-three years of Florida football before Spurrier, the Gators were ranked number one for one week (in November of 1985); after Spurrier, they've been ranked first for twenty-five weeks—all between 1994 and 1997, which are beginning to look like Spurrier's glory years. Before Spurrier, the Gators had a losing record in the SEC (.473 winning percentage between 1933 and 1989); after Spurrier, Florida's SEC winning percentage is .880. Florida played in three major bowls in all the years before Spurrier; since he arrived, they've played in a major bowl practically every year—and, of course, won the national championship in 1996. He is one of two coaches to win at least nine games every year in the 1990s; the other is Bobby Bowden.

To list all the passing and scoring records that Florida has set under Spurrier would take half a dozen pages. Suffice to say, the Gators light up the scoreboard—though their proficiency has lately been falling. During the 1990s, Florida QBs threw far more TD passes than any other team in the country. (Brigham Young was a distant second.) The 1996 team led the nation in scoring (46.5 points a game)—the best in SEC history. And for the decade just finished, the Gators offense scored an average of 37 points a game, and racked up 463 yards of offense. During the 1990s, Florida led the SEC in passing six times, and in scoring six times. That actually surprised me: I'd swear they led the SEC in those categories every year. It sure seemed like it.

What accounts for this success? I talked to Spurrier, and watched his team practice a few times, to find out. What I found was that The Head Ball Coach is very much as he seems: intense, demanding, flinty, ferociously competitive—more likable up close than he is from afar. Just before I was ushered into his spacious second-floor office adjacent to Ben Hill Griffin stadium, Spurrier's squeaky voice greets me.

"Is that Richard?" he says, sight unseen, sounding as if I was one of his favorite former QBs. "Come on in." Spurrier stands and we shake hands. He is dressed casually: short-sleeved knit shirt, gray coaching shorts, tennis shoes. His desk is large and cluttered with paper. To the right, a putter stands upright near the window. There is a row of SEC championship caps on a high credenza behind his desk. There is also a row of game footballs, starting with

Florida's 17-13 victory at Alabama in 1990 that started the Gator juggernaut. He told Florida assistant coach Carl Franks after that victory: "Whatever black cloud or curse hindered Florida football, I think we blew it away."

With pride, Spurrier points to a cluster of championship team photos hung on the walls. It's a Florida tradition, he says, to take a team photo immediately after winning the SEC title. Some of the players are sprawled happily inside the Georgia Dome like kids. There are a few game photos of individual players. "That kid up top on the left," he says, "is Chris Doering. He caught more TD passes than any player ever in the SEC." He then points to a photograph of another Florida wide receiver, Travis McGriff. "He totaled more passing yardage in one season than any SEC player ever."

Spurrier is renowned as a quarterback coach, but he understands that there are two sides to the passing game. He works closely with Florida's receivers. And the Gators have had some good ones: Reidel Anthony, Ike Hilliard, Jacquez Green, and Willie Jackson, to name a few. Hilliard and Anthony were first-round NFL draft choices. But Doering and McGriff are obviously two of Spurrier's favorite players, and the reason is simple: like most coaches, Spurrier has a special affection for overachievers, for guys who are not enormously talented but who work hard and "buy into the system."

That means that they listen to the coach, and then perform. Doering was a non-scholarship walk-on when he started at Florida. McGriff was on scholarship, but he was small and, as Spurrier acknowledges, not a head-turning athlete. Still, he had the qualities necessary to be a good college receiver: he was quick off the line of scrimmage, ran precise routes, and, of course, had soft hands. "He came a long way his last year," says the coach. Spurrier makes a point of reviewing practice tapes with both the quarterbacks and receivers, "so they all hear the same thing. I think that's important. A lot of teams, the quarterbacks will meet in one room and the receivers in another. And the quarterback will say, 'I think the receiver was too deep on that play.' And you'd respond, 'Well, now, is somebody telling that to the receiver?' So we go over everything together. It makes sense to me."

"We Have a Good System"

Carlson had warned me that Spurrier was a tough interview. "He gets fidgety after fifteen minutes and starts thrumming his fingers on his desk." Remembering this, I get right to the point with The Head Ball Coach. What, I ask him, makes the Florida passing attack so good? "We have a good system," he replies, fingering his horn-rim glasses. "We've got good players and coaches, and being here in Florida, the weather is conducive for passing. It's warm, which makes the ball easier to catch; we've got a good grass field, and there is very low wind. So it's all conducive to throwing and catching the ball."

As a former QB, Spurrier knows what quarterbacks experience on a football field: what they see, what they feel. But as Wuerffel puts it, developing quarterbacks takes more than mere knowledge of the position. "What makes him special," says Wuerffel, "is that he can transfer his knowledge to you. He teaches you what he knows. A lot of coaches can't do that." How true. Spurrier does not merely tell players what he wants, he often shows them, even though his knees now are a little gimpy. In the blazing Florida heat, his visor turned sideways (almost comically) to shade his face from the sun, he will quickly throw his body into reverse, demonstrating a three- or five-step "drop." He plants his legs firmly and then whips his arm forward, as if he is throwing a pass. (On the days I watched him he did not actually handle or throw the ball.)

Brian Fox, a former Gator quarterback (1989–1991), knows first-hand how demanding Spurrier can be. He says that most offensive coordinators will tell their quarterbacks: "On this play, throw the ball 25 yards down the field, and hit the receiver near the sideline." Spurrier demands more. "He'll say, 'I want you to throw the 20 to 22 yards deep, hit the receiver two-and-half yards from the sideline, and hit him from the chest up.' The trajectory of the ball and everything else has to be perfect. If you hit the receiver at the belt buckle, he'll let you know about it. That's what he expected of us."

Fox says that Spurrier "makes it so difficult for his quarterbacks in practices and scrimmages that the games are actually easy." Adds Doug Johnson, the Gators starting QB in 1999: "He tries to make us think like he would, if he were out on the field. He tries to make us go over the same things he's going over during games. That's why when you see Coach Spurrier on the sidelines, he looks like he's ready to run somebody over. He's in the game, totally focused on the game, as if he were behind center. A lot of people criticize him for throwing stuff, showmanship, but that's because he's totally in the game."

Spurrier stresses many things to his quarterbacks, says Fox, but the first is throwing mechanics—ball positioning. Getting the football "up" and "back" before a throw. "He has a certain idea of how the ball should be thrown, and it starts with the drop-back," says Fox. "With each step you are swinging the ball across your chest. Then, by the fifth step, the ball should be on your back shoulder. He wants the ball way back. It's all timing—that's what he is shooting for." Unfortunately, Fox, who transferred from Purdue to Florida, could never quite grasp the Spurrier technique. His natural tendency was to hold the ball lower, near his chest, before throwing. That did not help his career at Florida. "I *wanted* to throw the ball like Spurrier wanted," says Fox, "but I couldn't really do it." As a result, Fox didn't play very much. When Wuerffel was at Florida, he says that Spurrier often emphasized "face position—looking into areas, looking off the secondary. And we did a lot of audibling."

Steve Spurrier

Quarterback Essentials

Spurrier explained to me what one needs to play quarterback for the Gators. "First, you have to have some talent throwing the ball. And you've got to be courageous; you've got to have the courage to stand there in the pocket, with guys coming at you and flying at your knees. But mainly, it's the decision-making that's important." I ask him if his two top quarterbacks for the 1999 season, Doug Johnson and Jesse Palmer, are good decision makers. "Uh, well, I wouldn't say that they're as good as Danny Wuerffel and Shane Matthews. They were probably our best two." The coach also demands that his quarterback recognize defenses and run plays that he has mapped out to exploit them. Says Palmer: "Recognizing defenses is one of the fundamentals, like learning how to write and walk. We're always well coached up, and we always have a game plan when we come up to the ball, so we can audible if necessary."

Spurrier recruits a lot of quarterbacks. There are at least four scholarship QBs on the team every year. With such stiff competition, getting playing time can be tough. In fact, if you peruse the list of quarterbacks at Florida over the last ten years, very few played much at all. When Fox was a senior and buried on the depth chart, Spurrier told him he was not going to play and yanked his scholarship. It was, says Fox, who is now thirty and works in Orlando, "a traumatic experience." So much so that he could hardly watch Florida play for a few years after he graduated. "I had accepted my role as a backup. But to work hard and then have the rug pulled out from under you is tough. It was difficult to be a Florida fan for a few years. I almost felt sick."

Ironically, for all his talent as a QB coach, Spurrier has not had much success developing his most high-profile recruits, or turning out NFL-caliber signal-callers. Prior to 1999, Spurrier had recruited three *Parade* magazine All Americans—Luke Bencie, Bobby Sabelhous, and Tim Olmstead—and all transferred to other schools after no more than two years under his tutelage. Total passes thrown by the three in their years at Florida: one.

Critics says Spurrier's tough love destroyed their confidence. The coach disagrees, and says that when kids fail, it is mostly for lack of talent. None of the three who transferred played much—if at all—at their new schools. Bencie played for Spurrier only one year (1991) before transferring to Michigan State. But he said recently: "I learned more about offense and playing quarterback in one year at Florida than I probably did in four seasons at Michigan State." Sabelhous hopped from Florida to San Jose State to West Virginia to Maryland. He never took a college snap. Only two Spurrier-coached quarterbacks—Wuerffel and Matthews—have made an NFL roster, and both of them have labored mostly as backups.

Interestingly, Florida's chief rival, Tennessee, has had three straight quarterbacks with more physical talent than anyone Spurrier has ever had: Heath Shuler (third pick in the 1994 NFL draft), Peyton Manning (first pick in the 1998 draft), and Tee Martin (1998 national championship) were all outstanding college signal-callers. And yet, when Tennessee and Florida play, Spurrier's quarterbacks tend to have the better game—and Florida usually wins. Martin was the only Vol QB to beat Florida, and he did it only once.

"Take Your Steps and Throw the Ball"

This year, Spurrier has landed a hotshot high school star, Brock Berlin, a native of Louisiana. Berlin was the top high school QB prospect in the country. But that won't impress Spurrier much when he gets to Gainesville. What does? Well, when I talked to him, just before the start of the 1999 season, Spurrier seemed as excited about the play of Kevin McKinnon, a walk-on, third-string QB, as he was about his top two QBs. "I really enjoy working with guys who listen and do what you ask them to do," says Spurrier. "I like coaching McKinnon for that reason. One of the things I say to our quarterback, over and over, is: 'Take your steps and throw the ball.' You can't go back there and mess around. You don't have time. The defenses are too good. But if you'll go back, take your steps, and make a decision to throw it here, or there, or there, you can get rid of it . . . most of the time. And McKinnon will do that. He'll take his steps and [Spurrier's voice rises] *get it out*. That's not easy to teach, because most of 'em go back and hesitate a moment. Uh, uh. Threw it late. Threw it late . . . You can't go back downfield once you've hesitated. That's where interceptions usually occur."

He continues: "Our quarterback should have a plan when he drops back. If we send five guys out, he's got to make a decision: which one do I throw to? They sort of know which one to throw to, but a lot depends on how the other team plays their defense—what the coverage is and so forth. That's where the decision making comes in."

Spurrier must make a lot of decisions himself, in the days leading up to games. Steve Spurrier, Jr., Spurrier's son, was a Florida offensive assistant for a year before leaving to coach at Oklahoma. He said: "On Monday we'd go over the scouting report of the team we were playing that week. [Spurrier] would hand out a packet of plays—four sheets of paper with six plays on each page. He'd say, 'This is what we're going to do this week.' We never debated anything; we didn't argue. There might be a few suggestions here and there. And then we'd go over the plays with the quarterbacks and receivers." Not all of the plays make it into the game. If a play doesn't "time out right" when practiced—if the intricate timing between the quarterback's throw and the receiver's cut—isn't right, the play gets dropped. "By the end of the week," said Spurrier, Jr., "rarely did we have anyone confused. Everyone was well prepared."

Spurrier Jr. says that his dad almost always keeps his own counsel. But the son says that he suggested what may have been one of Spurrier's great offensive coups: in 1997 the Florida coach alternated quarterbacks on *every play* and beat a very good Florida State team, which had an outstanding defense. Doug Johnson and Noah Brindise—whom Spurrier Jr. calls "tough, but the least athletic guy to ever play major-college football"—took the Gators on a twelve-play scoring drive to open that game.

Spurrier Jr. says that his dad doesn't concern himself with the defense. "He didn't know what they were running week to week. His philosophy with coaches is that you need good coordinators and then a bunch of guys who can recruit, who are organized and who get along. For the most part he's not a loud, emotional guy. But he hates incompletions, hates holding penalties, hates sacks, and hates losing." Before Spurrier Jr. left for Oklahoma, a Florida official suggested that he should stay at Florida a few years longer and soak up his dad's knowledge. "I said, 'Shoot, he just calls plays. I see him do it, but I don't know how he does it. He just can.'"

When I watched Florida practice, the offense was playing the defense in 11-on-11 "skeleton" drills—plays are run, the defense reacts, but there is no tackling. After Palmer and McKinnon got some reps, Spurrier tells Tim Olmstead, a highly recruited QB out of Virginia, to run some plays. Almost immediately, Olmstead breaks Spurrier's cardinal rule: he drops back to pass, then hesitates, unsure where to throw the ball. At the last second he dumps the ball over the middle to a receiver who is not open and who gets thwacked by a waiting defensive back. Spurrier quickly waves Olmstead out of the huddle. Within weeks Olmstead has quit the team and transferred to Vanderbilt.

When Olmstead was a sophomore, his father was dying of cancer. He spent time in Virginia with his family, missed practice time. When he got back on the field, he said Spurrier didn't cut him any slack. "If I asked him questions, I got yelled at," Olmstead told me while sitting in a Vanderbilt meeting room. "He'd say, 'Don't you know the plays? Oh, that's right, you've haven't been here.'" He said Spurrier's coaching style is "negative," and that the coach is not into positive reinforcement. "If you do something well, he doesn't say anything. He expects you to do the right thing." And if you don't? "He yells."

Besides his difficulties with Spurrier, Olmstead found that being a football player at Florida had a downside. "You can't be a regular student," he says. "You have to watch your image. If you do anything at all you're in the papers. You can't be a party person, which is good. But you want to have a good time occasionally. But if you get seen out twice a week, they'll call you a drinker. You can get labeled pretty quickly."

BRAGGING RIGHTS

A Tennessee Boy

It may pain Tennessee fans to hear this, but Spurrier wanted to play football for the Vols. He was a Tennessee boy: he grew up in Johnson City, Tennessee, and attended Science Hill Academy, where he was an exceptional all-around athlete. As a senior he was All State in three sports—football, basketball, and baseball—a rare feat. He was a high school All American in football. Spurrier has two older siblings—a brother, Graham, who's fifty-eight and still lives in Johnson City, and a sister, Sara, who's fifty-five (a year older than Steve). Their father was a Presbyterian preacher. The Rev. John Graham Spurrier liked sports—and he liked to win. He died last April in Green Cove Springs, which is thirty miles southwest of Jacksonville, where he lived with his wife, Marjorie. He was eighty-five. "I taught Steve everything he knows," the Reverend chuckled to me over the phone a few months before he passed away.

And that is apparently true. J. Graham coached Steve's youth-league baseball and basketball teams in Johnson City. The Reverend enjoyed playing tennis—and had a reputation for throwing his racket at the fence when he made an unforced error. Steve Spurrier would pick up his dad's habit of throwing things, most notably his visor. Spurrier recently told Mike Bianchi, a Jacksonville columnist, a story about his dad. The Reverend was coaching Steve's Babe Ruth baseball team, and on the first day of practice he asked the group: "How many of you boys believe that it's not whether you win or lose but how you play the game?" All but one boy (Steve Spurrier) raised his hand. "Well, you can put your hands down because I don't believe in that statement," said the Reverend. "I believe it *does* matter if you win or lose, and we're going to try to win. Any time you keep score, you're supposed to try and win." As Graham Spurrier says, "A lot of Steve's competitiveness came from Dad. Steve likes to win, always has. That's a family trait."

Sara Spurrier—who asserts that she was faster than Steve when they were young—calls her brother "intense." She contends that he's not a perfectionist, but rather someone who just works mightily to improve himself. Is there a distinction? "Growing up, once Steve set out to do something, he would practice and practice and practice to be the best that he could be. Some may consider that the definition of a perfectionist, but it's not mine."

The Spurriers had a big side yard in Johnson City, and a basketball gym behind the house. Sara's strongest memory of Steve is him out in the yard, or in the gym, practicing by himself—kicking footballs, shooting baskets. "He loved sports. He was content trying to improve himself individually." That inner drive to excel, she thinks, is why golf appeals to Spurrier—and why he gets so crazy on the football field. "With golf," she says, "it's all him. He is the one who makes the shots or makes the mistakes. He is in control on the golf course—it's his destiny. It's an individual sport. With football, you can only hope that the players do their best, that what you taught them and tried to instill in them will result in production. It's like being a parent."

According to Spurrier's mother, Marjorie, "Steve dreamed of going to college at Tennessee." The Reverend took both of his sons to watch UT play in Knoxville, which is 100 miles southwest of Johnson City. But there was a problem with Tennessee: in the early 1960s, Bowden Wyatt, the Vols coach, was still running the single-wing offense, which featured a running back, a blocking back, and an all-purpose tailback—who was expected to run, pass, and kick. Spurrier could pass and kick, but as Graham says, "Steve was not a runner. He was a plodder. He could not have played tailback there. So he had to look elsewhere." What's more, Wyatt had a drinking problem, which did not help Tennessee's chances. The Vols suggested that Spurrier play basketball (on scholarship), and, according to Marjorie, hinted that Wyatt would not be coaching the Vols much longer." That turned out to be true: a year later, Wyatt was out at UT and the new coach, Jim McDonald, installed the T formation—with the quarterback under center. But by then Spurrier was gone.

Spurrier wanted to play in the SEC, so he looked at other schools in the conference. He visited Alabama, when Joe Namath was the Tide quarterback. And he visited Ole Miss, when the Rebels were coached by Johnny Vaught and were an SEC power. Ray Graves, the coach at Florida, began to recruit Spurrier.

Here's more irony: Graves grew up in Knoxville—played at Central High School—and then played center on some of Tennessee's best-ever teams, coached by General Robert Neyland. Graves was on the 1939 UT team, which was undefeated and unscored-on in ten games, then lost to Southern California in the Rose Bowl. He was captain of the 1941 UT team. He later coached with Bobby Dodd, a legendary Vol player, at Georgia Tech. (Dodd quit coaching because he didn't like the scholarship rules at the time, when teams could sign 100 players every year!) Graves was named coach at Florida in 1960. "In those days it was a running conference," he says. There were complaints in Gainesville when Graves was hired. Some Gator fans wondered why the administration had hired a defensive coach. And Graves's first few teams did not score many points. So he vowed to open up the offense.

"Sign That Spurrier Kid"

The coach's brother, who was the postmaster in Knoxville in the early 1960s, suggested one way to do it—sign that kid over in Johnson City, Steve Spurrier. "I gave him a call and got him down here for a visit," says Graves, who now lives in Tampa. "I sold him on the idea that we wanted a wide-open offense and would give him the opportunity to run it." There were two other factors that worked in Florida's favor. Like Spurrier, Graves was a preacher's son; his father was a Methodist minister. And the University of Florida had built a golf course next to the campus. "I'm beginning to like that golf," Spurrier told Graves. So the coach sent him over to the course and got him a bucket of balls. "That might have done it," quips Graves. "But he liked a challenge, he liked the Florida climate—and the golf might have helped a little bit."

Spurrier got sick during his Florida visit. The school flew him back to Johnson City on a private plane. Spurrier's mother told Graves: "We wouldn't have given him that much attention—I'm glad he got sick down there." Later, Graves came up to Johnson City to visit the Spurrier family. They all sat down to dinner, which started with shrimp cocktail. Graves dug in—prompting Reverend Spurrier to raise his brow. "Do you know we haven't yet blessed this food?" asked Rev. Spurrier of Graves. Graves was ashen: "I thought, 'I've come all this way and blown it.'"

He hadn't. Spurrier decided to go to Florida. Needless to say, it worked out well. He was a two-time All American and won the Heisman. "He was our leader on and off the field," says Graves. "Steve tried to think what the defense was doing. I coached a lot of quarterbacks, and tried to give them help, calling plays from the sideline." The coaches sent plays in to Spurrier, too—but he often ignored them, checking into other plays he felt had a better chance to succeed. "If he saw that a cornerback was a little weak, he'd try to take advantage," says Graves. "He was always thinking. He'd cross his legs before the huddle, and it looked like he was resting, but he was thinking."

Graham Spurrier, who works for the Johnson City recreational department, goes to almost every Florida game. He stands on the sidelines, and sometimes goes up to the Gator Room, on the west side of Ben Hill Griffin Stadium, where Spurrier meets recruits. Graham says that Steve might have coached at Tennessee, too, had he been given the chance. Spurrier wanted an SEC head coaching job, and while he was at Duke interviewed at Mississippi State. But he didn't like it. Then, one weekend when Duke was playing Tennessee in Knoxville, Ben Hill Griffin, Jr., the influential Florida booster, flew into Knoxville, met Spurrier, and told him, "We've got to have you at Florida." Griffin died before he saw Spurrier coach the Gators.

Steve Spurrier visits his brother in Johnson City, Vol country, about once a year. "He's still got a lot of friends up here who pull for him every game but one," says Graham. Spurrier will go golfing in the nearby mountains of North Carolina—on Elk River, where Bob Griese and Don Shula (the Dolphin greats) have homes, and on Beech Mountain. It's a pleasant change from the flat, sandy courses in Florida. Once in a while, Graham takes Steve to a old pub in Johnson

City called the Cottage. There, Spurrier banters with Tennessee fans. "He sat around one year and answered all their questions," said Graham. "They dog him around here, but when they see he's a regular guy like they are, they're impressed. A lot of people don't like him because he beats Tennessee all the time, and because they think he's cocky. But they don't know him. He's just confident."

Spurrier's vaunted brio got dented in 1999. His Gator offense still led the league in scoring, but by Florida's standards it sputtered. According to one source, who asked not to be named, "The whole offense depends on really good quarterback play, and Doug Johnson didn't really give it to them. He was average. Because they haven't had good quarterback play, they haven't won an SEC championship [in three years]." In addition, "I'm not sure the team got along very well. There were factions, sideline incidents."

Indeed, last year was the first time Spurrier failed to win ten games since 1992. "He didn't have much fun," said Graham. "He was frustrated. The defense played well. That helped a lot. But he couldn't figure out [the offense]."

Jesse Palmer, who's a senior, will probably run the offense this year. Berlin is waiting in the wings. Berlin is not tall, but he's said to have a quick release and strong grasp of the game. If he develops, Spurrier might regain his magic and run roughshod over his rivals again. But it won't be easy. Everybody in the SEC has become accustomed to the Florida offense—and some teams [see Alabama in 1999] are even playing their own brand of the Gator "Fun-and-Gun." If Berlin does not develop, Spurrier might soon begin to drift toward retirement. Last year he seemed a little frustrated and impatient with his troops. At one point he blamed the media for being negative about the team, when in fact he has moaned for weeks about players making "stupid" mistakes. Still, the Gators are hauling in lots of high school talent, and good players tend to make coaching a lot more fun.

I asked Spurrier how it felt to be the senior coach in the SEC. "Yea," he replied, "coaches don't last a long time nowadays because everybody can't win. Everybody wants to win and win big—that's just the way life be's. We all know that when we get into coaching."

Is he still a "hungry" football coach? "I hope so," replies Spurrier. "I hope so. I get away a lot in the off-season to avoid burnout. I'm pretty good at avoiding burnout." Still, he said, "I don't think I'll be a long-term coach. I know, coaches who are seventy now said the same thing when they were age fifty or so. But nowadays you're able to make a lot of dough, so maybe you [can] retire when you're sixty or so. It depends on whether it's still challenging and fun. But right now, life is just too good in Gainesville to leave, unless they make me leave. Somebody asked me what could make me leave. And I said, 'Well, shoot, I could get fired.' We know that." Spurrier doesn't expect that to happen to him. But, as he notes, "the situation could change. Maybe we get a new president who raises academic standards so that we don't have a chance to compete. Or we get a new athletic director. You don't know what's going to happen."

Spurrier will burn out on the college game long before he gets fired. And even that wouldn't be such a bad thing. For one thing, he's a happy family man. His wife, Jerri, is an aerobics instructor at Florida. The couple met when they were students at Florida and got married just before Spurrier's senior season. They have four children: Steve Jr.; married daughters Lisa and Amy; and son Scotty, who is adopted. Beyond that, Spurrier has already established a formidable legacy at Florida—which means he could take a pro job and leave Gainesville a hero. He has turned down professional offers in the past, but doesn't rule out making the jump to the NFL. Most friends and family don't think he'll do it—unless a real good opportunity pops up with a Florida-based team—Tampa, Jacksonville, or Miami. "I think he'll stay in Gainesville and retire," says Graham. "He's had some attractive offers from the pros, but he enjoys coaching kids. You've got some control, whereas the professional athletes go their own way every day. My gut feeling is that he won't coach as long as a lot of them do." Of course, without financial wants, he could just retire to a happy life on the links.

Speaking of which, Chris Harry, the *Orlando Sentinel* sportswriter, recalls a 1994 tournament in which both Spurrier and John Reaves were playing. Reaves was Florida's quarterback between 1969 and 1972, and played for Spurrier on the Tampa Bay Bandits. He was a talented passer. At the time of the golf tourney, he was South Carolina's tight end and running backs coach. (He was let go a couple of years ago.) According to Harry, Reaves told him that he'd played well in the tourney. "I shot an 84 and I tied Spurrier," he said. Reaves then recounted how he and Spurrier were splitting up the financial pot afterwards. There was a dollar left over. Reaves told Harry: "I just figured Steve would let me have it. But Steve said, 'Flip ya for it, Johnny.'" Harry checked Reaves's account of the tale with another coach who was at the tournament. He confirmed that the two men did, in fact, flip for the remaining money on the table—but it wasn't a dollar, the coach told Harry. It was a quarter. Harry wrote the story, and it was published. Spurrier read it. The next time Spurrier sees Harry, he walks up to the reporter and says: "I don't know who told you that golf story, but it's wrong. John Reaves never shot a friggin' 84 in his life." Ever the competitor. That is Steve Spurrier.

Steve Spurrier

GUIDELINES FOR A GOOD BALL COACH

1. Treat all players fairly; the way they deserve to be treated.
2. After chewing out a player, say something positive to bring him back tomorrow.
3. Support your players every chance you have.
4. If you must criticize, do it to a player's face, not downtown or to the media. End all criticism with something positive.
5. Try to make all your players feel important.
6. Stimulate your players to be the best they can be.
7. Stay in control; don't lose your temper or your emotions.
8. Coach, coach, and coach some more before you criticize.
9. What your players learn is what's most important, not what you know.
10. Your practice plans are very important. Know what you're doing each practice.
11. Enthusiasm is contagious. Practice this every day.
12. Fundamentals are the most important factor you can teach.
13. Coaches should never argue with or criticize another coach in front of another. Never allow a player to be disloyal or criticize another coach or player.
14. Be concerned about injuries to all players.
15. Don't ever allow any player to loaf, no matter who he is.
16. Don't ever threaten a player or team unless you plan to back it up.
17. Encourage and demand that your players do well in their academic work.
18. Make the game fun for your players.
19. Do not berate the referees.
20. Don't ever use foul language in front of your players.
21. Be willing to suspend or remove a star player if he is disruptive to the team.
22. Always be open to new ides and techniques that can make your player and team more successful.
23. Be sure to listen to your players and maintain a balance between being a friend and the boss.
24. If you have been a good coach, your former players will stay in touch and will feel comfortable and appreciated around your current players.
25. Honesty is the centerpiece of a coach-player relationship.
26. Your priorities should be God, your family, then your team.
27. If you are a good coach, your players will play very close to how you teach them to play.
28. Good teams get better as the season progresses, and their ability, commitment, and confidence grow stronger.
29. When things are going good, you must stay on their butts to improve everyday. When things are going bad, you need to lighten up a little.
30. Your favorite player should be the most well-conditioned and the most unselfish player on the team.

Steve Spurrier, Florida Gators

FIVE

ONLY GATORS GET OUT ALIVE : TENNESSEE VERSUS FLORIDA

I've got a friend whose body temperature goes up three degrees on game week-ends, he gets so worked up.
—The Lizard Man, also known as Gainesville house painter Bruce Doyle

A lot of people say it tastes like chicken. But I say it tastes like gator.
—Jeanne Britton of Hawthorne, Florida, who sells genuine alligator heads on University Avenue in Gainesville

We said before the game, this is going to be a fifteen-round heavyweight fight.
—Jon Hoke, Florida defensive coordinator

September 18, 1999

Spencer Rygas had an idea. Wouldn't it be great, he thought, to grab a few friends, hop in the family recreational vehicle, and drive from Pulaski, Virginia, to Gainesville, Florida, to watch the Florida-Tennessee game? What college football fan wouldn't want to watch this game? Florida and Tennessee were the two lions of the SEC in the second half of the 1990s. Their annual, early season showdown was not just a huge game in the Southeastern Conference—giving the winner a big boost in the race for conference champion—but also had become a contest with important national implications. The Gators and Vols are two of the best teams in the country. Florida, largely because it had beaten Tennessee, won the 1996 national title. Tennessee, largely because it had beaten Florida (for the first time since 1993), went undefeated in 1998 and won the national championship.

One thing the Vols hadn't done in the 1990s (or since 1971, for that matter), was beat Florida at Ben Hill Griffin Stadium, which is so noisy that it's been called the football equivalent of Dante's *Inferno*. Four times in the 1990s, Tennessee brought a team ranked number eight in the nation or higher into

Tennessee vs. Florida

Gainesville—and four times the Vols had returned to Knoxville a loser. Would things be different in 1999?

Tennessee was certainly optimistic, coming off a national title season and with an all-star lineup of talent. Coming into this game, the Vols were ranked number two in the nation, but they'd only played one game, beating an over-matched Wyoming team. Florida, led by coach Steve Spurrier, had waxed two season-starting creampuffs and was ranked number four. While Tennessee seemed to have the talent edge coming into this game, Florida certainly would not lack for confidence. The Gators had won ten games seven times in the 1990s. And, of course, they had their trump card: They were playing at home, in the notorious Swamp, which is probably the toughest place to win a game in the country. The fans practically sit on the field, but certainly not on their hands: they are L-O-U-D, and deserved partial credit for Florida's twenty-nine-game home winning streak. Florida hoped to make it thirty victories in a row at home by beating the Vols, who were challenging Florida for supremacy in the SEC.

Spurrier has had his way with Tennessee. Coming into this game, he was 6-3 against the Vols since taking over at Florida in 1990. The Florida coach likes to play head games with his SEC opponents, and he'd already issued a challenge to his counterpart at Tennessee, Phillip Fulmer. "You tell Coach Fulmer that the Swamp is going to be loud this year," Spurrier told me before the season, "as loud as it's ever been."

I conveyed that message to the Tennessee coach over the phone a few weeks prior to the game. There was no response. Fulmer hasn't done well against Florida, but he and the Vols did manage to put the Spurrier hex to rest in 1998, when Tennessee beat Florida in an overtime thriller. Still, Fulmer has not shown, tactically, that he's a match for Spurrier. Here was his chance to go into the Swamp with a power football team and teach Steve Superior—as his foes called him—a lesson.

Rygas, twenty-nine, couldn't wait to watch. A graduate of the University of Florida law school, he works as an attorney in Pulaski, which is fifty miles from Roanoke, Virginia. Rygas had no trouble finding a few friends to make the trip. Chris Davis, a thirty-two-year-old golf pro from Wytheville, Virginia, signed on. So did Marco Ruas, twenty-two, a funeral home director in Pulaski. The final member of the foursome was Matt Gardner, a twenty-one-year-old student at Ohio State University, who'd been persuaded that he would never see a real college football game until he saw Tennessee lock horns with Florida. Gardner left Columbus, Ohio, on Wednesday at 2:00 P.M., drove eight hours into Virginia, and joined up with the others. The group roared out of Pulaski about midnight, gung ho for a 620-mile SEC road trip. They had beer, they had cash, they had $200 worth of junk food (chips, pretzels, soft drinks, Cheese Doodles, Sunny Delight), and they had . . .

7 3

BRAGGING RIGHTS

... A 1977 Dodge Swinger, which was their four-wheeled steed for the journey. Like many fun seekers, Rygas and his pals did not iron out *every* detail before hitting the road. Tickets? They'd buy them in Gainesville. Weather? Yeah, there were reports of a big storm roiling the south Atlantic and threatening the Florida coast, but so what? And the Swinger? True, she hadn't been driven in three years—but how often do you get a chance to travel with the boys in something that the Bee Gees would appreciate—a real 1970s-style funkmobile?

When Rygas was a graduate student at Florida, in the mid-1970s, he lived in the Swinger. Even then the old RV was having mechanical problems. After graduation it took him three days to get the Swinger home. When he did, Rygas parked it on a farm—and there the RV rested for three years. Rygas's father had recently refurbished the engine. "This," said the Pulaski attorney, "was the maiden journey. Not many people would say, 'Let's get in a twenty-two-year-old RV and go.' We did—for this game. Let's just say it's not a high-tech, tight-handling machine."

That was an understatement. The Swinger was a little short on luxury options: it had no water hookups and no TV. It had a massive dashboard, with enough knobs to resemble a 747 cockpit, but "only three of the buttons work," said Rygas. The interior lights had shorted out, and the glove compartment box wouldn't shut. Rygas estimated that the fuzzy orange interior carpeting had soaked up three gallons of vodka punch over the years. There was no CD player, but as Rygas noted, "We've got a jumpin' 8-track system." It was only after they got on the highway that the guys came to realize that the Swinger got about eight miles to the gallon—and that they were driving straight into Hurricane Floyd.

Gainesville: Thursday, September 16

Florida is wrapping up its last full practice before the big game. There would be a brief workout on Friday, but this was the last day to iron out any offensive or defensive kinks before the "mighty Vols," as Spurrier liked to call them, came rolling into town. A chainlink fence surrounds the Florida practice field, but it was covered in a Gator-blue tarp to block out inquisitive eyes. SEC teams fret about spies who might try to steal plays or gather vital intelligence for the opposition, and so most practices are closed during game weeks: no press, no visitors, no chances. A couple of beefy, yellow-shirted security guards patrol the perimeter. At 5:30 P.M., practice concludes and the gates are thrown open. About 100 Florida players—hollering and teasing one another—start to trudge off the practice field, which is located next to the Florida basketball coliseum

7 4

and a short walk from the football stadium. About fifteen press people pass through the gates to ask Steve Spurrier a few questions.

"Quotes, quotes, quotes," says the clever Gator coach to himself as he ambles over to the media contingent. He is tanned and fit, as always, wearing blue coaching shorts, athletic shoes, a knit shirt, and a Florida cap. The weather is mild—in the mid-70s. There have been predictions of cool, possibly rainy weather for Saturday's night game, which might help the Vols. Florida's withering humidity can be hard on visiting teams.

A local reporter asks Spurrier a question: Did he realize that if Florida were to win, three teams from the state of Florida (Florida State, Florida, and Miami) would be ranked number one, two, and three in the nation? "Hadn't thought about that, don't care about that," snapped Spurrier in his quick, clipped style. "Just tryin' to get our kids to get a pass off, throw it in the right direction, and see if a guy can catch it." There is another silly question about whether Spurrier has talked to his team about staying out of pregame scuffles with Tennessee. The coach brushes that one off, too, saying: "We've never had an on-field scuffle with anyone but FSU, so why should I?"

Spurrier says that he was disappointed with the practice, and in particular with the Gator offense—which he dotes on like an obsessive parent. He seems not disgusted or exasperated but rather wistful. "We didn't do much today except throw to the air, and the air was tough on us. Better today than Saturday, right Mick?"

Mick is Mike Hubert, who is Florida's radio announcer and hosts the Steve Spurrier TV show. (Hubert's signature call, when Florida makes a big play, is to say "Oh, my!"—a locution Dick Enberg patented twenty years ago.) "We weren't particularly sharp in our assignments today," continued The Head Ball Coach, as Spurrier is known locally. "Maybe we got too much offense for these kids, I don't know. . . . It's not quite like it was with Ike (Hilliard) and Reidel (Anthony) and Danny (Wuerffel) and some of those guys. Yea, maybe we'll throw out half the plays tonight, and just give them a chance to line up. . . ." It's hard to know whether Spurrier's concern is legitimate or if his lamentation is merely a ploy to motivate his players, who will surely hear his comments later that night on local radio and TV stations.

Another press question comes: "Anything you want to say to the fans, Coach?" I'm sure he's going to wave off this question like the others—but Spurrier perks up. "Yeah. Be quiet when we have the ball, please. We gotta do some [play] checking and some signals, and we need to hear. But be as loud as you want when they got the ball. But try to be quiet when the Gators have it. I'll try to repeat that tonight on our TV call-in show with Mick Hubert—remind me of that, Mick, will you? Be loud when they have it. . . ." Spurrier is very serious about this request.

Spurrier then mentions something about Tennessee. "I hear," he says in his squeaky voice, "that they might be wearing their shiny orange pants for this game. I don't know if they will, but they might try to surprise us." He doesn't elaborate, but Spurrier is apparently concerned that the Vols might gain some sort of psychological advantage by breaking out a different uniform color scheme for the game.

Spurrier is a dyed-in-the-wool Florida man: he played quarterback at Florida, where he won the Heisman Trophy in 1969. When he makes a point to tell Florida's boisterous fans to be loud, and when he warns them that Tennessee might be breaking out orange pants, he takes on a second identity. In addition to being Florida's football coach, he also becomes the school's own version of Paul Revere, warning the faithful that pagan intruders will soon be pillaging Gainesville unless everybody grabs a weapon and joins the fight.

A reporter asks the coach if any Tennessee fans ever call in to his TV show. "Oh, sure. There'll be a bunch calling in tonight. They call up and tell our [producer] they've got a basic question—'how is Doug [Johnson, the Florida quarterback] looking this week' or something, then they get on the air and say, 'We're going to kick your butt!' Some of 'em do it."

And with that Spurrier concludes the brief press chat. "All right? Let's head on in, Mick." The two men must be in the studio to do the TV call-in show in a couple of hours. As Spurrier walks off the practice field, Joe Drape, a reporter for the *New York Times*, approaches him and tries to engage the coach in a conversation. Spurrier brushes him off—doesn't want to talk. Spurrier is all business most game weeks, but especially before playing the Vols. He is focused like a laser beam on football.

"Do It the Way We Ask"

Dwayne Dixon, the coach responsible for Florida's talented group of receivers, is horsing around with one of his sons after the practice. I asked him to explain why Florida's passing game had been so successful, so dazzling, over the last ten years—ever since Spurrier arrived. Dixon, who himself played receiver for Florida between 1980 and 1983, is a stocky man who did more blocking than pass-catching when he was playing with Gator running back John L. Williams. He says: "Throwing the football is fun. We try to keep a balance between running and throwing, but we're different from most other teams. We pass to set up the run; most everyone else does it the other way around. It works for us, and until we see that it won't work, we'll keep doing it."

What makes the Florida passing game so efficient? "We stress route running," he says. "We try to throw the ball on a timing basis. It doesn't always work out that way, but our routes are precise, exact, and sharp. The ball should get to you [the receiver] the moment you're creating space between you and the defender. That's what we try to do, and we put a lot of emphasis on that. Back when I was a kid, that's all I could do—run a route the way the coach asked me. I wasn't fast, so that was the only way I could get on the field. These guys have a little more speed and God-given ability. So if they do the little things, like staying on the route until you get to a certain point and then actually separate from a defender, at the right moment, you get more opportunities to get into the end zone."

Dixon says that pass plays go wrong, sometimes, because receivers rush their routes. "Kids get excited about scoring, because they know this offense has a chance to score, and sometimes they rush what they're doing. That throws a play's timing off, and the receiver is not in the right spot when the ball is supposed to be arriving. That [causes problems] with this offensive scheme. Our job as coaches is to find guys who will do it the way we ask them to do it. That's why we've been successful. These guys understand that if they don't do it the way we ask, if they want to run routes their own way, then they won't be doing it for Florida. That is encased in their minds."

Dixon calls Spurrier a "wonk," adding: "He's a guy who pays close attention to detail. He is very meticulous. We watch tapes together, and he goes over things with the quarterbacks and receivers. My job is to fine-tune those little things that the receivers aren't doing, or that he may not have time to see. He'll say, 'Coach Dixon, yesterday so-and-so didn't get all the way up to the end of the route.' So today, we'll run that route [repeatedly] and get it corrected. Maybe a really fast kid has to run a pattern two yards deeper than the other receivers [to maintain the timing of the play]. So we work on those types of things. Repetition really helps this offense; when you do it over and over again, it becomes second nature to you. You don't have to think about it. You just do it."

Dixon has coached at Florida for ten years, and says he's never had a bad relationship with a receiver. "That's the good thing about coaching, when you can develop a relationship with players who relate to you as a person, as a counselor and as a brother. You've got to be there for them and help motivate them and keep them on track. You can't save them all. Those that will listen to you are the ones you want to go out and prosper."

What can Florida expect from Tennessee? "They have a good football team. Tennessee has excellent defensive linemen and defensive backs. They've won thirteen straight games. We'll try to execute our plays based on what they give us; find the open areas of the field. We've really been concentrating on protecting the ball. If we hold onto the ball, we've got a chance." After two games—easy wins against Central Florida and Western Michigan, Dixon asserts that "the passing game is humming. We are on track. The opportunity is here. Tennessee is a team we have to go through to even think about the SEC championship."

Friday, September 17

There is a palpable sense of anticipation in Gainesville. The city, located in north-central Florida, is a short drive from Tampa, Orlando, and Jacksonville. On North-South Drive, which runs past the Florida stadium, both CBS and Sunshine Sports trailers are parked. Thick cables snake from the trucks inside the stadium. CBS will broadcast the game nationally; Sunshine Sports, a southeastern cable network, will rebroadcast the game on Sunday.

Ben Hill Griffin Stadium seems a little like Fenway Park in Boston. Because the field and most of the seats are below ground level, it's inconspicuous. From the front it's hardly noticeable. The stadium's benefactor, Ben Hill Griffin, Jr., was a major landowner and citrus grower in Florida. His son, Ben Hill Griffin III, is a major contributor to UF and its athletic department. He likes to eat fried chicken in his luxury box before every home game. George Steinbrenner, the New York Yankee owner who's from Tampa, has his own parking place near the trucks. (Steinbrenner has contributed money to Florida.)

Recreational vehicles—a sure sign of a football game—are seen chugging around Gainesville. Workers are dropping off big round trash bins around the stadium; vendors are unloading soft drink canisters; a few people are milling around a ticket window, though this game was sold out long ago. Archer Drive, the main commercial road leading from Interstate 75 into the Florida campus, is chock full of cars sporting Florida flags and bumper stickers, which weren't visible four months earlier when I was in Gainesville. But that was in April. Now, in September, one could feel a major atmospheric change. It was a football weekend—and a big one. A pair of radio talk-show hosts are discussing Spurrier's postpractice comments from the day before. One is concerned that Spurrier's criticism, which was rather tepid by his standards, will eat at the team's confidence level rather than galvanize the players. His partner believes the coach's comments could have the opposite effect—motivate the Florida players to prove that they can play.

At Wilbur's Deli, a small shop across from the Florida law school, students are loading up on beer.

At Calico Jack's grill, a lunch spot a couple of miles down the road, radio talk-show host Steve Russell is talking football. When I walk in, he's chiding Tennessee fans for their "revisionist" attitude toward Peyton Manning, the outstanding Vol quarterback who preceded Tee Martin. (Russell's point, I surmise, is that after Martin beat Florida last year and led UT to the national championship, Tennessee fans didn't revere Manning, who didn't beat Florida, quite like they used to.

Nearby, Sheila Melton, a middle-aged woman from Williston, Florida (twenty minutes west of Gainesville), is having lunch with her friends Janet Smith and Jim and Betty Parish. Betty is wearing a T-shirt that shows a Gator sitting on top of a hound dog named Smokey, the Tennessee mascot. Sheila is perky and brash. She's wearing a sleeveless Florida-orange knit top, and she's adorned with a panoply of Gator jewelry—a Gator pin, a Gator belt buckle, an alligator broach.

I note that both Florida and Tennessee have orange as one of their school colors. This prompts an immediate reaction from Sheila, who is not a Florida grad (none of the four is) but who, with her husband, has had season tickets for twelve years: "Theirs is a *burnt* orange," she says derisively—"it's faded." Her accent stretches out the "a" in faded for a second or so. "If you take Gator orange and wear it for ten years, wash it and dry it more times than you can count, that is Tennessee orange. Faded. *Faaaaaded.* . . . That would be Tennessee orange." She has clearly given the color comparison some thought.

When I ask the women if they are excited about the game, they look at me as if I were a Martian. "Apparently, you've never been here," says Sheila with a sarcastic smile. "You *will be* impressed. Your ears will ring for days. There is something to be said when it's 100 degrees outside—and yet when the team runs through the tunnel you get chill bumps. There is something to be said about that."

Adds Janet, who's had Florida season tickets since 1971: "This is one of the biggest games of the year. It used to be FSU, but it's kind of become Tennessee. I've got chill bumps right now, just thinking about it."

Says Betty: "There is no way to explain it to people. You just have to experience it."

Sheila is so pumped up, she'd probably pull on some pads and take on the Vols herself. "We *have got* to be extremely loud when Tennessee has the ball," she tells the group. (Had she heard Spurrier's plea?) "We've seen it work before: we've forced teams to call a time out, or their play was totally messed up. Nobody on their team could hear anything because the fans were so loud. You'll get a taste of that tomorrow. I'm glad you're going."

Betty says, "A lot of people drive a long way to come to these games. Our son-in-law is coming from Alabama, and we know another young man who's coming from Kentucky. We lived in North Carolina for eleven years, and kept our season tickets and didn't miss a home game. It was a nine-hour drive from Raleigh."

The group, which calls itself the Sand Hill Lizard Tailgate Crew, is planning to eat a Cajun meal on Saturday. "We cook Cajun so that we can go to the Sugar Bowl in New Orleans," says Sheila. The Sugar Bowl is where the national championship game will be played. "We're just getting ourselves prepared." The ladies then begin an extended discussion on SEC fans. To wit:

> *Sheila:* "Last year we were in Tennessee, and we had a section of Gator fans. Where we were sitting there was one aisle leading out of the stadium. After the game, the stadium was literally rocking. And Tennessee fans blocked the aisle—they would not let Gator fans leave. So we had to walk down on the bleachers to get out. It was awful, and we were really high in the stadium."
>
> *Janet:* "Every school has them [obnoxious fans]. It depends on whom you encounter. If you encounter adults like us, we are very civil."
>
> *Betty:* "The adults in Tallahassee are bad."
>
> *Sheila:* "I went up to Tallahassee one time with my sister-in-law. We were sitting in an FSU section, and there was a lady behind us old enough to be my mother. And she bent down between us while I was doing the Gator chop and said, 'I *haaaate* it when y'all do that.' She was in our face, and I thought she was old enough to be my mom. Her husband made her move to the end of the row so she would get out of our faces. That was pretty bad."

The Lizard Man

At a table near the ladies, I come face to face with . . . The Lizard Man. Bruce Doyle is a fifty-five-year-old resident of Gainesville, but he acts a lot younger on football weekends. Why else would he introduce himself to strangers as "the lizard man"? He's nursing a beer, wearing a purple T-shirt and a cap with a large fuzzy alligator on top. Doyle, who loves talking SEC football, says he's been a UF fan for thirty years—ever since he moved to the state with his parents in 1968. He grew up in Hanover, New Hampshire, which is home to an Ivy League university (Dartmouth), which also has a football team but (presumably) fewer people wearing funny hats and cracking jokes about those hillbillies from Harvard. Doyle claims to have both undergraduate (1969) and graduate degrees (1972) from Florida, which he says makes him "the best educated house painter in Gainesville."

Doyle is a member of the Fighting Gator Touchdown Club, which has almost 800 members. The group does charitable work, some of it for the university. "Over the years, we've done such things as buy lights for the [Florida] practice field, video cameras for the coaches—and then we decided to endow scholarships," says Doyle. "We've endowed over $200,000 in scholarships to the university—all from Joe Sixpack guys like myself who work for a living."

Tennessee vs. Florida

The club members sit together at Florida home games, and take buses to away games. "That's the most fun," says Doyle. "You can talk to Gator fans here till you're blue in the face and hear the same spin. But when you go on the road, you get a different perspective. Believe me, my blood pressure is much lower on the road and in the stadium than destroying my furniture at home when a game is on TV. The animals run for cover."

Doyle adds: "I've got a friend whose body temperature goes up three degrees on game weekends, he gets so fired up. It's kind of pathetic, in a way, but it's the reality. Unless you live here, you can't understand it. It's like this all over Florida, but especially here and around the SEC. There are three sports in the South: football, spring football, and recruiting. It causes you to alter your life at times; weddings and trips and such are scheduled around home football games. You can tell when somebody is not a football fan: they'll get married on a home football weekend, or even when there is a road game."

Doyle vowed to make 1999 a "nonmojo" year—meaning that he wouldn't be a slave to hoary game-day rituals that in the past had brought the Gators luck. He would *not* rummage through his chest of drawers, looking for the underwear he wore the last time Florida beat Tennessee. He would *not* try to eat the same meals that preceded past Gator victories. "This year I decided not to do that stuff. Now that I've hit the double nickel, maybe I'm maturing. I don't know."

But there are certain *routines* that he's not yet prepared to quit. "I'll get up and go get the Jacksonville paper. The Gainesville paper is delivered at home. Then I'll monitor the media: put on the TV and radio talk shows. I'll watch ESPN game day. I'm waiting for my son to come up from Orlando. He and I go to all the games together, and he sits with me. We'll go to some pregame parties and try not to look too nervous—a little false bravado. This year, with the weak defense we have, we'll be genuinely uptight. Hopefully, we can go find some Tennessee fans, congratulate them on winning the SEC championship; tell them, 'Atta way to keep it in the SEC East.' I sit high up in the southwest corner of one end zone. They are great seats. If you can't be on the fifty-yard line, sitting on the bias high in the end zone is the next best thing. You can see the line play; you can see holes develop, and just about call the plays. You know Spurrier likes to run isolation plays on the other team's defensive backs. You know pretty much who's going to get the pass."

Florida football has been large in the 1990s. But Doyle remembers the lean years, especially the 1979 team that did not win a game, and several brutal losses to Georgia. "There is a joke among Florida fans about 1979," says Doyle. "Question: What kind of year did you have? Florida fan: 'Ohhhh, ten and one.'" (In reality, the Gators were 0-10-1.) The next year, in 1980, Florida had a much better team. That year, Mike Shanahan was the Florida offensive coordinator, and he cracked open the musty Gator offense. He developed a slick passing game (characterized by a four-wide passing formation), which bamboozled opponents. To win its first SEC championship, all UF needed to do was beat its chief rival, Georgia. The Bulldogs had running back Herschel Walker, and had dominated the Gators in the 1960s and 1970s. But Florida seemed certain of winning the 1980 game. Suddenly, with only seconds left on the clock, Georgia quarterback Buck Belou hit Lindsay Scott with an improbable, 93-yard TD pass, and Georgia miraculously won the game. "I was sick, literally, until Thursday after that game," says Doyle. "It was a dagger through the heart. We could have won the conference. To me, Georgia is our biggest rival, and FSU, a former girls' school, is number two. I don't see any Tennessee fans on a day-to-day basis. I do work with Seminole fans, and one's life is made miserable when we lose to them."

I ask him to describe SEC football: "The one word I use to describe it," says Doyle, "is *passion*. Put that word in capital letters and underline it. And when you have a good football team, the fans want to give money. It's no accident that since Steve Spurrier has been coach, the UF endowment has gone up to $500 million."

Up the road, standing in the parking lot of the Church of Christ Methodist church, on Southwest Second Avenue, is a Tennessee fan named Al Humphrey. He's a thirty-two-year-old sergeant in the Broward County Sheriff's office. He and five friends have driven a rented RV up from Fort Lauderdale—a four-hour drive—to watch the game. Cost of the RV: $440 for three days. Cost for weekend parking in the Church of Christ lot: $20. You'd think that Humphrey would be with a Vol group, but Tennessee fans are scarce in south Florida. So he's brought along two University of Miami fans and two Florida fans. He grew up in Knoxville, never missed a Vol home game. Now, living in south Florida, he makes only two Tennessee games a year—and one of them is always the Florida game. "We either fly to Knoxville or drive to Gainesville. It's the best game of the year."

Swingin' Through the Rain

And guess who is parked beside Humphrey in the church lot? The crew from Pulaski. They'd made it to Gainesville—but not without a scare or two. They'd left Virginia on Wednesday night and driven straight toward Hurricane Floyd, which by then was roaring up the southeastern coastline. Except for a twenty-minute break, Rygas had driven the whole way. "I've had twenty minutes of sleep in a day and a half," he said. Because of the hurricane, the group found itself practically alone driving south. After arriving in Charlotte, the guys had to make a key decision: should they drive to Atlanta, stay clear of the hurricane, but lose time? Or should they rumble on toward Savannah, come hell or, ahem, high water? "We said the worst thing would be if we lost time," said Davis. "We just wanted to get on with the trip."

So they pointed the Swinger toward the coast, and prayed. The hurricane was supposed to hit Myrtle Beach. But by the time the intrepid Pulaski bunch got there, it wasn't even raining—just windy. They pushed on toward Savannah. "After we got on 95 South in Savannah, we probably saw five cars in 100 miles," said Rygas. They pressed on, nearly alone on the highway. That soon became a problem. The Swinger is a gas guzzler—and in the middle of the night, with a hurricane in the Georgia area, there were almost no gas stations open. "With half a tank of gas," said Rygas, "we started looking for a fuel station. From half a tank of gas to no gas, we didn't find one. They were all boarded up and abandoned. "Added Gardner: We said, 'we're screwed!' We kept going and going and there was nothing."

Nearly out of gas, the crew decided to take emergency action. There was a portable generator in the Swinger. It had a broken fuel pump—but there was gas in it. The group grabbed the RV's shower hose, stuck it in the generator, and siphoned off its gas—running it into the RV's forty-gallon gas tank. Doing that got the Swinger another twenty miles down the road. Still, it wasn't long before they were running out of fuel again.

Rygas pulled into a gas station at Exit 12 in Georgia. It was near dawn, and the station was closed. They crossed their fingers, and waited. In an hour or so, an employee showed up and opened the station. They were saved. They filled up the Swinger and motored on down to Lake City, Florida. They'd spent nearly $250 on gas alone, but no matter: they were in Florida. "We were lucky," said Rygas. "We didn't really see any rain south of Columbia, South Carolina. So we just kept on chugging. We were the only people going south." They got into Lake City in time for a round of golf! They looked like a bunch of vagrants by that time—eleven hours after starting out—but the manager of the golf course took pity and let them use the shower facilities.

All was well when they got to Gainesville. The Swinger had made it. "I'm sitting there driving and trying to stay awake," said Rygas, "and these guys are sleeping in beds; these couches roll out. It's spacious in here. It kills you on gas, but as long as somebody knows how to drive it, get in and out of parking spaces, it's not too stressful."

Now all they needed was food and tickets. For food, the men stopped at a Publix grocer and bought $127 worth of chips, beer, bologna, and turkey. "We stopped at a Taco Bell last night and splurged, and at a Dunkin' Donuts this morning," said Davis. They'd been on the Internet all week looking for tickets, and on the phone, but had no luck. So they just walked around the Florida campus. Not wanting to waste a day, they bought a block of thirteen tickets in the student section for $125 each. That was more tickets than they needed—and they had to scramble to find the money—but the group figured they could resell some of them for a profit. "We bought thirteen, sold five and have eight now," says Gardner. "Need a ticket?"

"Next time this thing hits the road," said Rygas, taking a swig from a Sunny Delight, "we bring the satellite uplinks. And there will be a TV and CD player." Hey, the Pulaski bunch was happy. It was Friday afternoon. They had a full day of partying ahead. And, said Rygas: "We've got $20 invested in the Florida lottery. We may not have to go back."

The Purple Porpoise

The Purple Porpoise is a fairly mundane looking bar on University Avenue, a short walk from the Florida football field. It's got old, faded windows, with lots of beer signs on the facade; inside, there is lots of unpolished wood—sturdy tables and chairs. It's the kind of furniture one needs in a rowdy campus bar, and the Purple Porpoise had a reputation for being loud. It's got a front room mostly for eating, and a back room mostly for drinking and dancing.

When I got there, early Friday evening, the front room was three-quarters full of Florida folk eating burgers and such, and the back room was mostly full of Tennessee fans. The place was rocking. A Tennessee sports talk radio host, Tony Basilio, had brought his show to the Porpoise's back-room stage. Vol fans were already full of themselves. They seemed confident—especially six young, orange-clad Tennessee supporters who'd driven down from Maryville, a bedroom community outside of Knoxville where Phillip Fulmer lives.

"We lost our voice down here today," yelled one of the UT fans over the din. The Maryville group suddenly breaks into a little ditty: "We've got spirit! We've got guts! We've got the Gators by the nuts! Roll, Smokey, Roll!" There is no shortage of testosterone on this night. I ask their names. "Brent Buckner—they call me the Maryville stud," said the first, his voice hoarse. His friends were Brandon Booker, James Hargrove, and Stacy Mables. Another young man pops his head into the group and hollers: "And I'm George Brendt from Lake City, Florida, and go Gators!" This provokes the Tennesseans, who crack a nasty Florida joke. "There is a lot of talk in Gainesville that Steve Spurrier was seen at a bar in a G-string and thigh-highs," says one. "This is what the Tennessee players sing in the locker room after the game," says Buckner. "Here we go gang," and the group roars: "We don't give a damn about the whole state of Florida, the whole state of Florida; we don't give a damn about the whole state of Florida, we're from Tennessee! Whew, whew! Go Vols!"

At this, a burly, bare-chested Florida student strides into the back room with a bullhorn up to his mouth. "No inbreds allowed in Gainesville," he bellows. Florida fans go wild. "All Tennessee fans, please leave immediately—no inbreds in Gainesville. Tony Basilio, please leave immediately. No inbreds in Gainesville!" Carson Kemp, a UT fan from Nashville, takes offense. "I can take some abuse," he says, "but not that shit. Don't put a megaphone in my face." Kemp left Nashville at 2:30 A.M. with a few friends and got to Gainesville at noon. "We drove directly to the Purple Porpoise," he said. "We were the first six people here." Ten minutes later, there is a scuffle at the Porpoise's front door between the bullhorn-toting Gator student and a few Vol fans. The ruckus is quickly over, and nobody in the Porpoise seems terribly fazed. It's early.

After Basilio's show is over, Max Howell and Ken Kincaid, who host a regional radio show called *SEC Conference Call*, take the stage. They will analyze the Florida-Tennessee game, interview guests, and take calls from fans around the southeast. Howell, a former football player at Auburn, says the Memphis-based show has gotten extremely popular. "We started in September of 1997 with eight stations and now we have eighty-one in twelve states. We're in all the SEC markets—and the larger stations take us into Texas and Oklahoma and up into Cincinnati, Ohio." The show runs from 6 to 9 P.M., Monday through Friday, and has 900,000 listeners. "College football is the lifeblood down here," says Howell. "They relish it. Pro football was long coming to the South; there was 100 years of college football before it got here, and that is the reason it is popular." Adds Kincaid: "Plus, if you look, a lot of SEC schools are in small markets. There is not a metropolitan team with the exception of Vanderbilt, so there is not any head-to-head competition with the pros. And the coaches all come from small towns—that adds character to it."

The Swamp, a pastel-colored corner bar just down the street from the Porpoise, is jammed with students on Friday night. Fred Sowder, promotions coordinator for radio station WRVV, takes me in for a drink. I estimate that there are 200 people inside, 300 outside on the bar's front yard, and another 100 waiting in line to get in—including many tanned, leggy female students, wearing plenty of big-weekend makeup. A lone troubadour, standing on a makeshift stage, makes snide Tennessee comments—but I can't make out much of what he's saying and neither can the crowd. This group will not really stop drinking until sometime on Sunday. "Why should we?" says one student in a Florida cap and khaki pants. "You gotta party the day before the big game, the day of the big game, and during the big game." "And," says a sandy-haired, twenty-something companion, "After we kick Tennessee's ass, we'll drink some more!" Much laughter, and they disappear into the crowd.

BRAGGING RIGHTS

Floyd Blows...

Along University Avenue, fans are snatching up new T-shirts. One shows Vol Coach Phillip Fulmer dressed up to resemble the Tennessee mascot, a bluetick coon hound. He's holding a box of Lucky Charms cereal. The words "five lucky turnovers in every box" are emblazoned on the shirt, along with: "Not this year, Phil-boy. Those [championship] rings don't mean a thing in the Swamp." The Lucky Charms box is Florida's way of saying that the Vols were fortunate to beat the Gators the year before, taking advantage of five turnovers. There is another T-shirt poking fun at Tennessee: SIX THINGS THAT YOU'LL NEVER HEAR A TENNESSEAN SAY, It reads:

1) "Checkmate."
2) "Shakespeare for $1,000, Alex."
3) "E-mail it to me."
4) "I can't marry you, you're my cousin!"
5) "Wrasslin' is fake."
6) "Ole Phil is gonna get us a win in Gainesville this year."

Adding insult to injury, there is a huge banner hanging in the front of the Delta Upsilon fraternity house: FLOYD BLOWS, VOLS SUCK.

A Tennessee fan walks down University Avenue wearing an insult shirt of her own. It reads on the front: I NEVER MET A MAN I DIDN'T LIKE—WILL ROGERS. Then, on the back: WILL ROGERS NEVER MET STEVE SPURRIER.

At the stadium, I run into Brent Hubbs, a Tennessee beat reporter for Volquest (an Internet site) and WIFK and WNOX radio stations in Knoxville. He tells me that his stations will have seven hours of *pregame* coverage of the Vols and Gators. He'll host a call-in show starting at 9:00 Saturday morning. The Vol Network—comprising more than eighty stations around the state—will add a separate six hours of coverage. Former Vol quarterback Jeff Francis is the network's sideline reporter. The *Knoxville News Sentinel* newspaper sent six reporters and one photographer to report on the game. "It's safe to say the coverage is intense," says Hubbs. Norm Carlson, Florida's sports information director, handed out about 200 press credentials for the game. "The number would have been much higher but our press box is small." Nearly fifty radio stations across the state of Florida will broadcast the game. On the day after the game, both Spurrier and Fulmer will be back on TV for their weekly post-game shows—seen state-wide in Florida and Tennessee, respectively—to narrate highlights and offer analysis.

Tennessee vs. Florida

On Thursday evening, Spurrier appeared on his weekly pregame UF call-in show. Even by cable TV standards, it's a little nutty. Fans dial in to ask the coach questions, to offer encouragement, or to make wacky statements. Spurrier, who does not suffer fools gladly, takes it all in stride. He gets perturbed with the press, perturbed with his players—but when Florida fans call in and wig out, he seems perfectly serene, sitting at a desk (in coat and tie) with the show's host, Mike Hubert. The coach knows they are well-meaning Gator fans—and besides, he is very well-paid for his shows. So he listens, and takes every call with aplomb.

Lou from Boca Raton calls in and makes a statement: "Coach, I'm begging you. Do not give up on the running game too soon, because this [Tennessee] defense is below average." Spurrier's response: "Okay . . . you may have a point, and you may not. I thought I called a bad game last year, when we ran into the teeth of the UT defense. But we'll see; it's a chess game." Spurrier begins almost all of his answers with a nervous, "Okay . . ." And he likes the expression "this, that, and the other." (Example: "We seemed to be playing well, and then this, that, and the other happened and the game was tied.")

Steve from Gainesville calls in with a similar suggestion: "I'd like to see more running out of the power-I formation with Roberts and Frazier in the backfield," he opines. Spurrier says that is something to think about. There's a break, and Spurrier appears again—this time in two taped TV commercials—one for the Florida Citrus Growers and another for a company called Osmose Wood. Next comes a public service announcement, directed at fans and alums, reminding them to "be aware of NCAA rules concerning interaction with student-athletes."

When the show resumes, Spurrier skates over various topics: "We're not wearing orange jerseys. Blue jerseys have been very good to us. . . . We're going to play the best we can every week and try to improve along the way." He then reminds Florida fans "not to be surprised" if Tennessee comes onto the field wearing "shiny orange pants." The idea that the Vols might try to upstage the Gators with a new color scheme is clearly a bee in his bonnet—he's mentioned it twice in a few hours. Responding to another call, the coach says: "Practice has been 50-50." He expresses "disappointment in our backup players," especially the play of the second-team offensive line in the previous game against Central Florida. "I was a little mad at 'em, upset," he says, sounding more and more like former President George Bush. He and Spurrier have the same clipped speech pattern. Spurrier mentions that quarterback Doug Johnson threw eight TD passes in the first two games, adding: "I'm beginning to think that Doug is like Danny Wuerffel. He plays in games better than he practices. Sometimes he doesn't throw the ball well in practice." Spurrier makes another appeal for a noisy crowd. "I hope we set a noise-level record this Saturday in the Swamp. Loud when Tennessee has the ball, quiet when we have the ball."

He says that "Tennessee is going to come in here and try to run it down our throats."

After that, the one-hour show starts to get peculiar. As Spurrier predicted, a Vol fan named Scott calls in—and though he makes an innocuous comment, Spurrier is irritated that a Tennessee fan has broken through Florida's electronic Maginot Line. "I don't know why we let these guys on our show," he says. "Scott, you need to call Fulmer's show." Mark from Melbourne calls in and says that in a dream the night before, he saw "positive molecules bouncing around in the Swamp." Spurrier: "Okaaay. . . ." Another caller boasts that "Gator fans are like a time bomb . . . tick, tick, tick."

Game Day

The game will not start until 8:00 P.M., but pregame drinking begins much earlier. Gainesville has officially become consumed by this game. In the early afternoon, the bars and restaurants along University Avenue are jammed. Music is blaring. Convertibles cruise by with Florida fans holding up signs— VOLS SUX—and honking their horns. You can barely walk down the sidewalk for the people. Tom Rider, who owns Goerings' Books and lives in College Park, a residential neighborhood near the stadium, told the *Gainesville Sun* that he went to the store at 11 A.M. and "you could already see the drunkenness. And it went on all day." Tell me about it: inside Joe's Deli, the crowd is cheek-by-jowl. Well-dressed alums from both schools are hoisting brews like bearded sailors. A male Vol fan is loudly explaining how he drove down from Maryland for this game, playing sixty-three holes of golf along the way. There is a picture in Joe's of a previous Vol-Florida game. It shows a Tennessee runner with about eight Gator defenders hanging off his neck. It's been that way for Tennessee in Gainesville.

Down the block a few yards, Brother's Pizza has set up a special counter on the sidewalk to feed slices to passers-by. Business is brisk. Every few minutes, an employee leaves the shop with an armload of large pizza boxes. Apparently, the Florida frats are having lunch. Across the street, many Greeks are already half-snockered (okay, *completely inebriated*) and having fun. Hundreds of students are gathered around coolers, drinking beer and poking fun at passing Vol fans. A chubby man in Tennessee orange, who is carrying a seat cushion, tries to pick his way through the young crowd. "Your ass is too big for that cushion," yells a student. There is much laughter.

Nearby, Jeanne Britton and her son, Justin, who live in Hawthorne, Florida, have set up their alligator stand. Britton has been selling genuine alligator heads, gator claws, full-size gators, and various other gator-hide collectibles for eight years. She says that gator meat is "a real delicacy" and sells for $8 to $15 a pound. "A lot of people say it tastes like chicken, but I say it tastes like gator." Most of it comes from alligator farms, which she says are a big business. Alligators are on the protected species list, she notes, and cannot be hunted without a special license. Britton sells gator claws for $10; an eighteen-inch gator head for $195 ("It's $300 in a retail store"); and a four-foot-long alligator for $495. "Some have red eyes," she says—"nighttime eyes." By kickoff she estimates that she will sell between 60 and 200 smallish alligator heads.

Just outside the stadium, ESPN, the cable sports network, has erected its game-day set. Despite drizzly weather, a small crowd waits for Chris Fowler, Lee Corso, and Kirk Herbstreit to make an appearance—and then make their predictions for this game. Someone behind the stage is holding up a very large, unflattering picture of Fulmer with the letter L (for loser) on his forehead.

Morrine Hadden, a fifty-two-year-old Florida graduate, is part of the ESPN crowd. "I think this is wonderful," she says of the atmosphere, which has come to resemble a mini–Mardi Gras. She complains that the UT band will play "Rocky Top" when Florida fans stand up (at the end of the fourth quarter) and sing the alma mater—"We Are the Boys of Old Florida." She is offended by what she presumes will be a breach of college-football protocol. I confess ignorance and ask her about the parking. She says she parked in the yard of a student house in the neighborhood. Price: $30. "Last year we paid $10 a couple of times, $15 once, and it was free a couple of times. Today it was $30, but I don't care. They're poor students." Her brother, Bill, who's sixty but looks eighty, hears this comment, takes a deep drag on a cigarette, and wheezes: "Ain't America great!"

"Hillbilly Fiddles"

Down the road, in a UF commuter parking lot, about 100 recreational vehicles are parked in what is a weekend community for traveling Gator fans—few of whom actually attended UF. Pace Arrows, Sun Cruisers, Cruise Airs—those motor homes and many more are gathered like a herd of metallic elephants a quarter-mile from the stadium. Many are flying UF flags. The Florida fight song is blaring out of somebody's sound system. These are not cheap rides: most of the motor homes cost between $60,000 and $250,000. Children whiz around the lot on scooters and bikes. Some of the motor homes have satellite dishes on the roof. Families and friends are milling about—some watching the Miami–Penn State football game on TV, others cooking—and chewing—the fat.

I meet the mother of Corey Yarbrough, Florida's starting center. The Yarbroughs are from Glen St. Mary, outside Jacksonville—and they travel to games as part of an eleven-motor-home caravan. The group of fifty or so people includes the families of two other Florida players—Ben Brown and Tommy Hillard—and calls itself the Champagne Gators. Mrs. Yarbrough is wearing a T-shirt that reads: SOUTHERN GIRLS KNOW THEIR PRIMARY COLORS. She is wearing lots of orange. She said she last talked to her son at 4:00 P.M. the previous day. "He hides a lot from me, because he doesn't want me to get upset. He said, 'Don't worry, Mom, we're going to do great and win the game. Don't worry about it.'" But she *does* worry, of course. "He's been here since 1996," says Mrs. Yarbrough of her son. "He started at guard but they moved him to center. He's been hurt several times." She says the group will be eating "hillbilly fiddles" today: black-eyed peas and rice, fried chicken, collard greens, corn, chicken-and-dumplings. I would eat all of it, happily.

The Yarbroughs own a thirty-eight-foot camper. Lee Lanier, a friend and fellow Champagne Gator from Crescent City, owns a forty-foot American Eagle from Fleetwood. Price: $275,000. "We've been coming to Florida games since 1979," says Lee. "I'm a transplant, originally from Michigan. My husband is from North Carolina. He's retired navy and now an insurance consultant. He's the one who taught me to be a Gator fan. We just adopted the team. It's the best thing going—the best football. We have season tickets and travel to all the away games." She is standing under a canopy, next to some upscale plastic chairs. There is smoke rising from a gas grill. "We've missed only one game since 1980—the Syracuse game up there—and the Gators lost. We sat home with our tickets in our hands."

Lanier is decked out in Gator jewelry. She's wearing a small helmet brooch with an orange F on it, a pendant replica of Florida's national championship ring, two Gator rings, a Gator bracelet, a Gator watch, Gator earrings, plus a Gator T-shirt and orange socks. "Anything underneath with orange?" I ask. "Not today," laughs Lee. "I'm a grandma. I'm fifty-five." Lee and her husband live on a lake. Lee says the home's party room has been "Gatorized." "You walk in the back of my house, and the floor is an orange-and-blue checkerboard. We have orange and blue vertical blinds. We used to have a Gator commode seat in the motor home, but it was well-used and broke."

On Archer Street, four guys in orange fright wigs are standing atop a motor home. I think they're Tennessee fans, but can't tell if the orange is *faaaaaded* or not. Sheila would know. On North-South Drive, a white stretch Lincoln Continental—with its top painted Tennessee orange, cruises by. One of the riders pops his head out of the roof and looks around. Bad idea. Florida "tailgators," who are spread out in front of the dorms, start jeering at him: "You're going the wrong way!" yells one man. "I-75 is the other way!" Somebody else screams, "Vols suck!" Most of the shouts are innocent bluster, but there are some mean-spirited comments.

Tennessee vs. Florida

A dilapidated orange car is sitting in front of the Delta Upsilon fraternity house. BASH TENNESSEE FOR CHILDREN'S CHARITY reads a sign in front. One hammer whack costs $1; five whacks, $3. The car is heavily dented, but most people seem to prefer spending their money on booze and pizza.

Back at Joe's, a mortgage banker and UF graduate named Terry Palmer is taking in the madness with a young son. "I live in Atlanta," says Palmer. "I got up at 7:00 A.M. and drove down here. I've been to every home game, and this will be the loudest, most unbelievable game here in practically thirty years. This is as good as it gets in college football. Tennessee is trying to take away our dominance in the conference, so it's going to be louder than ever—unbelievable." Palmer attended Florida in the late 1960s—the same time Spurrier was a student and football player. He claims to have known Spurrier, and played poker with him in college. "Spurrier was an Alpha Tau Omega, I was a Phi Delta Theta." Palmer calls the Florida coach "a good person. He's honest, and gives a lot of good quotes to the media. But he has laid off lately, gotten a little softer. He's not quite as brash. He doesn't make the predictions he used to. That kills him. He can't stand not talking." What was Spurrier like as a poker player? I ask. "Deadly."

With the game about an hour away, I wander to the rooftop of the Florida Gator Club. There, the top contributors to the athletic department, who are named Bull Gators, are feasting on barbecue, chicken, iced tea (sweetened and unsweetened), and coleslaw. I look down and notice a Hari Krishna band banging little cymbals and chanting—what an incongruous sight at an SEC football game. "They're here all the time," says a booster. I eat with the owner of a luxury-car dealership in Tampa and then wander out onto the field. By this time, Ben Hill Griffin III is surely in his luxury box, munching on fried chicken.

Inside the Swamp

It is a cloudy, overcast night. No matter: Ben Hill Griffin Stadium is *alive*. And yes, it is *loud*. It seems much like the Roman coliseum without the lions and togas, although I do notice a few Florida students wearing orange-and-blue Dr. Seuss hats. The crowd is right on top of the field—there is very little space between the sidelines and the bleachers. When Tennessee takes the field for its warmups, a huge chorus of boos rains down from Gator partisans. The Florida student section is right behind the Tennessee bench—and since many have been drinking for several hours, they are in a rowdy mood: "UT sucks! UT sucks! UT sucks!" I look up and notice a shirtless young man, pointing at me. What's he trying to say? I wonder. A second look makes it clear that he is cursing at me—apparently because I'm on the Vol side of the field. Tennessee offensive tackle Chad Clifton is so pumped up he's doing grande jetés during warmups—not bad for a 300-pound offensive tackle. Center Spencer Riley and running back Travis Henry taunt the crowd. Bad idea.

There had been the usual woofing between the two sides during the week. There is no love lost between these two teams. Cedrick Wilson, a UT wide receiver, had said early in the week that playing in the Swamp was no different than playing at Kentucky. Safety Deon Grant did not try to be diplomatic. "I just don't like Florida—period," he said during the week. "I never have liked them. I respect them and all that, but I just don't like them." Quarterback Tee Martin was pragmatic: "We know the crowd is going to be loud, but after everything this team has gone through, we should be able to handle things like that." Coach Phillip Fulmer said: "Florida is a difficult place to play, but no more difficult than any of the other places we go. Their stadium is pretty much like ours when it's rocking." Said Riley: "Everybody thinks it's a bad place to play. It's not. I love going to the Swamp."

"This is always a big game," said Florida quarterback Doug Johnson. "It's why you come to Florida. It's pretty much whoever wins this game is going to be in the SEC championship game." Added UF offensive tackle Kenyatta Walker: "This is it. This is the season for us. Last year was my first SEC starting game, and I didn't play very well. Now, I'm ready for [Tennessee defensive end] Shaun Ellis. Bring the mighty Vols on." Spurrier put the chest-beating into perspective. "Everybody likes to talk about the game. Players talk. Coaches talk. But once the game starts, I don't think talk matters much. It's who plays better; who has their team prepared to play."

Mr. Two Bits

Florida is leaving no stone unturned to excite the crowd—and who can blame them? The public address announcer informs everybody that golfer Steve Melnick is a Florida grad. So is the pro wrestler Rick Flair, and broadcaster Forrest Sawyer. And so is Sonny—who owns a restaurant chain named Sonny's Barbecue. Just before kickoff, a group of former Florida letter holders—men and women from all sports—form a human tunnel on the field for the team to run through. But before the team appears, an elderly man wearing brown slacks and a bright yellow shirt comes racing through the tunnel onto the field. The crowd roars! It's Mr. Two Bits—George Edmondson, who lives in Tampa. For more than fifty years, he had led the UF crowd through the old "Two bits, four bits . . ." cheer. Edmondson retired last year—but he's been brought back for this game. He stands at midfield and, using big cue cards, leads the cheer again. "Two bits, four bits, six bits, a dollar. All for

Florida, stand up and holler!" The crowd roars. Then comes another collective chant: "We are the proudest, we are the loudest, we are the Gators!"

Next, the big video screen comes to life with a foreboding image: several real alligators are seen crawling around on a river bank. There are ominous sound effects: "Dunh, dunh . . . dunh, dunh . . . dunh, dunh." The alligators slip into the water with evil intentions. A massive bull gator, with menacing eyes, suddenly opens his elongated jaw and snaps it shut. The crowd erupts at the sight. The video screen flashes the words: ONLY GATORS GET OUT ALIVE! Then the Florida team races onto the field. More deafening cheers. No, this is not an easy place to win a football game.

Inside the Tennessee locker room, coach Phillip Fulmer is calm. He tells his troops to "be soldiers. Play like you're in a war. Sixty minutes of football." The Volunteers are calm—there are a few scattered yells. When they take the field a few moments later, scores of sideline photographers train their long lenses on the visitors and begin shooting pictures. Tennesee was dressed in all-white uniforms; in the end they didn't wear the shiny orange pants. The whir of 200 apertures closing at once sounds like a plague of locusts.

The Game

Tennessee receives the kickoff. On the Vols' first possession, Jamal Lewis, the powerful Tennessee tailback, plows over Gator defensive back Marquand Manuel. Manuel's helmet goes flying off his head. The Vols are trying to do just what Spurrier said they would: ram the ball down Florida's throat. But because Florida knows what the Vols want to do, the Tennessee boys don't have much success. Though young, the Gator defense is geared up to stop the run. Forced to throw on third downs, Martin frequently misses his targets. The Vols are handicapped by the crowd noise, weak execution, and unimaginative play-calling. Vol center Riley breaks a bone in his right hand on the Vol's first offensive series. He walks to the sideline holding his hand gingerly. It is bloody and mangled. He takes a seat on the bench. The hand is quickly taped up. Riley keeps playing. "I was not going to come out of that ball game," he said later.

"Uh Oh"

The first half is ragged but competitive. Florida, taking advantage of good field position, moves the ball but can't finish off its drives. Johnson, working mostly out of the shotgun, completes a 38-yard fade pass to Travis Taylor, and a 41-yard up-and-out pattern to Darrell Jackson. But the Vols are blitzing a lot, and he hurries several throws. Johnson and Tennessee linebacker Raynoch Thompson jaw at each other after a couple of plays. Jeff Chandler kicks a field goal on Florida's second possession and the Gators take the lead.

Five personal fouls are called on both teams in the first half. Tennessee scores in the second quarter, after Andre Lott recovers a Jackson fumble at the Florida 32-yard line. On fourth and one from the UF 7-yard line, the Vols decide to go for the first down. Tee Martin had injured his shoulder earlier in the series, after a hit by Gator linebacker Keith Kelsey. Martin missed a play but returns and throws a 21-yard pass to Eric Parker to keep the short drive alive. Now, on fourth and one, he scampers right on a naked bootleg and squeezes into the end zone. The TD gives the Vols a short-lived 7-6 lead.

Florida comes back. Just before the half, Tennessee must punt out of its own end zone. Florida's students, delighting in UT's misery, begin chanting, "Uh oh, uh oh." They are prescient. It *is* "uh oh" time for the Vols. Florida takes over the ball at the Tennessee 31. Two plays later, Johnson hits Jackson on an 11-yard slant. That TD, combined with three Jeff Chandler field goals, gives Florida a 16-7 first-half lead. Florida might have scored even more points, but a smartly conceived TD pass to tight end Erron Kinney is called back by an offensive facemask penalty. The Gators have lost two starters to foot injuries—wide receiver Travis Taylor, their best offensive player, and defensive tackle Buck Gurley.

During the first half, as I am walking behind the Tennessee bench from one end of the field to the other, a female Florida student leans over and snatches my cap off my head. That's how close the fans are to the field. During the second half she leans over and places it back on my head as I'm walking by. Who says Gator students are obnoxious? Florida students have been known to leave the stadium at the half, hurry across the street to the Purple Porpoise, down a couple of shots, and return to their seats in time for the second half kickoff. I think that practice has been outlawed—and certainly no one is lacking courage (liquid or otherwise) on this night.

The game turns early in the third quarter. The Gators take the second-half kickoff. On their first drive, Spurrier ditches the passing game and starts running Earnest Graham—who, though only 5'9", is thick-legged, quick, and powerful. The strategy works: Florida drives seventy-eight yards in only eight plays for a crucial touchdown. Tennessee's defense seemed lethargic on the drive. Johnson caps the drive by throwing a 4-yard TD strike to Reche Caldwell, his first college TD. The score gives Florida a comfortable 23-7 lead. In the last ten Florida-Tennessee games, the team that rushes for more yards wins the game. That trend would hold true in this contest, with Florida rushing for 128 yards compared to 86 for Tennessee.

Tennessee, meantime, is struggling to cope with the noise. It is clearly having an adverse effect on the Vol offense—especially in the second half, when the Vols are behind and forced to throw. The noise rises to a crescendo every time the Tennessee linemen approach the line of scrimmage. Unable to hear Martin's signals, they frequently flinch before the ball is snapped, each time drawing a 5-yard penalty. To keep from incurring more penalties, Tennessee's offensive linemen begin holding hands at the line of scrimmage. They release them and block when the ball is snapped. That tactic helps eliminate illegal procedure calls—but the Vols are practically giving away their snap count.

Gator defensive end Alex Brown takes advantage. Several times he runs past Vol right tackle Josh Tucker like he's standing still—before the Tennessee lineman even gets out of his stance. Brown pressures Martin all night—sacking the Vol QB five times, and intercepting a pass. On this night, Brown was the best player on the field. Florida's defense also got big performances from linebacker Eugene McCaslin (who was the team's second-leading rusher the year before) and Gerard "Big Money" Warren, a first-rate defensive tackle who was playing his first game after serving a two-game suspension for marijuana possession.

And yet the Vols rally. A Deon Grant interception leads to a 1-yard scoring run by Lewis midway through the third quarter. That makes the score 23-14. Twice in the fourth quarter the Vols stop Florida on fourth-and-one gambles. After the second, the Vols take over and Lewis again scores from the 1-yard line, jumping up and over the Florida defense. The Vols, seemingly out of the game, have suddenly drawn within two points, 23-21.

With about three minutes to go in the game, Johnson attempts to pass. The Florida quarterback has had an inconsistent game, but a productive one— throwing for more than 330 yards. But this pass goes awry. Grant, an excellent center fielder, picks it off—his second interception of the game—and runs the ball back into Florida territory. With just minutes to go, Tennessee has the ball and a good chance to win the game.

But the Florida defense does not yield. On a crucial third and three, the Vols run Lewis on a "toss sweep" around the left end. He gets nothing. Facing a decisive fourth and three, the Vols run the same play. The play had been called to go right—toward Brown. But Martin wrongly checks out of the play at the line of scrimmage. He decides to send Lewis left rather than right. He explained after the game that he feared running at Brown, even though it was the Gator defensive end's *pass rush*, not run defense, that had bedeviled the Vols all night. It probably didn't matter which direction Lewis ran: the Gators are expecting another Lewis run—and they gang tackle the UT back short of the first-down marker with 2:10 to go in the game. It is over. Florida has beaten Tennessee—and in doing so jumps over a huge early-season hurdle. The game was not pretty, but very dramatic.

As soon as the gun sounds, the police K-9 corps takes the field. There is pandemonium in the stands, but few students dare venture out to challenge the dogs. Standing on the 20-yard line, I see Florida Athletic Director Jeremy Foley race by me with a look of utter jubilation on his face. He stops and jabs the air a couple of times with his arms. I'm a little surprised to see the Florida athletic director, who is one of the more sophisticated athletic administrators in the SEC, bouncing around on the field after the game. But then, this *is* Florida and Tennessee. And it *is* a big victory. A sweaty, tired Spurrier suddenly appears. A male CBS reporter (his face caked with makeup), begins to interview the coach. Spurrier seems relieved. He praises his defense, mentions a Gator turnover near the end that almost cost them the game, then says: "In the end the Swamp prevailed." About forty Florida and Tennessee players kneel at midfield to share a prayer. When it's over, a bunch of Florida players begin chanting rhythmically and jumping around together on the field. The Gators had foiled Tennessee's ambitions once again.

"Anybody See Tee Martin?"

In the Florida press room, while the media is waiting for Spurrier to speak, Kenyatta Walker pokes his head in the door and yells: "Anybody see Tee Martin? I didn't see Tee Martin tonight." There is laughter. Spurrier takes the podium. He seems frazzled, happy—and humble. "Our defensive guys played their hearts out," he says. "We're proud of the defense. Gosh, it was a game with a whole lot of penalties." He praises Brown, McClaslin, and Warren, and says he's given a game ball to defensive coordinator Jon Hoke. Asked about Doug Johnson's performance, he says: "Doug had some errant plays, but had a lot of good plays, too. He hung in there tough. We didn't play extremely well offensively—it was one of our worst offensive games overall. But somehow or 'nother, we beat 'em by two points. So we're very thankful. God smiled on the Gators tonight there at the end. The Swamp prevailed. We don't act like we're a whole bunch better than anybody. We know we were very fortunate."

Of Tennessee, Spurrier said: "They didn't get in the shotgun with four wide and throw every down, like other teams do. Tennessee is going to be Tennessee, as their coach says. Now, we can stack in against the run, we can close the gaps. Our players have a lot of pride and won't let teams run up and down the field. We'll treat this victory just like all of them. We won't celebrate like they did last year. We've got a lot of room for improvement. Tennessee has a chance to win all the rest of their games. They'll go back and say, 'Hey, the Gators screwed up in '97 and they may do it again.' So let's win the rest. We'll enjoy this tonight and then on Monday start getting ready for Kentucky."

Hoke makes a brief appearance to chat with the press. "Tennessee is a team that thinks they can run the ball," he says. "That's their bread and butter. They think they can be more physical than you are. We played run defense on both of those last two plays. We told our corners, 'Good luck, you're man for man, shut 'em down if they throw it, but we're going to hunker down and stop the run.' That's what we were counting on them to do. We said before the game this would be a fifteen-round heavyweight fight, and that it would take all fifteen rounds to win it."

Said linebacker Eugene McClaslin: "It was a territory game. We don't ever want to lose in the Swamp. Tee Martin made some statements about how he loved it when teams blitzed him. I'm pretty sure he's eating his words now. The noise definitely bothered Tennessee tonight."

Alex Brown reveals why he was able to pressure Martin so successfully. "I noticed during the game that Tee Martin shakes his hands before he gets the snap. He had to do that, because his center couldn't hear anything over the crowd noise. When I saw him shake his hands, I'd take off."

Walker, the young Florida tackle, is asked by a reporter if Florida is now a national title contender. "Let me get an SEC ring first. I don't have an SEC ring. My hands are still naked. Let me get to the SEC championship, win that, and then we'll talk about the national stuff."

Unsurprisingly, the mood in the Tennessee locker room is dark. Nobody is talking. Amid a sea of white tape, grim-faced equipment men are rolling black metal chests to waiting trucks. Black duffel bags, each with a piece of orange tape on the side and a number, are getting stacked outside the doors. The bags contain each player's shoulder pads, shoes, and helmet. Martin is getting medical treatment on his shoulder. Fulmer is off somewhere doing a radio show. "Sacks, penalties, and generally poor execution killed us," he said after the game. The Vols had a school-record fifteen penalties. Defensive coordinator John Chavis said that the difference in the game was the touchdown Florida scored to start the second half. "They came out and ran it at us, and what made it so bad was that we knew they were going to do that. You can't let them have it so easy."

The players are slowly filing out to meet waiting girlfriends and family members—hair tousled, shirts undone. Cosey Coleman, the Vols All-SEC offensive guard, is disappointed but not discouraged by the loss. "Both teams came out and fought hard. It was a sixty-minute battle. There were some ups and downs. We got behind and got away from what we like to do, which is run the ball." Of the noise, he said: "It hurt us some, but I don't think it was the deciding factor. It hurt our tackles at times. Alex Brown had the edge on our offensive tackles, not that they didn't fight their hearts out." What was the Tennessee mood at the half? "Heads were high, heads were high. We were confident. We were not intimidated."

Chad Clifton, the UT offensive tackle, said that Martin had given an impassioned speech to the team after the game. "It was uplifting. I had my head down, shedding a few tears, and Tee got up and spoke to the team. It uplifted me. He told everybody to keep their heads up. It is a long season." Of the crowd, he said: "The Gainesville crowd is always into it. But their offense and defense came out and played well—that's what won the game. I just wanted to come down here and win in the Swamp. But we couldn't pull it off."

When Martin finally emerges from the locker room and meets his girlfriend, four buses have their engines idling and are ready to roll. Chavis, sitting in the front row of the first bus, has a scowl on his face.

Around the corner, in front of the stadium, I run into Travis Taylor and his wife. He was injured in the second quarter and has a plastic cast on one of his feet. He had five catches in the game before jamming his foot into the turf and twisting his ankle badly. He is pleased with the win, but seems concerned about his injury. In the locker room before the game, he said that Spurrier was "pretty calm. He said to go out, have fun, and stick to the game plan." Every week a different Gator assistant speaks to the team before the game. Hoke had Tennessee, and Taylor says he gave "an emotional speech, and did a good job of pumping up the guys."

During the game, says Taylor, he and Dwayne Goodrich, the Tennessee cornerback, did a lot of friendly talking. "He is a good guy. He was asking me how long I'd been married and if it was good. I was kind of surprised. He's a really good guy. We had a few nice conversations walking back to the huddle." Did Deon Grant speak? "No, he said he didn't like Florida so I didn't expect him to talk much."

By the time I get back to my hotel on Archer, it is after 1:00 A.M. A groggy, middle-aged Vol fan walks in the lobby and asks: "Anybody catch the score? I haven't heard who won." That elicits a collective chuckle from a small group of weary football fans. The manager makes a batch of chocolate chip cookies. Everybody waits ten minutes for the cookies, and then eats.

Back in New York, I get a call from Bruce Doyle, the Lizard Man, first thing Monday morning. "The earth is back on its axis," he announces. "The Gators are on top in the SEC." He had not yet come down from Cloud Nine. He'd been up until 2:00 A.M. the night before, he said, breaking down videotape of the game.

And the boys from Pulaski? They had come through the weekend in fine shape. They'd sold their surplus tickets, made a tiny profit—and, of course, partied a lot. The Gators had won. And, best of all, they had no problems getting home. There were no hurricanes on the northbound return trip, and all the gas stations on the highway were open. The weekend was . . . swingin'.

THE MEMPHIS AVENGERS

Meet Logan Young and Roy Adams, two of the fiercest adversaries in the SEC. Football players? No. Coaches? Naaa. Both are aging college football zealots who live in Memphis. They've both got money to burn and axes to grind. Young and Adams were friends for nearly ten years. They'd see each other twice a week for lunch or dinner. Almost always their talk would gravitate from Crescent City goings-on to a topic that practically consumes both men—SEC football. In fact, the football rivalry grew too strong for the friendship, which ended in acrimony four years ago. Nowadays Adams and Young seldom speak except to take verbal swipes at one another.

Young is a wealthy Alabama booster. Though he's from Osceola, Arkansas (forty miles from Memphis), and attended Vanderbilt, he's a fanatical Bama fan. He gives a lot of money to the football program. His daddy (he does not say "father" or "dad," but rather uses the very old-South idiom "daddy") was a lawyer and banker in Osceola who, in 1946, started a successful food company that helped to popularize oleo margarine. Young sold the company, Osceola Foods, in 1999 for a large sum. Young owned the Memphis Showboats, a member of the short-lived United States Football League in 1983 and 1984—a $2 million investment. He managed to sell off a large stake in the team before it went out of business. He now spends his time running Logan Young Investments, which is based in the Columns, a modest two-story office building (antebellum columns in front) in central Memphis, across the street from the Greater Tabernacle Church and a few blocks from the Liberty Bowl.

When not making investments, Young spends a lot of time fretting about the Crimson Tide football program. His claim to fame is that he was a close friend of Bear Bryant, whom he calls "a great, wonderful person," adding: "I went to California with him a week before he died (in 1983) to accept the Alonzo Stagg Award." Young is a pal of Mal Moore, the new athletic director at Alabama, and Billy Neighbors, the former Bama All-America lineman. He knows Paul Bryant, Jr., the Bear's publicity-shy son, who owns several businesses in Alabama. When Alabama Coach Mike DuBose travels to Memphis, he stays at Young's house. Young's small office looks more like a kid's bedroom than a place of business for a sixty-year-old man—it's a shrine to Alabama football. There is a framed Alabama football jersey on a wall, an Alabama helmet (orginially purchased for his son) on a corner table, and a replica of the Bear's famous houndstooth hat. There are lots of pictures of Young and the Bear at various social functions—restaurants in New York, bowl-game soirees, including one at a black-tie dinner in Memphis just before the Bear retired. There's a Bear quote: "I used to be the meanest, toughest, and best coach in America. But now I've been coaching so long I'm like the director or chairman of the board." On a hall wall, there is a newspaper clipping that mentions the Bear vacationing at Young's (former) house in Palm Beach, Florida. There is a raft of newspaper clippings from Alabama's 1992 national championship season.

I visited Young at his office in Memphis last October, just before the Tennessee game. We exchanged pleasantries, and then, leaning back in an old green leather swivel chair (the arms completely worn away), he fixed a suspicious glance at me and said he'd gotten a call from an Alabama friend. "Somebody saw your name on the Internet," Young intoned gravely. "He told me you were having dinner with Roy Adams and coming here to stir up recruiting trouble." I gulped. He was right—sort of. I was curious about his reputed activities on behalf of Alabama, but I wasn't trying to stir up trouble. I just aimed to get a first-hand look at the protagonists in this SEC feud. (When I heard Young say "stir up trouble," I felt like I'd stepped into an Elmore Leonard novel.) A short man who wears a black hairpiece, Young seemed a little uncomfortable answering questions.

Adams is just the opposite. He's a garrulous, sixty-two-year-old Tennessee man with a penchant for wine, gossip, and southern football. "I'm a college football freak," he says. Paunchy and balding, with a rapier wit, he sometimes dresses the part. A graduate of Tennessee, he not only owns a bright orange UT sportcoat and white coonskin cap, but he'll wear them occasionally to social functions. He's got twenty-two televisions in his house—including four big screens and two separate satellite dishes. Many are in use on fall Saturdays, when he'll have about 100 people over for a day-long football party. Many are UT fans, but there are more than a few friends and acquaintances from around Memphis, including fans and coaches from the universities of Memphis,

Mississippi, and Northwest Community College (NWCC). "The bar is open from noon to 10 P.M.," says Adams—"free food and booze for football fanatics and friends of mine. And a few enemies have been known to come by, too."

Adams attends three UT games a year. When in Knoxville, he stays at the Days Inn, within walking distance of Neyland Stadium, and throws a pregame party for about fifty people. He makes an annual $500 contribution to the UT general fund, and has had season football tickets for thirty years. But he doesn't much enjoy traveling to games any more. "When I'm in Knoxville, I think of all the football games I'm missing on TV. We can watch five college games in my den at one time. I've got more TVs than any place in Memphis. College football is the only sport I follow, which is a good thing because it's an expensive sideline." In the middle and late 1980s, Adams attracted attention from both the NCAA and the Tennessee athletic department, which were worried that he was providing illegal favors to UT players and prospects in the Memphis area. "I've been accused of a lot," says Adams, "but I've never been guilty of anything."

The feud between Adams and Young is southern gothic. The last time the two men were together was in January 1996. They had dinner at Folk's Folly, a well-known steakhouse in town. Logan called Adams up and asked him to join him at the restaurant. Adams, who lives in a big contemporary house in the Balmoral subdivision in east Memphis, had a friend drop him off. Over drinks he and Young exchanged their usual jibes. Adams teased Young because Tennessee has beaten Alabama again that year—and the Crimson Tide has been put on probation by the NCAA. "I took shit from Logan for ten years because Alabama beat Tennessee all the time," says Adams, "and I'd accepted it."

That night Adams gave Young some verbal payback. According to Adams, Young "sat at the bar and sulked for two hours." Then Young got mad. "He went into an anti-Tennessee diatribe," says Adams. "He called me a fat fucker, he called Phil Fulmer fat, and he said Tennessee would start losing to Alabama again when Peyton Manning left Tennessee." Young then stormed out of the restaurant, jumped into his Jaguar, and left—stranding Adams without a ride for two hours. "It was the end of our friendship," says Adams—though he notes that Young sent him a $200 flower basket when his mother died.

Both may have allowed their football loyalties to get the best of them—Young because he cares a little *too much* about Alabama, and Adams because he seems preoccupied with Young. Long story short, Adams has repeatedly raised suspicions that Young cheats on behalf of Alabama. He has suggested many times on a Tennessee Internet site that Young has paid off high school coaches in Memphis in exchange for the coaches steering their star players to Alabama. Adams is not the only person to point a finger at Young, who is somewhat notorious in the South for his alleged activities on behalf of Bama.

BRAGGING RIGHTS

His name comes up in Oxford, Baton Rouge, and Athens—and not in a flattering way. Says a lawyer in Memphis, who asked not to be named, "The word on the street is that Young is a rich kid who drinks, loves college sports, and will do anything it takes to get prize recruits to attend Alabama. I don't know if the last part is true, but he is rich, he does drink, and he does love Alabama."

Tennessee fans and coaches fulminate at the mere mention of Young's name. The implication is clear. Dan Brooks, UT's recruiting coordinator, got flustered when I asked him about Logan Young and the Memphis recruiting scene. "I can't talk about that," he spluttered. "You'll have to talk to Coach Fulmer. I'm glad I'm not recruiting in Memphis anymore." Fulmer won't say anything.

Adams has no such compunction. He has insinuated that, in 1998, Young bought an expensive luxury car for Tim Thompson, the football coach for Memphis Melrose High School, in exchange for Thompson steering Kindal Moorehead, one of his star players, to Alabama. Both Thompson and Young deny the charge. Young says he has not given Thompson any gifts, and Thompson says he has not received any gifts from Young. Young told me that he had met Thompson, the Melrose coach, but did not know him very well. He may not have been completely truthful. I saw evidence—in Young's office—that suggests that the two men are more than casual acquaintances.

Adams and a Georgia booster suspect that Young made a similar deal last winter with Lynn Lang, the football coach at Trezevant High School. Like Thompson, Lang had a star player (Albert Means) who signed with Alabama. During the recruiting season, Adams, who is very well connected in Memphis, said that he'd heard that Lang's "asking price" for Means was, among other things, a Ford Expedition. Were Adams and the Memphis businessman blowing smoke at a rival SEC program?

It would be easy to think so—except that Adams knows Memphis, he knows Young, and he knows about southern recruiting. Just before Albert Means signed papers pledging to play for Bama, Lang acquired a 1999 Ford Expedition. He told me so himself. Base sticker price for an Expedition: $37,000. Lynn Lang's annual salary: $35,000. Lang wouldn't tell me where he bought the truck, but one of Logan Young's best friends, Tommy Kassee, is a principal at the Oakley-Kassee Ford dealership in Memphis.

The timing of Lang's Expedition purchase has raised suspicions around the SEC, which can be a hothouse of innuedo. There is no proof that Young helped Lang buy the vehicle, and both Lang and Young deny making any arrangement. Young told me he'd heard of Lang but never met him. Lang says the same thing of Young. "I've heard his name, but that's all I know about that." How did he finance the purchase? Says Lang: "I make enough to pay for my own truck. I have a note. It's the only payment I have. I go to work at 7:20 A.M. and get home at 8:00 P.M."

Adams and others do not put much stock in those denials. Rumors have circulated for years that Thompson's lifestyle got a sudden boost in 1998, right around the time Moorehead, a star defensive lineman, was deciding where to go to college. Despite being one of the best high school players in the country, and reputedly being a longtime Tennessee fan, Moorehead did not visit UT or any other universities during his senior year. That is highly unusual. He simply signed with Alabama.

In the fall of 1998 Thompson was seen driving around Memphis in a new Lexus, a luxury automobile that costs about $40,000. Thompson wrecked the Lexus and, according to Adams, did not have insurance. According to both Adams and the Memphis businessman, (who did not want to be named), Thompson now drives an ultra-expensive Range Rover. Adams calls the Young-Thompson collusion "common knowledge" around town, adding, "Young deals in cash, so how are you going to prove it? He's not going to admit it, and neither will Thompson." Adds the Memphis businessman: "Tim Thompson makes $30,000 a year, lives in a $100,000 house, and is driving a $50,000 Range Rover? Give me a break."

Last year, the Georgia booster says he had lunch with Lang and Georgia coach Leon Perry at an Applebee's restaurant in Memphis. Perry was recruiting Albert Means, the Trezevant lineman, for Georgia. According to the Georgia booster, Lang talked about Means's "poor financial situation and how he wanted to better the kid's life, that sort of thing." Lang didn't make any explicit requests, says the Georgia booster, "but it appeared to me that there was something going on. It was a gut feeling—you read between the lines."

Last March, after Means had signed with Bama, the businessman stopped hedging and made explicit his accusation. He was certain, he told me on the phone, that there had been foul play in the recruitment of Albert Means. Before and during the recruiting season, he asserted, Lang was driving "a blue Camaro with a dented fender. I saw it myself," he said. "When the recruiting season ended (last February), he was driving a new Expedition. I saw it, and so did Coach Perry. The situation is not on the up-and-up, and you and I know that."

I didn't ask Young about Thompson or Lang when we first met, last October. But I did bring up the charges last December, just before Alabama played in the SEC championship game. Four weeks earlier, Young had had triple-bypass heart surgery, which he said "put a crimp in my football going, but not my football watching." I asked Young if he'd ever given money, cars, or anything else to Tim Thompson. I expected him to shout an obscenity or slam down the phone. Instead, there was a short pause on the telephone line, after which he said, "Not true. I've been hearing that stuff for years. The same people have been saying that for years. It's probably from Tennessee. They think something is wrong when someone from Memphis doesn't go to Tennessee. Alabama is closer to Memphis than Knoxville. Football players from Memphis have been going to Alabama for 100 years. We just got a great one [Moorehead] two years ago. There are two Melrose players starting at UT, and I haven't heard any [accusations] about that."

Young did not seem particularly offended by the suspicion of cheating. But he did express anger at those whom he felt were behind the smear campaign: Adams and other Tennessee fans. "They got theirs coming," he said of his adversaries. "They'll be back where they belong in a couple of years." By that he meant under the foot of Alabama, which had beaten Tennessee for eleven straight years before the Vols started returning the favor, winning five in a row. "We used to beat their brains out," continued Young bitterly, "and it will turn."

I pressed on. Had Young ever given money or done any favors for high school prospects or coaches to sway players toward Alabama? "Never done it," he replied. "I don't care who says it." Had he ever been reprimanded by Alabama officials for illegal or unethical recruiting activities? "I have never been reprimanded by anybody. That is a bunch of b.s. If I had been reprimanded, I wouldn't be allowed to have a stadium box." Does money still get passed to players and prospects? I ask him. "I think it probably goes on," he replied, "nickle and dime stuff. I'd be naive to think it doesn't. I purposely do not talk to players, but a lot of people do." And, unprovoked, he volunteers a couple of ways in which college players acquire spending money. He said that athletes commonly apply for federal Pell Grants—and then use the money to lease cars. "I don't know how these players can afford to own a car, which can cost $300 or $400 a month, but I can see how they can get a Pell Grant and then lease one." He also volunteers that players can make money on bowl games. Players are given money by their school to fly to the bowl site, but some will opt to drive to the games with their buddies and pocket the airfare. "They can make two or three thousand bucks," offers Young. "That will make a few car payments."

When I was in Memphis, Young told me he didn't really follow recruiting. But he clearly does. He is familiar with the high school football scene in Memphis. He is familiar with both Moorehead and Means, whom he called "a helluva ballplayer." He drives to Tuscaloosa every August to watch Alabama's freshman football players work out. I asked Young if he knew Tim Thompson, the coach at Melrose. His response: "I've met him a time or two—but I wouldn't say I know him. I met him at a high school banquet in town, and at a Touchdown Club meeting where they have high school players and speakers." Does he talk to Thompson on the phone, or meet with him? Young's response: "I wouldn't say I talk to him occasionally. I wouldn't say I meet him occasionally."

In fact, Young and Thompson must know each other fairly well. When I first got to Young's office to interview him, around noon on a weekday, there was nobody there: the office door was open, but the rooms were empty. Young and his two associates (an accountant/partner and his secretary) had stepped out.

There was a message pad on the secretary's desk—one with carbon copies of all recent messages. Like a gumshoe, I flipped through it. I quickly came across two messages for "Logan" from a caller named "Tim Thompson." The caller had not left a return phone number, and the message did not identify "Tim Thompson" in any way. The two men are clearly more than acquaintances—or Thompson would have left his phone number. Young describes Thompson as "very reputable. He turns out good players and they go to schools and graduate." Interestingly, he mentions the Lexus, but suggests that Adams or a Tennessee booster may have given it to him. "Most of the players at Melrose have gone to Tennessee," said Young, "but [his tone becomes sarcastic] they don't do that [buy off high school coaches], do they? Roy would give them a damn airplane if he had the money. He's a sorry-ass man with problems."

Adams doesn't take issue with the first part of that accusation. "Am I crazy?" he asks. "I plead guilty to that, but [Young's] crazier—and wealthier." He says Young can be "a very charming person, but he's bitter because his team has been on a losing streak to Tennessee."

"Yeah, He'd Do It"

I called an individual who knows Logan Young, knows the Alabama football program, and worked as a top SEC administrator. I asked him about Young. The source said: "He's a passionate Alabama supporter. He had a drinking problem for a long time. Maybe he's quit. If he's not drinking, he's fine." I asked: Would Logan Young cheat on behalf of Alabama? Answer: "Probably so." Would he give gifts to high school coaches to get recruits for Alabama? His response: "Yeah, he'd do it." Why? "For Alabama, to put you on the inside." What makes you say he would cheat? I asked. "Because of my knowledge of him and a lot of others like him. . . . There are tons of people like him in the southeast. If you tell 'em to do it [get a player], they'll do it." Who would tell a booster to get a player? "Coaches." This source says that cheating—payments to high school players, high school coaches, and college players—was "pervasive" in the past. Does it go on now? "I think in isolated cases, yes. Mississippi is the worst, because it's poor. Alabama would be next."

Happy Talk

Adams spends considerable time on a Tennessee Internet chat board, Gridscape.com, regaling Vol fans with yarns about his encounters with the many current athletes, former athletes, and sports personalities he knows in the

Memphis area. And he knows a lot of them. Most of his tales of corruption go back many years. Adams told me, for example, that he knows Cassius Ware, who grew up in Batesville, Mississippi (where Adams was born), and went on to play football at Ole Miss in the mid-1990s. Ware later lived in Memphis. According to Adams, Ware once told him he was paid "around 50,000" by boosters during the two years he played in Oxford. "I swear to God," says Adams. "But nobody is going to admit this stuff. I'm just trying to tell you how the real world operates." Adams is a close friend of Cortez Kennedy, the all-pro NFL defensive lineman for the Seattle Seahawks. Adams often describes Kennedy's fondness for cognac and the girls at Platinum Plus, a nude dance club in Memphis. He'll often post messages on the UT board after he's been out partying—and he is more than happy to acknowledge when his thoughts may be influenced by drink. Bill Harper, sixty-two, who owns a house-and-garden trade show in Memphis and runs a couple of 900-number recruiting services, told me that some of what Roy says "is just the red wine talking. Roy exaggerates a lot."

Adams likes to talk. He'll happily converse about politics, government, or the economy. But the subject that really sets him off is Young and various football shenanigans in the Memphis area. Much of what he says has a ring of truth to it, especially to anyone who knows Memphis and the history of college football. In the past it was pretty much standard practice for boosters, who are typically wealthy businessmen, to provide material favors—cash, clothes, cars—to prominent players, who were often poor and usually black. The "twenty-dollar handshake" is part of college football lore. It happened everywhere, and was certainly prevalent in the 1960s, 1970s, and early 1980s. There is an old saw in college athletics: "If you ain't cheatin', you ain't competin'." Bear Bryant, in his autobiography, admitted that Bama boosters gave money to Alabama players and prospects. "I know some of our alumni went out and paid a few boys," Bryant writes. He later adds: "I'm not sure how many of our boys got something. . . . I didn't know what they got and I didn't want to know, but they got something because they had other offers and I told my alumni to meet the competition."

Last fall Albert Means, the high school star from Trezevant High School who was at the center of all the Lang rumors, attended a joint meeting of the Memphis Touchdown and Quarterback clubs. About 100 people were in attendance at the Chickasaw Country Club. Means was there to pick up an award. Adams and a few local Georgia fans, including Harper, were sitting at one table. When Means was introduced and took the stage, Adams told me gleefully that the people at his table started changing: "Logan Young! Logan Young! Logan Young!" I asked Adams who started the chant. He said he didn't know— it was spontaneous. When I asked Harper about the incident, he said that the instigator was Adams.

The Memphis Avengers

Adams started listening to UT football games on the radio in 1946, when he was eight years old. He grew up in Batesville, Mississippi, where his parents were tenant farmers. The family then moved to Memphis, and his dad became a railroad switchman. His dad was an alcoholic. "I started reading at an early age to get away from my dad's drunken world," Adams says. Starting his sophomore year in high school, he rode a bus for forty-five minutes to attend Central High School, which was much better than the blue-collar school in south Memphis in which he'd been enrolled. He made good grades. He became a senate page for Tennessee Senator Estes Kefauver, who had played football for Tennessee in the 1920s and later ran for the Democratic presidential nomination in 1952. (Kefauver beat Harry Truman in the New Hampshire primary, prompting Truman to drop out of the reelection race. But the Democratic bosses bestowed the nomination on Illinois Governor Adlai Stevenson, who was beaten badly by Dwight Eisenhower.) Adams says he was a socialist Democrat growing up, and had "a chance" to go to Yale on scholarship. "But because of my love of Tennessee, I went to Knoxville instead. I worked my way through. That shows you how stupid I was."

Not too stupid, really. When not partying or tossing brickbats at Young, Adams displays a lively intellect. He knows more than a little about American politics. Adams started classes at UT in 1956 but didn't graduate until 1963. In between he served in the army. After college he joined Goodyear Tire & Rubber Co. and became a store manager for nearly sixteen years. He invested in real estate on the side, and then opened an eponymous family-restaurant chain. "I had ten at one time in Memphis and Mississippi. They did great." But he sold out in 1988, and now spends most of his time managing the "several hundred" apartment units he owns. He's never been married.

"I live an open life," asserts Adams. "I'll take a lie detector test about anything." I asked him if he'd ever given money to athletes. "Yes, in the old days." In fact, Adams will readily admit that, in the past, he did small favors for "hundreds" of athletes and plenty of coaches, too. A few of the beneficiaries were UT players and coaches, he says, but most were associated with other schools—the University of Memphis, Ole Miss, Northwest Mississippi Community College, the University of Houston, even Alabama. He managed Goodyear tire stores in Memphis, and occasionally he'd give athletes and coaches free tires. He would hand out a little cash, take players down to bars on Beale Street, buy athletes and coaches a meal or two. He opened his first Adams family-style restaurant in 1975. He can't remember the number of meal checks he picked up over the years. (He says the only assistant coach who ever refused to accept a free meal was Ken Donahue, the one-time defensive coordinator at Tennessee.) "Coaches are worse than the players," he says. He recalls giving a former Tennessee assistant coach a bunch of small stereos for the Tennessee staff when the Vols played at the Liberty Bowl in the mid-1980s. "I went over to the hotel a little later and asked one of the assistants if he'd gotten the gift. He said, 'What gift?' Warren was selling the damn things!"

Like most boosters, Adams seems more the eccentric, slightly dissolute uncle than an insidious corrupter of youth. "Corruption is when you buy players out of high school and steer them where you want them to go," he says—an obvious dig at Young. "College players are already corrupted." That sounds a bit self-serving. Adams admits that the NCAA investigated him in the mid- and late 1980s, when he was dancing around more than a few minefields. "The NCAA has been to my home, and I have met with the NCAA on several occasions." Adams is almost proud to admit his indiscretions, which he believes were minor and took place when rules were far less rigid than they are today. In 1987, he sponsored a recruiting trip to the University of Houston for two receivers from NWCC, Royell Preston and Eric Smith, who were being heavily recruited. Preston went to Ole Miss, Smith to LSU. Adams later bought a car (cost: $3,000 to $4,000) for Smith, who flunked a drug test during his second year in Baton Rouge and was kicked off the team. "Of all the athletes I've known, he is one of the few I wish I hadn't associated with," says Adams. "I have no tolerance for drugs."

"Don't Talk to Roy"

Because he lives in Memphis, and loves football, Adams has been a benefactor to University of Memphis coaches. When Charlie Bailey was the Memphis football coach, says Adams, "I gave him $10,000 to play with on the options market." Adams bought a house for Buddy Geiss, the team's quarterback coach in the mid-1980s. "I put up the money," says Adams, "and he made the monthly note, which was the same as a rental payment."

Adams stopped associating with UT in the late 1980s, after he had run-ins with Doug Dickey, the Tennessee athletic director, and Vol coach Johnny Majors. Adams doesn't like either one of them, partly because they hounded him to stay away from college prospects and players. Says Adams: "Unofficially, the UT coaches have told people: 'Don't talk to Roy Adams.'" He's been sent warning letters by the UT athletic department, and in the mid-1980s Tennessee's chief counsel paid a visit to Adams. The lawyer said Adams's name had surfaced at the SEC meetings, and he presented the booster with twenty accusations. Among them: that UT players had eaten in Adams's restaurant. "That was amusing," says Adams. "Knoxville is 400 miles away. Now, University of Memphis players? Yes."

The Memphis Avengers

Unique Defense

Karl Schledwitz, who is the chairman of Southland Capital Corp., a real estate development company in Memphis, was Adams's attorney in the 1980s, when the NCAA was scrutinizing the Tennessee booster. "It was fifteen years ago," says Schledwitz. "I don't think anything ever went past the inquiry stage. I dealt with a Chicago attorney [for the NCAA]. We had several conversations." Schledwitz says that he had a "unique" defense for Adams. "As I recall interpreting the NCAA guidelines, it is improper for a booster or someone connected to a university to give that university preferential treatment. I pointed out that Roy is one of these guys who's helped student-athletes at ten to twenty universities. He doesn't discriminate for one school or another. He loves student-athletes regardless of their affiliation. If you looked at all the student-athletes that Roy had helped, it would have taxed the NCAA's staff, to say the least, if they'd decided to go down that path. The inquiry ended." Schledwitz, who is a former student-body president at Tennessee, believes there is a fundamental distinction between boosters who get involved with high school athletes and those who, like Adams, "are a friend of football players after they've chosen their college affiliation. At that point, you have to give him the benefit of the doubt." Schledwitz says that he doesn't believe Adams corrupts youth by doing small favors for athletes. "It's hard to figure out how it could be," he says. "In my mind, the corruption is more apt to take place during the recruiting process."

Adams is, by now, something of an expert on boosterism. He makes a point of giving me the definition of a booster: someone who is associated with a university because he or she attended the school, owns season tickets to a particular school sport, gives money to the school, or belongs to a student or university group. "Any one of those qualifies you as a booster," says Adams, "and schools can punish you or keep you in line" if they feel you've violated NCAA rules. "But if you're not associated with the school, they can't do anything. You can't limit the activities of an American citizen."

About twelve years ago, says Adams, Tennessee and several other schools were recruiting Eddie Blake, an outstanding lineman at NWCC. At the time, Adams was chairman of UT's Memphis/Shelby County Alumni Association. "I knew Blake, and was interested in talking up Tennessee." Adams then got a phone call from Dickey, UT's athletic director. According to Adams, Dickey had heard reports that Adams was involved in the recruiting of Blake. Dickey said to Adams, "We know you're a big Tennessee fan, and you're wearing that orange coat around." He warned Adams to steer clear of Blake. Adams was offended by Dickey's "sneering" attitude, he says, adding: "He's an arrogant [expletive deleted]. He talked to me like he was my boss. I told Dickey that I'd called the NCAA to make sure that I wasn't doing anything in violation of NCAA rules. Dickey's reply was, 'You don't call the NCAA, you call me.'" Adams says he stopped contributing to the UT athletic department that year. Blake ended up signing with Auburn. Two weeks after Blake had signed with Auburn, says Adams, "he called me up and asked me for help. I told him I couldn't give him any money."

"Mean, Cruel, and Vindictive"

In 1990, Adams had an unpleasant experience with Johnny Majors. Adams was wearing his white coonskin cap at a dinner-meeting of the Memphis Touchdown Club. The Touchdown Club is a small group of local college fans who invite sundry sports figures to speak at monthly dinners. Many major southern cities have them. Majors, the Tennessee coach at that time, was the guest. He got up to speak, says Adams—and then began to ridicule the Vol booster. "I don't know what that is growing out of Roy's head," Majors told the crowd. The coach went on: "Roy Adams has nothing to do with the UT program, and if you hear of him doing anything [wrong], I want you to call me." Adams was publicly humiliated. He now describes Majors as "mean, cruel, and vindictive—all the bad things you can say about a person are personified in Johnny Majors." Ever since that public dressing down, says Adams, "I have deliberately avoided associating with UT coaches."

Adams emphasizes that the booster business is not nearly as dirty as it used to be. "Most recruiting now is on the up-and-up. There is not as much cheating. Memphis must be one of the last places where it happens." What has caused the change? The threat of NCAA sanctions, primarily. Booster involvement with players and prospects was banned in the mid-1980s, though as many people acknowledge, there are a lot of gray areas. Universities now make a point of telling fans—in person and on TV and radio commercials—not to fraternize with players or prospects. And as Adams has learned, schools are quick to disassociate themselves from boosters with questionable reputations—deserved or not. Beyond that, says Adams, "There just aren't any secrets anymore. Kids now have recording devices and caller ID, and a lot of stuff gets on the Internet." Adams says he is largely retired from the booster business. "I don't get involved in UT's recruiting—haven't for years." He is close to Bobby Franklin, who played quarterback for Mississippi in the 1960s and is now the football coach at Northwest Community College. Adams says he does help out NWCC. "I give prospects $20 to go out on a date or go to Platinum Plus," he says. (Cortez Kennedy attended NWCC and then signed with Miami, where he became a star player.) But he notes that he isn't, technically, a booster for NWCC because he has no formal association with the school.

Dinner with DuBose

Young, who is divorced and has a son, has closer direct ties to Vanderbilt than Alabama. He attended the Nashville university—but did not graduate. Young's daddy earned two degrees from Vanderbilt (including a law degree), and he loved football. Too little to play the sport, Young's father became team manager for the Vandy football team in the 1940s, when Red Saunders was the Commodore coach. "My daddy knew Red Saunders very well," says Young, "and he knew Bear Bryant through connections in Arkansas. Bryant spent a year coaching at Vanderbilt, and eventually wound his way back to his alma mater, Alabama. He took over as coach of the Crimson Tide in 1958. "I've been an Alabama fan ever since," says Young. Even after his daddy died, his friendship with Bryant flourished. Of the Bear, he says, "He could be gruff, but he really wasn't. He was intense. He gave a lot and he expected a lot in return. He could motivate like nobody I've ever been around."

Young donates money to both Vanderbilt and Alabama, but his heart is with the Crimson Tide. He leases a private box at Bryant-Denny Stadium in Tuscaloosa, and Billy Neighbors often sits with him. Lee Roy Jordan, the great Alabama (and later Dallas Cowboy) linebacker, stops by during games to visit. Paul Bryant, Jr., who is a Civil War buff and behind-the-scenes power broker, sits a floor above. Young says that he contributed money so that the football team could buy new video equipment. In addition, he donates money to the football camp run by Alabama coach Mike DuBose. "You get a special dinner with the coach for doing that," says Young. He also says he was one of four boosters who donated money so that Alabama could hire Ronnie Cottrell, Alabama's recruiting coordinator, away from Florida State University.

As one might expect, Young is outspoken about the folks who manage the Alabama football tradition. Simply put, he likes people who will crawl over broken glass to maintain it; loathes anyone who does not pay it proper respect. He likes DuBose, and was glad that former Athletic Director Bob Bockrath and Alabama President Ted Sorenson didn't fire the coach after he became embroiled in a threatened sexual harassment lawsuit just prior to the 1999 season. "I get along with Mike," says Young. "I've heard people say he's hard to communicate with, but I haven't found that to be true. He's not as outgoing as some people you'd meet." After Alabama beat Florida last year, in what was a major upset, Young called DuBose and congratulated him. Young says that the only problem with DuBose is that some people want to compare him to Coach Bryant. "There are no other Coach Bryants and never will be."

Young abhored Bockrath, whom he says "was not a football man." He's not crazy about Alabama President Sorenson, either. He faults both men for trying to build up other sports at Alabama at the expense of the football program. "Most southern schools derive their income from football," says Young, "and you got to fix that before you fix women's softball. There are certain things you have to do to comply with Title IX, but you don't have to do more. Most SEC schools aren't trying to do more, but we are. Bockrath was hell-bent on spending money on every sport but football. He was a fish out of water at Alabama from the day he got there."

So when Bockrath was let go by the university last year, Young was pleased. He was even more pleased when his longtime friend Mal Moore, who grew up in Alabama, played football at Alabama (he was a nifty running back dubbed the Dozier Comet), and has coached at Alabama for many years, was named the new athletic director. "I'm really happy he got the job," says Young. "It's the best thing that could happen to us. He's an Alabama guy. We needed somebody we could trust. He knows the problems, and he'll fix them. We didn't need Bob Bockrath from California," he sneers. "We needed Mal Moore from Bama."

Alabama's football team rolled off the rails for a few years, what with probation and a few mediocre teams. But like the booster he is, Young is heartened by the recent turn of events. DuBose not only escaped the guillotine, he won the SEC championship in 1999. "We're headed downhill now," says Young. "Everything is under control." He's biding his time until next season—and in particular until October 2000, when Alabama will get another opportunity to whip the hated Vols.

Adams is not worried. Whereas Young is consumed with winning, Adams likes to have fun *and* win. That is the difference between the two men. Adams recently flew to Nashville for a night of partying with Cortez Kennedy. And, he says, he's gotten a new satellite service. College football season is coming, and it's never too early to make sure all the TVs are working.

SEVEN

THE DEVIL'S BREW OR DRINK OF HAPPINESS? THE VANDY EXPERIENCE

Woody Widenhofer has four Super Bowl rings. For any National Football League coach, winning one Super Bowl ring is nirvana. Widenhofer has *four*. Woody Widenhofer spent eighteen years in the National Football League, and was a key architect of what may have been the NFL's best defense *ever*—the Pittsburgh Steelers' so-called "steel curtain." Widenhofer was the Steelers' linebacker coach in 1974 and 1975, when Pittsburgh won back-to-back Super Bowls. He was their defensive coordinator in 1978 and 1979, when the Steelers claimed two more NFL titles. On those great Steelers teams, Widenhofer coached two of the best linebackers ever— Jack Ham and Jack Lambert. Widenhofer was the only professional position coach Lambert ever had. Picture Lambert for a moment: he is a medieval warrior—armour strapped across his chest, face bleeding—striding across a battlefield with a 100-pound sword. His face has a look of pure (toothless) menace.

And now, if you will, picture the team that Widenhofer coaches . . . Vanderbilt.

Actually, the Nashville-based school gave us some help last year, when it attempted to overhaul its athletic image. Vanderbilt produced a promotional poster for the 1999 football team. The poster shows five players standing in full uniform in front of an army helicopter, which has shark's teeth painted on the side of the cockpit. The players all have their faces painted black, so that they resemble a cross between military commandoes and members of the band KISS. Widenhofer is standing behind the players, wearing Johnny Cash black. The poster's background is dark, misty, foreboding. The message is clear: these Vandy guys are tough, maybe even a little *dangerous*. It's a perfectly good promotional effort, but outside of Nashville it would only elicit a derisive chuckle. The players just don't look like, well, Jack Lambert. They don't seem *mean*. Vanderbilt took its image makeover one step further. The school designed a new athletic logo, which Widenhofer described as a "combination of character, manliness, and violence." The character part, we buy. But the other two components still need proving on a football field.

The hard truth is that Vandy isn't very good at football. Who else offers a money-back guarantee to its season-ticket holders, as the Commodores did last year? (After the third game, only two ticket holders had asked for their money back.) In the 1920s and 1930s, Vanderbilt *was* a formidable football school. Dan McGugin, the school's first coach, was exceptional: between 1904 and 1934, he won 197 games and lost 55, with 19 ties. Tennessee hired Robert Neyland partly to beat its tough, in-state rival. And Vandy had a few good teams in the 1940s. "People who say we don't have football tradition are thinking about the last forty-five years," says Rod Williamson, Vandy's sports information director. Quite true.

After World War II, Vanderbilt's football fortunes began a long downhill slide. And despite coaching changes and periodic bouts of optimism, the school has never recovered. Vandy is, to be blunt, the milquetoast of SEC football—a ninety-eight-pound weakling in a conference full of Russian weightlifters. Vandy hasn't had a winning season since 1982, and has never won the SEC football title. The school has played in only three bowl games in its history, winning one (the 1955 Gator Bowl).

Why the football futility? The reason is simple: Vanderbilt is a small private school that puts a heavy emphasis on academics. Ranked one of the top twenty universities in the nation, Vanderbilt has about 10,000 students—half of them in graduate school. That's roughly half the size of the student population in the rest of the SEC. Vanderbilt's stadium holds 42,000 people—the second smallest in the conference (just above Mississippi State.) Vanderbilt's athletic budget is about $25 million—the smallest in the SEC and just half of what Tennessee and Florida spend on their sports teams. Last year the school sold a measly 12,000 football season tickets. Vandy is the southern equivalent of Ivy League—a place for people (here is the stereotype) who wear glasses, speak well, floss regularly, and average 1,300 on their SAT test. Al Gore, Jr., and Amy Grant are Vandy grads. Jack Lambert is not.

The school was founded in 1873 through a gift from Commodore Cornelius Vanderbilt. The famous financier never visited Nashville, but his $1-million donation endowed a charter that had been issued for "Central University." In 1875, Vanderbilt University opened its doors for classes, with 192 students enrolled. Nasvhille had 40,000 residents at the time, and the campus was part of a cornfield. The well-known stone wall surrounding the campus was built to keep cows off the grounds.

Today, what used to be a cow pasture is the football practice field. There can be found the SEC's brightest football players. Most SEC schools have lately been laboring to boost their graduation rates. Vandy has been there, done that. The graduation rates for its football players has recently been averaging more than 80 percent. That's not only much higher than Vandy's SEC brethren (whose graduation rate for footballers is on average roughly 50 percent), it's slightly better than the grad rate for regular Vandy students!

And Vandy degrees are not cheap: no country-music appreciation courses for this bunch. Brad Bates, a senior associate athletic director, says that the Vandy curriculum is "rigorous" and "not as broad-based and specialized as other SEC schools. Ours is more liberal arts. It's a little more challenging here." Last year Vandy's football players had a collective grade point average of about 2.9 compared to roughly 2.5 in the rest of the conference. The team's 1998 freshmen had an average GPA of 2.84, average SAT score of 1,113, and an average ACT score of 22—all significantly higher than other SEC schools. The football program has never been on athletic probation, and while its athletes aren't Boy Scouts, they rarely get into trouble—no drug-dealing or assault charges.

"There aren't a lot of places where the players are getting uptight about a calculus test," says Williamson. "They do here." And unlike players at other SEC schools, Vanderbilt footballers seldom quit or transfer to other schools. Most *don't* go to Vandy for the football. If their athletic career stalls out, they still *want* a Vandy degree. That fact hurts the football program, because the school can't improve its talent base by signing good players to replace weaker players who might drop off the team or transfer, as happens at other SEC schools.

Harvard on Monday, Bama on Saturday

Vandy is rightly proud of its academic prowess. It's got the right priorities. But make no mistake: the school is tired of having sand kicked in its face every autumn by the SEC big boys. As Williamson says, "We're not here just to brag about how smart we are. We want to win." The school has *ambitions*. That's why it hired Widenhofer (and his FOUR Super Bowl rings). He's arguably got the best coaching credentials in the SEC. Talk to Vandy officials, and they all say, "We want to be Harvard Monday through Friday and Alabama on Saturday." That's a favorite expression around McGugin Center, Vandy's athletic offices. Vanderbilt officials know full well that football is important: winning excites fans, boosts revenues, stimulates alumuni donations, and, generally, creates a "winning" image for a university that crosses over into the academic realm. Williamson bemoans the "glass half-empty image" of Vandy football, which obviously derives from losing too many football games. "Our kids lift as many weights, run in the summer, practice as hard as everybody else," says Williamson. "But football is the first sporting event of the year, and when you're not winning your reputation suffers. It affects a lot of things, most of which are not happy."

In fact, there are a lot of football fans in the SEC who look at Vandy and ask, "Why?" Why are they even *in* the Southeastern Conference, which consists mostly of big state schools with broad-shouldered football programs and so-so academic reputations? There is periodic talk that Vandy should drop out of the SEC and join another conference more suited to its horn-rimmed image. "There are some people who think we're only in the conference to get money," says Williamson. "Others think we're more of a basketball school, and say, 'Why don't they join the Atlantic Coast Conference.'" (Vandy did, in fact, win the SEC basketball title in 1993.) "But we compete quite well in a lot of sports. Our women's teams are strong. But football is a tough nut to crack." And while some SEC fans may watch Vandy lose and scratch their heads, SEC Commissioner Roy Kramer is one of the school's biggest fans. And well he should be: he was Vandy's athletic director for ten years. But beyond that, he knows that Vanderbilt gives the football-mad SEC something it sorely needs—academic integrity, much as Northwestern does for the Big Ten.

Sitting in his office in the McGugin Center, classical music wafting around the room, Bates flips the *Vandy shouldn't be in the SEC* argument on its head. "In a lot of ways," he asserts, "we have the model SEC program. We've got arguably the best academic reputation in the best football conference, and we're located in arguably the best SEC city. If Woody can get things on a roll . . . we could get some momentum." Vandy on a roll? The idea sounds far-fetched, but it's not. Bates mentions Northwestern as an example of what Vandy could achieve in football—if the gods ever smiled and a few more Renaissance men (brainiacs with brawn) ever made their way to Nashville. Northwestern, which is the academic standard-bearer in the Big 10 conference, was that league's champion in football in 1995, and played in the Rose Bowl. (How *did* they do that?) "Northwestern was such a good story because it has the balance between academics and athletics," says Bates. "It was an underdog story."

Bates knows a lot about big-time football. He played football at Michigan (appearing in three Rose Bowls as a defensive back), and then was a graduate assistant for two years under Bo Schembechler, the longtime Wolverine coach. Bates then spent three years as the strength-and-conditioning coach at

Colorado. He joined Vanderbilt in 1985, and over the years has been involved in just about every facet of athletic department administration—student-life director, compliance, academic support director. He now chairs an athletic committee on recruiting. Bates says he enjoys working at Vandy precisely because it has a strong balance between academics and athletics. While the school will never sacrifice its academic reputation to win a few more football skirmishes, he asserts, "We do care about football. And the intensity with which we want to succeed is about equal to other SEC schools. But because we haven't had recent success, I'd say the expectations here are not as high, particularly in the community. But we care deeply about winning."

"A Special Challenge"

Widenhofer, for one, thinks he can win. A cheerful optimist, the fifty-six-year-old coach calls his job "a special challenge." Melding Harvard minds with Alabama bodies is "a tough combination." But he is undeterred. "People tell me, 'You can't win with smart guys.' But I think you can build a winning program here. I think you can get it done. But you've got to broaden your recruiting pool—geographically, it's got to be coast to coast. When you don't have a football tradition, you lose a lot of guys [during the recruiting process]. Therefore, we have to go after a lot of players. You don't want to take people just because they can get in the school."

In three years as head coach, Widenhofer has compiled a 10-23 record. That's not very good, but he's got the Commodores heading toward greener pastures. Last year's team was 5-6—a good year by Vandy standards—and it might have been even better. Vandy played some excellent football in 1999— and with a couple of breaks might have earned its fourth bowl berth. Last year the Commodores beat Mississippi, a top-20 team for most of the year, on the road. Vandy led Alabama at the half, led Georgia going into the fourth quarter, and outplayed Florida in Gainesville. They lost all three games. In the last game of the season, the team was driving for a game-winning field goal against Kentucky. But trailing by two points with two minutes remaining in the game, Vandy fumbled the ball at the Kentucky 31-yard line (within field goal range) and lost another nail-biter.

For all its problems, Vandy is nowhere near the worst team in the SEC. South Carolina has lately been the caboose at the end of the parade. In fact, with a little luck and better second-half play, Vandy might well be primed for a breakthrough season in 2000. Vandy returns nearly its entire team—including linebacker Jamie Winborn, who is arguably the best defensive player in the conference. Widenhofer says that he "feels good" about Vandy's recent recruiting classes. "The talent is young, but we've got more athletes than we've ever had." In 1998 Vandy had sixty-one players who were redshirt sophomores or freshmen. They've now matured.

Widenhofer is a defensive specialist, but he's finally got some legitimate talent on offense—especially quarterback Greg Zolman and running back Rodney Williams. Zolman—a mobile, left-handed QB—has been a major addition to the Vandy offense. The best Vandy quarterback in years, Zolman was last year named the SEC's offensive player of the week—the first time a Commodore had garnered that honor in nine years. "We knew he could be a good SEC quarterback," says Widenhofer.

In the same way, Widenhofer believes Vandy can be a good SEC team. "I think our efforts will pay off," he says. "I just hope [the university] gives me enough time." He almost sounds worried about his job. Imagine that: Widenhofer—four Super Bowl rings, coach of Jack Lambert—fretting about getting fired by Vandy. Life isn't always fair. And they *do* fire coaches at Vandy. Watson Brown got fired after the 1990 season. Given the school's losing tradition, Vandy coaches get more slack than most of their counterparts in the SEC, but Brown won only ten games in five seasons. That brought out the ax.

Gerry DiNardo was something of a minor hero at Vandy (at least until he got into a contract dispute with the school after leaving for LSU), and he never won more than five games. But he posted three 5-6 records—and that's an achievement at Vandy. For many coaches, Vanderbilt can be a dead-end job. No matter how good a coach is, he's not going to get much acclaim for trying hard, for coming close. Winning matters. DiNardo was one of the few Vandy coaches to parley his Nashville performance into a better, more lucrative position. He was hired away by LSU—which with its football tradition, hefty budget, and great athletes, is really the antithesis of Vandy. Ironically, DiNardo did poorly at LSU, and he was sacked last year.

Call Woody

Maybe it's the losing, but things *are* different at Vandy. The school is not completely carefree in its dealings with the press, but you can get what you need without much hassle. Williamson promptly returns e-mails. You don't need a police escort and special ID card to watch a practice—although an assistant did drive up to me in a golf cart and ask if I was an NFL scout. "You want to talk to Woody?" Williamson asked me. "Here's his number, give him a call." I called the number and asked Woody's secretary if I could speak with the coach for a few minutes. Fifteen seconds later, Woody is on the phone! He's the most media-friendly coach in the SEC. (Maybe, with a name like Woody, he has to be. You can't be pretentious when you're named Woody and you're the coach at Vandy.) At other SEC schools, getting ten minutes with the coach means navigating through a small bureaucracy. But Vandy? Give Woody a holler; he'll talk to you.

Widenhofer has been around. In addition to his eighteen years of NFL experience (with the Steelers, Cleveland Browns, and Detroit Lions), he has had a few college stints. He has coached at Minnesota and Michigan State, and was the head coach at Missouri—his alma mater—for four years, leaving in 1989 to return to the pros (as defensive coordinator for the Detroit Lions.) After four years in the Motor City, Widenhofer spent two years as linebacker coach for the Cleveland Browns before taking the job of defensive coordinator for Vanderbilt in 1995. Two years later, he was promoted to head coach.

With his slicked-back, receding hair and black moustache, Widenhofer might easily pass as a casino manager or salesman. He's got an Everyman face. But he is every bit a football coach. More to the point, he's something of a defensive mastermind. Since he joined Vanderbilt, the team's defense every year has been rugged. "In 1997 we had the best defense in the SEC, and the eighth-best defense in the nation," says Widenhofer, "and we won three games. We had no offense." Peyton Manning threw eighty-nine touchdown passes in his four years at Tennessee—but he could manage only *one* against Vandy. Both Tennessee and Florida have struggled to score on Vanderbilt, though both powerhouses always muster just enough offense to beat the Commodores.

The Perfect Score

If he ever hopes to turn Vandy around, Widenhofer will have to start winning the close games. Last year's Georgia game was a classic heartbreaker. Early in the fourth quarter, Vandy was leading 17-3. But after throwing three second-half interceptions, the Commodores completely squandered their momentum. Georgia returned one interception to the Vandy one-yard line and quickly scored, narrowing its deficit to 7 points. In the second half the Bulldogs' defense was shutting down the young Vandy offense. Early in the fourth quarter, facing a fourth-and-sixteen situation deep in his own territory, Widenhofer decided to gamble. Looking for something to spark his faltering team, the coach called for a fake punt. The play called for Jonathan Shaub, a freshman reserve who was a blocking back on the punt team, to take the snap and run around the end. The idea was to catch Georgia off-guard.

I had heard about Shaub. Lots of people have. He'd scored a perfect 1,600 on his SAT score while in high school—and could play a little football besides. Shaub is 6', weighs 200 pounds. In two and a half seasons at David Lipscomb High School in Nashville, he rushed for about 5,000 yards. He was the most valuable player for the Tennessee side in the annual Tennessee-Kentucky high school All-Star game. Shaub wasn't a blue-chip prospect, but several big-name universities were interested in offering him a scholarship—Notre Dame, Purdue, Baylor, and Tennessee, in addition to Vanderbilt. They liked Shaub's football skills, loved his academics.

Son of an actuarial consultant (who got a master's degree in mathematics from Vandy) and a homemaker, Shaub says his parents "always encouraged me to read and think when I was young. And I still read a lot." Growing up, he played chess with his dad and older sister, who is also a student at Vandy and got a 1,530 on her SATs. "My only goal was to beat her," quips Shaub, and he did.

Despite the interest from better football programs, Shaub never seriously considered going anywhere but Vanderbilt. "I had grown up a Vandy fan," he says. "I used to go to every home game [in the 1980s] with my grand-dad—it's my earliest memory. They were not very good when I started going. I have memories of the team losing. A lot of the games were close, and I held out hope that they would have a winning season the next year and the next year and the next. . . ." Shaub looked at Harvard, talked to the Princeton coach. But the Ivies don't offer athletic scholarships, and as Shaub says, "it didn't seem worth it to pay [Ivy League] tuition when I could go to Vandy for free." Shaub seems to relish the memory of blowing off Tennessee—Vandy's in-state athletic tormentor. "The first time a Tennessee coach called, I told him that I wasn't going to UT. I had this deep hatred for UT, though most of my friends were UT fans."

At Vandy, Shaub immediately impressed the coaches. As a true freshman, he was the second-team free safety and starting "nickle" (meaning fifth) defensive back, and played on special teams. Did he catch grief from teammates about his SAT score? "Quite a bit. I can't do anything stupid at all or I get teased." Turns out that trying a fake punt against Georgia was, well, let's just call it *unfortunate*. With the ball on his 20-yard line, Widenhofer (four Super Bowl rings) sends Shaub in to fool Georgia and throw the game's momentum back in Vandy's favor. Shaub had run a fake punt against Duke earlier in the season—and it worked: he ran for 34 yards. In the Georgia game, he says, "the coaches had been mixing me in on the punt team. Georgia looked vulnerable." Here's why: on earlier punts, Georgia's outside defenders had been "peeling back" down the field after the snap of the football. Simply put, instead of rushing the punter, Georgia's defenders dropped back to block.

The Vandy Experience

Entering the field, Shaub had misgivings about the fake punt—the field position wasn't ideal for such a gambit. He had the option of checking out of the play once the team got into its punt formation, but that's not really an option when you're a *freshman*. "I thought about doing it, but decided against it," he says. The ball was snapped, Shaub snatched it, and started running for the short side of the field. Hoping for daylight, he instead found two Georgia players waiting for him. The ruse hadn't fooled the Bulldogs. This time, alas, Georgia didn't send its outside people back downfield to block. "They were not peeling out, they were rushing," says Shaub. In desperation he pitched the ball to the hapless Vandy punter, who got crushed and lost seven yards. Georgia scored again, and went on to the win the game. Despite the bitter setback, Shaub says he "was not really impressed by Georgia. Quincy Carter is a good quarterback, but I didn't think they were as good as they were hyped to be. We were obviously the better team. Anybody who watched the game would agree to that."

Shaub, who is majoring in philosophy, was not discouraged. "This team is extremely competitive," he said. "Every team we faced, we had a realistic chance of winning. We've got guys who work hard and overachieve." Does the losing tradition affect morale? "I think you can see the remnants of a bad attitude in the older players, especially when we get behind. But there is a strong core that expects to win and is very competitive. There is a mixture, but we're more of a team that feels bad when it loses rather than just accepts it." Shaub says that the only thing that would have kept him from choosing Vanderbilt was its lack of a winning tradition. "I had never been involved with a losing team, and that's one of the things I wondered if I could deal with. But talking with Woody and some of the other players, I felt we could turn it around. And turning a losing school into a winner would be a better experience than going to a winning school and winning."

Lower Standards?

For all his skills as a coach, Widenhofer would be the first to say that talent wins football games. There has long been a debate at Vandy about whether to compromise its admissions criteria to attract more talented athletes. (Notre Dame wrestles with the same issue.) Standing on the edge of the Vanderbilt practice field last year, Don Cherry, a fifty-six-year-old UPS truck driver and longtime Commodore fan, bemoaned the state of the football program. He blamed the school's administration—and stringent entrance policies—for the team's woes. He thinks the admissions standards for athletes should be loos-

121

ened a bit. "Until Vandy shows that they are sincere about putting a winning team on the field, they won't get the blue-chip athlete they need," said Cherry. "That's what Woody is trying to do, and he's making some progress."

Cherry, who lives in Joelton, Tennessee, has been going to Vandy games since age ten—when his older brother started taking him to games. "I grew up admiring what they stood for—academics and trying to field a good team—and it kept me coming back." He remembers when Steve Sloan coached the Commodores and took them to the Peach Bowl in 1974. "Vandy hasn't been to too many bowls," he said, "so they're easy to remember." But even Cherry was disillusioned by the firing of Brown, which he says was handled badly by the administration. "They knew he was gone and waited till the last game to fire him. They lost a few fans with that. There are a lot of wounds. We all liked Watson a lot. He was too good for his own good—very easy to talk to. Woody is the same way. He'll talk to anybody."

Cherry asserts that Vandy should start following the example of Duke, another tough academic university that has had great success in basketball. He maintains that the Blue Devils admit basketball players with borderline grades, adding: "You've got to give some kids a chance. It all comes back to having the university—the chancellor—committed to football."

Intangible Value

In fact, Vandy's admissions policy for athletes is not as tough as one might expect. It's the toughest in the SEC, for sure. Whereas most SEC schools will admit a football player if he meets minimum NCAA standards, that is seldom good enough for entrance to Vandy. But the Vandy admissions threshhold does get lowered a bit for athletes. "There is some leeway there," says Bates. "Athletics is viewed as kind of an intangible that the institution values to a certain degree. Schools that don't compete in Division 1 don't value athletics like those that do." Ainsely Battles, a senior defensive back for Vandy last year, told me he got an 880 on his SAT. That score would almost never get a regular student into Vandy.

According to Bates, the admissions office "scrutinizes the academic skills of student-athletes a lot more carefully" than other SEC schools. But the school takes into consideration a variety of factors. Traditional board scores and high school GPAs are important, of course, but so is something called the PGPA: the predicted grade point average. Vandy officials review a prospective student-athletes' GPA and test scores, how he ranks in math and English components. They also assess the quality of a prospect's high school. Is it good, or second-rate? Throw all these quantifiable items into a formula and out comes a PGPA for the prospect's first year at Vandy, which is tweaked depending on which academic specialty the candidate is apt to choose—arts and science as opposed to education, for example.

Widenhofer and his staff also have some leverage, and they use it. The coach is free to lobby the admissions office on behalf of specific prospects who, though borderline academically, possess what the coach believes is the requisite character and ethics to graduate from Vandy. Says Bates: "The coaches can see how a particular person might fit into Vanderbilt, and represent him [before admissions] in ways that the student himself could not. It absolutely puts that coach on the spot. There is a credibility issue there."

In other words, if Widenhofer really likes a player who is a borderline student, he might persuade the admissions office to let him in. But he is on the hook if the player flunks out or gets in trouble. So far, the track record has been good. Asked how he feels about the admissions policy, Widenhofer doesn't say much. "It can be a positive or a negative," he allows before veering off in another conversational direction. He says he enjoys coaching "these kinds of kids. We talk about a lot of things other than football." But he's just being diplomatic, really. As Widenhofer goes on to say, "Admissions is not my business. The bottom line is to keep your job, and that means winning." Is the Vandy administration committed to winning? "I had some questions a few years back," says the coach, "but with [athletic director] Todd Turner here, I think there is a commitment. They tore out the artificial turf at the stadium and put grass in. They're pouring money into facilities. That's what it's all about. Tradition and facilities are great selling points."

Shifting Priorities

Bates says that universities and the NCAA are shifting their priorities with student-athletes. Rather than place lots of attention on admissions standards and initial eligibility—which has been the primary focus for many years—schools are increasingly emphasizing academic "outcomes"—getting athletes the help they need while in school to earn a degree and to make the transition to life after sports. "Philosophically," says Bates, "our department would look at athletics as a diverse educational endeavor. To bring someone to an institution just for his athletic ability is exploitation. But if [a borderline student] has a good character, good morals, and the coaches think he can succeed academically, then he brings something of value to the institution. As long as that value is recognized, and the coaches and faculty and admissions feel that such students will have opportunities to succeed, then I think an outcomes-based approach is probably much more reasonable than an upfront accountability."

What Vandy really wants to do is not lower its standards, but rather get other SEC schools to raise *theirs*. Vanderbilt Chancellor Joe B. Wyatt has been an outspoken critic of corruption and academic deficiencies within major-college football programs. In a recent article in the *Chronicle of Higher Education*, Wyatt suggested that college presidents "had not maintained a continuing, focused involvement in the activities of athletic departments." He called the graduation rates at many football programs "appalling," adding, "We have a moral obligation to take an active role in the academic success of the athletes in those programs."

Wyatt says that university presidents are put in "a very difficult position" by the fanatical emphasis on winning, and by athletic officials who stretch or break rules. "The abuses are a frustration for administrators. And you can measure the frustration by the turnover in presidents at many of these institutions. This is my nineteenth year at Vandy, but many of the big SEC schools have cycled presidents through three and four times during that period." He says that the pressure to win football games has made many university leaders "so uncomfortable that they move on. The president can't in good conscience allow the abuses to go on and still square that with the values that bring students to a university in the first place. It's a question of a president saying, 'We are really an educational university first, and have to fulfill that obligation to our society.' We don't think universities should support athletics as essentially a minor-league franchise. We're an educational and research institution. We have a confusion of roles." Having said that, Wyatt maintains that it is possible for football programs to have high academic standards *and* still accomplish their athletic goals. But Wyatt's athletic goals would certainly be more modest than those at other SEC schools.

The Vandy chancellor contends that "youngsters are being cycled through school and being used for their athletic abilities. That is not what college is supposed to be about." Last year Vandy sponsored a national proposal that would penalize schools when student-athletes fail to graduate. The idea: if any athlete leaves a program in poor academic standing (meaning he quits, flunks out, or gets kicked out of school), his scholarship cannot be replaced until after his expected eligibility would have expired. In short, if an athlete leaves school after two years, the school will lose his scholarship for the remaining two years of his (four-year) eligibility period. SEC presidents approved the proposal by a vote of 9-1 (with one absention)—and so did the NCAA. But athletic directors and coaches, who opposed the proposal, seemed intent on watering down the final legislation. Many athletic administrators believe that a scholarship penalty should be imposed only if the graduation rate for a basketball or football program has fallen below a certain standard—say, 66 percent.

The Vandy Experience

Vandy will never have to worry about that. But the school does worry about how it can win more football games—kick sand in the faces of its rivals for a change—and still not lose its soul. It's the basic riddle of major-college athletics, and Wyatt alluded to it cleverly in his *Chronicle of Higher Education* article.

Many years ago, he wrote, a now unknown congressman sent the following response to a constituent who'd asked: Where do you stand on whiskey? "If you mean the Devil's brew, the poison scourge, the bloody monster that defiles innocence, dethrones reason and topples men and women from the pinnacles of righteous, gracious living into the bottomless pit of degradation and despair, then certainly I am against it," the politician wrote.

"But," he continued, "if you mean the drink that enables a man to magnify his joy and happiness and to forget life's heartbreaks and sorrows; if you mean the drink that pours into our treasuries untold millions of dollars, which are used to care for our little crippled children, our aged and infirm, to build highways and schools, then certainly I am in favor of it."

Vandy values athletics, appreciates winning, but the school perceives bigtime football as being more Devil's brew than drink of happiness. But the idea that the school can persuade bigger rivals to follow its lead, to take the high road (less traveled), is wishful thinking. Everybody wants players who are both good and smart, but they are in short supply. The big schools will continue to take good players *before* smart players. Vandy wants both, and there marks the difference between winning (with an asterisk) and losing (with dignity). Still, keep your eye on the Commodores this year.

EIGHT

IMPRESSIONS: THE TALENTED (TALKATIVE) SHAUN ALEXANDER

Forget (for a moment) his talent for running with a football. What Shaun Alexander is really good at is talking. "I'm a people person," he says—and it shows. I called his mom's home in Florence, Kentucky, one night on the cusp of his senior season. He wasn't home, but he returned the call an hour later. "Hey, this is Shaun, hiya doing? I'm sorry I missed your call—I was out having dinner in Cincinnati." And within seconds he's volunteering the name of the restaurant (Montgomery Boat House), what he ate (steak), the quality of the food (excellent), and what he'd be doing in two weeks (appearing at a Fellowship of Christian Athletes camp in Black Mountain, North Carolina). My first thought was: is this a college football player? Many major-college football players are low-key and laconic, and spend a little too much time playing video games. Alexander has got the perky personality of a talk-show host—and he's probably more articulate than many.

My second thought was: do I *know* Shaun Alexander? I *must* know him and not realize it. There was a tone of familiarity in his voice, as if we were old friends, not strangers speaking for the first time. Not long into the conservation, he says, "Hold on a second, I got another call." He was back on the line in a few seconds. And then a few moments later: "Ooops, I got another call. I'll be right back, I promise. I've got call awaiting." And so it went: five minutes of talk followed by a break to take another phone call. Two of his close high school friends had called; Alabama's running back coach, Ivy Williams, had called to check on him. A cousin had called, looking for Shaun's older brother. But Alexander never kept me waiting for very long—and always apologized when he got back on the line.

Here is a young man (twenty-two years old) with a head on his shoulders. And, I hasten to add, two of the best legs in college football. Going into his final season at Alabama, Alexander was not just the linchpin of the Crimson Tide offense, he was also a Heisman Trophy candidate. He didn't win it, but was nevertheless excited to be a candidate for the honor. "I was the first person in Alabama history to be pushed for that award," said Alexander. "Bart Starr, Kenny Stabler, Joe Namath—those guys are legends, and I get pushed for it?" He is humbled by the thought. He's much more concerned about team achievements, he says.

At 6'1", 220 pounds, there isn't much that Alexander can't do on a football field. He's a power runner with wiggle. He's strong enough to break tackles and fast enough to beat linebackers or strong safeties down the field and catch passes. "He's got great vision," Head Coach Mike DuBose told me, "and he has true speed with the football in his hands. You see some guys who have good track speed but don't play the game that fast. They run a 4.4 [second] 40-yard dash on a track, but run a 4.6 on the football field after they put the pads on. Shaun plays fast with pads on."

By the end of his junior season, Alexander held two Alabama records— most touchdowns in a game (5), and most rushing yards in a game (291). By the end of his collegiate career, he'd own a bunch more—including career rushing yards. That's no small thing at a school that likes to pound the football. And he got the one thing he so desperately wanted, an SEC title. Yet, for all his accomplishments, he displayed very little ego, no attitude, just a jaunty wide-eyed appreciation for the good things in his life—his family, his faith in God, and his football skills.

What was amazing about Alexander's career, in retrospect, was how slowly it got started. For all he achieved in two full years as Alabama's tailback, he could have done more. He seemed "underemployed" his first two or three years in the program. He got sidetracked by little injuries and odd personnel decisions. Curiously, he was redshirted as a freshman—held off out of competition for a year so that he could adjust physically to the college game and save a year of eligibility. In the end, that worked to Alabama's advantage because Alexander stayed in school for a full five years. Almost nobody with his talent—he was a high school All American, the Player of the Year in Kentucky, and obviously gifted from the day he stepped on the field—gets redshirted anymore, or stays for five years. They often turn pro after their third or fourth year. Plus, when Alexander was an underclassman, Alabama's offense needed help. His first year on the field (playing as a "redshirt freshman"), he was the third-string tailback, playing behind Dennis Riddle and

Curtis Alexander (no relation)—two good backs, but not as good as Alexander. Inserted in the LSU game, he dazzled everybody rushing for a whopping 291 yards on only twenty carries (an average of more than fourteen yards a carry.)

I asked him about that breakout game. "It's 10:14," he said, looking at his clock. "You ruined it!" Huh? I'd ruined his day, he joked, by asking about the 291-yard game. "I've been asked about that game four times a week ever since the end of that year." Even for the happy-go-lucky Alexander, it was a sensitive subject. For this reason: though he played in eleven games as a freshman, the twenty carries he got against LSU were more than a quarter of the carries he got all year. And he never came close to duplicating that performance; he squeezed out one other 100-yard game as a freshman, and that was it. "Every running back who's got fight in him says, 'Hey, I should be playing.' The coaches always believed in me, and in my talent, but it was about letting a freshman grow into situations. There were some good backs in front of me." And the team played well, anyway, compiling a 10-2 record.

Alexander's sophomore year, 1997, was disappointing—for him and the team. Alabama's record that year was 4-7, the Tide's worst record in about forty years. And Alexander got only limited playing time. Again playing behind Riddle, who was a grinder, he got a few more carries (ninety for the season) but fewer yards (415) than the year before. He missed two games with a bad ankle. Why didn't he play more? I asked. "The coaches just wanted me to grow up," he said. A curious comment from a kid who seems far more mature than most of his peers.

There were reports that the coaches were displeased with Alexander's blocking, and he confirms that blocking was an issue. "I just had to get better at it." But if there is one position where mediocre blocking skills are tolerated, it is tailback. That's because tailbacks are expected mainly to tote the rock; everybody else blocks for *them*. In any case, it was a poor year for the Tide, which had been penalized by the NCAA and lost scholarships because of a scandal involving former player Antonio Langham. (He'd accepted money from an agent after his junior year, and though Alabama found out about it, allowed him to play his senior year.) "We took our lumps," says Alexander. "We had only sixty-five guys on scholarship [teams are allowed a total of eighty-five]. My class had only fourteen scholarships; the class behind me, ten."

Was it tough to lose seven games? "Yeah, it was. We said to ourselves, we are Alabama and we're going to beat the other teams, but our guys were worn out." With fewer scholarships, there was no depth—a necessity nowadays—and the Tide would falter late in games. "If we'd had one more linebacker to make a fourth-down stop, another defensive back or wide receiver to make a big play, one more guy who didn't get tired, we would have won. I said, 'God, you've got some funny tricks.' But that season taught me about life. I've learned patience. When times get tough, you work harder and see who's standing at the end. That's what I learned." He is not one to dwell on negatives.

The Kentucky native got to be "the man" in 1998. And, he says, "it was awesome." He ran the ball 258 times for nearly 1,200 yards; scored five TDs against Brigham Young in the first game. He rushed for more than 100 yards in six games. "It was all pretty cool," he says. As much as playing the games, he fondly recalls playing on ESPN, and playing before larger crowds in Tuscaloosa (Bryant-Denny Stadium had been expanded from 70,000 to 85,000 seats). He also enjoyed seeing his runs replayed for the crowd on a giant end-zone video screen. "It was a bunch of firsts," he says.

Like most of his peers, Alexander gets juiced about performing in front of big crowds—which he asserts is by far the best thing about playing college football. "To have 85,000 people on their feet when you come out of the tunnel [before a game] is an amazing feeling. I told the guys, 'We have to put on a show every weekend for four months.' It's the greatest feeling in the world." He vividly remembers the 1998 LSU game, in Baton Rouge, when the Pachyderms (another nickname for Alabama) rallied to beat LSU. The Alabama fans in attendance lingered happily in the stadium right after the game. A coach told the team in the locker room that the fans were still out cheering in the stands. "We don't believe in showboating," says Alexander. "Alabama is very classy. But we stuck our heads out. It was wild to see them all yelling and cheering. We've got the best fans in the country."

Were it not for his poor aim, Alexander would likely have played football in the north, for Michigan, instead of Alabama. His brother, Durran, who is a year older, earned an academic scholarship to Notre Dame (and now works for the Campbell Soup Co.). He and Shaun watched a lot of Irish and Big Ten football growing up in Florence, Kentucky. Alexander says he was a "big" Michigan fan, and Desmond Howard was his hero. He relished the idea of playing for the Wolverines and beating Notre Dame. He visited Ann Arbor, and liked the campus. "I had a big feeling about going up there." Except for one thing—the cold weather. "It was snowing, and everybody was driving down the middle of the road, and I said, 'Man, this is not good.'"

When he got home, he picked up an Alabama media guide—which he says he received late in the recruiting process—and tried to chuck it in a trash can. "I missed." So he picked the guide up off the floor and put it back in the pile of schools still under consideration. On such minor quirks of fate are major decisions made. He then decided to visit Alabama, and—the rest, as they say, is history. "He asked me what I thought about Alabama being so far away," says his mom, Carol Alexander, "and I told him whatever made him happy made me happy. No matter how far away it is, I will support him."

That quote says a lot. If Alexander is well-grounded, it's because his parents are. Carol and Curtis Alexander are divorced, but they clearly made many positive impressions on Shaun. In particular, they emphasized the importance of education. "Education has always been stressed in my family," says Carol, age fifty, who works with troubled kids in a program in Covington, Kentucky. She herself is striving to earn an undergraduate degree in human services and mental health. When we spoke, last fall, she was doing field work with handicapped children and girding for a fifteen-hour class load at Northern Kentucky College. "I enjoy working with kids," she says. Curtis lives and works (for a chemical company) in Cincinnati. But both parents nearly always drove down to Tuscaloosa, separately, to watch their son play.

At Boone County High School, Shaun was an honor student (3.5 grade point average) and president of his senior class. "My mother didn't allow us outside until you had your homework done. I made the best of my time and if I didn't understand something, I found somebody to help. I jumped on problems right away. I just like doing things differently." He played football for Owen Hauck, a legendary high school coach in Kentucky, twice leading the team to the state championship game. (They lost both.)

Heading into the 1999 season, Alexander had already earned a marketing degree—in four years. "I said to my parents, 'I told you I'd finish in four years.' I was raised like that." He says that when he stepped up to the podium in Coleman Coliseum, in cap and gown, to accept his degree, "The crowd went crazy—buck wild. It's one of the greatest things that ever happened to me." With that out of the way, he planned to take some graduate business classes during his fifth year, "even though I hate starting stuff I can't finish." His long-term goal is to start a business, maybe a youth center, or possibly even go to work for a big company—"be a suit-and-tie guy. I was always one of those kids." Before he joins the business world, he'll be darting around on Sunday, playing pro football. For a time, he says, pro football "wasn't a strong desire. But the older I get, the more I realize it is something I really do want to do. I think it's a great honor."

How did Alexander like playing for DuBose? He says it was fun—"he's a good coach. All the guys were pumped up when he got the job." His previous two coaches—Hauck in high school and Gene Stallings at Alabama, who retired after the 1996 season, Alexander's redshirt freshman year—were stern taskmasters. "DuBose has been a twist," says Alexander. "He is open to opinions. He'll ask you what you think about certain plays or opposing players. There was none of that with Stallings." He calls DuBose an "inner motivator," adding: "He challenges you on the sidelines. He says, 'Shaun, is this linebacker soft? Can you whip him on this play? Can you beat that strong safety?' He's a tough guy—a let's-show-people-who's-boss kind of coach. He wants to control the line of scrimmage."

Shaun Alexander

Sneaky Agents

With his professional potential, it's not surprising that Alexander attracted a lot of attention from agents. But what he says about them is almost scary. Going into his final year, Alexander says he'd already been approached "at least thirty times" by agents or people who work with agents—so-called runners. "They didn't offer me anything, because I tried to make them understand that I knew the rules and I didn't come from a poor family. I just said, 'I can't get involved with this.' I told them, 'If you want any shot at me in the future, you'll leave me alone now.' After that, most of them did."

Alexander says that agents are everywhere and "sneaky." He'd be at a McDonald's, eating lunch, or at a department store, "and they'll run into you—just happen to be there." Most didn't identify themselves as agents, but rather told Alexander they were lawyers or legal-management types. A few offered to buy him things before he realized they were agents. Most weren't brazen enough to proffer cash or gifts. What they did, says Alexander, "is insinuate. They'd all say, 'Do you *need* anything? Can I *help* you *get* something?'" He says he turned them all down. "Mom has always stressed that you don't need to take anything from anybody. So it was easier for me to say no."

The coaches warned him to beware, but it was tough because "agents can be hanging out with anybody." They are, in fact, insidious. Alexander says that he'd often be walking along with a small group of friends—and some guy he assumed was a relative of one of his friends. "You'll turn to a friend and say, 'I thought *you* knew this guy? And he says, 'I thought *you* knew him?' You think you're walking around with somebody's uncle, and it's an agent."

Having been through the SEC wars for five years, Alexander says that he tried to pass on some advice to the younger players. "It's hard for them to understand how hard college is. It can be hard to keep up academically. You go to a big-time school, and you go there because you can catch a football. But you have to stress to some people that football might not pan out for them, even if they were studs in high school." That is the type of counsel one might expect a *fourth-stringer* to give a freshman—not a star who's going to play pro football. "I always tell the freshmen, 'If you get the first year out of the way and get off to a good start, you'll be all right.' They'll be good to go." Sounding almost like a young fogie, he opines that "kids nowadays don't want to play sports and they don't want to hear things. They are rebellious." Spoken like a true, er, *twenty-two*-year-old.

Certainly, Alexander helped hold Alabama together during some lean years, when the program didn't have the success to which it was accustomed. He was a mentor to some of the "young guns" on offense, who will carry on for the Tide now that he is gone. In 1998, the coaches tapped Andrew Zow, a young quarterback, to start against Florida—a daunting task for anyone, much less an inexperienced player. Before the game, Alexander tried to buck up the jittery Zow. "During warmups I pointed at Florida and said, 'There is the team you're going to dominate.' We joked with each other: 'You ready?' 'You ready?'" Bama lost by six points, but Zow played well. "He played a great game," said Alexander. "He was really hurt when we got to the locker room. I said, 'Dog, you just played great. We're going to need you from now on.'"

Alexander is that way—a silver-lining guy. He was pleased, starting his final season in Tuscaloosa, that the team's talent level had been restored after the years of NCAA probation. "The cool thing is that my freshman year, we had eighty-five scholarships, and my senior year we had eighty-five." The implication: the bad times were over, Alabama was back. "We have the talent to win the SEC this year," he said before the 1999 season—and his prediction proved true. Alexander helped turn a good season into an excellent one when he ran for a 25-yard touchdown in overtime to help Alabama upset Florida, 40-39, in Gainesville. The play was a counter-sweep, and Alexander said after the game that he'd suggested it to the coach. Bama had not run it much during the game, but said Alexander, "I told coach, 'If we get into overtime, we still got the counter.'" DuBose was just happy to have Alexander. "You just get the ball to number 37 and watch him play," said an elated DuBose after the game. "I've said it over and over again. Some guys talk the talk, but can't walk the walk. Shaun Alexander can talk the talk *and* walk the walk."

The Florida win was huge and unexpected—and Zow showed, in his second game against the Gators, that he'd learned how to play under pressure. He stood cooly in the pocket, and his accurate passing bedeviled the Gator defense all day. It was by far his best game at quarterback. Feeling their oats, the Tide went on to win the western division and then beat Florida, again, in the SEC championship game. "It was fantastic," said Alexander after the season. "An unbelievable way to end my college career."

And now he will begin the next phase. He was selected in the first round of the NFL draft (the 19th overall pick) by the Seattle Seahawks. Asked how he'll spend the interregnum between his college and pro days, Alexander replied: "I'll be working out and talking to people. It's just cool. God has given me the ability to play football, so you know He's got a sense of humor." And so ended my late-night chat with Shaun Alexander. Which is not to say that Shaun was ready to hang up the phone. There was somebody else on the line.

NINE

THE STRIVER: PHILLIP FULMER

Where is Phillip Fulmer? The answer is easy: he is everywhere. He's in Chattanooga, speaking to a Big Orange Booster Club—about 150 mostly middle-aged men who are avid fans of the University of Tennessee football team. He's in Nashville, signing autographs at a massive picnic for UT alumni and fans. He's in Johnson City, Tennessee, doing a public service announcement for the visually impaired; in Bristol, Tennessee, visiting hospital patients and elementary school students; in Atlanta, speaking to, say, the General Contractors' Association about the challenges of running a major college football program. He's in Knoxville, running the Phillip Fulmer Football Camp for teenagers. He's flying to Las Vegas to meet a blue-chip prospect; he's at a lakeside retreat in Tellico, Tennessee, brainstorming with his staff; he's coaching a high school All-Star game in Hawaii; he's being interviewed by ESPN; he's in sleepy Winchester, Tennessee, his hometown, visiting his seventy-five-year-old mother, Nan (who's got a full-size Vols helmet perched atop her mailbox post); he's doing the SEC coaches radio show; he's in New York for the Heisman ceremony; he's on the UT practice field—hair thinning, waist like a Southern sheriff, in his coaching shorts and orange Vols cap, twirling his whistle as Tennessee's football players are put through their paces. Whew! That just about covers, oh, a month or two in his schedule.

Where is Phillip (never call him Phil) Fulmer? Never in one place for very long. He will tell you that—and so will his family. I learned it the hard way. Last August, I tried three times to get him on the phone for a twenty-minute interview. Fulmer's exasperated secretary, Pat Pryor, would schedule a day and a time for the chat—and then the coach would miss the appointment. He was always too busy—a photo session with camp kids, a meeting with Athletic Director Doug Dickey, that sort of thing. I soon realized that my timing was terrible. The start of the season was less than a month away! Two-a-day practices had already begun. A trip to Gainesville to play Steve Spurrier's Florida Gators was looming. Battle plans were being drawn. It was a time of intense activity in the UT football complex.

On top of all that, Fulmer was then (and is now) in constant demand as a speaker. The invitations arrived by phone and fax, said Pryor, rolling over her desk like little wavelets. "People say they'll take him for breakfast, lunch, or dinner, it doesn't matter." Fulmer's speaking requests doubled in the months after Tennessee won the January 1999 Fiesta Bowl, and with it the national championship.

Talk to Fulmer for twenty minutes? I had a better chance of spending an afternoon with Bill Parcells. Finally, Pryor suggested that I ask for *ten* minutes with the coach rather than twenty minutes. It was a sensible idea, and it worked: next time I called, Fulmer was ready to talk. The conversation lasted about, oh, nine minutes. I got the message: if we were to have a long conversation, I surmised, it would have to be done incrementally, in short blocks of time. And that's what we did.

Fulmer is to college football what James Brown is to music: the hardest working guy in the business. He takes a week or two off every year, typically to go fishing with his buddy John "Thunder" Thorton in Jackson Hole, Wyoming, not far from Harrison Ford's ranch. (Thorton, who's an interesting story himself, once owned the largest area-rug manufacturer in America. He sold the company, and is now a real estate developer.) But even after a few days of horseback riding and fly casting for cutthroat trout, Fulmer begins to display what his wife, Vicky, and friends call "the look." The Tennessee coach becomes distant and distracted. His body may still be in the foothills of the Grand Tetons, but Fulmer's mind has drifted back to Knoxville and the subject that consumes him: Tennessee football.

Ask anyone about Fulmer, and it's the first thing they all say. "He works harder than anybody I've ever known," says Heywood Harris, Tennessee's veteran media-relations chief. "Everything he does races through his mind and settles in a place that will help him become a better football coach. I won't use the word 'obsessed,' but he is surely focused. He doesn't go through many experiences in life—a night at the theater, even—that he can't in some way relate to his job." Adds Fulmer's longtime friend Bob Kendall, a retired Procter & Gamble sales manager in Chattanooga: "It wouldn't be fair to call him a workaholic, but he borders on it. He's a completely driven person, partly because coaching Tennessee was for him a lifelong dream."

Phillip Fulmer

During the season, Fulmer typically leaves his spacious, custom-made house in Maryville, Tennessee, a bedroom community outside of Knoxville, at 5:45 in the morning. Twenty minutes later, he pulls his Lexus into his parking spot at Tennessee's posh campus football complex. Moments later, he's perched in his nicely appointed office on the second floor of the building. Condredge Holloway, Tennessee's star quarterback in the 1970s and now head of football operations, is stationed just across from the head coach's office. Just outside Fulmer's door, alongside a reception area, there are two trophy cases stacked with Vol memorabilia: Fulmer's Coach of the Year awards, various bowl trophies, a musty letterman's sweater worn by Vol great Beattie Feathers in the 1930s. Vast windows look out on the team's indoor practice field. On a table, there are a few brochures promoting Tennessee bangles—rings, earrings, and other baubles for well-heeled Tennessee fans.

Fulmer actually has two offices: the outer room, where he does most of his work, has an antique oak desk, a high-backed leather chair, and a lectern that's stacked with quote books—a staple in the coaching profession. On the wall behind his chair there is an oil painting of the 1996 Citrus Bowl, in which the Vols beat Ohio State. There's an original print of the 1997 Tennessee team—a montage featuring Peyton Manning, Marcus Nash, Jeff Hall, Trey Teague, and Al Wilson. There are photographs of his family and of special Vol moments—including his January 1999 triumph in Tempe when the Vols beat Florida State. The coach has been hoisted aloft by the Vol captains, and Fulmer has got his arm and forefinger raised high in the air—number 1. There is a look of utter joy on his face. Behind the main office there is an inner sanctum, where Fulmer relaxes (often in his casual coaching garb), watches tape, and during the winter recruiting season lays his persuasive Tennessee sales pitch on wide-eyed high school prospects. There is a picture of Gen. Bob Neyland, the great Tennessee coach, and one of Vince Lombardi.

In the morning, Fulmer sips coffee, reads his voluminous mail (he gets dozens of letters a week from Vol fans), and reviews his frenetic schedule, which Pryor has typed up the day before. She puts little yellow Post-It notes—appointment reminders—all over his door. Once every week or two, Fulmer will take a few minutes to autograph a stack of photographs and some footballs. Recently, radio station WREC in Memphis asked for eighteen autographed Fulmer photos. The coach obliged. Starting at 11:00 A.M., he'll start catching up on phone calls. On Thursdays from 1 P.M. until 2 P.M., he takes calls from the media. "He does one after the other," says Pryor. "They average about seven or eight minutes each." Like all coaches, Fulmer is constantly writing memos and notes—most relating to the team. Some are vaguely inspirational ("WE MAKES ME STRONGER"), but most are practical brainstorms about improving the team—"MUST WORK ON KICK COVERAGE." After the early morning routine, he begins a long day of staff meetings, phone calls, practices, chats with individual players, perhaps an evening speech. During the fall football season, it's often around midnight when he pulls back into his winding driveway in Maryville, where he lives with Vicky, his second wife, and their three daughters. For those counting, that's an eighteen-hour day. "This job is very demanding—very time-consuming," says Fulmer. "But it's a labor of love for me. It is hard on the family, very tough—but we're blessed here. My wife tells me, 'You're just a boy playing a game.'"

The CEO

Actually, college football is much more than a game nowadays. It's a high-profile, high-stakes business, and the men who run the programs are the equivalent of Chief Executive Officers. Fulmer has no problem with that analogy. He runs a football program that employs roughly 100 people and is the cash cow for the University of Tennessee athletic budget. Last year UT football generated more than $36 million in revenue (from operations, ticket sales, and fundraising for tickets)—71 percent of the university's $51 million athletic budget. After expenses are paid, the money helps fund athletic scholarships for nearly all of the twenty-two sports (men's and women's) sponsored by the university. Winning *is* important. Happy fans fill 107,000-seat Neyland Stadium (the second largest college stadium in the country), and are eager to donate money—to the athletic department.

In 1997 Fulmer co-wrote a book, titled *Legacy of Winning*, that is part football memoir, part management primer on the rigors of running a large "high performance" organization. There are two coaches on the book's cover: Fulmer, barking out instructions on the Tennessee sidelines during a game, and Neyland, the iconic coach who essentially created Tennessee football between the late 1930s and the early 1950s.

Fulmer caught some flack for that book. Some Vol fans felt it a little premature for him to associate himself with Neyland, who'd won a national championship, or to write about his "winning legacy." At the time the book was published, Fulmer's accomplishments were decidedly modest: one SEC title. The book was not Fulmer's idea, but a project of Gerald Sentell, who runs a management development company called Tennessee Associates International. Fulmer sat for interviews on Sunday nights, when he otherwise would have been at home eating dinner.

While the book won't win any literary awards, and only sold about 5,000 copies, it does contain some interesting background material on Fulmer. It also gives readers a peek under the big tent that is major-college football. And,

Phillip Fulmer

of course, the book now seems prescient: a year after it went on sale, in 1998, Fulmer won another SEC title and led Tennessee to an undefeated season and its first national title in forty-seven years. At the still-tender age of fifty, Fulmer has ensured himself a legacy.

Like Bear Bryant, Knute Rockne, and all great coaches, Neyland has taken on almost mythical status at Tennessee over the years. He was a West Point graduate, a general, a fanatic about football fundamentals like blocking and tackling. There is nothing mythical about Fulmer—yet. Until recently rival SEC fans often poked fun at his weight, deriding him as Phat Phil. (He is burly but by no means fat.) And there were unfavorable comparisons to Steve Spurrier, the Florida coach who's gotten the better of Fulmer in head-to-head competition. But you don't hear too many jokes about the Vol coach anymore. That's because he's won nearly 85 percent of his games since taking over at Tennessee in 1992—the third highest winning percentage among all active coaches (behind Bob Pruett of Marshall and Bobby Bowden at FSU).

Fulmer is, above all, a striver—an earnest good ol' boy with a wide streak of ambition, excellent management skills, and the determination of a mountain goat. Humble and soft-spoken, he is not the most dynamic personality in college football. He still answers questions from fans and reporters by saying "yes, ma'am" or "no, sir." His idea of a snappy quote is, "We've just got to be the best football team we can be." (Ugggh.) Fulmer doesn't have Bowden's affected "Aw, shucks, I'm just a country boy" shtick. And he's not one to needle his opponents. A few years ago, after Spurrier had taken several potshots at the Vols over the years, Fulmer returned fire. He mocked the Florida coach as "Saint Steve." SEC fans made a big deal about the remark because Fulmer had always been cautious with his public comments. The contretemps made Fulmer uncomfortable, and he has since returned to the safe haven that is his blandness.

In his early years as Tennessee's head coach, Fulmer seemed insecure in public and guarded with the media. He was certainly unaccustomed to serious press coverage. Jimmy Hyams, who covered Tennessee football for the *Knoxville News Sentinel* for many years, and who now works as a radio sports-talk host for WNOX, says that Fulmer often complained about his stories. In 1993, when Tennessee was in Tampa to play in the Hall of Fame Bowl, there was an incident involving a few players who'd invited a prostitute to a hotel room. Hyams wrote an article about it, and Fulmer took offense. "He got upset," says Hyams. "He said that 90 percent of the players do good things and all I was doing was focusing on the negative." Fulmer used to call Hyams regularly and complain about story headlines. "He kept ripping me about the headlines to my stories," says Hyams, "and I kept telling him that I didn't write them and didn't always agree with them myself. But he kept ripping me. He's gotten better, but we had some difficulties for a while. He's had trouble understanding the role of the media—and he's not alone in that respect. Most coaches do. To his credit, he sat down with me one time and said, 'What can I do better?' He doesn't think he has all the answers."

"He Will Not Be Outworked"

What Fulmer lacks in charisma or media savvy, he more than makes up for with his rock-solid, easy-going personality: he gets along with people, and he's brought stability to a program that wobbled too much under his predecessor, the mercurial Johnny Majors. "A lot of people underestimate Phillip; they view him as a big doofus," says Kendall. "But he is real sharp, very polished, and handles himself very well. He's the most genuine person I've ever been around. There is no put-on about him." Adds John Chavis, Tennessee's defensive coordinator: "Two things come to my mind about Coach Fulmer. First, he has great people skills; and second, he will not be outworked. A lot of times, when you say somebody is a hard worker, it throws up a red flag. But Phillip is as smart as anybody in the business. His football knowledge is second to none."

Those qualities have helped Fulmer transform Tennessee from a perennial bridesmaid, a team that could never win a big game, into one of the premier programs in college football. "I think winning the national championship validated our program," Fulmer says. And, of course, it validated Fulmer, who has now risen to nearly the top of his profession, with a pay package that tops $1 million annually. (Just above him, on both the pay and achievement scale, is Spurrier.) Fulmer has achieved cult-hero status in the state of Tennessee— but so far success hasn't much altered his laid-back demeanor. He still likes to fish, and he's still more than happy to stop at a homestyle Cracker Barrel restaurant for dinner when he's traveling around the southeast, even though he's sure to have his meal interrupted by autograph seekers. "The biggest change I see in him is that he absolutely has to budget his time now," says Wayne Sawyer, a Winchester resident and one of Fulmer's oldest friends. The two men talk about once a month. "His schedule is absolutely filled out. But his head has not swelled up, and he's done a much-appreciated job of staying the same and knowing who his friends are."

That perhaps is not easy when you've got streets named after you—and your own Web site. PhillipFulmer.com boldly displays the team's national championship ring, which is big and gaudy, but not as expensive as it seems. (NCAA rules limit the value of the rings to a few hundred dollars, so they contain not diamonds, as it appears, but cubic zirconium.) The Web site features biographical data on Fulmer and sundry information on the Volunteer football team. Last May the Knoxville City Council renamed Stadium Drive, which runs along the west side of Neyland Stadium, Phillip Fulmer Way. (Knoxville and the University of Tennessee are very excitable when it comes to honoring their athletic heroes. Peyton Manning, Lady Vol basketball coach Pat Summitt, and now Fulmer have all got campus streets named after them. It's a nice honor for the recipients, but invites obvious problems at a school like Tennessee, which has a lot of exceptional athletes. In fact, black leaders have complained that Knoxville, a city of roughly 100,000 people, has not yet named a street after former quarterback Tee Martin, who won a national championship. Martin was gracious about the controversy, and there was talk last summer that he'll be remembered with a Ripley's-style wax lookalike.) Fulmer's hometown of Winchester now boasts a Phillip Fulmer Parkway.

The coach was touched by both street-naming ceremonies—"It's probably the greatest honor that can be bestowed on somebody," he said. But Fulmer doesn't take the hero role too seriously, and deflects most accolades to his players. Not long after his street sign went up on the UT campus, Fulmer quipped that he hoped that the Vols would keep on winning because it would be awfully embarrassing to see it yanked down. Heywood Harris says that Tennessee's recent run of good fortune—the team was ranked in the top ten at season's end four straight years between 1994 and 1998—has made Fulmer a more confident individual. "He feels like he's earned the attention he gets more than before," says Harris. "He's got more self-assurance." Fulmer himself thinks the biggest change around Tennessee since the Vols won the national championship is how the fans perceive him. "They're a little more glad to see me now than in the past," he says with a grin.

"Antennas Up"

Perhaps because he lacks pretension, and is not very animated on the sidelines during games, it's easy to view Fulmer as a hands-off coach, a figurehead, a guy who delegates. Fulmer does leave offensive and defensive strategy largely in the hands of his coordinators, John Chavis and Randy Sanders (the offensive coordinator). During games, he is not the active decision-maker that Spurrier or Woody Widenhofer are.

But Fulmer is very much a hands-on administrator. "Phillip is on top of his program every day," says Doug Dickey, the UT athletic director. (Dickey was a longtime SEC coach himself at both Tennessee and Florida.) "At any given moment, he knows what's going on." Dickey calls Fulmer "quietly intense," and says that the coach is constantly getting briefed about various aspects of the program—academics, recruiting, strength and conditioning, game-day tactics, administrative matters. "He's always got his antennas up." In the end, says

Dickey, "It's the coach who sells the program, and Phillip comes across very well. He's a solid guy, and he's very honest. He's not trying to sell you last year's calendar. And he has a warm relationship with his players. They like the give-and-take he has with them."

When Bobby Bowden was asked at the 1998 Fiesta Bowl why he keeps coaching, the veteran Florida State coach responded: "Rings. I like rings. When you win the conference championship, you get a ring. When you win a bowl game, you get a ring. When you win the national championship, you get a ring." Fulmer likes winning as much as Bowden, but you would never hear him make such a nakedly ambitious, cynical remark. I asked Fulmer why he's a football coach, and he said simply: "Honestly, I like the kids, and I like the college environment. The players are between the ages of eighteen and twenty-two, and that is an interesting period. They are making the transition from adolescence to manhood. They are boys when they get here and men when they leave."

Fulmer considers himself a "player's coach," which means that he likes interacting with the kids himself, rather than relying excessively on his assistants. Fulmer talks frequently with his half-dozen team captains, and over the course of a year he'll have every player (there are about 100 on the team, including walk-ons) into his office for a one-on-one chat. Many players pay multiple visits to Fulmer's office, for reasons good and bad. Fulmer likes being with the players; he wants regular soundings on the team's psyche, and that of individual players. It's the best way to nip problems in the bud, before they blossom into major headaches. When you've got 100 kids in your charge, you'd better believe there are headaches.

To promote player-coach communications, Fulmer conceived of a group called the Unity Council. It is composed of about eight players who meet with Fulmer once a month or so to talk about—well, anything. The players at each team position (linebackers, for example, or defensive backs) elect one Unity Council representative, and Fulmer picks two or three additional players himself—"young men who I think could be future leaders."

The Vol leader says the idea was born of necessity. "We coaches are often busy recruiting or doing this or that, and there are times of the year when we don't get to spend as much time with the players as we'd like. So we formed the Unity Council to catch up with everything that was happening on the team: who's doing well, who's having problems. I might go into a meeting and say, 'Look, I hear Joe is missing classes or badmouthing another player; I need you guys to take care of it. He's on the wrong page.'" And if peer pressure doesn't work, Fulmer will step in himself. The coach says the meetings are candid, and the talk is not just about football. "We'll discuss anything—team issues, a personal problem—and what is said stays behind closed doors. The players will sometimes gripe, but I make sure they understand that the Unity Council is not a union. Still, it's a good way to relate to one another. They're not going to hurt my feelings, and I don't want to hurt theirs."

Fulmer preaches the value of spirituality and community service to his players. He has boosted the visibility of the Fellowship of Christian Athletes and instituted a Friday night chapel service during the season. It's not mandatory, but nearly all the players attend. Fulmer takes the team to various church services around Knoxville, including Mount Olive Baptist, one of Knoxville's largest black churches. Fulmer was born a Baptist but his wife, Vicky, "converted" him to her Episcopalian faith. They attend church services regularly, but not every week. "Spirituality is part of the program," says Fulmer, "along with academics, athletics, and social activities. We focus on all those things." Community service is also important: Fulmer strongly encourages his players to visit local hospitals, elder homes, boys' clubs, and other community groups as often as possible. Many do.

Like all coaches, Fulmer spends a lot of time trying to improve the "other side" of his football program—academics and graduation rates. With some justification, Tennessee has been labeled a football factory in the past, as well as a program with a poor graduation record. Like nearly every major-college football team, Tennessee's graduation rate varies widely, ranging anywhere from 20 percent to 70 percent for specific classes. Like all major universities, the Vol media office works hard to publicize the half-dozen or so UT players who make the SEC academic honors list every year. But what one discovers about almost every team's football "brainiacs" is that the vast majority are second-team players or walk-ons—guys who seldom play at all.

Fulmer bristles at the notion that UT's graduation rate is suspect. Says he: "Four of the seven years we've been here, we've graduated 70 percent of our class." He points out that players who turn pro early drag down a school's graduation rate unless they quickly get back to school in the off-season and obtain their degree. (The National Collegiate Athletic Association, or NCAA, defines anyone who has failed to earn a degree within six years of starting school as a nongraduate.) While only 2 percent of all college football players go on to play professional football, that number is much higher in the SEC. Tennessee lost four undergraduate players to the NFL this year—a fact that will certainly lower its graduation rate for the classes of 1995–96, when those players entered school.

"At-Risk" Kids

College football fans pay close attention to recruiting. Everybody is eager to know which top prospects the alma mater has corralled. What they don't notice is the tremendous effort that's needed to keep some of the kids in school after they sign scholarship papers. Like every other SEC school, Tennessee has installed a large support structure to deal with players who have academic, behavioral, or family troubles. "Keeping players in the program is very important, and we've done a good job of that here," asserts Fulmer. Pointing college football players down the straight-and-narrow path is a constant challenge, says the coach—a daily process. "You have to know who your so-called 'at-risk' kids are, and how they can be helped within the rules."

Fulmer says that out of the eighty-five scholarship players on his team, typically about half are responsible self-starters who don't need much supervision. An additional 30 percent are what he terms "average" kids. They need an occasional kick in the pants, a periodic butt-chewing, or require a disciplinarian action perhaps once during their college career. But by and large, they get with the program. And then there is the remaining 20 percent, who, says Fulmer, "you have to keep your eye on." Every team has them. When star running back Travis Henry was a freshman at UT, he'd hardly been on campus a month when he got caught (on videotape) stealing stereo equipment from a teammate's room. (Henry has not had any disciplinary problems since, which probably puts him somewhere between "average" and "needs watching.")

Fulmer considers himself a disciplinarian, but like most of his peers, he is a flexible one. He is largely understanding of mistakes, so long as they are relatively minor and the player does not repeat them. A player who fails a class will be warned and be required to get tutoring. A player who fails a drug test might be suspended for one or more games, but is generally not kicked off the squad for a first offense. "Kids get off-track, like I did in college, and you try to get them back on track." Even players who get into somewhat serious trouble—get arrested for disorderly conduct, or public drunkenness—tend to be given second and sometimes third chances.

"We try to build a family concept," says the coach. "You coach your best players the hardest, get them to practice the hardest, behave themselves, and set an example in the classroom. We've had some great young people come through here. You can't save them all; every now and then we have a problem. But most of the kids who've come through have done well—and they're a lot better off for being in the program. And that's what you like to see. It's not just the Peyton Manning types, who have a great pedigree and bring so much on the front end. It's also the guys in the back who are positively influenced by Manning and Tee Martin. Travis Henry is a good example. He's got a lot of good qualities, but he was tough [when he first arrived]. Tee Martin was tough."

The Vol coach chafes at the notion that nineteen- to twenty-two-year-old student-athletes should be role models, held to higher standards merely because they're football players. "People want to stick athletes in a different category, think of them as being different, but they're not. They're kids, no different than anybody else's children, and the same kinds of social problems come up with them—family issues, academic problems."

Is too much pressure placed on the players? Are there too many demands on their time? "I'm sure they feel pressure," says Fulmer. "But we tell them: 'All we expect is for you to be the best that you can be. If you're a C chemistry student, or an A geology student, fine. If you're a really solid second-team right guard, that's okay. Be the best you can be. But we can't let them underachieve." Is it hard to balance academics with the athletics? "No," says the coach. "You can't have one without the other, and you've got to consider social skills as well. If someone is off socially, he's not going to be good as a student or an athlete. If someone is off academically, he'll have trouble socially and athletically. They all affect the whole. If a player is focused, and all the parts are in synch, then a player can reach his potential."

The Nemesis

For Fulmer to reach his potential, he's going to have to start beating his archrival and nemesis, Spurrier. Truth be told, Fulmer has looked overmatched at times against the Gator coach. Though there is typically a rough parity of talent between the two teams, Spurrier has beaten UT six of the seven times they've played since Fulmer became the Vol coach—including five straight during one stretch. In fact, two or three times in the 1990s, Tennessee saw both its SEC and national title hopes dashed in losses to Florida. Last year was a case in point: Tennessee was loaded with talent, but the Gators won in Gainesville. The game has taken on huge importance every year precisely because each team is a powerhouse, and each stands in the way of the other's legitimate championship aspirations.

Despite his somewhat poor big-game record (he is 0-2 against both Penn State and Nebraska in bowl games), Fulmer takes losing in stride. "To him, losing a football game is just another step toward winning one," says Phillip Fulmer, Jr., the coach's thirty-one-year-old son. "He doesn't go in a shell after a loss." But he's not especially talkative, either. Phillip Jr., who works for Midland Employer Services Co. in Nashville, is close to his father, and the two sometimes talk after games—but not a lot, he says, if the Vols lose. "We don't go into great detail. He knows I know enough to see where mistakes were made." The two have more fun, naturally, on vacations. They try to go fishing at least once a year, sometimes for tarpin in Useppa, Florida (near Naples). "I once caught a sixty-five-pound tarpin," says Phillip Jr., "and Dad caught an eighty-five-pounder. He's a pretty good fisherman."

Fulmer's big break came in the 1998 Florida game, which was played before 107,000 screaming fans in Knoxville. The Tennessee coach will not admit it, but he was under enormous pressure to beat Florida. And by the skin of their teeth, the Vols did. Florida committed five turnovers and the game went into overtime tied at 24. Tennessee's Jeff Hall kicked a long field goal to give the Vols the lead. Florida had one last chance to tie or win the game, but Jeff Chandler missed a field goal and the Vols finally won the game they had to win. They went on to an undefeated season. Vol fans were so delirious after that victory that they yanked down the goal posts—each holding an expensive CBS TV mini-camera—and paraded them down Cumberland Avenue in Knoxville, two miles from the stadium. The street was closed, and thousands of people partied throughout the night. Fulmer and his staff celebrated that September 1998 night at the Texas Roadhouse restaurant in Maryville. "That damn monkey is gone!" shouted Fulmer as he entered the restaurant with the group. "You could tell beating Florida was a tremendous relief for him," says Kendall. "Losing to Florida was tough. There was always the implication that Spurrier was the better coach. It was a hump the fans expected him to get over." Adds Wayne Sawyer: "There was absolutely a sense of joyfulness when we beat Florida."

Ask Fulmer whether he feels the pressure to win, to beat Florida and Alabama, and he practically pooh-poohs the idea. "Pressure is what you make it," he responds. It's one of his favorite expressions. "I think my wife has more pressure than I do. I don't ever think of getting fired; it's more like, what can we do to get better. I don't worry about what the media thinks, what the fans think. I try to do what I think is best for the team."

Unlike Spurrier or Auburn's Tommy Tuberville, who are very animated and emotional during games, Fulmer is a model of understatement. He keeps his competitive nature concealed. He's not a screamer; he prefers to encourage people, clap backs. But when things are going poorly, on the practice field, during games, or even in meetings, he is quite capable of fixing a stony glare on someone, tightening his voice, and expressing—with a few terse words—his displeasure. "He knows when to push buttons, and he can crawl people if necessary," says Sawyer, using a southern expression for getting in someone's kitchen when they are underperforming. But more often than not, Fulmer values face-to-face, man-to-man discussion.

In His Element

Interestingly, Fulmer's competitive fires are most evident not during the season, but rather in January and February, when the fields are frozen and equipment is stored away in lockers. In the middle of winter the recruiting wars are raging—and that's when Fulmer is in his element. He likes to recruit, thrives on it—and he is arguably the best head coach in the business when it comes to winning the hearts and minds of eighteen-year-old prospects and their parents. Without Fulmer's recruiting skills, Tennessee would still be a top-twenty football program, but certainly would *not* be one of the elite football schools in the nation. Unlike his rivals in Florida, Georgia, and Alabama, the state of Tennessee produces very few top-quality high school prospects. So UT must scour the country annually for top players. In 1999, Tennessee signed players from sixteen states.

According to those who know him, the coach's personality takes on a slightly harder edge during the recruiting season. Gentleman Phillip Fulmer morphs into Phillip Fulmer, Big Game Hunter. "He's more aggressive," says Gerald Harrison, who is an aide to the coach. "When he hits the recruiting trail, he *hits* it. He lands one kid and then he asks the staff, 'How can we get the next one?' He's like a shark when there is blood in the water."Adds Hyams: "He puts tremendous energy into recruiting. If the gates to one state are shut, then he'll open them somewhere else. Tennessee is good enough to go anywhere and get players."

I saw Fulmer's recruiting edge during an interview with the coach in his back office. The interview was, of course, delayed. Before we met, he took a call from Sean Young, a Georgia prospect who would later sign with the Vols. Then he had to meet with UT compliance officer David Blackburn. There was an eligibility problem with a freshman player named Anthony Herrera. But I finally got in to interview the coach, who was wearing a knit shirt, coaching shorts, white socks, and sandals. We chatted amiably for about twenty minutes. And then, *whoosh*: I found myself confronting the Fulmer "look." Rather suddenly, like Bill Bixby morphing into the Incredible Hulk, his face tightened and his voice became edgy. "Anything more I can do for you?" he snapped, sounding like a desk officer at a police precinct. "I was supposed to meet with a recruit at 1:30, and I don't know where he is." It was a few minutes after 1:30, and the recruit was Casey Clausen—a blue-chip California quarterback who would later sign to play for Tennessee. Keep a big-time recruit waiting, or keep talking to an ink-slinger? Fulmer understands well his priorities. Earlier that day, he'd spent most of a morning practice session talking with Clausen.

Fulmer's prodigious work ethic comes into sharp relief during recruiting season. Head coaches are allowed to make one so-called in-home visit to every high school senior they're courting. The in-home visit is a vital part of the recruiting process. Most coaches might make, say, forty-five or fifty visits over a two-month period. Fulmer is apt to make seventy, crisscrossing the country, eating on the run, his cellular phone in his pocket, sometimes visiting two or even three families in one day. Last January he flew from Honolulu (where he had coached a high school All-Star game) to Knoxville. He landed on a Sunday, after twelve hours of flying, and drove straight to his office. There he met with three recruits who were visiting UT for the weekend. Most coaches would have done that. But after a twelve-hour flight and four hours at the office, most coaches would speed home and dive into bed. Fulmer didn't go home. He left the office and drove back to the Knoxville airport to catch a flight to Virginia. He was off to meet the family of offensive line prospect William Jernigan.

A Pulling Guard

Fulmer comes from a modest, small-town, working-class background. He grew up in Winchester, Tennessee, a one-horse town in the southern part of the state, near the Alabama border. His dad, James E. Fulmer, worked two jobs most of his life, one of them in a carpet factory that almost certainly killed him. He died of lung cancer in 1989. His mother, Nan, was a home-maker and mother of three. Phillip Fulmer has two younger siblings—a brother,Glen, and a sister, Kathy, who both still live and work in Winchester. The family didn't have much money, but they were close. Fulmer describes his dad as "a wonderful, kind, gentle man, who also had a determination and stubbornness about him that made him a winner. He was always involved in some kind of deal (trading cars, tools), and I don't remember one in which he didn't come out ahead."

Fulmer played football at Tennessee. He was a 220-pound offensive line-man at UT in the late 1960s and early 1970s. He was one of the last of the famous, undersized pulling guards, whose specialty was the so-called "roll block," also known as the "scramble block." According to Don Denbo, who was a teammate of Fulmer's and a guard himself, the technique was simple and *very* effective: "You threw your body at your opponent's knees and then rolled three times. If you didn't roll three times, the coaches would say you hadn't completed your block." Throw a few roll blocks and, before long, defenders were limping off the field with torn ligaments. "People got hurt so badly, the block was eventually outlawed and they started letting offensive linemen use their hands," says Denbo. Both he and Fulmer played weak-side guard, a position that required them to play on either the right or left side of the offensive line depending on where the split end was. Weak-side guards always played on the split-end side of the field.

In Fulmer's playing era, offensive linemen were expected to be agile. Blocking techniques were focused on the legs. Guards would scramble in front of linebackers and then essentially leg-whip them. "Fulmer and I were both undersized; we'd be playing defensive back today," says Denbo. "We were both great at cutting linebackers—that's what we did when we played odd-man, 5-4 defensive fronts. Then in 1969 teams started playing even-man fronts defensively—four defensive linemen and three linebackers—and that was a disadvantage for us. Instead of blocking linebackers, we were taking on 260-pound defensive tackles. That started a trend away from quick, explosive guards." Today, the emphasis is on "drive blocking," which means driving an opponent off the line of scrimmage with the upper body.

Denbo remembers Fulmer as a "good football player. We actually had a lot in common: I am intensively competitive, and so is he. In those days, the offensive linemen were very tight—we were all good friends. But Phillip wasn't around very much." Fulmer had gotten married right before entering college, to his high school sweetheart, Renee, and they lived in the married-student apartments while in college. "None of us knew him very well," says Denbo.

Fulmer played on some of Tennessee's best teams ever. During his four-year stint at UT, the team won two SEC championships. The talent was conspicuous: Jack Reynolds (nicknamed "Hacksaw" because he once sawed a car in half with, yes, a hacksaw), Steve Kiner (who once called Archie Manning's Mississippi squad "a bunch of mules," a comment that backfired badly when the Archie Manning–led Rebels crushed the Vols), Chip Kell, Bobby Majors, Curt Watson, Tim Priest, David Allen, Jackie Walker, Conrad Graham. The 1970 defensive backs intercepted thirty-six passes—an NCAA record. Denbo, who was a year ahead of Fulmer, says that playing football in those days was rugged. "When we started there was no water on the practice field; you were considered a wussy if you needed water. We got beat by UCLA in the opening game of 1967, and we came back and practiced in the blazing heat. And we kept practicing. And then, at one point, Bob Johnson (an All-America center) stood up after a play and passed out—fell flat on his face."

It's a frightening thought to Vol fans, but Fulmer came close to wearing Alabama's crimson jersey rather than Tennessee's orange. The Crimson Tide heavily recruited Fulmer when he was a high school star. Alabama wanted Fulmer to play linebacker, promised him he'd be a team captain by his senior season. Fulmer made a verbal commitment to the Bear. But like a lot of kids, he reneged and opted in the end to go to the state university in Knoxville. Growing up in southern Tennessee, Fulmer followed Swanee College (the University of the South), which was not far away. He also kept up with Vanderbilt, Tennessee State, and Alabama. "I went to Swanee games first," says Fulmer. "And then when I was a high school sophomore, my high school coach would take us up to Nashville to watch games. We watched Tennessee State play in the afternoon—they had some great teams—and then watched

Vanderbilt at night. That was my first exposure to college football." He walked to the Winchester library to read the sports page. At that time Alabama was in fine form: Fulmer recalls following the 1966 Bama team that won the national championship. Joe Namath was the Tide quarterback. Fulmer's high school football coach was an Alabama fan, a Bear Bryant fan. As Fulmer says, "Everybody was at that time." Fulmer attended an Alabama game as a sophomore in high school, and calls it an "eye-opening experience."

Fortunately for Vol fans, Doug Dickey began reviving the Tennessee program just about the time Fulmer got serious about football. "I had a chance to go to Tennessee games when I was a high school junior [in 1967] and really started following them at that time." In particular, Fulmer remembers the tragic 1965 car accident that killed three Tennessee football coaches. The team wore a black T on its helmets that year to honor the deceased. Tennessee won the SEC championship in 1967—and the following year, when Fulmer was a senior, the Vols really began to shine. Fulmer noticed, and signed on. But, he says, "I came close to going to Alabama. But the state pride issue came into play, and I thought Tennessee was on the rise. It's funny: when I went to UT I though Bryant was ready to retire. He was fairly old. Ten years later, I was coaching at Tennessee and Bryant was still at Alabama. It's odd how things happen."

Fulmer started coaching in 1972, working as a graduate assistant for the Vols. Even then he showed a talent for recruiting. Though only in his early twenties, he succeeded in signing more prospects than a couple of older, more experienced assistants. In 1974 he left Tennessee and joined the staff of Wichita State, a small university in the middle of Kansas. The football team had such a modest budget, the coaches would drive downtown and use the phones of a local business to make long-distance recruiting calls. After five years at Wichita State, Fulmer spent a year at Vandy and then, in 1980, joined the staff at Tennessee. Johnny Majors—a Tennessee hero—was the coach. Fulmer spent twelve years as a Vol assistant under Majors before grabbing the top job in 1993.

Majors had been hired in 1977, after Bill Battle was fired. Majors was a Tennessee man, and a popular hire. He was born in the state and became a star player at UT in the mid-1950s, finishing second to Notre Dame's Paul Horning (playing on a 2-9 team) in the 1956 Heisman race. He went on to coach at Pittsburgh, where he recruited Tony Dorsett and won a national championship before joining his alma mater. The Vols needed help in the late 1970s, and Majors was a tonic. He recruited better players and imbued the Vols with his toughness. After some lean years in the 1980s, the team's record slowly improved. But the program seemed always in a state of upheaval. There was a lot of turnover among Tennessee's assistant coaches. Every year, seemingly, there was a new offensive or defensive coordinator.

Phillip Fulmer

The reason soon became clear: Majors had serious "people problems." He was notoriously hard to get along with. If you look at the best college football programs, they all have one thing in common: a large measure of stability in the coaching staff. Some of Joe Paterno's assistants at Penn State have been with him for more than twenty years. Majors ran roughshod over his coaching staff and lots of other people, and eventually it caught up with him. He ran out of friends—at a time when he was trying to renegotiate his contract. Entering the 1992 season, Majors didn't like the fact that he wasn't one of the highest-paid coaches in the conference. Talks had begun to renew his contract. Early in the 1992 season, he entered the hospital for heart-bypass surgery. His contract extension was still up in the air. Fulmer, then the offensive coordinator, was appointed interim coach. The team seemed to flourish under his command. If Majors was the General George Patton of Tennessee football—a brash bully—then Fulmer was General Omar Bradley, a guy who could relate to the grunts.

Fulmer was not a casual choice: he was considered one of the top assistant coaches in the country at the time, and almost certain to leave Tennessee at the end of the '93 season. That worried Vol fans, Dickey, and university President Joseph Johnson. While they fretted about keeping Fulmer happy, Majors, recuperating in a Knoxville hospital, began to worry about his job. He rushed back to the team, with disastrous effect. The Vols went into a tailspin. Administrative wheels started turning. When they stopped, Majors had been replaced—effectively fired. Phillip Fulmer—soft-spoken, mild-mannered, the antithesis of Majors—was Tennessee's new coach. His hiring now looks like a stroke of genius. Majors, unfortunately, was outraged by his dismissal. He has bitterly accused Fulmer of conspiring to steal his job while he was in the hospital. Fulmer denies that. Majors went back to Pittsburgh for a second coaching stint (much less successful than his first with the Panthers), and then retired. He is completely estranged from the University of Tennessee.

A Football Wife

Nobody understands the demands of college football more than Vicky Fulmer, the Tennessee coach's energetic, forty-three-year-old wife. She and Fulmer have been married for eighteen years. But measured in "football years," it's probably been a little longer. "It's a crazy life," says Vicky, "a very full life. We get to do a lot of fun things, travel a lot, meet interesting people." That's the upside. The downside, she says, is that "it's very difficult to find family time. There are many, many sacrifices."

BRAGGING RIGHTS

The biggest is simply that she rarely sees her husband. "You're alone a lot," says Vicky, speaking in the second-person. "You don't have companionship, so you'd better be independent. Phillip works eighteen-hour days, seven days a week. It's not unusual for him to get home after midnight. He comes in, sleeps, showers, and leaves." The only days Fulmer gets off—open dates during the season—are consumed by fundraisers and speaking engagements. On those occasions when the coach does get home for dinner, he's sometimes got a busload of players with him. The day I spoke with Vicky, she was preparing to entertain Tennessee's freshman players at the Fulmers' home. The menu (catered): steak, chicken, vegetables, Caesar salad, and strawberry shortcake for dessert. The seniors had been over the night before. The team captains share occasional evenings with the Fulmers, too. It's not a burden; Vicky enjoys being around the players. "I adore them all," she says. "I travel with the team. Phillip will crack the whip and they'll get mad at him now and then, but they never get mad at me."

Inquiring minds want to know: with the coach gone so much, how much family business must Vicky handle? The answer arrives in a split-second. "I do *everything* for Phillip," she says. "He handles football, I handle everything else"—bill paying, investments, social arrangements, car repairs, keeping tabs on the kids. "I juggle the whole other part of our life. I've picked up more and more of the slack over the years so he could concentrate on football." She doesn't mind it, she says, because "I'm really dedicated to him."

Vicky calls her husband "a very easy-going guy who takes things in stride. I probably get more stressed out than he does." She appreciates the fact that, for the most part, he doesn't fret too much about football when he's at home. With three teenage daughters—Courtney, Brittany, and Allison—there is a lot to catch up on. "He doesn't bring his problems home," says Vicky. "He's a softy here; the girls call him a big teddy bear. I don't think the players realize he has another side. I'll ask questions, and he'll talk. If there are things that are bothering him, I'm his backboard." At Vicky's request, all of the girls have served separate stints as Tennessee ball girls, standing on the sidelines during games. Courtney went first, followed by Brittany and then Allison. "They have to keep the balls dry, give them to the referees, and stay out of the way," says Vicky. "They are very much into the games, and don't miss a thing. A coach's children live and breathe football, too. It affects their lives. They love being involved." One of the girls is always at Fulmer's side at the end of games, when he walks across the field for the ceremonial handshake. That caused a problem three years ago when Georgia Coach Jim Donnan cursed out Fulmer after a game because he thought the Tennessee coach had run up the score.

Vicky, who sits in Athletic Director Doug Dickey's box during games, says that winning the national championship has relieved her husband of some pressure. "He's had the goal of doing that for the university—he wanted to take the program to the next level—and now that he's done it he's more relaxed and receptive to family needs." She says that going through the undefeated season was "stressful," adding: "But after getting through it we feel like we can handle anything. It was such a relief to finally win it. You're just so thankful—that's the way I would put it. It's something that no one can take away from you."

Coaches catch a lot of flack when the team loses, and so do their families. Vicky has seen and heard the anger of fans. "You have no control over the outcome of games," she says. "You're at the mercy of the team, fans, and the community." Fortunately, the Vols win most of their games, and Vicky has many friends—some of whom don't care about football—who allow her to step into other dimensions, away from the glare of Tennessee football. "In order to survive," she says, "you've got to establish a life of your own."

Like most coaches' wives, Vicky does a lot of charity work. She's on the board of directors of the Friends of the Smokies, an organization that raises money to protect national parks. She's also on the board of Kid Fit, a public-service group that promotes fitness in elementary schools. "I get involved in anything Phillip volunteers me for," she quips. Like her Florida counterpart, Jerri Spurrier, Vicky Fulmer is a fitness buff. It's her "escape" from a high-pressure life. She lifts weights, practices yoga, bikes, hikes, and "cross-trains" a lot. Two summers ago she biked 610 miles across the Canadian Rockies.

She and Fulmer met in St. Petersburg, Florida. In 1980, Vicky was working in the mortgage banking business in St. Petersburg when Fulmer came to town to speak to a UT alumni group. The two met and were married a year later. Vicky still keeps a finger in business; she and the chief executive officer of Cornerstone Bank in St. Petersburg started a new bank last year. She flies to Tampa once a month to catch up on the bank's activities.

Fulmer is, of course, proud of his family—and sensitive to their needs. "I can go in my office and close the door, read the paper, watch film, take calls or not, and get ready for the next game. They've got to go to school and the grocery store and interact with the [community]." That said, Fulmer doesn't think he could be in a better situation, or at a better school. He was very close to former UT President Joe Johnson, whom the coach says "was very supportive of all the athletic programs at Tennessee. He saw the importance, and I think our new president [J. Wade Gilley] feels the same way. President Johnson always said that athletics—not just football, but athletics—was the 'front porch' of the university. I thought that was well put. It is the first thing people outside of the university notice about us."

Fulmer himself has gotten noticed. At a pregame press conference at the Fiesta Bowl in January 1999, just before the national championship, a reporter leaned over to a colleague and whispered: "Which one's Fulmer?" The Vol coach was almost anonymous. Now, he's a high-profile coaching star—still driven to achieve, but never far from the country values he learned in rural Tennessee years ago. "I just try to do what I think is best for Tennessee football," says the coach. "Somebody said if you can lay your head on the pillow at night knowing you've done the best you can, you don't have anything to worry about." Fulmer still worries, but only during his fourteen-hour days. And now that the 2000 season has arrived, the Vol coach need not feel guilty if he drifts off into his football world when a friend, fan, or family member tries to engage him in a nonfootball conversation. It's okay to get "the look." Everybody understands.

Neyland Stadium, University of Tennessee

Travis Taylor,
University of Florida

Raynoch Thompson,
University of Tennessee

Steve Spurrier, head coach,
University of Florida

Woody Widenhofer, head
coach, Vanderbilt

Shaun Alexander,
University of Alabama

Phillip Fulmer, head coach, University of Tennessee

Alabama's Dabo
Swinney (right) and
Ronnie Cottrell (below)

Quincy Carter, University of Georgia

Bobby Lowder, Auburn booster and trustee

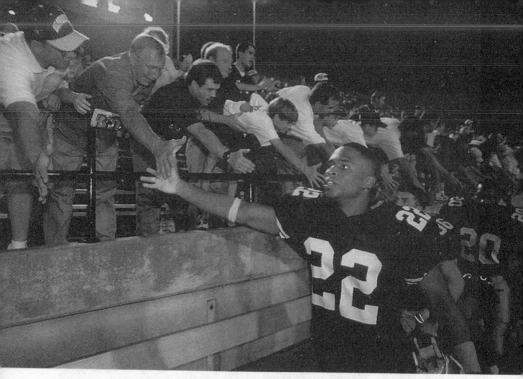

Ainsley Battles,
Vanderbilt

Jim Donnan, head coach, University of Georgia

Gerry DiNardo, ex–head coach of LSU

from LSU:

Joe Domingaeux

Tommy Banks

Fred Booker

Mike DuBose, Alabama's head coach, at the SEC championship game

TEN

IN THE CROSSHAIRS: JUSTIN SMILEY

Bunk Beds, Chocolate Labs, and Football's Second Season

Justin Smiley was in the crosshairs. Last fall Smiley was not much different than most other seventeen-year-old high school seniors. He lived in Ellabell, Georgia, a tiny town about fifteen minutes outside Savannah, and attended Southeast Bulloch High School, which has only 600 students. A country boy, Smiley enjoyed hunting deer and hanging out with friends on the Ogeechee River when he wasn't at home or in school.

He also enjoyed playing football. When he was a sophomore in high school, Smiley was a talented, strong, but somewhat undersized lineman. He was 6'4", weighed about 240, and played both offense and defense. Then, suddenly, he started to fill out. By the end of his junior year, Smiley's weight had climbed to nearly 300 pounds—and suddenly a kid whom SEC recruiters had been watching but not drooling over was dubbed a bona fide high school star—a classic blue-chip prospect. Unlike many other bulky teenagers, Smiley maintained his mobility as his weight increased—a huge plus for a lineman. And, though he was a polite boy off the football field, Smiley had a nasty disposition on it. That, too, endeared him to SEC recruiters. Heading into his senior year at Southeast Bulloch, various recruiting services rated Smiley as the third-best offensive-line prospect in Georgia (a talent-rich state)—and one of the ten best linemen in the Southeast.

And then came . . . the madness.

Smiley became the focal point of a brutal, nine-month recruiting war. Nebraska, Georgia Tech, and Notre Dame all targeted Justin Smiley. But they were outsiders in the battle for the young man's services. The real combatants

153

turned out to be four SEC rivals—Lou Holtz of South Carolina, Steve Spurrier of Florida, Mike DuBose of Alabama, and Jim Donnan of Georgia. The first three made Smiley a priority recruit; the fourth unwisely hedged his bet. Spurrier and Smiley got to know each other fairly well. But in the fall of 1999, the talented teenager was trying to manage a dozen or so new adult friends—who were very solicitous and very good about staying in touch.

The young Georgian enjoyed the attention—at first. Smiley comes from a football family (he has a first cousin who plays for the Buffalo Bills). He enjoys the contact of the sport. He wanted to play for an SEC school. But it's not easy to keep your head with recruiters practically throwing rocks at your bedroom window at night. Think of a commodities trading pit in Chicago: a couple-dozen people screaming frantically and waving their arms. Now imagine placing a young man and his mother in the middle of that pit, and all the traders are screaming at them, trying to get their attention. That's the kind of recruiting pressure the Smileys experienced, and they say it took its toll. During one especially intense period, Smiley says, he was getting phone calls from fourteen or fifteen schools *every night*. "When the calls started, it was cool," says Smiley. "But then I'd be on the phone till midnight. I'd tell one guy I had to get off so I could talk to another. You think it's the best thing in the world, but it gets tough. It was a crazy process. Just talking about it brings back memories."

Smiley's mother, Terri White, has got memories, too—bad ones. She got sucked up in the vortex of promises and backbiting that swirled around her son. When it ended, she was embittered. "What started out as a thrilling experience turned into a nightmare," says White, forty-two. She runs a day-care center out of a garage on the ten-acre plot where she lives with her second husband, Paul, and two sons—Justin, who's now eighteen and a freshman in college, and his younger brother, Nicholas. "No one could prepare us for what we went through. It was ugly—dog-eat-dog. If you sat me down beforehand and told me what it would entail, I would have laughed at you. What's weird is that the coaches warned us that it would get bad, and sure enough it happened. It was like they were talking about themselves."

By the time the hostilities were over, and Smiley had picked his school, we would learn the following: that Steve Spurrier does not like having his pants wrinkled by Labrador retrievers; that a bed can be a major factor in where a kid decides to go to college; that high school coaches are influential in the recruiting process; that moms are more influential than high-school coaches (and, sometimes, dads); that kids ain't dumb—they know when they're being jerked around; that Spurrier grew suspicious of DuBose and Alabama's recruitment of Smiley; and finally, that recruiters *never* take no for an answer.

Things started out simply enough. South Carolina was the first team to show interest in Justin; the school sent him a letter when he was in the ninth grade. By May 1999, the Gamecocks had been joined by a dozen other schools. Smiley was then a rising senior, a blue-chip prospect—and the fight for his signature was on. *Let's get ready to ruuuummmmble!*

Smiley can remember when his life started to get a little crazy. "A recruiter from Nebraska came to [spring] practice and offered me a scholarship that night. That was pretty overwhelming. I started getting attention from schools I never thought I'd be able to go to." Recruiters from Georgia, Florida, Alabama, and Auburn, to name a few, soon followed. They'd watch practice, return to a motel near Ellabell, then call Smiley's house. Says the Ellabell teen: "They'd say, 'We saw you practice, talked to your coach, and we're ready to offer.' I had thirteen Division 1 offers." Smiley talks rapidly, as if he's been guzzling Cokes all day, or maybe he's still wired from the recruiting process.

Know this about southerners. When it comes to college football, *nobody* is neutral. *Nobody* is indifferent. *Everybody* has a favorite. And if they tell you they don't, they're lying. And in Justin Smiley's case, everybody he knew wanted him to go to a *different* school. His father, who separated from Justin's mother many years ago and lives forty-five minutes from Ellabell, liked South Carolina. But, says Justin, "He told me, 'I'm not going to make you do anything.'" Terri White, Justin's mom, is a huge Bama fan (and so is her dad). Justin's high school coach, Ron Flott, favored Florida. Flott knew Jim Collins, Florida's recruiting coordinator, and had previously sent one of his players to Gainesville. Nearly all of Smiley's friends, classmates, and neighbors were Georgia fans, naturally, and urged him to be loyal to his home-state university. Justin says that "I had my [school] favorites from the beginning." But like so many kids, he would be buffeted by heavy winds and heavy personalities. He would make things interesting before officially signing a "letter of intent"—a binding commitment to a particular university—in early February. (We'll come back to Justin Smiley.)

The Recruiters

It's easy to see why Alabama's Ronnie Cottrell is one of the SEC's best recruiters. It's the voice. Cottrell has got a southern drawl as thick and as sweet as molasses. When he speaks, consonants and vowels loll on his lips for a second or so, then roll off slooooowly, like sap sliding down a maple tree. The word "get" becomes "git." He says "nosir" and "yesiree." One listens, strangely mesmerized by the sound. "He has a voice that puts a smile on your face," Florida State cornerback Reggie Durden said recently. It's true.

Before joining the Alabama staff in 1997, Cottrell spent nine years at Florida State—he was instrumental in building the Seminoles into a national power. But he's a native of Brewton, Alabama—born and bred a Crimson Tide fan. So when

BRAGGING RIGHTS

Alabama Head Coach Mike DuBose pleaded with him to return to his roots and become recruiting coordinator for Alabama, dangling a salary of well over $100,000 in Cottrell's face, he was preaching to the choir. Cottrell took the job.

Nobody appreciates Alabama football, or SEC football, more than forty-one-year-old Ronnie Cottrell. His dad, an electrician, was a dyed-in-the-wool Bama man. "He spent his whole life working for Container Corporation of America," says Cottrell, sitting in a second-floor office overlooking the Bama practice field. "He provided for his family, but he followed Alabama sports. He loved Alabama. And I don't think he was any different from 90 percent of the people in this state. The biggest days of their lives are Saturdays, when Alabama and Auburn are playing football. When you are born in Alabama, it is like a rite of passage: you have to be for one of those two teams. That's the way it is. And fans are the same way everywhere in the Southeastern Conference. I mean, you drive across the state line and Tennessee fans are just as rabid as ours. You go into Florida and their fans are just as intense. When I was in Tallahassee, people talked about the Florida–Florida State rivalry. Well, to me, the Alabama-Auburn series is unmatched. Then throw in the tradition of Alabama versus Tennessee . . . I mean, it is hard to imagine bigger games than those. The history and legacy of this conference is pretty amazing—unbelievable."

When Cottrell came to Tuscaloosa for an interview, he was reminded of his youth and Bama's large football legacy by all the photographs and Daniel Moore paintings he saw hanging around the town. "I realized that I saw in person or on TV, or listened on the radio, to virtually all of them," he says. He recalls attending an Alabama-LSU game at Legion Field in Birmingham in the pouring rain. "The weather was s'bad you could hardly see the field. There were tornado warnings, but nobody left." He recalls watching the Bear Bryant TV show at 4:00 P.M. on Sundays. "Coach Bryant would open a Coca-Cola [on camera] and a bag of Golden Flake potato chips, and he'd pour 'em out and mumble for thirty minutes, and they'd show a few highlights. But it was so exciting to me—he was an icon. So to be at the school where he coached is truly a thrill. My dad's hope was for my brother and I to get a college degree and get good jobs. He never dreamed that I'd have the opportunity to coach at a junior high school program, much less Alabama."

It now falls to Cottrell—as it does to other SEC recruiting coordinators like Rodney Garner at Georgia and Dan Brooks at Tennessee—to maintain the Bama tradition. Good coaches are vital, of course—but they'll all tell you that great teams are made by great players. There are no coaches good enough to win consistently without the horses. Once, after losing to Notre Dame, Penn State Coach Joe Paterno was asked by a reporter if the Irish had been helped at certain times by "divine intervention." Paterno's response: "God is on the side of the team with the best defensive tackles." And that's where recruiting coordinators come in. Like stable owners, every year they must find new thoroughbreds—quarterbacks, linebackers, offensive linemen, defensive backs, and yes, defensive tackles.

That means winning what has become the so-called "second season" in college football—the recruiting wars. There are lots of good recruiters in the SEC—among them, Greg Adkins at Georgia, Eddie Gran at Auburn, Charlie Strong at South Carolina, Mark Bradley at Tennessee, Buddy Teevins at Florida, Tony Franklin at Kentucky—all of whom could sell air conditioners in Alaska.

Garner (of Georgia) is acknowledged as probably the best recruiter in the SEC. A native of Leeds, Alabama, he's a chunky, charismatic thirty-four-year-old man with a big smile. Garner played football at Auburn and coached on the Plains for five years, leaving for Tennessee in 1995. He relates very well to young men, and he is particularly skilled at charming the "mammas"—who have a large say, in many cases *the* say, in where their babies go to college. While in Knoxville, Garner recruited three players from Georgia who helped the Vols win a national title—safety Deon Grant, offensive guard Cosey Coleman, and running back Jamal Lewis. Losing three in-state studs to a rival was too much for Georgia coach Jim Donnan: in 1998 he lured Garner away from Tennessee, boosted his salary, and made him recruiting coordinator for the Bulldogs. Garner's decision to leave Tennessee was controversial—not because he left, but *when* he left. He quit at the height of the recruiting season, at a time when he seemed close to luring another batch of Georgia boys to Tennessee. When Garner switched loyalties, so did the kids he was recruiting that year—among them, David Jacobs, Cap Burnett, and Jessie Miller. They signed with Georgia instead of Tennessee.

The Crème de la Crème

To describe recruiting as a "war" is not an overstatement. Every year, the 107 biggest universities in America—Division 1 teams—dole out scholarships to roughly 2,200 high school football players. Every school is allowed to sign a maximum of twenty-five kids to scholarships annually. That, fundamentally, seems a pretty easy thing to do. There are thousands of good football players around the country, and many are eager to play for SEC schools. But here's why recruiting is so fascinating: top-tier SEC schools don't want just good players—they want the best players, the "blue chips," the crème de la crème. They want the Justin Smileys. But those players, naturally, are few in number—and picky about which school they choose to play for. That makes the winter battles among top SEC schools for the top-tier talent nearly as intense as the actual games are in the fall. There is a natural synergy between the two. "If you win the recruiting battles in December and January, you have a chance to win football games in the fall," says Cottrell.

Coaches are not the only people who have made that connection. Thanks to extensive press coverage by magazines, Web sites, 900-number phone lines, TV stations, and sports talk radio, fan interest in recruiting has exploded in recent years. In the past, only a school's most hard-core devotees would inquire about the new crop of freshmen—and that *after* they'd signed scholarship papers. Nowadays, tens of thousands of SEC fans—mostly men aged twenty to fifty— follow every twist in the helter-skelter recruiting campaign, which starts in earnest in September and peaks on the first Wednesday in February. That is National Signing Day, when the high school players sign their letters of intent, or LOIs, which are written pledges to play for a particular school.

Kids being kids (meaning capricious and impressionable), there is no shortage of excitement. "Recruiting has gotten to be big stuff," says Bill King, who along with partner Bob Bell hosts a three-hour evening sports-talk show on Nashville radio station WLAC. During the winter, King's show, which can be heard in twenty-eight states, devotes its last hour to recruiting. "We have to limit it to an hour because if we didn't, it would dominate the broadcast," says King, who is thirty-eight and a biochemistry major from David Lipscomb College. "Southern fans are so attached to college football that, when the season is over, they're not able to put it to bed. Even though recruiting is a very inexact business, it's a way for the fans to keep competing with one another." And who *are* these "recruitniks"? King calls them "typical testosterone-over-loaded men. On our show, the male demographics are strong."

A Nutty Ritual

As King suggests, recruiting is not an exercise in rationality. In fact, it's arguably the nuttiest ritual in all of sports. Confusion and indecisiveness are its hallmarks; disinformation its handmaiden. With a half-dozen schools jockeying for the attention of certain star players, recruiters throw out more propaganda than the KGB did during the Cold War. Imagine a corporate chief executive officer *beseeching* seventeen-year-old kids to come to work for his company! That is essentially what college recruiters—and head coaches—must do to attract talent. "You're at the mercy of teenagers," says Gerald Harrison, an aide to Tennessee Coach Phillip Fulmer. It's sometimes not a pretty sight. High school prospects are besieged by letters, phone calls, and personal visits from coaches. What results, typically, is a three- or four-way tug of war between southern schools for hotshot prospects, with plenty of complications: many of the very best high school players tend to have trouble qualifying for college—their core grade point average is too low, or they can't make the minimum standardized test score. Two years ago, a Miami kid named Jason Geathers was considered one of the best high school players in America. But he was a poor student, could not get into a four-year college, and, last I read, was working for a car wash in Florida.

That kids get confounded by the many recruiting pitches they hear is understandable. That's why parents play a vital role in the process. More often than not, parents offer the guidance any child needs when making a big decision. But fathers and mothers can also be overbearing. Rather than let the kid decide where he wants to go school, they effectively make the decision for him. Many parents practically insist that their son stay close to home, so that they can watch him play football in college. One can appreciate the instinct, but they are basically railroading the kid into signing with *their* favorite school. Last year Michigan linebacker prospect Marco Cooper was high on Tennessee, but his mother seemed not at all comfortable with the prospect of her son going to a southern college. "He doesn't know anything about the South," she complained after her son returned from a visit to Knoxville. "He wouldn't be comfortable down there." He signed with Ohio State, which was closer to home.

In Justin Smiley's case, his mom played an active role in his decision-making process. She didn't tell Justin where to go to school, but she clearly influenced his decision—paved a road along which Justin would follow. "My mom intervened a lot," said Smiley, "and it made me mad sometimes. She'd say, 'You ain't going to promise anybody anything.' But I knew everything was for the best." Terri White says that she and Justin formed a "plan" for his recruitment—that he would visit three or four schools before making his decision—and that she simply demanded that Justin "stick with the plan. I don't think any young man could make the right choices without parental support."

Sometimes, strong-willed parents disagree about where Junior should go to college. Result: chaos. Last February, for example, Jonathan Colon, a heavily recruited offensive lineman from Miami, became so flummoxed that he signed with two schools on February 3—first with Miami, then with Florida, sparking a major controversy. Both schools claimed to have won his services. Turns out that Jonathan and his mother were keen on the Gators, but Colon's dad practically insisted that he go to Miami. Guess who got caught in the middle?

Predicting where a prospect will go to school can be risky. During the recruiting season, many kids will make an early, nonbinding "verbal commitment" to one school (typically after being dazzled by a visit to a university), then later renege and commit to another college, then in February make an entirely different choice when the time comes to make an official decision. Justin Smiley did just that: he committed early to one school, and then pulled back. He committed to a second school, and then pulled back. And, ultimately, he signed with a different school.

BRAGGING RIGHTS

Recruiting fans revel in such drama. As the process builds to its February climax, they hunger for news. Says Cottrell: "Fans will ask me, 'How we doin' with that ol' six-foot, seven-inch boy over there in Ragland? I heard he's leanin' to Auburn.'" In fact, at the height of the recruiting season—in November, December, and January—recruitniks are clamoring for just such news—and if there is no news, a rumor will do. Above all, they want to know to which colleges top prospects are "leaning." A kid may be "strongly leaning" to one school—meaning it's a clear favorite for his services. Or he might be a "soft lean"—meaning he likes one school but is still considering others. Or he may not yet have a favorite at all. Justin Smiley had a leader. "I'm going to tell you the truth," he says, as if he's revealing a big secret. "Florida was my leader all throughout the process."

The Internet Gurus

To get the latest scuttlebutt, fans now flock to the Web. With its informational speed, the Internet is ideal for keeping up with the fast-paced recruiting process. Every university has at least one cyber-fan who runs a recruiting Web site—it's really a recruiting fan club with no official connection to the college. Recruitniks gather on the site to gossip, complain, and beat their chests. The bigger, more successful SEC programs have multiple recruiting Web sites. Florida and Tennessee each have at least three, and in the winter they're buzzing with recruiting chatter—including more solid information than traditionalists would like to acknowledge. Somebody will mention that he's talked to the uncle of a prospect, who told him that the kid really loved the linebacker coach at Mississippi State. A lot of such second-hand intelligence is on the mark. Fans hang on cryptic utterings by anonymous sources as if they were bond traders trying to interpret a few vague market comments by Alan Greenspan.

It's all a cheap form of winter entertainment. "Recruiting is a segue for college football fans," says Bobby Burton, a thirty-one-year-old Texan who has lately become the biggest recruiting guru on the Internet through his affiliation with Rivals.com, a big online sports network. "It stretches over the lull between the end of the football season and the start of the basketball season." (One wonders how Burton ever got started in the business, given that he grew up a big fan of [drum roll] . . . Rice. It's a fine school—but it's got almost no football tradition.) Asked which fans follow recruiting most avidly, Burton's answer is quick in coming. "There is no question that the SEC is the ultimate; they live and breathe college recruiting. I think football recruiting draws as much interest in the SEC as the basketball season. It's a fever with them."

And with Burton. Over the course of a year, he and his Rivals.com colleagues will follow upwards of 1,000 high school prospects as they wrestle with their college decisions. One third of the kids will merit close attention—meaning they will get called regularly by recruiting services as they get buffeted by recruiters, careening from one school to the next. Among the questions: "Have you made a commitment to anybody yet?" "How did your visit to LSU go?" "Will you trip to Mississippi?" "Are you still leaning toward Georgia?" It's all posted on the Web sites, and then consumed by caffeine-laced recruiting junkies.

In the past, fans bought recruiting magazines to scrutinize the athletic credentials (size, weight, speed, and assorted stats) of college prospects. Nowadays, it's all available on Web sites for free—pictures, interviews, awards, and player rankings. Jamie Newberg, one of Burton's colleagues at Rivals.com, is a self-described "recruiting geek." He lives with a phone in his ear from November to January, making at least twenty-five calls per day to high school players in the southeast. "It's a good thing Rivals pays for my phone bill," he says. He came to know Justin Smiley rather well.

Newberg used to publish a recruiting magazine called *Border Wars*, which was devoted mostly to the states of Georgia and Florida. But two years ago Newberg and a partner ditched the magazine and transferred *Border Wars* to the Web. It's been a hit across the southeast. Newberg, thirty-two, is not merely a Web denizen; he also appears on radio talk shows and co-hosts a fall/winter cable TV show called *Countdown to Signing Day*. On the TV show Newberg shows video clips of, and interviews with, top players. Justin Smiley was featured on the show at least twice. A wrapup of recruiting news, *Countdown to Signing Day* is broadcast weekly throughout the South (except Florida) between Thanksgiving and early February. Separate *CSD* shows are produced for Mississippi, Georgia, and Alabama. There is also a weekly *CSD* show for the combined North and South Carolina markets, and one for the combined Tennessee and Kentucky markets. "The TV show started in 1992," says Newberg, "and from there it friggin' exploded. Every year it's gotten a little bigger. It's got a cult following."

Newberg and Burton don't just track the college preferences of high school players. They also evaluate talent themselves. Just as college football stars attend "combines" prior to the NFL draft, at which they perform agility drills and take psychological tests, so now do high schoolers. Burton attended eleven combines last summer—some open to all comers; others, including one sponsored by Nike, invitation-only camps. There is a combine at halftime of the Georgia-Florida game in Jacksonville. Anywhere from 100 to 1,000 kids typically attend one of these events, at which they run timed 40-yard dashes, throw and kick footballs, lift weights, jump, and essentially showcase their athletic skills. Some kids are videotaped.

Based on those and other tryouts, and input from other recruiting gurus around the country, Rivals.com and other Web sites attempt to rank high school players across the nation—listing the top 100 at every position. A two-star player is considered "top 500 caliber"; a four-star, "top 100 caliber." The top twenty-five players are elite five-star athletes. "It's nothing more than a best guess," says Burton. "I'm not perfect, and I certainly don't have the budget of the New York Giants—and they make mistakes." Newberg even sells information to recruiters. "I e-mail info to schools that I've gotten from the kids." He claims that nineteen universities—SEC and ACC schools, plus Notre Dame and Ohio State—have signed up for his service, which he calls The Recruiting Edge. "I think a majority of the colleges buy up almost anything. They get a new name and—boom, send out a letter and start the recruiting process." Newberg ranked Smiley as a four-star player.

Some kids are discovered at the combines, or by the gurus. Willis McGahee, a running back out of Miami, did not have stellar stats as a high school player, partly because he was sharing playing time with another back at Miami Central High School. But McGahee turned heads at a Nike camp, running a blistering 4.4-second 40-yard dash—and last year he was one of the hottest prospects in the country. Florida quarterback Jesse Palmer credits Newberg with "discovering" him four years ago, in the pre-Internet age. Newberg heard about Palmer's exploits in Canadian club football, wrote up the kid in his *Border Wars* magazine, which was read by Florida's coaching staff. They did some research on the young Canadian, liked what they saw, and started courting him.

"You'd Better Root for Evangel!"

Burton is quick to find the humor in his helter-skelter job. He tells me, with a laugh, that there is a high school coach in Osceola, Arkansas, named Clinton Gore—"and he always has good players." He tells me about a bizarre comment he heard a public-address announcer make last fall at a game played by Evangel Christian High School in Shreveport, Louisiana. "I was up in the press box, and it was a sultry night," said Burton. "At the end of the third quarter, a player gets hurt. During the pause in the action, the PA guy says to the crowd: 'If you think it's hot on the field, it's hotter in hell and you'd better root for Evangel!'" As Burton says, "Football is different down there. Say what you want about SEC football. But it's woven into the fabric of southern society at an early age—by high school at least."

Newberg grew up in St. Petersburg, Florida. He attended the University of Florida, was a big Gator fan, then transferred to South Florida, where he graduated in 1990. Because of his affiliation with Florida, Newberg has had to work extra hard to prove his fairness to other SEC schools. "I was a staunch Florida fan before I got into this, but I'm not like that anymore," he insists. "I'm a huge football fan, though I don't consider myself an all-knowing football person. You look at my rankings, and there is no bias toward anybody. I call it like I see it."

By late in the recruiting campaign, Newberg will have a computer database of 1,500 kids. He boasts that through the combines and Rivals' network of Web sites—Rivals.com now owns hundreds of college and recruiting sites around the country—"we're trying to revolutionize recruiting." He says the business has lost credibility in the past because of bad information. Kids who are said to be 6'5", 280 pounds often turn out to be only 6 feet tall and weigh 250. "High school coaches often oversell their kids because they're trying to get them scholarships," says Newberg. "We don't rely on rumors or hearsay. We try to go out and see players. I could go on the Web and make up something, and it would be splattered everywhere in fifteen minutes. Information spreads like wildfire." That's especially true in the closing days of the recruiting season. In 1998, the first year for the Border Wars Web site, Newberg says he got 500,000 "hits" on signing day—"and all I did was list who signed where." Last year, says Newberg, Border Wars got 755,000 viewer "hits" on the big day—and two million during the first four days of signing week. "Every SEC team has an unbelievable following," he says. "The Internet has made it a full-time job."

"I'm Very Picky"

It is certainly a full-time job for Cottrell and Dan Brooks, the recruiting coordinators at Alabama and Tennessee. For them, recruiting is a year-round effort. The essential task for any recruiting coordinator is to find roughly 100 good high school football players who have a moderate to strong interest in his school. That must be done relatively early—nearly a year before signing day—typically in the summer months between a high school player's junior and senior seasons. The early start is necessary for two reasons. First, high school players must be evaluated thoroughly—not only for their athletic potential but also their academic skills and personality traits. In past decades—when teams could sign thirty-two or more players and there was less attention paid to graduation rates—schools would throw out scholarship offers willy-nilly. Lots of bad students and bad apples—troublemakers—would annually make their way to SEC campuses. That still happens, to be sure. Newberg and his partner, Tom Culpepper, recently received a letter from an SEC player—a kid who in 1998 was one of the top high school prospects in the South. "Every word in the letter was misspelled," says Newberg. "It was terrible. There was no grammar. We wanted to cry. He is playing for an SEC school today."

SEC schools are trying to be more selective. With the annual scholarship limit down to twenty-five, there is more pressure on universities to find mature kids who not only *can* earn a degree, but *want to*—in addition to playing football. Player evaluation has become paramount. A prospect's academic eligibility is now highly scrutinized. And so is his personality. Says Dabo Swinney, a Bama assistant and one of Cottrell's most valuable recruiters: "When I bring a guy into Alabama, I am accountable for him. If he isn't successful, if he comes in here and is busted for drugs or flunks out or is a problem guy, I take it personally. I'm very, very picky about who I recruit." Swinney recruited Justin Smiley, and they developed a good relationship. Smiley calls Swinney "very straightforward."

The second reason for compiling a pool of potential prospects early is that the actual recruiting process—the courtship—is very volatile and takes months to complete. "We'd all like to find the twenty-five guys we want, give them a scholarship, and get them in here," says Brooks of Tennessee. "But the problem is, Florida and Alabama like some of our favorite players and recruit them hard. We all like the same guys. So you have to be realistic and do a good job of showing prospects what sets your school apart." Cottrell agrees: "Most of the guys we fight for are obvious talents; even a layman can see that they're great players. Where you earn your money is on the next group, making sure you select players who will develop. The NFL is full of them."

Recruiters are salesmen. They have territories, work contacts, make a huge number of phone calls, travel a lot. They must be good communicators who can charm kids (and parents) from all types of backgrounds—a rural kid from Kentucky, a suburban Nashville boy, an urban teen from a one-parent family in Atlanta. As one writer put it last year, "They must walk a fine line between being themselves and something of a chameleon." And there are lots of rules to follow. Schools cannot make any official recruiting contact with a high school player until he is a junior. One letter may be mailed before September 1 of a prospect's junior year. After September 1, a prospect may be sent an unlimited amount of mail (or e-mail)—and top prospects will accumulate stacks and stacks of correspondence. "Justin's got a hamper full of mail," says his mom. "We were getting six or seven handwritten letters from South Carolina *every day*."

Schools can call a senior prospect once before the fall—in May. After September 1, a senior prospect can be called (*and will be called*) once a week. Starting December 1, coaches may visit senior prospects in their homes—and may make up to seven in-home visits in the roughly two months before signing day. That's when the real fun begins. The process can be a thankless grind, but some coaches love it. Swinney, thirty-one, is one such coach. He was a 1988 walk-on at Alabama who eventually earned three football letters. He is now Bama's wide-receiver coach and, in Cottrell's words, a "relentless recruiter." Two years ago he snatched two of Bama's most promising young players—linebacker Saleem Rasheed and offensive lineman Alonzo

Ephraim—both from Birmingham (which means they weren't exactly coups).

There is a lot of cynicism in the recruiting business. There are a lot of coaches who don't much like the travel, don't much like dealing with hard-headed parents and quirky teens, don't much like the psychological games, the sales pitches, the bluffing and bluster. Swinney is *not* one of those guys. He truly likes recruiting for Alabama. He finds all the inspiration he needs in his office. He's got a plaque on his wall with one of Bear Bryant's favorite aphorisms: YOU'LL BE A WINNER. It reads: "The price of victory is high, but so are the rewards. If you have dedication and pride, and believe in yourself and never quit, you'll be a winner."

Swinney gets sentimental when talking about the Bear. "I never met him, but I feel like I know him—like I've known him all my life. He was my hero." He carries a couple of Bryant sayings in his wallet (and the Bear had a lot). When Swinney was a tot, one of his uncles gave him a five-part *Sports Illustrated* series on Coach Bryant. "He gave it to me for Christmas. It was unbelievable." Swinney still remembers where he was when Bryant died. "I was walking down the hall after my eighth-grade civics class. There was a buzz in the school, and somebody said that Coach Bryant had died. I couldn't believe it. *I could not believe it.*"

Swinney recruits in five states. He is responsible for Maryland, along with parts of Alabama, Tennessee (the eastern side, from Bristol to Chattanooga), Georgia (south-central, from Augusta to Savannah), and central Florida. That's his territory, and it's his job to get to know as many high school coaches and players in his area as possible. It's a big job: there are about seventy-five high schools in just the eight Alabama counties that he covers. (He rattles off the county names—Blunt, Jackson, Shelby, Marshall, Coleman, Jefferson, Jackson, and DeKalb.) Throw in the other four states and, as he says, "I've got a ton of schools, and so I have to do a ton of research." The state of Alabama is his first priority: "I try to go to every school in my territory every year, regardless of whether they've got a player we're recruiting, just to maintain relations within the state."

Tapes and Relationships

What's the biggest key to recruiting? I ask Swinney. "It's establishing a relationship with the prospect and his family," he says. "If you can't do that, you're going to have a hard time recruiting certain guys because there *will* be a coach out there who can. You want to make it hard for a player to say no to you." Cultivating relations with high school coaches is equally important; after parents, high school coaches usually have the biggest influence on a kid's college decision. And high school coaches are good at spotting talent. If a high school coach has got a promising player, he might call one or more college recruiters, or send them a videotape of the kid in action. In Justin Smiley's case, his high school coach, Ron Flott, had a lot of college connections, and used them to help call attention to his star player.

When Dan Brooks, Tennessee's recruiting coordinator, first called me, he was in Daytona Beach, Florida. Vacation? Nope. He was attending the Florida Athletic Coaches Association conclave—a gathering of 1,000 high school coaches from around that state. Brooks and Auburn's Tommy Tuberville were two of several college coaches who had been asked to speak. A month earlier, Brooks had attended the North Carolina high school coaches' extravaganza. With some 5,000 attendees, it's the biggest in the nation. Brooks is a North Carolina native, and he recruits North Carolina for Tennessee. He's got a lot of friends in the state—and when the time comes to find and evaluate prospects, those old ties are invaluable. In recent years he has plucked a lot of talent from North Carolina for the Vols. O. J. Owens, the top prospect in North Carolina this past year, signed with Tennessee. "The meetings give you a chance to visit with high school coaches, catch up with guys you know," says Brooks. "Relationships are important."

So, oddly, are videotapes. They are a vital tool in the recruiting business—especially in the early part of the process. Typically, tapes are used to make the first evaluation of a prospect. In both Cottrell's and Swinney's office, there is a TV, VCR, and stacks of tapes. High school coaches routinely send recruiters game tapes or highlight tapes featuring "star" players. Every SEC school will receive hundreds every year—most are stored in tape libraries. Sometimes parents will send Cottrell videotapes of their sons. But as Cottrell explains, tapes have limitations. "You watch a guy on tape, and he's just a jersey number and a helmet. And there are lots of variables. How big is a kid, really? How fast is he really?"

Cottrell calls recruiting "a process of keeping up." That is an apt way to put it. The process starts in the spring, when recruiting coordinators compile a "master list" of prospects. There can be anywhere from 300 to 500 players on the initial list, which will shrink continuously until February as players fall off—either because they are not interested in, say, Alabama, or because Alabama is not interested in them. Others—late bloomers—will be added. Cottrell notes that William Floyd, a fullback who helped FSU win a national championship (and later the San Francisco 49'ers win a Super Bowl), was virtually unknown as a high school junior. But a year later Floyd was one of the hottest players in America. Everybody on the master list gets letters (typically one a week) and a media guide—a thick, splashy promotional book that lists every football accomplishment in a university's history. Middling prospects get form letters; top prospects, handwritten notes—"some more encouraging than others" says Cottrell. (He's got albums full of old recruiting letters and questionnaires. He

Justin Smiley

pulled out one during my visit and showed me the first questionnaire filled out by Woodrow Lowe, a star Bama linebacker in the 1970s.)

An Inexact Science

In addition to being good salesmen, the best recruiters have an eye for talent. Actually, what the best recruiters have is an eye for *potential*. Essentially, kids are labeled as a "take" (offer a scholarship), a "hold" (keep an eye on him), or a "reject" (no potential to play SEC football). Here's a not-so-secret reality about major-college recruiting: it's an inexact science. As Cottrell points out, it's easy for recruiters to zero in on the lions and toss out the lambs. But the vast "hold" group—borderline kids who may or may not develop into solid SEC players—often holds the key to a successful class. The reason: half of the top high school prospects—the automatic "takes" whom coaches swoon over when they're eighteen years old—are destined to become SEC busts after a year or two in college. Flame-outs. They will turn out to lack the talent, attitude, or work ethic that everyone thought they had a year or two earlier. They couldn't make the jump to big-time college football. That makes it imperative that a school's second-tier signees—the B crowd, if you will—contains several kids who *will* sparkle. Asked the biggest difference between high school and college, Casey Clausen, a top quarterback signee with Tennessee last year, put it perfectly. "In college," he said, "you learn that everybody is as good or better than you are." That is the Darwinian reality of major-college football.

As important as tapes are for spotting prospects, they are a secondary tool in the evaluation process. The primary arbiter of talent is the naked eye. Schools rarely offer a kid a scholarship until at least one coach has seen the prospect perform—in person. "We'll watch a guy play football, run track, play basketball—doing something athletically," says Brooks. These days, many prospects are uncovered at an early age at summer football camps. Every summer thousands of kids—most ages fourteen to seventeen—spend a few days at the Lou Holtz, Tommy Tuberville, David Cutcliffe, or Hal Mumme camp. Every coach has one. For universities, the camps raise a little revenue and help promote the football program. They've also become a major recruiting tool. While the kids are running through drills and learning basic football techniques, they are also being scrutinized by SEC coaches for their athletic and personal potential. "Camps are great because you get to meet the kids and get to know something about them as people," says Cottrell. "You find out if a guy has a personality, how coachable he is. If you're going to spend four years with a kid, you want to like him. You want him to be a guy who you're going to have fun coaching—not just somebody who can run with a football." But talent helps.

BRAGGING RIGHTS

"Count Me In"

In the summer of 1999, Justin Smiley attended two football camps—one at Georgia Tech and the other at South Carolina, presided over by Lou Holtz. By then Smiley was a hot commodity. Mail was piling up at his house. Smiley didn't much like Atlanta, where Georgia Tech is located. It was too big for a rural kid. But South Carolina was a different story. The Gamecocks' offensive line coach, Dave Deguglielmo, was recruiting Smiley, and both Justin and his dad, Gerard Smiley, liked him. "He was real cool," says Justin. Smiley spent two weeks in Columbia, at the South Carolina camp, showing Lou Holtz his skills. Holtz was impressed with the kid's size, attitude, and especially his 4.9-second time in the 40-yard dash. "That's what set me apart," says Smiley.

One day after camp, the former Notre Dame coach told Smiley to go shower and then come back to see him. When Smiley returned, Holtz offered him a scholarship. When Smiley first saw Holtz, he says, "I thought, 'He's frail, what does he know about football?' But he's a mastermind. He's a competitor and a motivator. He was reciting Knute Rockne and everything. I was overwhelmed." Smiley liked South Carolina, and when Holtz asked him to commit to the Gamecocks, he happily obliged. "I told him it would be a great experience. I said, 'You can count me in.'" That was the first verbal commitment that Smiley made—and it did not please his mom. "I raised holy hell about that decision," says Terri. "He wasn't sticking to the plan."

Recruiters travel a lot. During the spring "evaluation period," recruiters visit high schools in their territory. (Every SEC school has ten coaches—including the head coach—and seven can be traveling at the same time.) Southern high schools practice football in May, and Swinney gets to as many schools as he can. He watches workouts, talks to coaches, hands out tapes (a gift to cash-strapped high schools), and picks up tapes to view later. Swinney doesn't just look at high school juniors and seniors; he's also eyeballing freshmen and sophomores—fifteen- and sixteen-year-olds—who may become blue-chip prospects in the future. "I've worked my territory for four years, so I know where the great [high school] freshmen and sophomores are," he says. "I've seen a lot of them, and already have them on my future list."

What does he look for in a prospect? "There are obvious things—speed, the potential for size, how well a kid plays a position. If they are linemen, I look at their feet [to see if they're agile]. Some kids may not have an ideal weight right now, but they may have potential to hold weight." Swinney says he does not pay much attention to player rankings, publicity, or "who is recruiting who." Because he was one himself, he likes finding diamonds in the rough—players with potential and good attitudes. "I evaluate everybody the same," he says. "There are certain guys who are not great players when they walk on your campus, but they turn out to be great players. There are a lot of those guys out there." Two years ago he signed an offensive line prospect from Georgia named Lannis Baxley. "He was six-foot-seven, two-hundred-and-fifty pounds when he signed," says Swinney. "Now he weighs 300 pounds and he's second-team left tackle as a red-shirt freshman. He's got four years left. He was offered by Virginia, Central Florida, and us." Last year he signed a lightly recruited offensive lineman named Danny Martz, who attended DeMatha High School in Hyattsville, Maryland. Martz was offered a scholarship by other Division 1 schools, such as Rutgers and Maryland, but was not, Swinney acknowledges, a blue-chip prospect. "We offered him late," says the coach. "I took Coach Callaway [Alabama's offensive line coach] up to Maryland with me, so he could sit down and talk with Danny, and he really liked him." What did Swinney and Neil Callaway see in Martz that others didn't? "We liked his size and his potential," says Swinney. "He's only played two years of football. He's got good flexibility, good feet, and he's a strong kid. We thought he'd be able to help us at some point."

Eyeing Transcripts

Swinney also has a sharp eye for academic abilities. "I am well-versed in reviewing transcripts," he says. "I can look at one and tell if a guy is going to have a chance to qualify for admission or not. I've recruited some kids who people said didn't have a chance of getting in. And I was able to come up with an [academic] plan for them and get them qualified. They were admitted. Others, you look at their transcript and say, 'No way. No way.' It can be tough sometimes with borderline students."

All universities have academic and admissions officials who review transcripts, too, and they advise the coaching staff on whether specific kids are likely to qualify or not. It's a sad comment on America's educational system and misplaced priorities—by which I mean this country's habit of glorifying athletes and movie stars—but of the top 200 high school prospects in America every year, at least 30 percent will struggle to gain entrance to college. Many will not make it. They'll have to attend a junior college or prep school if they hope to get into a four-year university later. Others will be partial qualifiers, so-called Prop 48s, who are admitted to a college and can practice with the team as freshmen—but cannot play in games. They typically have an adequate grade point average but fail to pass the standardized SAT or ACT test. Every college is allowed to accept two partial qualifiers a year. Some of the best players in the SEC were partial qualifiers. John Henderson, a defensive tackle at Tennessee, was a partial qualifier.

Swinney says that qualifying problems can often be traced to a kid's early high school years. "It's not the junior or senior year—it's the freshman year," he says. "A guy goes into high school and screws up—doesn't work hard. The last thing high school freshmen are thinking about is college. They're thinking about their next meal. Then all of a sudden the guy blossoms into a great athlete—and when he's a junior, he's paying a big price for what he didn't do as a freshman"—passing a required class. "They end up short on some core classes and have to go to summer or night school." Swinney is sympathetic to kids who falter as high school underclassmen. He thinks the NCAA should have a "forgiveness policy" for such kids, enabling them to gain entrance to college. "Now, if he's a junior or senior and not getting it done in the classroom, that's a different story. But I have a hard time telling somebody who had freshman grade problems that he has to go to junior college."

How were Justin Smiley's grades? "They were mediocre," he says sheepishly. "I just did qualify." He was lagging academically as a high school sophomore, he says. "In tenth grade, I said: 'I'd better pick it up.'" He managed to raise his final GPA to 2.5, and scored an 890 on his SAT, which he only took one time. "I'm good to go, but I was pretty much borderline. I wished I had focused and done better. Grades are mega-important; if you don't have the grades, you'll be sitting there in JUCO [junior college]."

Grades and talent are not the only things that recruiters scrutinize in prospects. They also evaluate a kid's personality—his attitude. Swinney insists that he will not recruit kids who have attitude or behavioral problems. "There are a ton—a ton—of great players out there that I don't even recruit," he says. "Bad apples. Or I will call them, talk to a guy a couple of weeks, and then say, 'No way. I'm not going to waste my time.'" Will he truly ignore a stud athlete with an attitude? I ask him. "Absolutely. Absolutely. That is just me. I'm not going to sell my soul. Maybe it's because I went to school at Alabama. I know to be successful at Alabama, you have to have the right kind of people. Not everybody can play here. There is a lot of pressure. You've got to have the right guy. I'm not saying we don't have a few bad apples, because we do, and we have to keep our thumb on them. But if you have too many of those guys, they are going to turn the good apples bad. If you bring in enough good guys, the few bad guys you get will either get good or get gone."

After he returns to Tuscaloosa from his May trips, Swinney will sit down with Cottrell, Head Coach Mike DuBose, and Bama's other coaches to give rising high school seniors a more definitive recruiting ranking. By the summer, coaches have watched kids on tape and in person, seen them play games or perform at camps. They've got a pretty strong sense of who can dazzle, and who can't. Alabama ranks kids from 1 to 5. A 1 ranking is best; it signifies that a kid is a bona fide Division 1 prospect. He is expected to get a lot of scholarship offers—and merits an immediate scholarship offer from Bama. A 2 is a "probable" Division 1 prospect, who Bama will *not yet offer*, but rather "watch." A 3 is a borderline Division 1 prospect, who probably won't be offered. A 4 is "a great player with bad academics," says Swinney. And a 5? "Reject. Can't play for us." Smiley got a ranking of 1.

The Three-Coach Approval Rule

Before Alabama offers a kid a scholarship, he must be "approved" by three coaches—including the prospect's position coach. Swinney may love an offensive linemen in his territory. But unless Callaway, Bama's offensive line coach, is sold on the kid, too, he won't get an offer. "By now I have a pretty good idea what Callaway likes in a lineman," says Swinney. "When I bring him a tape of a line prospect, I have a good sense of who he's going to like and not like." And it works the other way. If Callaway is keen on a wide receiver prospect in *his* territory, he must sell Swinney and one other coach on the kid's talent; otherwise, it's no-go.

Tennessee uses a consensus system, and Coach Phillip Fulmer has the last word on scholarship offers. Brooks says there is often disagreement among the staff about whether to offer a certain prospect. The coaches will sit around a table and debate a kid's potential. But Fulmer is the ultimate arbiter; until he nods the head, there is no offer. And there have been a few cases where he has given a thumbs-down to kids who a majority of Vol coaches wanted to offer.

By August, the recruiting train is starting to gain some steam. Prospects are gearing up for their senior season. The master list has already been winnowed drastically. By late summer, says Cottrell, "I've seen probably fifty super players"—top blue-chippers. "Half don't give us the time of day; they're in other areas of the country or like other schools or whatever. But there are about fifteen that we're looking real good with, and those are the guys you lock in on and try to hold. At the same time, you continue to recruit guys who, right now, are not interested in Alabama."

When I spoke to him last summer, Swinney had chopped his master list to seventy. "That's fewer than I've ever had," he said, "but we have fewer scholarships to give." But after shaking the boughs for months to find seventy prospects, many quickly disappear. "My list will dwindle and dwindle and dwindle," says Swinney. "Some guys will eliminate us; others will eliminate themselves with poor academics." There is a lot of rejection? "Oh, yeah," says the Bama recruiter. "But you can't wear your feelings on your sleeve. But it also works both ways. There are a lot of good players who want to come to Alabama, but I have to tell them, 'Look, you gotta go to Clemson or wherever because we don't have a scholarship for you. They are good players, but we're full because we took other kids."

The period between September 1 and December 1 is the so-called "calling period." Recruiters can call a prospect once a week. After December 1, recruiters can make unlimited calls up to signing day (except for a few days over Christmas), and says Swinney, "you'd better call them every day or you are behind." He enjoys talking to prospects on the phone, getting to know them and their parents. "It's not just, 'Hey, hiya doin', Roll Tide.' I get to know as much about prospects and their families as I can. And I try to tell them as much about me as possible. Then, in December, when you can meet them face-to-face, you've got a foundation."

Beginning in September, the head coaches will start getting seriously involved in the process, too. In military parlance, it's time to roll out the big guns. Many assistants will give the head coach a list of prospects to call, hoping his stature will sway the prospect. Swinney is a little different. "I want to build a relationship with a bunch of guys and find out who is interested in us pretty strongly. Coach DuBose will call anybody for you at any time. But I don't want him to call a kid cold. I want to find out a few things about a prospect, and give that information to the coach. Some coaches are different; they'll call everybody. But I like handling things myself in the initial stages."

Recruits can also call coaches—any time they want—to ask questions or just chew the fat. Every recruiting office has an 800 number that's given out to top prospects. "We absolutely encourage recruits to call; we send them letters and make sure they have our 800 number," says Swinney. If a kid calls Swinney, it's a good indication that he's serious about Bama. If he doesn't, one can assume that his interest is lukewarm. Knowing which kids are truly interested in your school, and which are merely flirts (intrigued by the idea of being recruited by Bama but inclined to play for, say, Auburn), is important. That's because, in the fall, invitations are issued to prospects to make a so-called "official visit."

Swinney says that "sometimes you have a feel for a guy," and in the fall and winter of 1999, he had a good feeling about Smiley. By then Smiley had pulled back from his verbal commitment to South Carolina. "I really liked South Carolina," he says, "but I jumped the gun." He was being courted by the SEC's musclemen, and they were too strong for the Gamecocks, who were the worst team in the conference. Besides, Smiley's mom did not like South Carolina. She reproached Justin for committing to Lou Holtz. The Gamecocks were fading from the race for Justin Smiley. Meantime, Alabama was coming on. Swinney was calling Smiley regularly, and they established a rapport. He even persuaded the Georgia boy to call him a couple of times. And Smiley agreed to visit Tuscaloosa in January. "It was going good with him," says the Alabama coach. "I felt all through the recruiting process that we were leading for him and that we'd get him."

Funny thing: Jimmy Ray Stephens, Florida's offensive line coach, felt good about Smiley, too. He and Jim Collins, Florida's recruiting coordinator, were doggedly pursuing the big boy—and their efforts were paying off. When Florida coach Steve Spurrier got involved, he tried to seal the deal. One day last fall, says Smiley, "I was waiting on a call from Coach Stephens and lo and behold Coach Spurrier called. He was pretty blunt and to the point. He said, 'Justin, we want you here [in Gainesville].'" Spurrier told Smiley what other offensive linemen Florida was recruiting—among them, Shannon Shell, whom Spurrier projected would play tackle, and one other guard. "Spurrier told me they needed guards,'" says Smiley, "and they were going to sign two. And he said that one of the freshman guards would no doubt play as a freshman." He suggested Smiley would be that guy. "That was a pretty good feeling," says Smiley. Spurrier concluded his first call by telling the prospect, "We're going to do whatever it takes to get you here." Smiley was smitten, and agreed to visit Florida on December 5.

The Visits

There are two types of college recruiting visits—unofficial and official. An unofficial visit is a casual visit: a prospect and his parents might drive to Oxford or Athens to watch a game, hang out with players—some of whom they may know—meet with coaches. They get a feel for the campus. It's a good way for "in-state prospects"—Georgia kids who are most interested in the University of Georgia, for example—to cement their relationship with a school. The families must pay for the trip themselves. Official trips are different. They take place in December and are highly coveted by prospects as a sort of status symbol. Official visits are first offered to kids who live out of state, who have never seen, say, the University of Alabama. Prospects may make up to five official visits—to five different universities—if they wish. Most top recruits will make between two and four.

During an "official" weekend, anywhere from three to thirty prospects will tour a campus. They're given red-carpet treatment—the school will do everything it can to impress the high school star and his parents. Some prospects are flown in on private jets—many schools do it. There are free meals, flirty hostesses, nights on the town, an evening at the coach's house. The school picks up the tab for airfare, hotel rooms, and meals for the prospect and his guardians. The NCAA imposes a limit on the number of official visits a team can sponsor—fifty-six annually. That forces schools to be picky with their invitations. They don't want to offer official visits to borderline prospects who don't seem terribly enthusiastic about the school. On the other hand, Swinney and all other recruiters work assiduously to persuade the big dogs—the best prospects—to make an official visit, no matter how indifferent they may seem.

The reason: official visits can be very compelling to kids. Give a teen and his parents a tour of the stadium, some ribs and cornbread, show them the education or business school, visit the sports museum, watch video clips, lavish them with affection—and boom, prospects that were shunning you for months suddenly topple like ten-pins. "You can tell kids on the phone about Coach Bryant and all the rest," says Swinney. "But kids today don't remember that stuff; they have a hard time sensing the tradition. But then they come here [Swinney's voice rises] and see all the national championships and the facilities and meet the players and the academic people, and they go, 'Wow.' I hate it when this is the only place they visit. I like for them to go to other schools, because it gives them something to compare us to. Most guys have never been here. I tell them, 'Just take your visit. If you come here and don't like it, I wish you well.'" Brandon Miree, a running back out of Cincinnati, Ohio, was not much interested in Bama until he made a visit. He liked the experience, and now plays for the Tide.

Smiley made three official visits in 1999. His first was to South Carolina, but it was more of a courtesy visit than anything. Smiley says he didn't really want to go—he'd ruled out the 'Cocks by the late fall of 1999. But the Gamecocks wouldn't take no for an answer, and so Smiley and his dad (who is a Lou Holtz fan) made the trip. "I went up, and I really didn't care for it that much." says Smiley. "I liked the team and the coaching staff was awesome—great people—but I just didn't fit in good there. I felt I should go elsewhere." South Carolina was out.

All schools try to get their top prospects to see a game—and, if possible, a big game. Last year Tennessee invited six prospects to make official visits the weekend of the Notre Dame game—a high-profile contest that was televised on ESPN. With 107,000 fans rocking Neyland Stadium, and the Irish in town for a night game, the "wow" potential was high. All the prospects arrived by 12:30 P.M. on Saturday. They were given lunch, then a bus tour of the university. The group, which included New Jersey wide receiver Rashad Baker, then met with Tennessee's academic-support staff—including Judy Jackson, the assistant director of student life, whom Brooks says "does a good job of getting personal with the parents of prospects." She visits with all of them, telling them what their sons must do to qualify for admission. After that, a couple of prospects were whisked off to the UT business school—the focus of their academic interest. There, they met with a professor or two. Others were taken to the library to meet UT students. "Most of Saturday is geared toward academics," says Brooks.

In the evening, the focus shifted back to football. The prospects met briefly with their prospective position coach. Then they sat in on pregame meetings with the Vols. "They just jump into our game-day ritual," says Brooks. Two hours before kickoff, they also participate in the Vol Walk—the team's quarter-mile stroll from the UT football complex to the stadium. Thousands of fans line the path, cheering the team. The prospects were shown the locker room, then taken out on the field with Fulmer for pregame warmups. During the game, they sit in the stands. It's a heady experience for anyone, but especially for impressionable teens.

After the game, which Tennessee easily won, the six official visitors were again ushered into the Vol locker room. The prospects ate sandwiches, then went out on the town with player-hosts. Such socializing has two purposes. The first, of course, is simply to show the prospects a good time. Schools generally pick their most responsible and prepossessing players to fill the "host" role. They show the high schoolers around, introduce them to other players, answer questions about the team and program. The second reason that socializing is important, says Brooks, is that it gives Tennessee an opportunity to further vet the prospects. Says Brooks: "We tell our kids, 'You make sure he fits in [with us.] If he doesn't, you tell us.' Our players know what we want and expect, and if a kid is a jerk, they'll tell us. We don't want a rotten egg in the barrel. One of our greatest recruiting assets is our players." Last year Lynn McGruder, a top defensive line prospect from Nevada, signed with Tennessee partly because he got on so well with his Vol host, John Henderson.

The next day, Sunday, Fulmer put on his charm offensive. He gave the prospects a bus tour of Knoxville. Those kids who so wished were taken to church—by either a UT coach or player. "We have all denominations here," says Brooks, sounding like a Chamber of Commerce official. "Parents want to know that their children can continue their spiritual development." For lunch UT prospects are often taken to the Varsity Inn, a favorite player hangout. Before they leave for home on Sunday, every prospect has a fifteen-minute or longer sit-down meeting with Fulmer in his office. It is the Moment of Truth. Fulmer touts Tennessee—its academics, its football prowess, its espirit de corps. "You can win football games and get a good education here," he says. "We're graduating players." He'd mention Darwin Walker, a hard-working defensive lineman with an electrical engineering degree. Then comes the football hard-sell, and Fulmer can be very persuasive: "We're recruiting the best kids in the country, and we think you're one of them. We're excited about your interest in us." Fulmer tells the prospect where he stands with the Vols: "you've got a scholarship, if you want it." Or: "we're recruiting several linebackers, and you're high on the list." He then probes the prospect for his level of interest in Tennessee: "Where do we stand with you? Are we first on your list? Second? Third? In the top five?" Many recruiters and coaches will remind prospects that if they wait too long to make a decision, there might not be any scholarships left. That's often true, but it's sometimes used as a ploy to get a top prospect to commit. In fact, schools always keep a few scholarships in reserve for the very best players.

Spurrier and a 140-Pound Labrador

Smiley's second visit, to Florida, went well—at least as far as he was concerned. He liked the campus, liked the weather, liked the program, liked the players and coaches. His mother felt differently. "She hardly talked to me on the Florida visit," Smiley said. "She said, 'This is up to you,' and went on and did her own thing." Terri insists she wasn't biased against Florida, but there were things about UF that bothered her. In particular, she didn't like the living arrangements—hated them, in fact. Florida officials showed her where Justin would live as a freshman—in a high-rise dormitory, sharing a room with one other football player, and sharing a bathroom with three others. "The rooms were small, about the size of my walk-in closet," complains Terri. "And they had hard, cold concrete floors." When Terri saw where Justin would sleep—on a bunk bed—she went through the roof! According to Smiley, when she saw the bunk beds she blurted out, "My son ain't sleeping on a bunk bed!" She turned to her son and said, "You play football, don't you want to sleep good at night?" Smiley says he was "embarrassed" by his mom's reaction.

Clearly, mother and son had divergent opinions about Florida, and about Steve Spurrier as well. Smiley liked the Gator coach. But Terri is not a Spurrier fan, and neither is Smiley's father. And Spurrier didn't endear himself to Terri when he visited the family's house. When the Gator coach got to Ellabell, in the afternoon, Smiley was in school. But Terri was home, and so was the family's 140-pound chocolate Lab, named Drake. The dog saw Spurrier and went galumphing up to the Gator coach, who was wearing green pants, and tried to get friendly. Spurrier, according to the family, did not want to play with the dog, and certainly did not want Drake slobbering all over his green pants. He said, "Uh-uh," and pushed Drake away. This turned off Terri, who told her son later that day, "Justin, he don't like your dog!" She added: "The other coaches wallowed down with the dog, but Spurrier didn't want our Lab touching him. I knew then that I didn't like him."

Justin Smiley

Lap Dances and Legal Trouble

What's more, Terri wasn't crazy about Florida's reputation as a social school. "We are strictly country people. My boys are home and in bed by 10 P.M. every night. In Gainesville, everything was fast-paced. It was a whole different world. Justin calls it a partying town." That's certainly what Smiley did on his official visit to Florida. Gator players took him out to bars on both Friday and Saturday night. He returned to his hotel room after one prolonged social session at 4:00 A.M. (After his South Carolina visit, Smiley came home and blurted out: "Mom, I got lap dances." He'd been taken to a Columbia bar named the Zoo, where students hang out, and apparently things got risqué. "I said, 'Pardon me?'" recalls Terri. "That's not what a mother wants to hear. That's not what college is all about." Smiley, hearing his mom, retorts: "That's pretty much what it's like, Momma.")

Jason Respert, another top Georgia prospect, also made a recruiting trip to Florida. He was a *Parade* All American last year, and perhaps the best offensive-line prospect in the South. Like Smiley, Respert partied late into a Friday night (Saturday morning) with his hosts from the Florida football team. And he got into serious legal trouble. On Friday, January 28, Respert spent the first part of his Gainesville visit drinking in the apartment of Florida defensive lineman Alex Brown. Gerard Warren, another Gator player and Respert's official host for the weekend, was also at the apartment, as was then-seventeen-year-old Tre Orr, a Lake City, Florida, prospect who would later sign with Florida. The four young men left Brown's apartment and went to the Purple Porpoise, a popular campus bar. There the guys continued drinking, though three of the four were under Florida's official drinking age of twenty-one. After some youthful carousing, three of the guys—Brown, Respert, and Orr—separated from the others. The three men eventually made their way to an off-campus apartment where at least three female Florida students lived. It was 3:15 in the morning. The group turned on a PC to confirm the star-prospect status of Respert and Orr. Then, reportedly, Brown and Orr paired off with a couple of the women. Respert fell asleep downstairs, at the foot of a pull-out couch. Around dawn on January 29, as the men were preparing to leave, a third woman in the apartment, who had neither met nor partied with the players, was awakened in her bed by a man who, she later charged, was fondling her. She went to the police and identified Respert as the assailant. The eighteen-year-old prospect was arrested the next day, while he was inside the Florida football complex, and charged with attempted sexual battery and residential burglary—both felonies.

Respert, an honors student, vehemently denied the charges. However, he did tell police, according to the arrest report, that he had been intoxicated and

177

did not remember much about the evening. Last June in a Gainesville court-room, he pled "no contest" to reduced misdemeanor charges of battery and trespassing. As punishment, he was given two years of supervised probation and forty hours of community service. The Georgia prospect maintained his innocence, and said he reluctantly agreed to the plea bargain. "It was some-thing my attorney and I discussed over and over, something we felt we had to do to get [the case] over with," Respert said. "With me, personally, I always knew it would leave a black cloud over me. But if I would have fought it, it was going to take three or four months just to get a court date. I wouldn't have been able to go to school, wouldn't have been earning any credits, and, most importantly, wouldn't have been playing football."

His ordeal over, Respert signed with Tennessee. Vol coach Phillip Fulmer defended his decision to offer Respert a scholarship, saying at a press confer-ence: "We talked to everybody who had a relationship with Jason. Everybody around him feels very, very positive about him. If it was an isolated incident, which we're convinced that it was, and if we trust him to come here and do the right things, which we do, then he's worthy of getting a second chance." Fulmer acknowledged that assessing a prospect's character can be as inexact as evaluating someone's athletic potential. "You're never sure," he said. "There are great young men or young ladies who take a wrong step from time to time, and you've got to make a calculated decision as to what is best for the pro-gram. That's what we're looking at first. Whether it's a person already on the team or not, you ask yourself if you are putting the program at risk. I don't think we're doing that."

Smiley told me that what happened to Respert did not surprise him—and might easily have happened to him. "I'm not going to lie to you: on these recruiting trips you're free to do what you want, and you have to be careful to stay out of trouble. The alcohol and the girls were there. Anything was possi-ble. I was in the same situation [as Respert] many a time. That is college life. I felt bad about what happened to him."

By the end of the Florida visit, both Smiley and his mother were growing weary of the recruiting grind. Coaches would drive five hours to get to Ellabell, pull into a BP gas station near the Smileys' house, and then call and plead with Terri to let them come by for a visit. Sometimes Terri would say yes, sometimes no. When Smiley was visiting South Carolina, a Georgia coach called Terri and said that he'd heard that Justin had liked South Carolina. He asked if he could come by soon to talk to Smiley. "I said I don't know when he'll be home," said Terri. "And the coach said, 'I do, he can only be on a college campus for forty-eight hours.' Sure enough, Justin pulled up in the car just about the time the Georgia coach said he would. He knew more than I did." She says a South Carolina coach visited the home one evening and, under the pretense of being interested in her nephew, plopped down on a couch—and sat there till 10 at night. "I felt like I was in a used-car lot," said Terri. "Everybody had a sales pitch."

For all that bothered her about the University of Florida, Terri recognized and respected her son's attraction to the Gators. "Justin was real impressed with Florida," she says. "There were several things we didn't like, but the good outweighed the bad. And at that point, we were so tired of it all, we said, 'We'll end the recruiting right here.'" During his Gainesville visit, Smiley strongly suggested to the coaches that he'd be coming to Florida. He told me that he didn't make a verbal commitment—but if not, he certainly came awfully close. Terri was *almost* resigned to the fact that Justin would be a Gator—but not quite. "We've always been big Bama fans," she says, and for that reason she kept pestering Justin to make a visit to Tuscaloosa. The young man wasn't inclined to do so, but thought about it.

Position Rankings

Colleges rank prospects at every position—they will have a list of, say, ten cornerbacks, ten linebackers, and so on. During recruiting season, Alabama has a big board in a football meeting room, and on it are listed the school's top prospects at every position. There is a magnetic nameplate for each prospect, and it is moved up or down, or removed entirely, as the recruiting process moves along. Everybody wants to sign the top players on their board, but that seldom happens. Let's say Bama wants to sign four cornerbacks out of the ten it has ranked. The number 1 cornerback has indicated he probably won't sign with Bama. The number two–ranked cornerback seems only mildy interested in the Tide. The number three–ranked cornerback seems strongly interested, but he's also serious about one other school.

Meantime, the cornerbacks ranked five and seven are sold on Bama—ready to commit if offered a scholarship. This is where recruiting gets tricky. If a recruiter thinks he has a chance of signing a "can't-miss" prospect at a specific position, he's reluctant to offer a scholarship to a lesser player at the same position. In this case, the cornerbacks ranked five and seven are typically put on "hold" until it becomes clear where the blue chips will commit. Now recruiters must morph from salesmen into diplomats. What the top schools will do, typically, is a little bit disingenuous. The must try to keep the lower-ranked fish on the hook—still interested—even though Bama may eventually decide not to reel them in. In other words, a top B-level prospect could wait around for weeks, expecting a scholarship offer, and then not get it in the end if a position player ranked above him commits. So both the schools and the prospects must take risks.

Cottrell asserts that he's always upfront with prospects about their status. If he decides to put a kid on "hold," he often calls on the high school coach to help reinforce his message. "I know a lot of high school coaches in northwest Florida," says Cottrell. "They're my friends, and they trust me. I'll go to one and say, 'Here's where we are: we like the kid a lot, but we're not ready to offer him yet. We're going to come back and see him in the fall, but it looks good. We'll offer him an official visit.' When you've only got fifty-six official visits, that's a pretty strong endorsement—even though you haven't yet offered him a scholarship." Some kids will press a school for a decision, says Cottrell: will you offer me a scholarship? Then, says the Bama recruiting coordinator, "you have to be honest and say, 'No, not right now. But hang in there with us.'"

Some kids will, some won't. Last year, a West Virginia player named Ronnie Rodamer was strongly interested in Tennessee. The Vols put him off while they chased higher-rated wide receivers in Michigan and Texas. The Vols struck out on the other athletes, but remained cool to Rodamer. After weeks of biding his time, Rodamer started looking at other schools. He eventually accepted a scholarship to Notre Dame. Swinney says coaches must sometimes gamble on losing lower-ranked prospects until they've at least gotten the true blue-chips on campus for a dog-and-pony show. "If you turn down number three," says Swinney, "he could be gone. He says, 'Hey, I'm trying to commit and you don't want me. The reality is you want all three but can't have them. And if you turn number three down and then the first two don't come, then you're left holding the bag and you've got to go to a second-tier player. So we're forced to decide how badly we want certain guys."

Georgia's Gamble

Georgia found itself in just that position with Justin Smiley. Georgia rated Smiley a conditional "take." The Bulldogs were not desperate for offensive linemen last year, but they were strongly pursuing two studs from Georgia ranked more highly than Smiley—Respert and Sean Young, an offensive tackle from Cohutta, Georgia. Both were high school All Americans and ranked among the top 100 players nationally. Young was a first-team offensive lineman on USA Today's All-America list. Georgia Coach Jim Donnan wanted to sign two offensive linemen in 1999—and Respert and Young were his targets. Georgia liked Smiley, but apparently considered him a fall-back prospect—insurance, in case either Respert or Young fell through. Because

Justin Smiley

Young and Respert were in-state boys, Donnan and Garner thought they had a pretty good chance of signing them. They guessed wrong. Like Smiley, Young was a capricious prospect who liked almost every school he visited. He would commit, change his mind, commit, then change his mind. Respert played his cards closer to the vest. So while the Bulldogs chased Respert and Young, they kept Smiley on hold.

This annoyed Smiley and his family—especially because friends and classmates were all pestering Justin to sign with the Dawgs. "I told people, 'I would love to go to my home-state school.' But I felt like they were yanking me around." And, truth be told, Georgia *was* yanking Smiley around in the way that all the major programs yank around B or B+ prospects. Donnan and Georgia Coach Greg Adkins recruited Smiley, expressed their strong interest in him—but kept an official scholarship offer dangling just out of reach until it became clear where Young and Respert would sign. Says Smiley: "Coach Donnan called me and said, 'You want to stay in Georgia, don't you?' And I said, 'Are you gonna offer me? You've seen me play.'"

Indeed, the Bulldog coaches had seen Smiley on tape, on the practice field, and in games, just like everybody else. By November, it became clear that Georgia's chances of getting either Respert or Young were slipping. Tennessee was a strong player for both kids, and seemed certain to get at least one. Sensing this, Georgia renewed its interest in Smiley. The Bulldogs asked Ron Flott, the Southeast Bulloch coach, for more videotape of Smiley. That decision only compounded Georgia's problems. Flott told Adkins, "You don't need any more film of Justin. You've seen him play." By the middle of November, when it looked like Young and Respert were headed out of state, Georgia finally offered Smiley what he'd expected months earlier—a scholarship. But by then it was far too late. Georgia had long since lost its leverage. Says Smiley: "My high school coach told me: 'I'll never speak to you again if you go to UGA.'" Smiley refused the Georgia offer, telling Coach Adkins, "Looks like I've been your third wheel all along." Georgia was out.

Decisions, Decisions

For kids and their families, picking a college is equally tough. They must weigh numerous factors. What is a school's football reputation? What is its academic reputation? Does it graduate its players? Does it have the academic specialty (engineering, music,) that the prospect is looking for? Will a school let the prospect play a position he likes—give a kid a chance to play, say, quarterback, even though the recruiters may project him to be a defensive back in college?

Does the kid want to play for a major program—where football is king but the athletic competition is so fierce that he may not ever play a down? Signing with a top SEC school is a high-risk, high-reward proposition. If the prospect pans out, wins a starting job, then his college-football experience is apt to be very rewarding. But the competition is stiff—one reason for a high attrition rate. Three years ago Steve Shipp, a wide receiver from Charlotte, was one of the most heavily recruited prospects in America. Tennessee and Florida battled mightily for his signature. The Gators got it. But when Shipp got to Gainesville, he learned he was just one of about ten receivers on the squad. All, like him, were stars in high school. And it soon became evident that he wasn't quite as swift, wasn't quite as talented, as many of the others. After a frustrating two years, he talked with Florida Assistant Coach Dwayne Dixon. The two agreed that, given Shipp's interest in playing, a transfer might be in his best interest. And that's what he did. There are a lot of Steve Shipps in the SEC.

In their conversations with recruiters, prospects often ask about playing time. Many top prospects want to be assured that they will play early—it's another validation of their talent. Last year Shyrone Carey, a lightning-quick athlete out of Louisiana, talked at length with Tennessee offensive coordinator Randy Sanders about "PT." Could he play as a freshman? Carey asked. Sanders said yes. Carey pressed the matter. *Would* he play as a freshman? Sanders assured him—in repeated phone conversations—that he would. Carey signed with the Vols, but did not qualify academically. Last year Ronnie Brown, a late-blooming prospect from Georgia, seemed like a lock to go to Tennessee. In high school, Brown was a talented running back and linebacker. The Tennessee coaches told Brown that he'd get a shot at running back—but they also suggested he might be needed at linebacker—a "need position" for the Vols. The Vols already had three good running backs on their roster. Brown listened, and then took a visit to Auburn, the only other school he was considering. There, Auburn Coach Tuberville convinced Brown not only that he would play running back for the Tigers, but that he'd play early. Unlike the Vols, the Tigers needed help at running back. Wanting to play offense more than defense, Brown committed to Auburn.

Lear Jets and Cleat Chasers: A Tuscaloosa Visit

By around Christmas, with Alabama preparing to play in a bowl game, the word was out that Justin Smiley was a Florida commit. Smiley had told Swinney that he'd visit Alabama on January 7, but two nights before he was supposed to leave, he canceled the trip. He'd talked to Spurrier, who, accord-

Justin Smiley

ing to Smiley, urged him not to take his Bama visit. Smiley, feeling pressure, put a message on Swinney's phone line: "I want to think about my decision for a week," he said on the message, "and decide what is in my best interest." Terri says that, at that point, "even though it was my dream, we weren't going to Alabama. And I said to Justin: 'We'll just have to work things out with that [Florida] bed.'" By now Smiley was dodging phone calls from half a dozen recruiters "who wouldn't take no for an answer."

Swinney, when he heard the news that Smiley was a Florida commit, was stunned. "Sometimes you have a feel for a guy, and know when he's leaning one way or another. I never had any indication that he was considering Florida. It was out of the blue, and I was caught off-guard." Smiley says he got an alarmed message from Swinney on his answering machine. "He was all upset. He said, 'What do I have to do to get you to take this visit? We won't say one word against Florida.' It was against my wishes, but my mom wanted me to go and take a look." And so he did.

Smiley made his visit to Tuscaloosa in late January. But he didn't drive to Tuscaloosa. Alabama flew him and two other prospects there in a private Lear Jet. Along with Smiley, Jason Rawls and Hobie Holliday (a top prospect who signed with Georgia Tech), made the trip. "It was fun, a straight shot, a fifty-minute flight from Statesboro," says Smiley. When they arrived in Tuscaloosa, on a Friday afternoon, the group went straight to Swinney's house, where they ate lunch and sat around. Smiley played with Swinney's young son, Andrew. He says Swinney talked to him about growing up in Alabama. "They wanted to get personal," says Smiley. That night, Smiley and other prospects had dinner at a bar and grill named Wings. It was an all-you-can-eat buffet, which is the only way to feed high school football players. That night, Alabama players Jared Johnson and Matt Lomax took Smiley to various bars around town. They went to Pounders, where the football players hang out. "It was a good place—full of cleat chasers," says Smiley. He describes a "cleat chaser" as a "girl who follows players around. There was a lot of that on my visits. The girls got aggravating after awhile. I thought, maybe the school has paid for them—but if that were true there would be different girls paying attention to me on Friday and Saturday nights. I got the feeling that finding a girlfriend in college wouldn't be hard."

Girls are an important part of the recruiting process. It's an old (and outdated) tradition, but all major universities recruit pretty female students who serve as prospect hostesses during recruiting weekends. Their job is mostly to flirt with the prospects for two days. For Smiley, Alabama had lined up a hostess—a so-called Bama Belle—whose name is Emmy. It turned out that the Smileys knew Emmy—she'd attended a private school with one of Terri's nieces. "I asked the Alabama people," says Terri, "'Did you do your homework on that, too? Was that a coincidence?'" She seems skeptical. Georgia had an escort for Smiley, too. Her name was Stephanie—the same name, it turns out, as Smiley's first and only girlfriend (who broke his heart). Stephanie wrote five or six letters to Smiley, telling him what a great place Georgia was. "She matched right up with him," says Terri. "A twenty-year-old girl writing my son. It's all part of the game, part of the package."

While Smiley was fending off cleat chasers at Pounders, Terri was taken to dinner then squired over to Coach DuBose's house for dessert and coffee. She is practically breathless at the memory. Big house? "It was a mansion," she said, sounding like she'd spent a weekend at Buckingham Palace. "They had servants open doors for you, put your coat on for you. It was immaculate."

On Saturday, Smiley spent his morning and early afternoon checking out Alabama's academic scene. He toured the tutoring/life skills center for student athletes, met with criminal justice professors (his area of interest), filled out questionnaires. He learned that every freshman player must study for two hours a night in a computer lab. "My mother liked that," says Smiley. "It didn't register with me." He and his mom toured the Bear Bryant museum, which he described as "awesome." That night, the prospects were taken to Bryant-Denny Stadium. They toured the facility, then had dinner in the press box. Smiley and the other prospects wore Alabama jerseys all day with their names on the back—another recruiting tradition. "Every school does that, but it felt great," says Smiley. Smiley said Alabama was the only school that promised him his high school number, 78. "That was a minute factor." The stadium lights were turned off, and then the stadium's big video screen came to life. An announcer dramatically introduced a video clip for every prospect: "Justin Smiley, an All-Star offensive guard from Ellabell, Georgia—" And there, on a big screen atop Bryant-Denny Stadium, in color, was Justin Smiley in action. (The big-screen highlight experience is pretty much done by everybody nowadays.) At the end, the Alabama fight song resounded triumphantly through the night. Smiley says he asked several players about their Bama football experience. "I'd talk to a first-teamer and then a guy who walked on." The responses were positive, "and even the walk-ons said they hoped one day to get a scholarship." Justin was even taken out to the country and shown places were he could go hunting. The weekend went well, and Terri nudged Justin along. "She told me, 'You can't go wrong with Alabama.'"

On the trip home, Smiley pulled out a piece of paper and paired off Alabama and Florida, jotting down the advantages and disadvantages of each university. Florida got a thumbs-up for its location—it was closer to home, a two-and-a-half-hour drive from home. Tuscaloosa was seven hours away. But everything else had turned in Bama's favor. The living arrangements were more comfortable, said Terri. Alabama had bigger apartments for its ath-

Justin Smiley

letes—and queen-size beds! Florida was fast-paced; Bama was laid-back but, in Smiley's words, "hard-core football." And though Smiley was once entranced by the idea of playing as a freshman for Florida, after his Tuscaloosa visit that promise rang hollow. "Florida promised I'd start," he said. "Alabama didn't promise me one thing. You can't promise anything in the SEC, except that you're going to get your butt whipped day in and day out. Alabama said the best five would be on the field. That attracted me. Alabama outweighed Florida big-time. I've still got the piece of paper."

Suspicions

There is a lot of so-called negative recruiting in college football. When certain coaches find out that a prospect is considering a rival program, they waste no time throwing mud. It's very common for recruiters to denigrate their rivals. For example, if a rival recruiter hears that a prospect is seriously interested in South Carolina, he might say to the prospect: "Lou Holtz is a good man, but do you really want to play for the worst team in the SEC? You're not going to win many games." Tennessee? "Do you know how many linebackers they've got? You might have trouble playing there." Florida? "Yeah, they throw the ball, but Spurrier is not much fun to play for." Swinney claims he doesn't do it. "I don't believe in negative recruiting," he says. "I believe in selling Alabama. I will do everything I can to sell this program, and if that's not good enough, fine. But negative recruiting happens, and I've had to fight it several times. A kid will say, 'This coach said such and such about Alabama.' Well, if another team is so interested in talking about our program, that ought to tell you something. If you're going to a Ford dealership and all they talk about is Chevrolet, then maybe you ought to check out the Chevrolet." He adds that he doesn't tell recruits to attend Alabama because of him. "Don't come here because of me, because I may not be here next year. I may get fired or take another job. Choose a school because that's where you want to go to college, not because of me. If a kid chooses a school strictly because he likes a coach, and then suddenly the coach leaves, then the kid is going to be unhappy. So that should not be the main reason to choose a school." That said, "I do want the guys I recruit to feel like they had a positive experience with me, to trust me, to know that I care about them. I won't sell my soul for my job."

Perhaps Swinney should make that pledge to his rivals in Gainesville, because a minor scandal erupted around Alabama's recruitment of Justin Smiley. Before leaving Tuscaloosa, Terri and Justin met with Coach DuBose. The three sat at a table. DuBose gave them his recruiting spiel: "We're not going to promise you anything, Justin, but this is a great opportunity to come here and have fun and play football." At one point, says Smiley, DuBose pulled his hands out from under the table and, with a dramatic flourish, placed them on the table as he "laid out the facts." Smiley still remembers it. Smiley committed to Alabama.

The happiest person in the room was probably Terri. Excited, she told DuBose that Justin would need a new car to make the long drive from Georgia to Alabama. Smiley had been driving an '85 Ford truck, but Terri declared that it wasn't reliable. She claims she was talking to herself, or to her son, but not to DuBose. In any case, according to Terri, DuBose said there were mechanics in Tuscaloosa who could fix the truck. Smiley then returned to Georgia and announced—three days before signing day—that he was signing with Alabama. Smiley said something to his brother, Nicholas, about getting a new truck. Nicholas relayed this information to folks at Southeast Bulloch High School. And soon the word had reached the Florida coaching staff: Justin Smiley was going to Alabama—and he was getting a new truck.

To put it mildly, Florida's coaches were not pleased to hear the news that Smiley had defected. And when they heard about the new truck, well, that little piece of information (or innuedo) was a loaded stick of dynamite. SEC recruiting wars can be nasty—and they are complicated by suspicions of cheating. Last year Florida's offensive tackle, Kenyatta Walker, rolled a hand grenade toward the Crimson Tide, saying: "We all know that Alabama takes care of its players." One day after she and Justin got home, says Terri, "All hell broke loose. Florida could not accept the fact that Justin had changed his mind." Spurrier himself called Smiley. "I've heard a few things," said the Florida coach to his prospect. "I heard you're going to Alabama. That breaks our heart down here. I would watch your back," the coach continued. "Justin, you're going to get in trouble. The word is out that Alabama is getting you a new truck." Smiley told Spurrier that he was going to Alabama, but he said, "I don't know anything about a new truck." Spurrier said, "Is there anything I can say to make you change your mind?" Smiley said no. "It was hard telling him; I like him."

That wasn't the last of it. The next morning Terri got the first of a few letters from the University of Florida, asking for information about conversations between her and Bama coach DuBose. There was also correspondence from the NCAA—the collegiate governing body. Florida had asked the NCAA to investigate Alabama's recruitment of Smiley. An NCAA official called the house and took a statement from Terri. Coach DuBose's secretary called and asked her to make a statement. "Several people called and wanted to know what transpired in Coach DuBose's office," says Terri. "There was absolutely nothing to the controversy. I'm the one who said, 'We'll have to get you a new vehicle.' I was really just talking to my son." She got an attorney, and asked him to call "Coach Steve" and reiterate that her son *wasn't* going to Florida. Spurrier listened, said he respected Smiley's decision—but added that he would be at the high school in the morning. And the next morning, four Florida coaches arrived at Southeast Bulloch and gave Smiley one last pitch. "All those hugs and kisses turned into stares and glares," said Terri ruefully. "It got ugly."

In the end, nothing came of the NCAA investigation. How much of it was a genuine concern by Florida that Bama was cheating, or a last-ditch attempt to sway Smiley to Gainesville, is unknown. The recruiting business can be murky. Those in a position to influence the decisions of prospects have been known to ask for favors, and sometimes receive them. This makes losing a key prospect even more annoying. In the end, Smiley signed with Alabama at his high school library. He was the first kid ever from Southeast Bulloch to earn a Divsion 1 scholarship. TV news cameras were there. So was his high school coach, Ron Flott, who though disappointed with Smiley's decision, told him: "I'm happy for you. You did well."

Looking back, Swinney says that Smiley's recruitment "was quite a ride. Everybody was doing their job. Florida does a great job of recruiting. The whole thing is being persistent with these kids. If you're going to beat Florida, you'd better work, because they will stay on a guy." He says the key to nabbing Smiley was simply getting him to Tuscaloosa. "All he had to compare Florida to was South Carolina, and that was clear-cut. He didn't think anything could match Florida. He still thanks me for taking his visit." The Alabama coach remembers being burned by Florida two years ago, when he seemed to have landed Daryl Dixon, a top defensive back—only to lose him to the Gators at the eleventh hour. Newberg described Smiley as "fickle" and "naive." Maybe, but it's hard not to be when you're the focal point of a recruiting war.

Signing Day was good to the big three in SEC football—Florida, Tennessee, and Alabama. They all had monster recruiting years. Despite losing Smiley, Florida put together what analysts agreed was the best recruiting class in the nation. Tennessee was right behind, signing Young and Michael Munoz, a blue-chip offensive lineman and the son of NFL Hall of Famer Anthony Munoz. The Vols also snatched heralded North Carolina safety O. J. Owens, Nevada defensive lineman Lynn McGruder, and two of the best quarterbacks in the country—Casey Clausen and John Rattay. Brooks said that "while you can't get everybody, we're very pleased."

According to Swinney, Alabama had "a phenomenal year. We got who we wanted at every position. I can't think of any major disappointments." He himself signed ten players—including three receivers (Leonard Fulgham, Triandos Luke, and Derrick Woods). Alabama actually makes a habit of signing more players than it has room for every year. The practice, called oversigning, is ethically questionable, but Swinney says that "it's a common thing nowadays" because, sadly, so many recruits will not gain admission to school. Though teams can only sign twenty-five players to scholarships every year, Alabama got thirty-two prospects to pledge to the Crimson Tide in 1999 and the school signed twenty-eight last year. Bama does that to protect itself—to ensure that it gets its full allotment of twenty-five players into school every year. If Bama only signed twenty-five, certain academic casualties would cause it to fall short of its quota. Oversigning is, really, just another example of what SEC schools do nowadays to gain competitive advantage.

There are other examples. In the past, it was somewhat rare for schools to pull scholarships from athletes once they were in school. Though all athletic grants are renewed annually, and though a university is not *legally obligated* to pay an athlete's expenses for four years, it's long been an unwritten rule that scholarships were four- or five-year commitments by both the university and the prospect. But, increasingly, schools are pulling scholarships from players who are failing to meet either athletic or academic expectations. It, too, is an ethically questionable decision. Tommy Tuberville pulled six scholarships from Auburn players soon after he took over as coach in 1998. The players weren't troublemakers; apparently, they were just not good enough to play football for Auburn—though they were all recruited heavily by Auburn in the recent past. "It goes on, a lot more than people think," says Swinney. He asserts that Coach DuBose will not take a scholarship from a kid "if he's going to class, is a good citizen, and is giving us good effort. If a player is not good, then that's our fault, but he keeps his scholarship. But if he's a problem, we may not renew it. We've definitely had guys that we have not resigned."

And what of Smiley and his mom? Terri says she's still reeling from the rough-and-tumble recruiting process: "We're still paranoid." Smiley enrolled in Alabama's summer sessions to get a head start on his classwork and his football. It's a common practice nowadays. (Again, somebody figured out a few years ago that it was a way to gain an advantage, and now everybody does it.) Florida offers to pay for a summer session for its incoming freshmen football players. Alabama does not. "I will be out-of-pocket $1,000 to get him there for the summer," says Terri. "But that's fine with me." She's happy because her son will be living in those big, comfy Alabama rooms, sleeping in that queen-size bed—while Florida's freshmen are scrunched up in those bunk beds. "I just hope he has a prosperous four years," says Terri. "He's a good kid with a tender heart."

Justin Smiley

Epilogue

Last May I talked to Terri for the last time. There was talk that Alabama was being investigated for recruiting violations. Spurrier's reaction was interesting. "I'm not surprised," said the Florida coach. Terri wanted to know what I knew. Not much, I said. She and Justin had just returned from Tuscaloosa, she said, where they had bought *two* new vehicles—a Ford F150 for Justin and a new Ford Expedition, which Terri planned to drive to Bama games. She mentions car payments of $700 a month. She seems defensive about the purchases. "I got proof that I bought 'em," she says. "They videotaped me signing papers at the dealership." Why drive all the way from Georgia to Alabama to buy cars? "I shopped around," she said. "We got a better deal in Alabama."

ELEVEN

A HOUSE THAT MOVES: LYNN LANG AND ALBERT MEANS

NOTHING HAS CHANGED ABOUT WHAT MAKES A WINNER. A WINNER WORKS HIS BUTT OFF AND IS DEPENDABLE. HE'S NOT ALWAYS THE MOST TALENTED BUT HE GIVES EVERYTHING ON EVERY PLAY.

That's the message on a recruiting card sent by Auburn University to Albert Means, a top defensive line prospect last year at Trezevant High School in Memphis. There was an accompanying handwritten note: *Albert, Just a note to say hello and wish you the best. We really like the way you play football! Good luck and please come to our camp! We are thinking about you! [Signed] Coach Don Dunn*

The University of Texas also sent Means a card. On the front is a picture of the Longhorns lined up against Texas A&M, just above a line reading 1999 COTTON BOWL CHAMPIONS. Inside is a handwritten note: *Albert, I watched your high school tape and I wanted to drive to Memphis to get you! We need you to help make our defense special. Good luck. Hook 'em. [Signed] Coach Carl Reese*

Lynn Lang had lots of recruiting cards like that on the walls of his austere Memphis office. Cards from Georgia, UCLA, Nebraska, Arizona State, Ohio State. They weren't for him, of course, but for Albert Means, his star football prospect at Trezevant. Means is a 6'5", 310-pound lineman who can move. He was an All-State football player in Tennessee three straight years. More to the point, he was one of the most highly coveted line prospects in the country—and one of the more mysterious ones. You see, Means didn't really have much to say about where he chose to go to college. Lang, the Trezevant coach, essentially made the decision for him.

Lang is a thirty-year-old high school football coach in Memphis. A native of Greenville, Mississippi, he is a friendly man. As he said, "I can get along with a stop sign." Lang played football at Alcorn State, he says. He was on the same

190

team with Steve McNair, who is the quarterback for the Tennessee Titans. He shows me a lavender-colored class ring to prove the point. Lang was a nose-guard in college. Though he's getting a little soft around the middle, he doesn't seem quite beefy enough to be a former noseguard. Lang is married; his wife is a paralegal who's working on her law degree. The couple has two children—one who's two years old and the other, says Lang, "nine or ten."

Trezevant High School is a public school located on the north side of Memphis, in the Frazier neighborhood. With 1,400 students, it's a large 4A-classification school. Only 5A schools are bigger. Trezevant looks like a lot of urban schools—it's old and architecturally bleak. The facade is mostly dull brick. There are weather-beaten windows and rickety chainlink fences. The grounds around the school are mostly dirt, relieved by a few patches of grass. In the distance lies the football field—a green swath bracketed by bleachers. There are metal goal posts and a blocking sled—its plastic pads are torn in a few places. I wonder if Means is responsible for the tattered look of the sled. The kid has a reputation for being a bruising tackler.

Lang and his assistant, Milton Kirk, share a little office beside the Trezevant basketball court. Barbells and sundry weightlifting equipment is scattered around the gym. In the evening lots of kids—some Trezevant students, some not—whoop it up on the basketball court (no nets on the rims). You can hear them whooping from the parking lot—it's one of those predictable suburban sounds. The walls in Lang's office are concrete. There are a few wooden plaques along with pictures of his football team, the Trezevant Bears, clad in purple-and-white uniforms. There is a little poem, courtesy of Crimson Tide football, called "One Day at a Time." It begins: "Don't worry about yesterday or tomorrow." The office floor is cement. There is a small couch, a wooden desk, a small refrigerator, and a space heater whose coils were glowing when I visited in November 1999. There is a bottle of Pepto-Bismol on Lang's desk, and on his door a sticker that reads No Deals. Lang has worked at Trezevant for six years, and coached the football team for four. When he first started as coach, he says, there were only about thirty kids on the Bears. He has since boosted partici-pation to about fifty students annually—and gotten the team into the playoffs every year. The team practices every day in the fall from 4:00 P.M. "until they get it right," says the coach.

I spoke to Lang several times on the phone last summer and fall—and then paid him a visit. While most prospects of Means's stature get recruited heavily, there was talk early in the recruiting season that Means was headed to Alabama. Tennessee and Georgia fans speculated that the fix was in for Albert Means. Means's recruitment had been "arranged." Was there any truth to the rumors? Or were the rival fans just peeved that they hadn't had much success lately with top Memphis prospects? The number one prospect in Memphis the last three years has chosen to go to Alabama—and of the three, only Means bothered to take any recruiting trips. Such a situation certainly merited a look-see, especially since Jamie Newberg, who runs a recruiting service called Border Wars, called Lang's Svengali-like relationship with Means "disgusting, the worst I ever seen."

Late August, 1999

My first phone chat with Lynn Lang. The coach has already had countless conversations about Means, mostly with recruiters, but he seems more than happy to talk. Lang enjoys bragging about Means's athletic ability—and about his own paternalistic role in the boy's life. Means was seventeen when the coach and I first spoke. Means lives in a Memphis neighborhood called Raleigh, which is not far from Trezevant. According to Lang, "Albert is one of seven or eight kids, so sometimes he stays with me. Albert doesn't have a father, so I'm Daddy." Means's mother does not work, and apparently has little money. Lang makes it clear that when it comes to Albert's recruitment, "I'm taking care of this 100 percent by myself—total control." He says that nobody talks to Albert without first getting clearance from him. "Recruiters call me," says the coach. "I generally don't let people talk to him. I bring him by the office once in a while." Newberg once tried to get hold of Means at his home, circumventing Lang. Means's mother answered the phone, then called Lang to report the transgression. Newberg prides himself on his ability to cultivate relationships with top prospects—the better to follow their recruitment over the course of several months. But when Lang heard that Newberg had tried to contact Means directly, he cut off the analyst. Newberg would have no access to Lang or Means.

Lang and his star player had spent part of the summer on the road. They attended four different college football camps—at Nebraska, Georgia, Texas, and Kentucky. Lang drove his 1995 Camero to the camps, and the two spent three days at each, during which time Means showed off his considerable skills and Lang helped out with coaching duties, receiving a modest amount of money for his efforts at each camp. (Colleges typically pay high school coaches $200 to $300 for a couple days of works—but *some* schools give *some* coaches more than that, which has become a controversial issue.)

To break the ice at the start of our first conversation, I tell Lang that Means is considered an excellent football prospect. "Of cooourrrse," responds the coach, stretching out the second word like a rubber band. For the coach, it was patently obvious from the start that Means was a star. Lang answers many questions by saying, "Of cooourrrse." He continued: "Albert is beyond a good high school player. At Nebraska the kids wore pads and he beat everybody down there in one-on-one drills. People were getting in line at the camp to get his autograph. I am serious. The way he moves for his size is unbelievable."

In high school, Means played middle linebacker, defensive end, and offensive tackle. But, says Lang, "on the college level he will be a defensive lineman, and in the pros, too. That's what [Ohio State Head Coach John] Cooper said. Cooper told me he doesn't believe Albert can play for him for more than two years. He's definitely going to make it [to the pros], barring injury. There is no doubt about that. He's an excellent player, and a good kid." He describes Means as "pleasant and quiet. He doesn't say two words, but when he puts the pads on he means business. He doesn't have any fat on him. You won't find many kids with the build he has. I know, I'm a coach. I have to stop him from hitting in practice because he can hurt peple. He's a punisher—a natural punisher."

Lang says that he accompanied Means to the camps because "this kid has never been anywhere. He's never been outside of Memphis. Whenever any of my players goes anywhere, I will be there with them. I want to show him what's going on, see the big picture. The big thing about me is, I've been there. I know what Albert's facing [with recruiters]. A lot of parents have not been to college; they don't about [recruiters] pulling you this way and that. If a kid doesn't have a coach like myself who shields him and shows him what is important, he doesn't know what is going on."

I ask Lang who will decide where Means goes to college—him or Means. This is a tricky question, as evidenced by his response. "The decision will be totally his—as long as he satisfies my [criteria]. I will have an influence. It could come to that. He's kind of thinking in the same mode as I am about what to look for at the schools. So when he talks to guidance counselors, he asks them legitimate questions. He knows how to handle himself." And what is Lang/Means looking for in a college? "The first thing is academics," says the coach. "That's very important. Albert has about a 3.0 grade point average, and he made 20 on his ACT, so he's ready. He will qualify. Second, socially, he has to fit in off the field as well as on. I want a place where he will be accepted without the pads on. And the third thing I'm looking for is the player-coach relationship. He needs someone to confide in if he has a problem."

According to Lang, "Means hasn't narrowed down his colleges yet. He just went out this summer and had fun. I wanted him to experience different environments. I drove him to all the campuses." Why did he choose the camps at Nebraska, Georgia, Kentucky, and Texas? Simple: "They were the first four that contacted me about working at the camps. Every school in the country wanted me to come, but I had already filled my days."

I ask Lang if the recruiting pressure is a distraction to Means. "It's not bur-

densome because I keep a lot of pressure off him—shield him from things."
But he enjoys the attention? "Of cooourrrse. What kid his age wouldn't?"
Trezevant classes start in a few days.

September 7, 1999

Lang tells me that some recruiters have had their eyes on Means since he was
a sophomore. By now the Trezevant player has received enough recruiting letters to fill two large plastic mailboxes. Rodney Garner, Georgia's recruiting
coordinator, has sent Means a card with a quote from Vince Lombardi. It
read: *The difference between a successful person and others is not a lack of
strength, not a lack of knowledge, but rather a lack of will.* Garner goes on to
wish Means good luck with his exams and his last high school football season.

Besides Garner's note, there's a card from former Georgia defensive coach
Eric Ramsey. It reads:

> Dear Albert,
> I want to wish you the very best this upcoming season in all you do.
> Remember that discipline, dedication, desire, heart, fight, tenacity, and
> toughness are what got you where you are—and above all God giving you
> these abilities. I look forward to recruiting you to our "go get 'em" style of
> defense.
>
> Go Dawgs!
> Coach Ramsey

"He gets something in the mail every day," says Lang, "sometimes two or
three letters in a row from the same coach. He looks at his mail, and once he
does that, he can dispose of it." He says that he and Means talk every day after
practice for thirty minutes. "We talk about life, going to class, growing up, not
just football. Right now, he's the big man on campus, and I have to keep [suc-
cess] from going to his head." Means was All-State as a junior. "I make him
understand that he still has to work. He tries to impress me. I pat him on the
back, but still try to keep him motivated. A hungry dog is a good dog, because
he wants to eat."

The coach tells me that Albert can bench-press 400 pounds. That's pretty
strong for a high school player, I suggest. "Of cooourrrse. He'd live in the
weight room if I let him." Lang says he likes to play Albert at middle linebacker so that recruiters can see how well he moves for his size. He says that
Trezevant has had some good football players in the past—including Xavier

Crawford, a running back who signed with Memphis—"but nobody of this magnitude."

On September 1, coaches are allowed to call prospects or their guardians. Lang says that several assistant coaches called him on that day. Representatives from Kentucky, Alabama, Michigan State, Auburn, UCLA, Nebraska, and Texas all rang him at the office and raved about Means. So did Georgia Coach Jim Donnan. "He's the only head coach who called on the first day," says Lang. What did Donnan say? "He said he wanted Albert." Lang insists that "nobody will know where he's going till signing day in February. He doesn't have a choice because I'm not going to let him make a choice. That's the whole process. The family is not involved."

Trezevant has won its first two games, beating Greenville (Mississippi) High School and Memphis East. Against East, says Lang, Means played middle linebacker. He had thirteen solo tackles, two assists, caused a fumble, and recovered it in the end zone. "He played excellent. The biggest thing about Albert is, he's going to give it his all. He will empty his tank. I don't have to worry about him too much. I critique him pretty hard, especially on the defensive side of the ball. I tell my players, 'If you want to take a break, make it for all three plays.'"

The coach says his players watch a Tennessee national championship highlight tape to get motivated before their games. In addition, he and Means watch tapes of Trezevant games together, and on Saturday watch college games on TV. Lang says no recruiters are talking personally to Means at this time. "I don't want him to break with anything he's doing. I'm sheltering him right now. It's game week. I want him to concentrate on football." Indeed, the biggest game of the season is just ahead: Trezevant plays Melrose, its biggest Memphis rival. "I believe we are more physical than they are," says the coach. "If we can slow down their offense, we'll be okay."

September 28

Two weeks earlier, Trezevant beat Melrose by a score of 24-22. "The score wasn't that close," said Lang. "We were ahead 16 to nothing through three quarters." Trezevant's size was apparently too much for Melrose's run-and-shoot offense. Means, again playing middle linebacker, had a strong game: ten solo tackles, a pass interception, and two sacks. For his effort, he was named Memphis area Player of the Week—the fourth time he received that honor. There were about 12,000 people at the game, played at Charles Greenhill Stadium, among them about twenty-five college coaches. They were watching not only Means, but also another talented Trezevant player, running back–cornerback prospect Leonard Burress, along with Melrose lineman Mondre Dickerson. Lang said that he talked to about ten coaches before and after the game—including representatives from Georgia, Kentucky, Alabama, Tennessee, and Arkansas. "No coaches talked to Albert. I don't let anybody talk to him right now." He said the coaches were "amazed at how graceful [Means] is for his size. They said he could come and start for them right now." He says he knows some of the coaches, including Ivy Williams at Alabama—who was recruiting Means.

Lang and Means had just returned from a visit to Lexington, Kentucky, where they watched the Wildcats play Florida. "It was a good environment," said Lang of Lexington, "a good setting. We talked to the players, checked out Kentucky's facilities, which are excellent." At this point, said Lang, "Albert's mind is wide open. He hasn't narrowed anything down. He hasn't got to that point yet."

October 21

I meet Lynn Lang in his Trezevant office. He is wearing Nike workout shoes, a Kentucky football T-shirt, and nylon track pants. It's late, about 8:00 P.M., but Lang works late most nights. "I'm happy doin' what I'm doin'," says Lang of his job. "There's no pressure here, except what I put on myself." The talk quickly turns to Means, who has left school for the evening. I'd missed him. "He's never had any luxuries," says Lang of his star player. "Everything he has, I have to give to him—clothes, underwear, everything." Lang clears up a couple of hazy points about Means. He's one of eight kids—seven boys and a girl. His father "pops up once a year or so, but I have no reason to communicate with him." Lang says Means "never gets into any trouble. I shelter him from a lot of things. Recruiting can be overwhelming, but it comes with the territory." He mentions Newberg trying to reach Means at his home, and views this as an affront. "I'll be respectful of anyone," he says, "but they must be respectful of me. If you try to go behind my back, you'll have to deal with me. The kid ain't gonna move unless I tell him."

Lang mentions that he has talked to many head coaches, including Ohio State's John Cooper, Donnan of Georgia, Phillip Fulmer of Tennessee, Hal Mumme at Kentucky. I mention to Lang that I attended the University of Tennessee. I do so because SEC folk are a suspicious bunch: they assume that everyone has an agenda, and that anyone asking questions must be a spy or toady for some school. It becomes clear that Lang seems to have a chip on his shoulder about Tennessee. That's his perogative. I listen. "Tennessee treats

Memphis like it's not part of the state," he says. Memphis, in fact, is a long way from Knoxville—about a six-hour drive. Memphis sits on the Mississippi River, at a point where four states (Arkansas, Mississippi, Alabama, and Tennessee) converge. The city is home to lots of alumni from Mississippi and Tennessee, along with healthy contingents of Arkansas and Alabama graduates.

Lang, Milton Kirk, and I chat amiably about college football for a half-hour. We all agree that Texas football is overrated—both high school and college. We chew over various SEC topics. Lang makes a point of noting that Tennessee has lost the top player in Memphis the last three years. "Alabama has come in here and gotten the top recruit the last three years." He then pulls a VCR into the office and we watch tape of number 77—big Albert Means. "You're gonna see something," says Kirk. After Means's junior season, Lang put together a highlight tape and sent it to thirty-two universities. Most got back to him within a week, the coaches drooling over Means and ready to offer him a scholarship. "Every play he's ever made I put on tape," says Lang. "Some of the things he does on the field still amaze me."

The tape begins. After such glowing remarks, I expect to see a Superman on the field. Means is no Superman, but to my untrained eyes he seems good. He is certainly bigger than nearly all the high school players in Memphis. He's not as nimble as I'd imagined, but then Means weighs 310 pounds and he's playing linebacker. The kid moves reasonably well for his size, and when he tackles ball carriers, they go down *hard*. He flattens them.

Lang and Kirk, who have no doubt seen this tape 100 times, are practically coming out of their seats with excitement. "Some say he's the number one recruit in Tennessee, and you can see why on that play," says Kirk. Adds Lang: "Look at him run down that ball carrier. Look at the big guy run!" Then: "Watch him run down the receiver on that hitch pattern!" And: "After he hit that running back, he didn't want the ball any more that night." Lang says that if he plays Means at nose tackle, "all the other team does is try to cut him"— meaning dive at his legs. "They can't block him up top. He's the type of athlete who will have to play fairly quickly. He's a natural defensive lineman, but I stood him up to show people how good he is. He could be the starting defensive end at Bama next year."

After the tape, Lang and Kirk talk about kids. They must be taught early, the coaches say, about the importance of studying and staying out of trouble. "If I can't get a kid to listen to me by the ninth or tenth grade," says Lang, "he's not going to make it." He makes all his players fill out biweekly "progress reports," listing their grades, classes missed, school attendance, that sort of thing. "We don't believe in kids with talent [ignoring] the program," says Kirk. "You've got to do all the other things. Coach Lang gets 'em when they're young and instills discipline." Adds the coach: "I'm from the old school. I don't believe in pacifying kids, no matter how much talent they have." Trezevant players who goof off, or don't listen, are made to run extra after practice.

Lang tells me that he and Means will be going to the Alabama-Tennessee game this weekend. He says that they will later attend the Tennessee-Notre Dame game. Before I leave his office, Lang cuts to the chase: he tells me that Means "will probably end up going to Alabama or Tennessee—or Kentucky. Kentucky is still in there." He had volunteered the information—there was no prompting. We talk a while longer and break for the evening. I'll return to Trezevant in the morning to meet Means. Before leaving the office, Lang asks me in a sincere tone of voice, "So what do you think about Alabama?" "Fine place," I respond, "but I must stay neutral on all this."

The next morning, I drive back to Trezevant and meet Albert Means. He stops by the office with a couple of friends. He's wearing a blue flannel shirt with a Jim Donnan Football Camp T-shirt on underneath, cargo pants, tennis shoes, and a straw hat. He's got a key around his neck—the key to his house. He is carrying a wood paddle that looks like a boat oar and has the names of Trezevant's football players scribbled all over it. His name is on it, too: "Big Means." It's one of Lang's motivational tools for his players—they each carry it around periodically as a "reminder" to work hard and stay straight. Means is bulky, but not heavy. He takes a seat and answers questions politely, in almost a whisper. I must lean forward to make out the words.

I ask, How's your senior season going?

"Excellent."

I hear you've been a good player for a few years.

"I'd say three years, ever since the tenth grade."

Can anybody block you?

"No, sir."

Not yet?

"No, sir."

Do you read all this mail?

"When I get a chance."

Do you have a favorite college?

"Not really. Coach is helping me with that."

When will you decide where you want to go to school?

"Probably at the last minute."

Do you talk to college coaches when they call?

"Yes, sir."

What do they say?

"They basically just ask me questions about how I'm doin' and stuff. They ask me about life and my grades—how I'm doin' in school. They ask me about the season. Basically, just that."

What do you think about all this attention?

"I really don't pay it no mind. I try not to get too stressful about it."

How's school?

"It's doin' good."

Have you got any classes today?

"I just have one class today, English."

What's your favorite class?

"I'd say English."

Got a girlfriend?

"No, sir."

Are you still growing?

"Yes, sir."

Do you think college football will be tougher than high school?

"Well, not really. I believe I could play now, but I guess I gotta wait till I'm a freshman in college."

Has Coach Lang been helpful to you?

"He's like an extra dad for me. He's helped me through this recruiting stuff ever since tenth grade. If I need something and he's got it, he'll give it to me. He's been a big part of this for me."

And with that, he stands up with his paddle, exchanges a few words with his coach, and strolls out of the office and, presumably, off to class. And I take my leave of Memphis. On the way out of town, I see a car with a bumper sticker and a small drawing of the American flag. It reads "You burn it, I'll burn you." And on the radio, I hear this song: "I'm walkin' in Memphis, with my feet ten feet off the ground. Do I really feel the way I feel? . . . I saw the ghost of Elvis on Union Avenue . . . followed him up to the gates of Graceland and watched him walk right through. . . . They've got catfish on the table, gospel in the air, Reverend Green will be glad to see you when you haven't got a prayer."

October 26

Lang and Means are back after watching Tennessee beat Alabama in Tuscaloosa. "It was a lovely visit," says the coach. There were a lot of prospects at the game. They stood on the sidelines during pregame warmups, then moved up to the stands on the Alabama side of the field to watch the game itself. (I attended the game myself.) Lang said that Alabama Coach Mike DuBose talked to Means on Saturday. DuBose told Means that Alabama was interested in him, and that he (Means) was the best defensive lineman he'd ever seen. DuBose talked about the university, and about the Alabama football tradition. Lang interrupted the coach, telling DuBose: "Hey, I already know about your tradition." I ask Lang if he likes DuBose. "Of cooourrrrrse. I think he has a lot to offer. He seemed energetic about the program. I think he's getting things headed in the right direction." Means and some of the prospects (but apparently not all) were invited to spend time in the Alabama locker room. Lang says that he spoke to Tennessee assistant coach Pat Washington before the game, and both Washington and Phillip Fulmer after the game. According to Lang, he told the Vol coaches that he and Means would travel to Knoxville in a couple of weeks to watch the Notre Dame game.

Tom Culpepper of Border Wars has interviewed Lang and posted the Trezevant coach's comments on the Border Wars Web site. Lang tells Culpepper that "Albert had a great time at Alabama. We were surprised by the spirit of the fans. Albert thinks he can play right away at Alabama." Lang tells Culpepper that Kentucky, Georgia, Texas, and Tennessee are still in the mix for Means's signature on signing day. Culpepper writes: "In fact, Lang mentioned the possibility of a late announcement. He then quotes Lang as saying, "We're going to Tennessee for the Notre Dame game. We're a long way from making an announcement. It probably won't happen before Signing Day." Some of what Lang tells Culpepper is obvious hooey: Lang is *not* a long way from a decision, and Means is *not* going to sign with Texas or Georgia—despite the fact that Leon Perry, a Georgia assistant, is working assiduously to "get in" (a recruiting expression that means curry favor) with Lang. Means is almost certainly not going to Kentucky, either—despite the fact that Kentucky has impressed him. I say this based on what Lang told me with evident candor a week earlier. Lang tells me that his other Division 1 prospect, Burress, may go to Kentucky.

November 29

Lang and Means did not visit Knoxville for the Tennessee–Notre Dame game. I ask the coach why he canceled the trip. He nervously starts casting around in his mind for an answer. "I believe I may have lost that game," he responds vaguely. "Something happened, and I didn't make it. Albert got sick or something like that. I didn't want to put him on the road. We'd been going somewhere every weekend and he needed a break, that's all."

Lang tells me that Means will be making four official visits in the months ahead—to Alabama, Clemson, Kentucky, and Georgia. And Tennessee? "I haven't heard from them in awhile. I don't know why. Maybe they are stacked up with defensive linemen. (Dan Brooks, UT's recruiting coordinator, later tells me that the Vols did not chase Means very ardently, but he just huffs in frustration when I ask him why.)

I ask Lang if he knows Logan Young, the Alabama booster. I mention the suspicions among some UT fans about Young's involvement in the recruitment of Albert Means. "My response is that I don't know who Logan Young is," says the coach. " Second, if you ask me Tennessee people do a poor job of recruiting the Memphis area. They treat Memphis like it's a whole 'nother state—that's the way I see it. People think that because it's Tennessee, that kids automatically want to go there. Go pull up the graduation rate for Tennessee. Back before this process started, someone sent me a piece of paper showing their graduation rate—and they were at the bottom for graduating black athletes. [He later says that the letter came from Florida State.] They want to address something? They have to address that. Most of these players are coming from poverty and are out of the mainstream. You're going to take them and throw them into the mainstream? That doesn't suit me."

Lang goes on: "Football doesn't last long, let's be realistic. My main thing is that Albert's prepared academically to take care of himself. That is the big picture. Football is just part of it—it's not the end of the world. If he goes out and breaks his leg, what's going to happen to him? Let's talk about the whole thing. He's only gonna spend 10 percent of his time on the field. How will he fit in with everybody else? Tennessee needs to work on the academic part, plus the way they recruit Memphis. That is without a doubt." I ask the coach if he liked Pat Washington, the UT coach who recruited Means. "Of coourrrrrse. My biggest problem is why can't another school just do a better job of recruiting?"

Lang starts talking about Mississippi kids, who he says have been "left by the wayside academically. The biggest thing Mississippi has got going for it is its junior colleges." He mentions a few junior colleges in Mississippi—Hinds, Northwest, Northeast—and notes that Billy Brewer, the former Ole Miss coach, "got all of his linebackers from junior colleges." He is impressed by that fact. He criticizes the state of Tennessee for not having more junior colleges, and believes that is the reason why UT recruits players from other states. This obviously is a sensitive issue with the Trezevant coach.

Lang returns, unprompted, to the topic of Logan Young. "I've never in my life met him. I've never met him, never talked to him on the phone, don't know him. The University of Alabama is recruiting Albert Means. I like the way they recruit, and I like the way Kentucky recruits and Georgia, but for somebody to sit back and say something like this [the Young rumors], I have a problem with that. That's wrong. Albert's mild-mannered, never been in trouble, so that is wrong. I believe these Tennessee people need to stop pointing fingers and get their act together." He then begins talking about the UT football team. "I have seen them, they are average. They should have lost to Memphis. They remind me of the Oakland Raiders; they have a bunch of talent, but it's not organized right. Can you name me one time they got a sack against Florida? That defensive end from Florida, he made All-America in one game."

Lang's anti-Tennessee diatribe ends there. He mentions that Means will take official visits in the winter—to Clemson, Arkansas, Georgia, and either Kentucky or Texas. "There is no clear-cut winner yet," he says. "Everybody is neck and neck. Normally, I like to have a kid make a decision after he's made all his official visits and sees everything about a university. I like what they're doing at Kentucky. That's a program that's on the move. I like Coach Mumme and their coaches, and the same thing is true with Georgia. Donnan is a couple of players away. A lot of kids make a decision before they have a chance to look at the whole picture."

I wonder why Lang persists in pretending that Means's decision is still wide open. It clearly isn't. Having ruled out Tennessee, it's reasonably clear by now that Means will sign with Alabama. One needn't be Sherlock Holmes to make that deduction. Lang may have kept on with the "it's still a horse race" charade for two reasons. First, it's a way to stretch out the recruiting process—and the attention he's receiving from various schools and recruiting analysts. Lang's mind is probably made up by now, and probably was long before late November. But like a lot of parents, coaches, or guardians, he's come to enjoy being courted. The second reason is that there is a tendency among recruiting targets—and *Lang* has always been the target, not Means—to tell recruiters what they want to hear. Both probably applied to Lang.

December 11, 1999

Lang confirms the obvious. He tells Border Wars that "Alabama is number one right now. Kentucky and Georgia are co-number twos. Clemson would be three; Florida, four; and Mississippi State, number five. Culpepper asks Lang why he skipped the Tennessee–Notre Dame game. "We haven't heard from them, so we went to the Alcorn State–Mississippi Valley State game instead." Lang added that "we're going to the Georgia-Auburn game in Athens this weekend."

December 18, 1999

Trezevant's season is over. The team lost in the second round of the playoffs to East High School, 22-14. The team finished with a 9-2 record. Means had an excellent year: he finished the season with eighty-five solo tackles, nine sacks, three interceptions, caused four fumbles. He is named Prep Player of the Year by the Memphis Quarterback Club. He is named All State in Tennessee for the third straight year. He's also named a *Parade* magazine All American—a top national honor.

Lang and Means skipped the Georgia-Auburn game.

Means himself tells Jeremy Crabtree of Rivals.com that "I'm leaning on my coach to help me make a decision. I'd say I'm still looking at Alabama, Clemson, Florida, Georgia, Kentucky, Tennessee, Mississippi State, and Texas." (Eight schools!) "But I'm going to sit down with Coach Lang next week, and he's going to help me pick my final five." Means adds that he's looking for a "good coaching staff and a good atmosphere."

February 3, 1999

After taking three official visits, to Alabama, Kentucky, and Georgia, Means signs with Alabama. Until the end, Lang maintained that the school choice would not be made until the very end of the recruiting process. It was a game. On Signing Day, Means sat at a table in the Trezevant auditorium. About 200 people, including his mother, attended the show. On the table in front of Means were three caps—one from Alabama, one from Kentucky, and one from Georgia. To signal his choice, Means would pick one and put it on his head. After a pause, he grabbed the Alabama hat. The crowd applauded. The recruitment of Albert Means was over.

February 5, 1999

I ask Lang if Albert is happy with (his?) the decision. "Of coourrrrrse. It was Alabama all the way for him. When he went down there, coach [for some reason, Lang calls me "coach" throughout this conversation], and heard Bear Bryant's voice . . . well, the history and tradition pretty much got him. The academics, the social environment, all that played a part. The big part is tradition; you can see what they have accomplished." He calls Ivy Williams, his chief contact at Alabama, "an excellent recruiter. He sells the university real well."

What did he think of Georgia and its recruiter, Leon Perry? "I liked Perry, but they are still in the building process. I wanted Albert to be surrounded by people at his level. I didn't want him coming out of high school and being a man. I want him to work to be a man. If you want a thoroughbred to run, you gotta surround him with other thoroughbreds, not a bunch of mules." (Ouch!) "I want him to step out with other people on his level."

I mention that Bama has stockpiled a lot of linemen. Is he worried about playing time for Means? "I got the number one lineman in the country; why would I worry about playing time? Alabama is losing two starting linemen. Albert will be starting as a freshman—you can put your money on that. He's six-foot-six, three hundred and fifteen pounds, and runs a 4.9 [second] forty. Competition brings out the best in some players. He's a house that can move. He can chase down a running back. Everything he's ever gotten, he's had to fight for. I want his college process to be the same way. I want him to work for what he gets, fight for it. I don't want anything handed to him. This is my son."

May 2000

I first became interested in Lynn Lang because certain SEC fans, who live in Memphis, started mentioning his name on the Internet. They were suspicious about the recruitment of Albert Means. They suggested that Lang would receive a new vehicle—specifically, a Ford Expedition—from an Alabama booster in exchange for sending Means to Tuscaloosa. Why would anyone pay attention to such insidious insinuations? Because, first, there is a long history of recruiting shenanigans and rules-breaking in college football—especially in the South, and especially in Memphis. Because, second, the people making the accusations were longtime residents of Memphis and extremely familiar with the city's recruiting "culture." And because, third, high school football coaches don't make much money, and Expeditions are expensive. If a high school coach were to suddenly acquire an Expedition, right around the climax of the recruiting season—well, it would be a rather interesting coincidence.

Last fall Lang scoffed at the idea that his intentions were anything but pure. He was driving a Camero at the time. After the recruiting season, I was told by an irritated Georgia fan that Lynn Lang was suddenly driving a new Ford Expedition. No way, I thought. I called the coach and asked him. Lang confirmed that he had recently acquired a 1999 Expedition. Base price for an Expedition: at least $37,000. Lang said that bought the vehicle himself—with his $35,000 salary. "I make enough to pay for my own truck," he insisted. "I work every day. I go to work at 7:20 A.M. and get off at 8:00 P.M. This is the only thing I have to pay for. It's not paid for; I have a note every month. I don't have any kids." Huh? He'd told me months ago that he's had two kids! He went on: "If you can't afford an American car, what can you afford? I had a ball player who signed with Kentucky. I don't hear anybody saying anything about that." Logan Young? "I've heard his name, but that's all I know about that. I grew up a fan of Alabama and Bear Bryant and if I want to send a player there, I can. Those Georgia people should just line up. We'll see who wins the next national championship."

Lynn Lang and Albert Means

Lang went on to say that he decided against sending Means to Georgia because "they have too many problems on the coaching staff. There is too much dissension. Kids can see and feel that. That's what we felt when we were down there [for a visit]. They weren't together." (There has been some coaching turmoil at Georgia. Head Coach Jim Donnan has been casting around for a defensive coordinator. Two years ago he demoted Joe Kines and hired Eric Ramsey away from Tennessee to run his defense. That didn't work out to Donnan's satisfaction, so a few months ago he demoted Ramsey, which sparked a confrontation between the two men in Donnan's office. Ramsey has since left Georgia.)

The Trezevant coach confessed that the recruiting process "had gotten tiresome," adding: "Now I can go back to being a nobody. It's all over." And so it was. What to make of Lynn Lang and the Means situation? When we first started talking, I was put off by Lynn Lang. He seemed blustery, a braggart. He clearly had a portion of his self-esteem tied up with Means. But over time I grew to like him. Beneath the occasional blather, he seems a more than decent man. Lang, like nearly all urban high school coaches, does good work. He imparts important values to kids who often grow up without positive role models. That's what he did with Albert Means, apparently. He mentored the kid, served as his surrogate dad, and for that he deserves praise. Was the coach right to tightly control every aspect of the kid's recruitment, as he clearly did? That is debatable. Parents or guardians strongly influence their children's choice of colleges—and in Means's case, Lang was the de facto guardian. So long as he chose Alabama for the right reasons, Lang's motives should be above reproach.

And they would be—except for the Expedition. What are we to make of that Expedition? Was it pure coincidence, mere happenstance, that a man of modest means decides to buy an expensive new sport utility vehicle—the exact same vehicle that cynics pointed to from the beginning—at just the time when his star player decides where he's going to college? It's possible, yes, but the timing of the purchase (not to mention the expensive pricetag of the vehicle itself) is very curious. Were Means now a student at, say, Western Kentucky, would Lang be driving a new Expedition? Ummmm. Or is there, as many SEC folk suspect, something rotten in Memphis? Will we ever know the truth? As they say on *The X-Files*, the truth is out there.

TWELVE

LIONS AND TIGERS AND BEARS (OH, MY!): RATING THE COACHES

We are a nation of armchair quarterbacks, and we like lists. We thrive on making quick judgments about athletes, coaches, and teams. It's part of our entertainment-oriented, sports-obsessed culture. During the run up to January 1, 2000, we saw rankings of the century's most influential people, the century's best athletes, the most significant entertainers and musicians, and so on. Each year the critics rank the best movies, and the worst, and fashion mavens regale us with lists of the best (and worst) dressed. There are now plenty of services that rank college and high school football and basketball players. Much of this list-mania is fatuous—but also undeniably fun. Sports fans love to banter.

In this spirit, I rank the current crop of SEC head coaches. Actually, rather than rank them, I have divided them up into large groups, or tiers, which seems a better way to separate the gold from the gravel. I mean, who's to say why somebody is stuck in the number eight slot, and someone else, number nine? On what do I base these tier rankings? Good question. Obviously, win-loss records are a reflection of coaching prowess—but, in my estimation, not the final word. In fact, records can be misleading. Going into the 2000 SEC football season, South Carolina had the nation's longest losing streak—twenty-one games. But there is no doubt in my mind that Lou Holtz is an excellent coach. Lots of coaches can win with talent—the tradition at universities like Alabama and Tennessee is almost self-perpetuating. But you really find out who can

Rating the Coaches

coach when a team's talent level is mediocre, as at Vanderbilt. I have also factored in such issues as how well a coach manages his program (crucial to success), his attitude toward player discipline, his abilities as a recruiter, and his personal traits. Toss in a little personal bias and you've got . . . another list!

The Lions (Top Tier)

1. Steve Spurrier, Florida. He's fidgety in person, a savvy play-caller on the sidelines, and a poor loser—but Spurrier still gets the nod as the SEC's best coach. But his aura may be fading. The Gators haven't won an SEC championship in three years, and last year's team really struggled down the stretch. He's beginning to seem a little too impatient with his players. I still like Spurrier for the job he did at Duke—that was telling. The Gator leader—better known as The Head Ball Coach—is a Heisman winner, acknowledged offensive guru, and passing-game perfectionist who turned a hard-nosed, run-oriented conference on its head by flinging the ball. He has won five SEC championships and one national title (1996). A loyal Florida man, Spurrier has forced opposing coaches to recruit good cornerbacks—or die. The Head Ball Coach is hard on quarterbacks, but can turn middling or above-average talent into stars (for instance, Danny Wuerffel). The question now is: has the league caught up with him? Florida's passing game last year was abysmal at times—and the Gators played horribly in the SEC championship game. Is Spurrier slowing down? The next year or two will tell us a lot. If Brock Berlin develops, Spurrier could be poised for another stretch of SEC dominance. If not, well, he might start playing even *more* golf. The 1990s will be a hard act to follow.

2. Lou Holtz, South Carolina. How can a guy who has won *one* game in two years, who was *winless* last year (zip and 11) make the top tier? Easy—his lifetime record qualifies him for this spot. Holtz, who is equal parts Woody Allen and Woody Hayes, has won everywhere but USC—William & Mary, North Carolina State, Minnesota, and Notre Dame. And let's remember, those first three schools are not exactly football factories. He stalks the sidelines during games, then afterwards enjoys making self-deprecating quips about his team's performance. Probably the best all-around teacher in the SEC—and by far the most articulate coach.

3. **Phillip Fulmer, Tennessee.** This former offensive lineman is in many ways the antithesis of Spurrier. He is low-key and easy to underestimate. Beneath his broad exterior, he is ultracompetitive (as every major-college coach has to be). He and Spurrier dominated the SEC in the late 1990s. Fulmer's strength is that he's a relentless recruiter, which Tennessee needs to compete with its more talent-rich neighboring states. He's also put together a very solid staff, which together with the talent influx has transformed Tennessee from a good program into a powerhouse: back-to-back SEC titles (in 1997 and 1998) and the Vols first national championship (1998) in fifty years. He also sets fairly high moral standards for his players. Fulmer's weakness is that he's not an exceptional strategist—and he can't beat Spurrier. Yeah, the Vols beat the Gators in 1998, but not impressively. They seem never to play well against Florida—which is their biggest game. He may be loyal to a fault to certain players; in last year's Florida game, Fulmer used a senior kicker who clearly did not have the strongest leg on the team, and it cost him. So long as he keeps recruiting, the Vols will remain formidable.

4. **Woody Widenhofer, Vanderbilt.** This guy deserves respect. Despite being the SEC's academic standard-bearer, Vandy was the SEC's most-improved team last year. The Commodores lost tough games against both Georgia and Florida. Widenhofer is a bona fide defensive genius. He can shut *anybody* down, and has consistently caused problems for offensive high fliers like Florida and Tennessee. In four games against Vanderbilt, Peyton Manning threw *one* touchdown pass. Last year, Florida players said that the Vandy defense knew their offense better than they did. He coached Jack Lambert and the Pittsburgh "steel curtain" defense in its heyday. Enough said. He also gets high marks for being very accessible with the media. He may never win the SEC, or even post a winning SEC record, but he is a very good coach in an unenviable situation.

The Tigers (Tier Two)

1. **Houston Nutt, Arkansas.** He has a funny name, but there's nothing cute about his Hogs. Nutt is a no-nonsense Little Rock native (and former Arkansas quarterback) who appreciates power football. The Hogs beat Tennessee last year to knock the Vols out of the national title hunt. The Hogs were 8-4 in 1999, which was considered a rebuilding year.

Rating the Coaches

Nutt coached for four years at Murray State and was a former 1AA Coach of the Year. He has done a lot with a program that has tradition, but with the wrong leader could very easily be a disaster. Not a lot of kids are clamoring to spend four years in Fayetteville, Arkansas.

2. Tommy Tuberville, Auburn. Tuberville is a fiery taskmaster who took over a motley, undertalented Auburn squad last year and whipped LSU (hastening the demise of Gerry DiNardo). Before taking over at Auburn, Tuberville compiled a 25-20 record in four years at Ole Miss, which was on probation when he started. Tuberville, who coached with Jimmy Johnson at Miami, lied to the Ole Miss administration about his interest in the Auburn job; then, after moving to the Plains, kicked six kids off scholarship because he didn't think they could play. He pretended to have signed twenty-six players in 1995 at Ole Miss—but actually listed twelve walk-ons as signees. Ummm. With talent, Tuberville will give hated in-state Alabama all it can handle. He's old-school, tough, and *he can coach*.

3. Jackie Sherrill, Mississippi State. What can you say about a guy who has the balls of a bull cut off at a practice to motivate his team? Who knows why he did it. Sherrill is an old-school survivor. He spent five years at Pittsburgh, then seven at Texas A&M before getting sacked. He's got a career record of 169-89-4—the eighth-highest victory total in college history. He's built a solid winner at what is easily the most obscure university in the SEC. Does Starkville really exist—or is it just a town in a Stephen King novel? (It's a joke!) In nine years at Mississippi State, his SEC record is 36-34-1. Sherrill's speciality is finding the biggest offensive linemen in football—sumo wrestlers in shoulder pads.

4. Mike DuBose, Alabama. Forget football: here is a man who epitomizes the frail human condition. DuBose was a standout linebacker in the 1970s for Alabama. He played for the Bear, won a national championship. But he also played with his secretary and then lied about the affair, almost killing his coaching career. He found salvation last year when Alabama surprised everyone by winning the SEC title—beating Florida twice. His best move: hiring Ronnie Cottrell as recruiting coordinator. He has found some skilled players for an offense that had no passing game for years. Like Tuberville and Spurrier, he's developed a bad habit of signing an excessive number of recruits every year. This seems a questionable ploy to upgrade the football team every year at the expense of players who don't live up to their high school billing. But Bama fans are now beating their war drums again. A sure sign the Tide is back: artist Daniel Moore has painted a picture of Shaun Alexander scoring the winning touchdown in last year's regular season game against Florida. Having now won an SEC championship, DuBose's star is rising.

The Bears (Tier Three)

Tie: Hal Mumme, Kentucky. Mumme is the Elvis of the SEC. His team throws the football so much, he makes Spurrier seem like a Big Ten coach. Mumme, who coached at Valdosta State before moving to Lexington, deserves kudos for pumping life into what had been the SEC's most boring program. But he will need to find a defense to make a mark in this league. Mumme is a student of American history, but he looks like a WWF flunkie on the sidelines, with his wraparound sunglasses and a white towel around his neck. What's next: a rhinestone jacket and white shoes? He's prone to making foolish gambles during games. But for all that, he is interesting—and so is Kentucky football for the first time in years.

Tie: Jim Donnan, Georgia. The best thing about Donnan, who was a quarterback in college (N.C. State) and the offensive coordinator at Oklahoma during some of its glory years, is that he likes throwing to the tight end. After that, there are questions. (He accused me last year of stealing plays during a Georgia practice, so he's *a little* paranoid.) His offensive philosophy seems too cute for the SEC: he has never had a strong running attack, and doesn't seem to like power football. Georgia has talent—but it's been playing third fiddle in the eastern division so long that Athens may soon become more well-known for bluegrass music rather than progressive rock. Donnan is under increasing pressure to beat Tennessee and Florida. His best move: hiring recruiting guru Rodney Garner away from Tennessee. His worst move: hiring defensive back coach Kevin Ramsey away from Tennessee and making him defensive coordinator. Vol fans are still chuckling about that one. For Donnan, 2000 could be a make-or-break year. If things go south, he can always head north—to Atlanta, and do talk radio with Steak Shapiro and Ray Goff.

Rating the Coaches

NOT RANKED:

David Cutcliffe, Ole Miss. He's only been a head coach for one year, so it's too soon to assess his skills. Cutcliffe was the longtime offensive coordinator at Tennessee. He looks to be a good fit at Mississippi, but lost some close games last year. He'll need to recruit and develop Eli Manning, the younger brother of the QB who made his job so easy at Tennessee.

Nick Saban, LSU. Saban will have talent; the question is, can he keep his players in school and out of trouble? That's always difficult in Louisiana. Saban did a good job at Michigan State, a second-tier football program in a tough conference. In the SEC, the same challenge awaits.

THIRTEEN

IMPRESSIONS:
QUINCY CARTER

"I Want to Leave a Mark"

Q uincy Carter has broad shoulders. It's a good thing, because the strapping Georgia quarterback has got to carry a heavy load these days. Carter's essential duty is to lead the Georgia offense—and he does a good job of that. But Carter also has a symbolic importance to the Bulldog faithful. They want him, maybe even *expect* him, to put Georgia back where it belongs—at the top of the rough-and-tumble SEC. That is not so easily accomplished, despite Carter's considerable talent. It's been eighteen years—eighteen *long* years, they will tell you in Athens—since Georgia was the top dog in the conference. Herschel Walker was Georgia's star player in those days—and he's now retired from *pro* football.

Georgia has a good football program, a top-fifteen program nationally, but it's been living in the shadows cast by Tennessee and Florida, its powerhouse eastern division rivals, for a long time. They've had their way with Georgia the last ten years—but perhaps not much longer. Georgia returns nineteen of twenty-two starters from last year's team—and with Tennessee rebuilding and Florida trying to recapture its once-magical passing game, 2000 could be a breakthrough year for the Dawgs.

Though only a junior, Carter is the marquee performer. He's a big, mobile quarterback somewhat in the mold of Tee Martin, the former Tennessee QB. And while Carter is eager to throw the Georgia football team on his back and lead it to an SEC title, he may not have to do everything this year, as he seemingly has the past two years. Georgia's defense, though young, might be its best in years. What's more, Georgia's top rushing threat, Jasper Sanks, is back. Put it all together, and you have a team that some pundits are predicting will win the SEC. "The fans are excited, and the team is excited," says Carter, who was born in Chicago but grew up in Decatur, Georgia. "We'll be careful about making a prediction. We want to stay level-headed and work hard. But there is a lot of pressure. This is a critical year."

Carter has been Georgia's star attraction since 1998, when he grabbed the quarterback job as a freshman. That is not easily done in major-college football, but Carter's athletic skills are surpassing. He is big (6'3", 215 pounds), athletic, and a gifted runner. His freshman performance would have made a senior signal-caller proud: he threw for nearly 2,800 yards and fourteen touchdown passes, and was named the Associated Press SEC Freshman of the Year.

Last year Carter improved his game, though the team was inconsistent (posting an 8-3 record). He became more adept at reading defenses, and more comfortable with Coach Jim Donnan's sophisticated offense. This year he is arguably the best returning offensive player in the SEC. In two seasons he's already thrown for more than 5,000 yards. He doesn't throw too many deep passes, but he's a very accurate mid-range passer. Watch him roll out and hit the tight end over the middle—it's Georgia's bread-and-butter play. And like Martin, he is not averse to running when necessary. Unfortunately, many of his scampers last year were not planned. Playing behind a young offensive line, Carter was often *fleeing* defenders. The less he does of that in 2000, the better off Georgia will be.

Carter long ago learned to deal with pressure. Georgia began talking him up as a Heisman candidate last year, a fact that Carter called "weird" because it was only his second year of college football. But Carter is a little older, and a little more mature, than many college athletes. For one thing, he's already twenty-two years old. After graduating from Southwest DeKalb High School, outside of Atlanta, he signed a professional baseball contract with the Chicago Cubs. He got a $450,000 signing bonus.

But after three years of minor-league baseball, during which time he did not hit very well, he opted to attend college and play both college football and professional baseball. Right now, he's concentrating solely on football. He didn't play baseball last summer, as he had after his first two years in college. He stayed in Athens, took classes, and practiced football. "My love of football is so much greater than baseball right now," Carter said. During the summer, he trained almost every day—running, watching tape, and throwing footballs with teammates four times a week. "I go from 9 A.M. to 1 P.M. every day—just football. It is a lot of work, but I love it. I want to be fed football. I look at it as working on my future for four hours every day."

"No Special Recipe"

Carter has ambitions—for himself and for Georgia. "When all is said and done [with my life], I will have to look in the mirror. I want to like what I see. I want to bring this program up to a level where it's respected again. I want to leave a mark here. There are bigger goals than just being on TV." And the main one is? "Winning. I want to win."

Georgia does win—just not against Tennessee and Florida. In their last nineteen games against those two teams, the Dawgs have won *one* game. They've lost nine straight to the Vols, and nine out of their last ten to Florida. How to beat them? "I don't know if there is a special recipe," says Carter. "It's a matter of believing and then going out and making plays." He says the Bulldogs tend to focus too much on those games, try too hard—"treat them like the Super Bowls." As a result, he says, the team tends to play tight. "We just have to play those teams like they are any other teams. When we press we play bad. We have to relax." But he acknowledges that losing too often to the same teams can create psychological barriers. "[Losing] is in the back of our heads, and we have to get it out of the back of our heads," he says. "I've only lost to Tennessee twice. I want to stop it right there. I want to stop it bad."

More practically, Carter says that Georgia will need to improve its running game and make more big offensive plays to dethrone the Gators and Vols. "You can't just throw and throw. You've got to sustain some drives." He thinks that Sanks is primed for a 1,000-yard rushing season. And Georgia has a deep group of receivers—among them LaBrone Mitchell, Michael Greer, and Terrence Edwards. Durrell Robinson, a Prop 48 freshman, is a talented young receiver—and Carter's best friend. Robinson lives in a dorm, while Carter now has an off-campus apartment. But Carter has two bedrooms, and he says Robinson is often occupying one of them. "He's supposed to be in the dorm," laughs the Georgia quarterback, "but I told him as long as he gets his grades, he can stay with me."

For all that he wants to accomplish with his athletic career, Carter knows that there is more to life than football. He's got a deep reservoir of spiritual strength, and says, "I like to look at the big picture in life." Like so many black athletes, Carter grew up in a one-parent family. His biological dad wasn't around much in Chicago after his birth. When Carter was two, his mom, Sherry Carter-Embree, moved the family to Decatur, about ten minutes outside of Atlanta.

When he was twelve, the two went back to Illinois for a family funeral. He saw his dad then—for the last time. "He went out and promised to buy me some tennis shoes." He never came back. "It hurt me," said Carter, who is an only child. "But now I understand people. I look to the man above for everything now. I ask Him to watch over and guide me." Carter also depends on his mom, who works as an insurance claims investigator. The two are very close. "She has been my backbone, my spine. She holds me up and keeps me going. I thank her for everything." A few years ago, Carter's Mom gave him a cloth bracelet with the words "What Would Jesus Do?" stitched into it. He wears it during games. "It's a reminder," says Carter, "that you always have to keep going forward, keep believing in God, and let life take care of itself." He and his mom still go to a Baptist church together in Decatur.

Carter, who's a sports studies major, admits he's not the most dedicated college student in America. "I'm not your best student, or somebody who stays up late studying. But I will do my work and take care of business. If you can't do your school work, why even be here?" He says he makes Bs and Cs without really trying, though he did less well in a computer science course last spring. Going into the summer of 2000, he has a 2.9 grade point average. "If I put out a little more effort, I could make As. I wish I had a 3.0. Some people look at college as difficult, but it's not."

Unlike many young athletes, Carter says plainly, "I want to be a role model. Leadership is my strength. I don't just want to be known for making plays. I want to do the right things. People look at me to set an example." It's a noble thought—but Carter hasn't always done the right thing, or the smart thing, himself. At age seventeen, he fathered a child out of wedlock. His daughter, named Khai, is now five. Carter no longer has a relationship with Khai's mother, but he sees his daughter regularly because "I know how it feels to be lonely and not have a father." Khai lives with her mom, and spends "a lot" of time with Carter's mother. It's obviously not an ideal situation, but Carter proclaims that "we'll work it all out."

The Bulldog QB might very well turn pro after this year. But, he says, "I don't want to think about that now. I'm very excited to come back to school and have [football] experience. I'm really looking to benefit from it this year." He says that one of his goals is to hit more deep passes, make more big plays. "I overthrew a couple of long passes last year. I want to make the big play, the big play, the big play—that will really complete my game."

However his football career turns out, he says that he wants a degree, and wants to give back to the community. He aims to be a head coach one day, he says, and work with kids. "I love kids. I've always wanted to work with them— show them what's going on in the world. I grew up in the ghetto. I know how it feels to not have everything." That said, he doesn't intend to coddle anybody. "There is no excuse now to sit back on your heels and not get on with your life. There are too many opportunities."

He's got a few big ones in front of him this year. But first Carter has got to find his wallet, which he lost somewhere between breakfast and the end of his summer workout in the Butts-Mehre sports complex. "I don't even have my driver's license," he chuckles. "I was frustrated, but you can't worry about things. It's just life. I believe in God and just keep going forward. Life is too short to worry about the bad things. There are too many good things in life."

FOURTEEN

BEHIND THE SCENES:
THE VIDEO GUY

Joe Harrington is the Video Guy. It says so on the cap he's wearing at Tennessee's fall practice. While the Vol players run through their individual and team drills, Harrington is working just as hard. He's supervising six cameramen who are standing on tall (orange) towers high above the Tennessee practice field. There are three towers, and two cameramen on each. Using sophisticated Sony BetaCam cameras (the same ones used by TV stations and networks) they tape all the action—individual and team—from the start of practice to the finish. When a thirty-minute tape is finished, a cameraman immediately stashes it in a sack and drops it to Harrington, who is waiting on the ground below.

The operation seems like a scene from some spy caper. It's not quite that dramatic, of course—but there is a sense of urgency. Harrington collects a half-dozen videos and then hustles off to his office on the second floor of the Neyland-Thompson Sports Center. There, in the roomy Tennessee video production center, he'll get a head start making seven or eight copies of each tape. Speed is important. "After practice, some of the coaches will shower and come right up and start watching videotape," he says. "I'll have copies sitting right outside the door of the production room." Players do the same thing. They'll take a tape, eat lunch, and then go to a meeting room to watch the practice. They do so because later, they'll watch the tape again with their position coach, and the players want to have questions in mind. Did I block the wrong guy? Did I block the wrong shoulder of the defender? What's my assignment when the middle linebacker is blitzing? You have to understand the game of football before you can play it. In fact, while Harrington is explaining his operation, Vol center Spencer Riley strolls into the UT video center, a dip of Skoal in his mouth, and retrieves a tape of the offensive line's performance an hour or two earlier.

In their no-holds-barred quest to win football games, major-college football teams spend a lot of time watching videotapes. It's one of the vital, unseen learning tools in the football business. And, according to Harrington, nobody places more importance on tapes than Tennessee. "Coach Fulmer is by far the worst coach as far as wanting to save tapes," he says. There is evidence: the video center—a large room that looks like (and essentially is) a TV editing studio—is teeming with tapes. On a top shelf of a wall, there is the archive of original Tennessee game tapes going back to 1988. It runs almost the length of the thirty-foot-long room. Fulmer's favorite tape is up there: the 1991 Sugar Bowl, when the Vols scored 20 fourth-quarter points to beat Virginia, 23-22. Fulmer loves that tape because it shows the UT offensive line manhandling the Virginia defensive line in the second half. Every new Tennessee offensive lineman will see that tape more than a few times before his Vol career ends—in addition to a few hundred other tapes. On a shelf below the UT archive can be found the row of opponents' tapes. "I talk to my counterparts at other schools," says Harrington, "and saving tapes back to 1988 is way longer than anybody else. In fact, if another school needs a tape, their tape guy usually calls me because they know we have such an extensive library."

Harrington and his crew capture practically everything the Vols do on a football field. The Vols use six cameras. "We shoot everything that takes place after the players finish their stretching—every bag drill, every running drill, every catching drill, any kind of team preparation such as pass scale, blitz, team period [meaning offense versus defense], that kind of stuff." Every player is shot performing agility drills—running around "cones" and through "ladders." Before every practice, Harrington gives each cameraman a specific assignment. During the morning practice I watched, there were twelve "periods," and every play in every period was shot from two different cameras: one in the end zone and another a wide camera shot from the sidelines. "We shoot from the end zone because it enables you to see what the offensive and defensive lines are doing," says Harrington. "You can shoot a lot closer and tell what the offensive blocking scheme is, where the defensive linemen are rushing from. You can't really see that stuff with a wide shot. We look at every play from two different angles."

BRAGGING RIGHTS

A Competitive Advantage

Watching movies is nothing new, of course. Football coaches have been doing it for decades. Years ago, they would watch film—and then store it in metal canisters. Film was not easy to work with; rewinding and forwarding it was a laborious process. Not anymore. Coaches still tend to use the word "film" when they mean tape (and Harrington does it himself)—but college football has gone digital. Harrington spends most of his time perched in front of a large video editing system from Avid Technology—the biggest maker of video editors in the world. Eighty percent of all TV shows and movies are edited with this system. Harrington uses the system—which costs about $1 million and with 55 gigabytes of storage capacity is the largest computer on the Tennessee campus—to store and categorize virtually every play that Tennessee has run in recent years, from games and practices. The software can gather into one video file every long pass the Vols threw last year, for example, or show every fumble, or every corner blitz, or every goal-line offensive play. Opponents' games are likewise broken down.

The data is all stored on a massive hard drive and then networked out to viewing terminals—Macintosh computers—scattered in meeting rooms around the Tennessee complex. With a mouse, coaches and players can go directly to the plays they want to see—no rewinding or fast-forwarding with a VCR. "When you've got twenty hours each week to teach kids football," says Harrington, "you've got to get right to the point. This system lets us jump from one play to the next, and saves time. It can give you a competitive advantage."

While coaches spend considerable time studying taped performances of their own team, videos are crucially important to the process of analyzing an opponent. Coaches strive to find what their opponents' offensive and defensive "tendencies" are—in other words, which plays they like to run in specific situations. Says Harrington: "Coaches want to know how the other team defends its own goal line, what they do on fourth down and short yardage, third and short, third and long, how they defend a three-wide formation, and so on."

Here is where Harrington and his staff, not to mention the Avid software, are invaluable. They visually break down opponent tendencies like mathematics professors. Harrington is the only full-time employee of the video department, but he's got six part-time paid assistants. All are at their busiest on autumn Sundays. That's when tapes of Tennessee's next opponent arrive in Knoxville, typically by air, and the process of visually dissecting the opponent begins. Teams sign contracts whereby they exchange tapes, and typically send each other their previous eleven games. Harrington is so concerned about receiving tapes promptly that he makes his colleagues around the SEC detail on the contract precisely how and when their tapes will arrive in Knoxville. "And I want names—of drivers and couriers." This is serious stuff!

Finding "Tendencies"

With the tapes in hand, two graduate assistants (one for offense, one for defense) set to work. If Georgia is next on the Tennessee schedule, the grad assistants will take laptop computers and log every Georgia play for the year. For each play, they take note of the down and distance, what offensive formation or defensive alignment Georgia is in, what play was run, Georgia's field position on the play, what coverage Georgia's defensive backs were in, and whether there were any special defensive wrinkles—blitzes by defensive backs, for example, or stunts by linebackers. "They put in twenty-five pieces of data for each play," says Harrington. Using Avid software, Harrington and the staff then match each log entry with the actual video of the plays themselves. Next, the editing system will "filter" all the plays in whatever way Harrington wishes—gather all passing plays, for example, or all goal-line defensive plays. Harrington then creates "cut-ups"—actual tapes of the opponent in specific situations.

Last year, for example, Harrington composed a fifty-seven-minute tape showing all of Wyoming's first-down plays. It won't win any Oscars, but it did help Tennessee's defensive coaches get a solid feel for what the Cowboys like to do on first down. Harrington said compiling the tape was "easy. You tell it the system to give you all the first downs, or all of the second-and-short-yardage plays, and it will make the tape." Accompanying each play is an on-screen description—in football shorthand—of the offensive formation Wyoming was in when it ran the play, and what defensive tactics were employed by Wyoming's foe. (A formation might be described as "twins weak," or a defensive front might be lined up in 42 G Sam.) Similar cut-ups are produced for an opponent's secondary and defensive fronts. Beyond that, Harrington can create tapes that are even more finely honed. So-called "situational cut-ups" show, say, all third-down corner blitzes, or all offensive plays by the opponent in the red zone (within the 25-yard line).

Glen Grimes, whose official title is "data integrity clerk," is one of Harrington's assistants. He adds another crucial dimension to the scouting effort. Grimes creates a paper report on the opponent. Thick as the Los Angeles phone book, it is a *quantitative* analysis of tendencies—and almost impossible to decipher. Look in that book, and you can find out how many times Georgia used a two-tight-end formation in third-and-short situations last year. By 4:00 or 5:00 P.M. on Sunday, says Harrington, "our work is done and we're ready for the next opponent." The coaches' work is only beginning, however. They must take Harrington's tapes, study them, and formulate game plans.

Teams don't just scout other teams. They also scout opposing coaches and, oddly, themselves. Before last year's Florida game, Tennessee coaches scrutinized tapes of Missouri's defense. Why Missouri? Because Florida's new defensive coordinator, Jon Hoke, worked at Missouri before moving to Gainesville. That was the only way to get a fix on his defensive philosophy. Before Fresno State played Oregon State last year, Fresno's video director called Harrington and asked him for his 1993 Alabama versus Miami tape. Oregon State's new coach, Dennis Erickson, was once the head man at Miami. Teams also take a hard look at their own tendencies, to keep from being too predictable. Says Harrington: "In third-and-long yardage situations, are we throwing the ball every time? Am I coming out in a three-wide [formation, meaning three receivers] and throwing to the same guy every time? Am I giving away too much? We want to know."

When Tennessee plays, three cameras are used to tape the game—home and away. One is a wide-angle shot, usually taken from atop the press box, which captures all twenty-two players. The other two cameras are situated in the end zones and focus primarily on line play. Finding proper camera locations can sometimes be a problem at away games. When Tennessee played Florida State in the Fiesta Bowl in 1999, the game was played in the Arizona State University stadium. It doesn't have a camera deck in one end zone, so Harrington obtained permission to shoot from the roof of an ASU athletic building adjacent to the stadium. All seemed well until the Tennessee cameraman tried to make his way to the building's roof just before the game. He was stopped by a secret service agent. Vice President Al Gore was attending the game, and the secret service wouldn't allow anyone on the roof for any reason. So, says Harrington, "we had to go down one floor and shoot out of a window. Our end zone shot is a little crooked because the vice president was there." For a UT game against UCLA in Pasadena a few years ago, a Tennessee cameraman had to shoot from the middle of a student section in the end zone. Like Sun Devil stadium in Arizona, the Rose Bowl stadium did not have a camera deck in both end zones. "We shoot from rooftops, out of windows, wherever we can get it," says Harrington.

Harrington started working in Tennessee's video department ten years ago, right after he graduated from UT with a broadcasting degree. He jokes that he might have been better off with an elementary school education. The reason:

The Video Guy

"In this business, you're working with ten type-A personalities—coaches with short fuses who are under intense pressure six months a year. It's like working with kids: they want what they want, when they want it, and they throw fits when they don't get it. You get used to that, and try to stay a step ahead of them. There are no thank-yous or pats on the back. The fact that they don't blow up at you is your reward. They'll let you know if something's wrong."

He calls Fulmer "super-intense," adding: "When he was offensive coordinator, he was always creating these weird tapes and changing things and looking for some extra edge. He was really into it, and it was a lot of extra work. When he became head coach, he didn't have time to fool with the film anymore, and I got a break. He was so overwhelmed with all the head coaching duties that he backed off all the film stuff. But when he got his arm around the new job and got all the public relations stuff under control, he was right back into the films."

Harrington is justifiably proud of his work. He's got an operating budget of about $200,000 annually, which is used to buy cameras and other equipment, upgrade software, and buy tapes. (UT spends $25,000 annually for blank tapes alone.) Harrington gets a kick out of seeing visitors get wide-eyed when they walk into the video room. Says he: "They expect to see a big weight room, they expect to see a big training room. When they come in here, it's kind of cool to see their reaction. They have no idea that coaching is so sophisticated. This stuff is important."

So much so that Harrington is always the principal cameraman for Tennessee games. He handles the wide camera. "In eight or nine years, there has been one time when I didn't shoot a game, and on that occasion I was completely worried that the guy wasn't doing it right. The coaches don't want anything missed. It's up to me to get it. I could never do this job and not shoot."

He's so paranoid, in fact, that he has a recurring nightmare: "They're kicking off to start a game and I'm standing on the sideline. I see my camera up there, atop the stadium, by itself. I'm freaking out because I can't get to it, and I'm letting everybody down by not doing my job. I have a phobia about missing something." He almost never does. Look for him at the next game—high in the press box. He's the man with a camera in his hand, and a hat on his head: an unsung hero. The Video Guy.

FIFTEEN

REFLECTED GLORY:
AUBURN VERSUS ITSELF
(AND ALABAMA)

*[They] are peckerwood Machiavellis, ravenous rubes, toads and sycophants,
feckless fobs and duplicitous dons—all stereotypes crazed by sports, small-
mindedness, and a pathetic lust for power.*
>   —Jerry Brown, Auburn University graduate and former
>   head of the school's journalism department, on the
>   Auburn board of trustees (July 1999)

A uburn University is a story. You want southern provincialism, southern
scandal, southern intrigue? Make your way, ladies and gents, to the
Loveliest Village on the Plains, better known as Auburn. The university
is tucked away in a rural corner of southeastern Alabama. It's only an hour's
drive from Atlanta's Hartsdale Airport, but culturally Auburn is in a world of
its own. I drove down from Birmingham, along the torturously slow Route 280,
and it took me four hours to make a 120-mile drive. During the trip, the number of radio stations picked up by my rental car dwindled to a precious few.
Fearing a complete loss of entertainment, I stopped at a dilapidated roadside
shop selling fish bait and beef jerky. I'm here to tell you, beef jerky is *not bad*.

Located in the quaint town of Auburn (population 39,000), adjacent to
Opelika, Alabama, Auburn is a land-grant university with 21,000 students and
a budget of $480 million. As you drive into the campus, you pass several agri-
cultural "experimental stations" that conjure strange images in one's mind. I
wondered if Auburn students were inside the low-slung brick buildings
cloning cows or growing genetically modified okra with grants from
Monsanto and Archer Daniels Midland—Frankenstein food for the grits
crowd. I kid. Auburn's campus is a wonderful surprise. It's arguably the pret-
tiest in the Southeastern Conference: a collection of charming, colonial-style
brick buildings built around a self-contained and charming little town.

Auburn vs. Itself (and Bama)

Auburn's intense football rivalry with Alabama intrigued me. But truth be told, football is not the most fascinating thing about Auburn. The culture—which gives us Robert "Bobby" Lowder and a bruising internecine fight between the Auburn board of trustees and Auburn's students, faculty, and alumni—is much more interesting. Lowder is not the football coach. Tommy Tuberville—an Arkansas native who once managed a catfish restaurant and then coached with Jimmy Johnson at Miami when the Hurricanes were at their thuggish best—is the Auburn football coach.

Tuberville is already making a name for himself. In 1998 he was coaching Mississippi when Terry Bowden quit his job as coach of the Auburn football team. Rumors began circulating that Tuberville might be offered the job. Auburn has a bigger and more ambitious football program than Ole Miss—and is willing to shell out more money for its coaches (past and present). Tuberville publicly reassured Ole Miss officials that their worries were unfounded. He was not leaving, by damn. "They'll have to carry me out of Oxford in a pine box," he said at a speech to the (get this) Ole Miss Loyalty Foundation. Two days later, Tuberville was in Auburn accepting his new position. He neglected to tell his Ole Miss players that he was changing jobs.

After getting to Auburn, one of the first things Tuberville did in his new position was to yank athletic scholarships from six football players—violating an unwritten ethic in college athletics. Auburn's football program has been stained by a plethora of character problems in recent years—players who've gotten into criminal and academic trouble, a head coach who simply quit midway through the 1998 season. Some of the problem players have made their way back to the football team. None of the six players Tuberville sacked was a bad character, apparently, but their football skills were found wanting. Asked about the scholarship cuts, Tuberville blithely responded: "It's a business. They just weren't fitting into what we're trying to do. Some of these guys we wouldn't have recruited."

Interesting thought, but a little off the point: *they had already been recruited by Auburn*, with the implicit understanding that the scholarships would be renewed annually. That's not a rule but rather a tradition in college athletics—one that is being broken increasingly by schools, sometimes for legitimate reasons (when a player gets into academic or legal trouble) and sometimes for dubious reasons (when players are considered without sufficient talent to help the team). (Note: Florida is beginning to pull scholarships.)

Without financial aid, some of the Auburn Six might drop out of school because they can't afford the tuition. That is a possibility. But that is of no concern to Tuberville: he's a *football guy*, and football guys don't dwell too long on the messy downside of college athletics. They tend to react to problems or controversies with a shrug of the shoulders—as if to say, "It couldn't be helped," as if some random, omnipotent force was responsible for those kids losing their grants-in-aid or getting into trouble. There is a clause in Tuberville's contract stating that he gets a $100,000 bonus each year if he runs a clean program. Apparently, coaches need ethical "incentives" these days.

Southern Napoleon

Bobby Lowder needs no financial incentives—and, to the people and students at Auburn, no introduction. He's a rich Montgomery banker—the chairman of and major stockholder in Colonial BancGroup, a major financial services company in the southeastern United States. Lowder is an Auburn business school graduate—and an Auburn booster. Though small and soft-spoken, he is said to possess Napoleonic power—over the football program and over the university. Every university has powerful boosters who throw their money around. But as a former Auburn board of trustees member (who requested anonymity) told me: "Usually it is ten people who try to call the shots. In our case, it's just one guy—Lowder. I don't think there has ever been a situation in America where one man controls a university like he controls Auburn."

Critics call Lowder a "dictator," a "bully," and a "thorn in the side" of the university. Stan Tiner, the former editor of the *Mobile Register*, described Lowder as Auburn's version of Huey Long—the autocratic former Louisiana governor who meddled in college football. Whether Lowder "meddles" with Auburn, or makes smart decisions of benefit to the university, depends on one's perspective. But there is no disputing the fact that he is a lightning rod for criticism. Some people love him, many people hate him, but everybody agrees that at Auburn, Lowder is the boss. It seems, in many ways, his personal fiefdom.

The diminutive banker, who has something of a cartoon smile, was responsible for the hiring of Pat Dye as Auburn's football coach in 1981. He was instrumental in the hiring of Terry Bowden in 1993—and was lauded for the decision when Bowden got off to a fast start. Then, five years later, Lowder certainly played a role in Bowden's demise. Tuberville was named to replace Bowden largely because Lowder and his Auburn allies wanted to hire him. David Housel, Auburn's athletic director, favored Auburn defensive coordinator Bill Oliver for the job. Tuberville got the nod—and not long afterwards he acknowledged that Lowder calls him regularly, sometimes with "advice on who to play." Critics say that's just the problem with Lowder: he tries to micromanage the university, and therefore is a divisive force. "He wants everybody to be afraid of him," says Jerry Brown, who recently left Auburn, where he'd taught for twenty years, to run the journalism school at the University of Montana.

Auburn vs. Itself (and Bama)

Lowder's critics say that many AU leaders are cowed by the powerful banker, starting with Auburn's twelve-member board of trustees, who have the power to hire and fire any university employee. Many of the trustees have financial obligations to Lowder and his bank, raising serious concerns among alumni and faculty of old-fashioned cronyism. Auburn Trustee W. J. "Jimmy" Samford is a lobbyist for Colonial Bank. His law office is in the bank's Montgomery's headquarters. Trustee Paul Spina, a businessman from Hoover, Alabama, is a Colonial Bank board member who's acknowledged receiving "a sizable loan" from Lowder's bank. Trustee Lowell Barron, who is president pro tem of the Alabama state senate, has received political contributions from Lowder. Alabama Governor Don Siegelman is an Auburn trustee and major Lowder ally. His political career has benefited greatly from Lowder's contributions. Auburn Trustee James "Jimmy" Rane, a colorful character who owns the Great Southern Wood Preserving Co., is a Colonial Bank board member. (Rane has hired many SEC coaches to endorse his "ol' yeller" pressure-treated lumber in TV ads.) Trustee John Blackwell, a Huntsville businessman and former Auburn basketball player, is a partner in a real estate development company that is building an office complex in Huntsville. The primary tenant? Colonial Bank.

Auburn trustees are appointed by the governor and confirmed by the state senate. Lowder was first appointed to the AU board by Governor George Wallace in 1983. When his twelve-year term expired in 1995, then–Alabama Governor Fob James, who had clashed with Lowder over various issues (James is a Republican, Lowder a Democrat), decided to replace Lowder on the board. That proved to be a problem: Lowder did not want to be replaced. He filed a lawsuit petitioning the state to keep him on the board until a new trustee was appointed and confirmed by the Alabama state senate. The Alabama Supreme Court eventually ruled in Lowder's favor: he could remain on the board until a new trustee took his place.

Money, Money, Money

That never happened. James *twice* nominated candidates to replace Lowder—but neither ever made it out of the Alabama senate confirmations committee for a vote. Reason: according to the former Auburn trustee and other sources, Lowder had influence over three of the five members of the confirmation committee. In particular, both Barron and Siegleman (who was then lieutenant governor) worked to scuttle James's nominees. So Lowder remained on the Auburn board. Eventually, four years after Lowder's term had expired, it was time to elect a new governor. Siegelman ran for the office and won—thanks largely to Lowder, who was his biggest political donor. Lowder, his wife, and Colonial Bank reportedly donated $57,000 to Siegelman's 1998 campaign. Lowder also contributed $300,000 to various political action committees, which in turn contributed money to Siegelman's campaign.

After becoming governor, Siegelman last year returned the favor: he reappointed Lowder as an Auburn trustee. "Lowder needs Auburn," says Brown, who though now 2,000 miles away from Lee County still simmers about what he perceives to be political shenanigans at his alma mater. Why? "I don't know why; that would be a question for somebody who analyzes him. He has an obsession with Auburn, and he's got to be a trustee. If he weren't a trustee, he'd be nothing."

Siegelman recently appointed a new Auburn trustee—Jack Miller, who is head of the Alabama Democratic Party. Miller is *not* an Auburn graduate—but he *is* on the Colonial BancGroup board of directors, and has served as Lowder's personal lawyer. He is also on the Colonial BancGroup compensation committee, which sets salaries for Colonial executives (including Lowder). With Miller's appointment, eight of twelve Auburn board members have direct connections to Lowder's bank. Critics say that in addition to giving Tuberville football advice, Lowder has strongly influenced Siegelman's decisions about board appointments. A spokeswoman for Siegelman called that charge "absurd." Until last May, when a board reform bill was passed, Auburn had no formal procedure for naming new board nominees. The process was driven, Siegelman's spokeswoman told the *Mobile Register*, by "informal discussions."

A Scared President

Lowder does not just make waves in the athletic department. He's raised the ire of many faculty members in recent years by spearheading a reorganization of Auburn's curriculum. Trying to save money, Auburn's board has been streamlining academic programs. It eliminated Auburn's Ph.D. program in economics and moved aviation management from the engineering school to the business school. The board seems prepared to merge Auburn's well-regarded journalism program into the communications department. That, and the other moves, have sparked a faculty outcry. "Lowder wants Auburn to be like he knew it in the 1950s," says Brown—"strong in agriculture, strong in engineering, and strong in football. He's not a friend of liberal arts." In a recent editorial, the *Auburn Plainsman*—the student newspaper—accused the

Auburn vs. Itself (and Bama)

board and certain administrators with "slicing away at liberal arts" and making a "pathetic" attempt to turn Auburn into a polytechnic school.

Auburn President William Muse is also scared of Lowder. Muse and Lowder have been at odds since Muse was hired in 1992. (Auburn has had five presidents since Lowder became a trustee in 1983.) According to the former board member, Lowder never wanted to hire Muse in the first place. But after Lowder's board term expired in 1995, the board sidestepped the powerful banker and gave Muse a new five-year contract. "Lowder has been fighting Muse ever since," says the former trustee. Brown goes so far as to accuse Lowder of "jerking Muse around."

When I visited Muse in his capacious campus office in Samford Hall, I asked him about Bobby Lowder. He got red in the face, mumbled something about being late for a meeting, and politely ushered me from the room. "A lot of people have strong feelings about Mr. Lowder," I said to him. "Absolutely. I do, too," replied Muse. "But you don't want to talk about them?" Muse: "I don't see any reason to." Muse could not even muster a diplomatic response. According to Paul Davis, a local newspaper publisher and Lowder critic, Muse was set on quitting Auburn at one time because he got tired of trying to deal with Lowder. Five hundred supporters gathered at the university's on-campus conference center and persuaded Muse to stay. Muse has twice applied for jobs at other universities—first at Minnesota and more recently at the University of Florida. That's how bad things are at Auburn.

Friday, November 19, 1999—2:00 P.M.

A train of humpy recreational vehicles lines the right side of Donahue Street in the middle of Auburn's campus. They are waiting for students to jump in their cars and leave school. When they do, the RVs will lumber inside the Beard-Eaves Coliseum parking lot. Traffic is already bumper to bumper. Despite the commotion—middle-aged folk putzing around their vacation homes with a sense of nervous anticipation (hanging Auburn and Alabama flags from their vehicle windows, rechecking their supplies of ice, booze, and propane gas)—many students can be seen ambling casually off to class, past Sewell Hall (a dorm for athletes and regular students) and the baseball stadium, their backpacks a form of generational identification. Others are jogging—seemingly oblivious to the fact that Auburn and Alabama play here tomorrow.

It is a big game in many ways. First, the game carries with it bragging rights for the state of Alabama, which is probably the most fanatical college-football state in America. Auburn and Alabama are bitter rivals. Alabama is the more prominent program, and leads the in-state series 36-26. But those facts only make Auburn, which has won a national championship and five SEC titles, play even harder. Say what you will about Auburn, the football team always plays hard.

Alabama needed a victory to clinch the SEC Western Division crown and earn its first trip to the SEC championship game since 1993. Auburn came into the game with a 5-5 record. With a new coach and meager offensive talent (especially at the skill positions), the Tigers had played respectably well—whipping favored LSU, giving mighty Tennessee a decent fight (despite playing with an inexperienced quarterback), nearly beating a strong Mississippi State team, and waxing Georgia 38-21. Not bad, considering that Tuberville had joked prior to the season that his most important player might be his punter. (In Auburn's game against Tennessee, Tuberville got into a heated dispute with his punter, Damon Duval, in the first half and sent him off the field.)

A victory over Alabama would give the Tigers a winning record, an in-state recruiting fillup—and a huge psychological boost heading into the year 2000. Despite its offensive woes, Auburn had considerable talent on the other side of the ball: their defensive line—seniors Marcus Washington, Leonardo Carson, Jimmy Brumaugh, and Quinton Reese—were all formidable players and the strength of the team. Linebackers Kenny Kelly and Rob Pate were also solid. Their job would be to stop Shaun Alexander, Alabama's All-America running back.

Led by Alexander, Alabama was having a surprisingly good year. The Crimson Tide was expected to rebound from a mediocre 1998 season, but had played even better than expected. Going into this game, Alabama was 8-2 and ranked number eight in the nation. Alabama had rallied to beat Vanderbilt in its first game, vanquished a mediocre Arkansas team, then made its season by beating Florida in Gainesville, 40-39. That game showed where Alabama had made its most significant improvement—on offense. For the first time in years, Alabama had found some skill players at quarterback and receiver, and the team was scoring points. The Pachyderms were beaten by Tennessee but bounced back to grind out an ugly win over Mississippi State and take control of the SEC West. Alabama was not a powerhouse, by any stretch, but it was expected to beat Auburn. That's what the pundits said. Alabama fans may ridicule "Awbarn," as they call it, for its agricultural focus, but they know this: when you throw a bunch of country boys out on a football field in Alabama, there are no easy wins. This would be another in a long line of old-fashioned slobber-knockers. Other than Tennessee, nobody has beaten Alabama more often than Auburn.

Bobby Lowder's dad made millions running the Alabama farm bureau. Auburn's business school is named after Lowder's parents, who were Auburn grads and major contributors to the university. Lowder himself is a big contributor to Auburn—both to the academic and athletic sides of the aisle.

Auburn vs. Itself (and Bama)

Lowder told the *Dallas Morning News* that he donated $4.25 million to the university in 1998 alone. He helped fund the recent expansion of Auburn's football stadium and the installation of skyboxes. He loans money to board members. But while Lowder talks about the millions he's given to Auburn, critics say he does not talk about the money he has made *from* the university. Alabama law says that no public official can obtain personal gain from his public office. For years Auburn's lobbying offices in Montgomery were located in Lowder's bank building. Until recently, Colonial Bank issued all Auburn vanity credit cards—MasterCard and Visa. There were no competitive bids. Lowder once owned five radio stations, including WLWI in Montgomery, which was the flagship station for the Auburn sports network. There were no bids for the contract. Most recently, those contracts were put up for bid. Lowder sold the radio stations, and Colonial Bank no longer issues Auburn credit cards. Auburn's football stadium has many luxury skyboxes. The center box is for the university president. On one side of Muse's box is the AU trustee box. On the other side is Lowder's personal skybox.

Money buys influence. The former AU board member describes Lowder as a "control freak." Lowder has disputed that characterization. He says that he doesn't micromanage the Auburn board, because he's too busy running his $10-billion business. Some Auburn trustees assert that they don't rubberstamp all of Lowder's ideas. Around Auburn, it's almost conventional wisdom that Terry Bowden quit in 1998 because he got a strong sense that Lowder was ready to sack him. Lowder has said that it is not true. "I did not plot, plan, conspire, or encourage Terry Bowden to quit," Lowder told the *Dallas Morning News*.

John Denson, an attorney in Opelika who has clashed with Lowder, has a different viewpoint. According to Denson, "Lowder had a problem with Bowden." Denson contends that Bowden's resignation (or firing) was "the work of one trustee." (Putting aside for a moment the question of whether he quit or was effectively fired, Bowden was rapidly falling out of favor with many people at Auburn. The football team was floundering partly because, say Auburn sources, he recruited too many troubled kids from the state of Florida who had not been offered scholarships by universities in that state—often a red flag signaling possible behavior problems.)

When it comes to football, Auburn and Alabama seldom agree on anything. The two teams played for the first time in 1893 at Birmingham's Lakeview Park. An estimated 2,000 fans watched Auburn win that game, 32-22. But a dispute began immediately after the game. For some reason, Alabama wanted to count the loss as the last game of the 1892 season, while Auburn claimed it as its first victory of the 1893 season. The two programs have been jousting over various issues ever since. The rivalry went on a forty-one-year hiatus after 1907, follow-

ing a seemingly minor conflict. The schools couldn't agree on how much of a stipend each player should receive for making the trip to Birmingham for the game. Auburn wanted an expense of $3.50 per player, but Alabama offered only $3.00. There was also disagreement on who should officiate the 1908 game: Auburn wanted a neutral northerner, while Alabama insisted on a southerner. Both sides dug in their heels, and the two teams didn't play each other for forty-one years. In 1923 Auburn President Dr. Spright Dowell said the game should not be played because "football would tend to become the all-the-topic of both institutions." In 1944, the University of Alabama board of trustees declared that the game would "result in an accelerated over-emphasis of football in the state." If only they knew! It took a resolution by the Alabama House of Representatives to resume the rivalry in 1948.

Hush Money?

I tried to talk to Lowder, both on the phone and at his bank. He wouldn't speak to me by phone—and when I visited Colonial Bank headquarters in Montgomery he was off negotiating a financial settlement with Bill Oliver, the former defensive coordinator at Auburn. Oliver threatened to sue Auburn because, he said, he had been promised the football coaching job by Lowder and Auburn Athletic Director David Housel after Bowden quit. Oliver claimed that the two men "purposefully and willfully" misled him. Lowder disagreed, but he nevertheless signed off on a settlement package by which Auburn agreed to pay Oliver $220,000. The only stipulation for Oliver is that he not talk about his case or Auburn football, publicly.

Oliver is one of four former Auburn football coaches still getting paid by Auburn (out of booster and other funds) for not coaching. Former coach Pat Dye, who was fired after Auburn got caught in a major player-payment scandal in the 1980s, gets $8,000 annually from Auburn. Dye is a Colonial Bank board member, and reportedly owns about $1 million of Colonial stock. Wayne Hall, a former defensive coordinator at Auburn, was fired by Bowden in 1995. Lowder liked Hall, and he made arrangements by which the former coach would be paid a $100,000 annual salary. The payment has since dropped to $50,000 yearly. In return for that money, Hall is supposed to solicit contributions from former Auburn athletes in the pros.

According to the former board member, Hall's salary was never approved by the board: "It was supposedly handled by Housel and the president, but Lowder calls all the shots." And, the source continues, "It's never been revealed if Hall has raised a penny." When Bowden quit, Auburn agreed to pay him a $620,000 settlement. On top of that, Auburn agreed to make the mortgage payments on Bowden's $850,000 house (for five years) and pay for automobiles for both Bowden and his wife. Not a bad deal, if you can get it. Muse says that given Bowden's hefty salary, the settlement amount was not excessive. As with Oliver, the Bowden settlement stipulates that the former coach not talk about Auburn. "It's all hush money," says Davis, who's the publisher and editor of the *Tuskegee News*, a weekly paper.

Davis, who was active in Alabama's civil-rights movement, has felt Lowder's wrath. He once owned the *Auburn Bulletin*, a weekly that ran articles critical of Lowder. Lots of people will tell you: Bobby Lowder does not like criticism. Lowder owns the biggest shopping mall in Auburn, and according to Davis, he halted all mall advertising in the *Bulletin* for two years. Davis says that Lowder encouraged some local car dealers to withhold advertising from his newspaper as well. "He didn't run me out of business, but he tried," says Davis. "The loss of advertising really did hurt." Asked about the no-talk clause in Bowden's contact, Housel says: "Both attorneys [Auburn's and Bowden's] wanted it. The attorneys said it was more or less a standard clause in contracts like this."

3:35 P.M.

The Beat-Bama parade starts in twenty-five minutes. Families, couples, and students are beginning to line Magnolia, College, Thach, and Duncan streets to watch. Stuffed versions of Big Al, the Alabama mascot, are being treated rather harshly. A van passes the crowd dragging a Big Al clone by the neck. One woman in the crowd "walks" Big Al with an Auburn leash. Then an Alabama car—there are Crimson Tide flags in the windows—drives down Thach. The Auburn fans take notice. Shouts of "War Eagle"—the battle cry whose origin dates back to the Civil War—pierce the air. (There is much confusion, apparently, about Auburn's nickname. Many people ascribe at least three nicknames to Auburn—the Plainsmen, the War Eagles, and Tigers. The university takes pains to point out that it has only one name—Tigers. The confusion arises from a poem published in 1770 by Oliver Goldsmith, who was rhapsodizing about the area that would later be occupied by Auburn. Titled "The Deserted Village," the poem includes the line: "Where crouching tigers await their prey. . . ." Hence, the nickname "tigers." Goldsmith goes on to write, "Sweet Auburn, loveliest [sic] village of the plain." Hence, Auburn's earliest athletes were Plainsmen. But they are simply Tigers now.
And what about the eagle? The fable of the war eagle, as recounted by Jim Philips, a former editor of the Auburn Plainsman, *is wonderful. In 1864, an*

Auburn student went to fight in the Civil War with troops under the command of Confederate General Robert E. Lee. In the fierce Battle of the Wilderness in Virginia, the Auburn student was wounded and given up for dead. But he survived, and when he regained consciousness the only living thing he saw was a baby eagle—it, too, was wounded. The soldier nursed the bird back to health and returned with it to Auburn. The soldier became a faculty member. In 1892—twenty-eight years later—Auburn and Georgia played the "game of the century," the first game of what would become the South's oldest football rivalry. The unnamed faculty member brought the by-now elderly eagle to Atlanta's Piedmont Park to watch the game. When Auburn scored the first touchdown, the old eagle broke free from its master and began to soar above the field. Auburn people looked skyward, saw the regal bird, and yelled "war eagle!" At the end of the game, which Auburn won 10-0, the old eagle collapsed and died, having given his all in pursuit of victory for Auburn.

Religions have been founded on less fabulous tales.

4:00 P.M.

The parade begins. Auburn cheerleaders, perky ingenues in their blue-and-orange outfits, start a familiar cheer: "Two-bits, four-bits, six-bits, a dollar. All for Auburn, stand up and holler!" (It's a mystery, but that ancient cheer is still popular.) The cheerleaders are followed by the band, playing "War Eagle." Next comes the Tiger Pause dance team. In their wake follow the beauty queens (sweet joy of youth!): Miss Auburn, Miss Auburn University, and Miss Homecoming. All are wearing suit jackets and skirts, and riding in Mazda Miata and BMW convertibles. All are chosen by student elections. Miss Auburn, Jamie Harder, is the official hostess for Auburn. Miss Auburn candidates must go through one interview with students and one interview with faculty. Five finalists are picked. They then campaign for a week, and the entire student body votes. Miss Auburn University is actually a beauty contest, which serves as a preliminary to the Miss Alabama pageant. There is a pageant—complete with evening gowns, a talent demonstration, and interviews. Miss Homecoming is solely a popularity contest. Katie Day won it.

Next in the parade is Aubie, the Auburn tiger mascot. He's driving a BMW convertible. Auburn President William Muse and his wife follow, riding in a turquoise Bronco convertible. (How did the mascot rate a Beemer, and the university president a Bronco?) The floats are next. Scores of freshmen fraternity pledges are lugging a half-dozen floats on their shoulders down the thoroughfare. (About 22 percent of Auburn's students are in either fraternities or sororities.) While the men do the heavy work, sorority sisters are singing cheers such as

Auburn vs. Itself (and Bama)

Bodagetta and War Eagle. Each float is a collaborative effort between a fraternity and sorority. The frat builds the wooden platforms and the sorority gals add the creative touches—a mix of chicken wire, streamers, and spray-painted napkins that are made to resemble a football field or goal posts or the like. They won't be confused with Rose Bowl Parade floats, but they are heavy—about 300 pounds. It takes about six frat pledges to haul one down the street. Floats display themes like "Aubie Says Roll the Tide" and "Trash the Tide." One displays graves for Andrew Zow (the Alabama quarterback) and Shaun Alexander.

The Greeks are supposed to spend a week working on the floats, but (here's a dark secret) they don't. Alabama-week partying tends to slow down the construction effort. The Kappa Delta sorority did not start working on its float until Thursday, I was told, because its partner, the ΣAE fraternity, was too busy hoisting beers to complete the platform. (Hey, they've got their priorities in order.) No matter: the Kappa Delta/ΣAE float looks perfectly, uh, collegiate, and is greeted by a cheering crowd. At the tail end of the parade, a large group of Auburn freshmen walk in support for the team. The parade ends at the entrance to Jordan-Hare Stadium, where the football game will be played before 85,000 people.

4:30 P.M.

There is an old-fashioned pep rally in Jordan-Hare, which is named after Ralph "Shug" Jordan, Auburn's most successful football coach, and Clifford Hare, who was a member of Auburn's first football team and later president of the Southern Conference (precursor of the SEC). Half of the student section is filled by Auburn fans. A few Alabama fans are mixed in the crowd. Three Auburn players—Heath Evans, Damon Duval, and Marcus Washington—begin the pep rally by thanking the fans for their support. They lead the crowd in singing the Auburn fight song the way the football team sings it, in locker-room style—fast, with rapid-fire hand clapping. Auburn students also let loose with another cheer, this one directed derisively at Alabama: "Round the bowl and down the hole, roll Tide roll!" Coach Tommy Tuberville speaks after the players. He thanks the band and the cheerleaders, then says: "Auburn's had tough times. These guys have struggled. It's been tough getting balls across goal lines, but it's great when you can look up into this [student] section and see the support and cheers. You've helped pull us through. Thank you for coming. We have a chance to win tomorrow and the reason is the twelfth man—the people in the stands." After the coach's speech, the cheerleaders, Tiger Pause, and majorettes perform. Everybody seems excited.

BRAGGING RIGHTS

5:10 p.m.

After the pep rally, there is bumper-to-bumper traffic around Auburn. It's not all for tomorrow's football game; Auburn's number-one–ranked basketball team is preparing to play the University of Alabama-Birmingham. The students are caught in traffic and having trouble leaving campus. But the older football fans are comfortable. They've settled in and around their RVs, which are resting like George Lucas creatures in grassy areas cordoned off with pink, yellow, blue, and orange flagging tape. Inside the vehicles, bottles can be heard clanging. Whiskey and beer are being pulled out of cabinets by fans following old football-weekend instincts. This is a veteran crowd. Outside, the atmosphere is festive: fans are sipping beers, snacking on chips and chicken wings, and chortling confidently. Auburn verus Alabama: it's little more than twenty-four hours away.

Auburn's athletic complex is an impressive, 88,000-square-foot facility that houses football and administrative offices. On one side of the lobby is the Lovelace Athletic Museum. On the other side is a lounge that looks like a businessman's club—leather couches, bronze busts, and football portraits. The complex was opened in 1988, but seems almost new—pristine. Athletic Director David Housel, a large, courtly gentleman who graduated from Auburn in 1969, works on the second floor. He's got a huge office with all sorts of Auburn sports paraphernalia on the walls—including panoramic shots of Jordan-Hare stadium. I talked to Housel, briefly, about the various problems that afflicted the football program in 1998 and 1999: a player was arrested for selling cocaine; a player was charged with having sexual relations with a minor (he later pled guilty to a lesser charge of contributing to the delinquency of a minor and was reinstated on the team); a few players had flunked out; half a dozen 1998 Auburn football signees did not meet the NCAA's initial admissions standards and therefore did not get into school.

In addition, James Brooks, a former star running back at Auburn, had admitted in court that he was illiterate—though he does have a degree from the university. After all that, Auburn paid out $500,000 last year to cancel its season-opening football game with Florida State. The university apparently feared getting embarrassed by FSU, whose coach is Bobby Bowden, father of Terry. Housel justified the game cancellation by saying, "If you go through an ugly divorce, as long as you're having dinner with the in-laws, it's not over. We wanted to close the book on the Terry Bowden era." It was, in fact, a wise—if costly—decision. Why should Auburn—which was not served well by Terry Bowden, despite his cumulative record—allow itself to get humbled by the Bowden family in a nationally televised game? Still, Auburn's critics lambasted the school for backing out of the game. Alabama fans started clucking that Auburn's battle cry, War Eagle, had been changed to War Chicken.

Housel is a bright man in a tough spot. He's spent thirty-four years at Auburn, working his way up from the ticket office to sports information director to his current job. Everyone says it: he loves Auburn. Housel has an affection for birds, books, and Broadway. In fact, in 1992 he performed in New York in the Cameron MacIntosh production of *Five Guys Named Moe*. (That has *got* to be an SEC first.) Housel and Paul Davis and Lewis Grizzard (the late southern comedian) used to drink together on Saturday nights. Davis says that "I don't think David would sit down now and have three whiskeys, because he'd talk." Housel's boss is Lowder. Last year Tuberville explained the Auburn chain-of-command. "When I took this job," said the coach, "Bobby Lowder was described as the guy who pulled the trigger on everything. But, actually, he runs things through David [Housel]." It was a curious comment—confirming everyone's worst fears about Lowder and, at the same time, denigrating Housel's position. Was he trying to make Housel feel good?

Housel himself does not refer to Lowder as Bobby, which seems a little odd given their close relationship. He is more deferential, always using the names "Bobby Lowder" or "Mr. Lowder." Asked about Lowder and the many recent difficulties at Auburn, Housel did not want to say too much. He, like Tuberville and others around the SEC, has become quite deft at the brush-off—blaming most everything on happenstance or society at large. He preferred looking ahead, saying somewhat poetically: "It's a new beginning, owing much to the past. Our great debt is ever to the future."

Uh, okay, but what about this big mess on the Plains? Pressed, he allowed that 1998 was a "traumatic and tumultuous year. It's been tough for everybody, and we hope the worst is behind us. But if you look back at the SEC over the last fifteen years, virtually every school has had a year like we had. It's almost like a virus going around the league. It's part of big-time college athletics." Housel did not explain what "it" is, but he later alludes to broad "societal problems" that tend to rear up on college campuses.

I asked Housel about the six players Tuberville kicked off scholarship. He said, "That is allowable under NCAA rules, and happens at every school every year." That is true. He didn't offer any specifics, however, on why the players were removed from scholarship, saying only: "Maybe they were not academically sound, or maybe some were not as athletically gifted as presumed. It's our experience that the more successful a player is on the field, the more successful he is in the classroom." (That is a dubious statement, given that the most successful SEC players tend to leave after their junior years, without a degree, while a team's academic stars tend to occupy lower rungs on the depth chart.)

BRAGGING RIGHTS

I asked Housel if Lowder was responsible for the hiring of Tuberville and the departure of Bowden. "I don't think that is fair to me or Mr. Lowder," he replied. "I am the athletic director, and any decisions or recommendations to the president are mine. I don't think Bowden would have been fired at the end of [1998]." Housel added that "hard decisions" were needed about the direction of the program, "but the departure of Bowden was guaranteed to be one of them." Asked about Tuberville's hiring, Housel asserts: "I hired Tommy, but obviously you don't hire somebody whom your people don't support. I don't operate in a vacuum. I get input from a cross-section of people, and Mr. Lowder is one of the people I talk to." How often does Housel speak with Lowder? "It varies," he says. "Sometimes often, sometimes not very often." Asked if Lowder effectively runs the Auburn athletic department, Housel replied: "That is not true. He's keenly interested in all aspects of Auburn University—the football program and basketball, facilities and the upkeep of the physical plant, and the business school. People may agree or disagree with Mr. Lowder—that's the American way—but nobody can say that he doesn't want to be helpful to Auburn. I think when people [talk about] Mr. Lowder, he's either great or terrible. I happen to think there is a middle ground with all human beings. I think he's done good things with this university. Period. Others disagree, and that is their right."

8:00 P.M.

Eight middle-aged Alabama tailgaters are gathered off Donahue Street, in a field less than a mile from the stadium. Six had driven up from Mobile in RVs—Pete and Kiddy Dobbs, Bob and Cecilia Turner, and Don and Doug Melton. Bub and Louise Hadding, from Orange Beach, are also with the group. On this cool night, they are all sitting around a gas-tank flame bundled up in University of Alabama blankets. Heads and feet are all that can be seen. They'd been in Auburn since Sunday (five days)—the women shopping, mostly, and the men playing golf. "Some of us don't go shopping," says Pete Dobbs with a chuckle. "The men usually stay away from that."

On trips to away games like this, the group eats dinner together. "Tonight we had spaghetti," Dobbs says. Adds Louise Hadding: "We don't go out to eat in Auburn. There aren't any good places." Her comment prompts a collective guffaw among her friends.

There it is—the SEC football dig! The zinger! The verbal jab! It takes less than forty seconds to emerge. Talk to almost any SEC football tailgater, at any venue, and they can be counted on to hurl brickbats at the opponent—and especially the opponent's fans. Running down the other team's fans is traditional—as much a part of a tailgating weekend as buying a bag of chips.

When the Alabama group is asked if they like being in Auburn, they all answer unanimously: "No!" "It feels like we're in a foreign land," Louise Hadding says.

Adds Cecilia Turner: "We're treated like aliens. They won't even let us park in the ROTC drill field until 8:00 in the morning. The field is empty, and we still can't park in it."

Kiddy Dobbs jumps into the conversation: "They egged some Alabama motor homes last night. They also stole flags. This is a terrible game."

"This is the only campus I've ever been to that treated us like we were not here," Cecilia says. "People don't speak, and they turn their heads. The last Auburn-Alabama game I came to, we were sitting in the Auburn section. Fans looked me in the eye and said, 'I hate you.' I had tears they were so ugly to me. Auburn is the top of my list [for being rude]. We went to Florida, and they could not have been any nicer." The group says they've been following Alabama for twenty-five years—and have traveled to Texas, Tennessee, Kentucky, Arkansas, Florida, and other states. "We've been to every game and we know how everyone is," Louise Hadding says. "Auburn has the rudest fans."

"I'm in a silent prayer [for Auburn]," quips Pete Dobbs, making everyone laugh.

"There's nothing wrong with the school," says his wife, Kiddy. "I have two grandchildren who went to Auburn. It didn't bother me too much, as long as they got a good education."

The Haddings and the Dobbs have been going to Alabama games since they graduated from Alabama in 1962. "We didn't have motor homes then," Louise Hadding explains. "We've been carrying children and grandchildren ever since we graduated. We've all been friends for years." Bob Turner has only missed five games since 1986.

After a brief interlude, there is more complaining about Auburn—this time about the university's lack of visitor services and general lack of organization. "Auburn needs designated parking areas and signs on the interstate telling you where to go and where you can park," Cecilia says. Adds Louise Hadding: "I called the Auburn Police Department twice to find out where we could park, and they didn't even know. Auburn doesn't try to go out of its way to show Alabama fans any courtesy. They don't do anything to accommodate visitors." All agree that Auburn tailgaters are equally irritated with the parking situation. "The Auburn people are as mad about it as we are," Cecilia says. "It's unorganized. You can't just put one of these things [RVs] anywhere."

A champagne brunch is planned for Saturday morning: bacon, eggs, grits, biscuits, and bubbly. Energy will be needed to get through the game. Everybody has great fun on these trips, but the game itself is serious business—three hours of

high anxiety. Not fun—anxiety. That's the way it always is, says the Mobile group,
when the Tide plays. That the opponent is Auburn only makes the tension worse.

Lowell Barron is an Auburn board member—and a stout defender of both Lowder and what he often refers to as "the Auburn family." A resident of Fyffe, Alabama (population: 1,400), Barron is a major real estate developer. He's also, in his words, a "veteran" political operator. He's president pro tem of the Alabama state senate. His state senate district is so Democratic, he says, that a Republican hasn't even been nominated for election in more than a 100 years.

Barron helped keep Lowder on the Auburn board. Last spring he was criticized for holding up a bill that aimed to reform the AU board—but it eventually passed. The bill, which was introduced to reduce some of the Japanese-style backroom dealmaking at Auburn, mandates a new selection process for AU trustees. No longer will the governor make board appointments. Instead, a new five-person nominating committee will pick new trustees and send their names to the state senate for confirmation. The committee will be comprised of two trustees, two alumni, and the governor. The AU national alumni association was a big backer of the bill, and wants to boost its involvement on the board of trustees. That may happen—but the current board probably will continue to call the shots on new nominees. That's because, if one assumes that the two alumni and the two trustees disagree over a candidate, the governor (who is also a trustee) can cast the deciding vote. The reform bill limits new board members to two seven-year terms. "I think the Auburn family is on the same page," said Barron after the bill was passed by the state legislature.

Everybody, that is, except those who Barron refers to as "malcontents." He speaks mainly of the Auburn journalism department, which he says "has declared war on the trustees." But Barron shrugs off the criticism of both the board and Lowder, saying "It's totally wrong. These [critics] are poorly informed, and they make no effort to get informed." Barron, who graduated from Auburn in 1965 with a pharmacology degree, is proud of the fact that the AU board is composed mostly of businessmen who, he says, "cut to the chase, make decisions, and carry them out. People don't like that, but they are well thought out decisions."

One example: Barron says that when the Auburn faculty controlled the university budget in the early 1990s, not nearly enough money was being earmarked for building maintenance. "They were putting all the money into academic programs. They didn't care if the roof leaked. You couldn't get into some rooms because there were no knobs on the doors." With businessmen now running the school, he says, that problem has been fixed. The budget for building maintenance has been boosted substantially. And, says Barron, "Auburn has never been in better financial shape." He insists that the board does not make arbitrary decisions. Everybody—students, faculty, and alumni—is consulted before major policy decisions are made. "That's what makes our family so strong."

Barron calls Lowder "one of the brightest, most capable, and caring individuals I've ever worked with. He's a man who makes good decisions. If he makes a bad one, he's willing to make another decision to correct it. And we get his financial expertise on the board for nothing. I don't know how you can criticize positive results. Auburn is much stronger than it's been in modern history." Barron acknowledges that Lowder is powerful, but says: "He's not as powerful as the governor or lieutenant governor or the powerful [Democratic] forces that threw me out of the senate in 1983." He acknowledges that board members are friends, but asks: "What does that mean?" He asserts that neither he nor other board members are reluctant to challenge Lowder on specific AU issues. "We've got some of the most powerful personalities imaginable on the board. There is not a stronger personality in this state than me. I have no problems opposing people if they're wrong. It just so happens that Lowder's right 97 percent of the time."

Asked about board conflicts with President Muse, Barron is candid. "Dr. Muse is a wonderful man, but he just won't make a decision. He'll form a committee and after it produces a report, he'll appoint another committee. He's likable, pleasant, a nice man, but he doesn't show leadership." Barron said that the AU board had to force Muse to fire the head of the Montgomery campus, after the president had studied the situation for two years. "We forced him to make a decision. AUM languished for lack of leadership."

In the end, Barron makes clear that in this sometimes bitter family squabble, he and the board hold the big cards. They hear the critics, but they will not be deterred from doing what the senator calls "the right things. People can criticize, but there is nothing they can do about it. I been through all the [political] wars and battles, and I've been called everything known to man. Auburn is in every respect better off now than I can ever remember it being. Our academics are good, and our athletic teams are at their apex. We've had a deluge of student applicants. You don't have that when things are all wrong at the university."

8:30 P.M.

Here is another group of Alabama supporters. Among them are Mr. and Mrs. Jim Berryhill of Tuscaloosa. Their son is the assistant band director of Alabama's Million Dollar Band. Mr. Berryhill seems a little, well . . . happy. The Berryhills

BRAGGING RIGHTS

arrived in Auburn on Wednesday. They are part of a twelve-motor-home convoy that has parked in a circle. Apparently when in enemy territory, fans circle the RVs. A five-foot-long, lighted elephant is mounted on the roof of one of the RVs. The University of Alabama fight song is blaring in the background.

"We've been eating and drinking," Mrs. Berryhill brags. "We've eaten thirty-five pounds of crab legs. We're just here to have a good time. We've been to every Alabama game since the early 1980s."

Though Mrs. Berryhill says Auburn is a beautiful place, and she has no problem with the people, Mr. Berryhill feels differently. He says he hates it. He seems serious.

Before leaving, Mrs. Berryhill shows off her good-luck charms. One is a gorilla wearing an Alabama jersey and holding an Alabama flag. When pushed, the gorilla waves the flag and plays the fight song. She also has a frog wearing an Alabama hat. It croaks the fight song.

9:00 P.M.

Two tents are perched just outside Auburn's basketball coliseum. One is a party tent; it's about 100 feet long and has covered sides. The other, right next to the first tent, is smaller and has no sides. In the middle of the small tent, a security guard sits in a folding chair eating from a Burger King sack. Her name is Andrea Jackson. She works for a security company.

Jackson is guarding the tent. What's in there? "I have no idea what's under there. I just have to guard it until midnight, and then I'll be moved to another area." Jackson says 'round-the-clock security began Thursday and will continue through Sunday. "Somebody will be watching this tent all night. We just make sure no one bothers anyone else's belongings."

Jackson says she's an Alabama fan. "I've just been sitting here trippin' on everybody coming through and complaining about parking and everything else. I've been trippin' on Auburn people. They are funny just to sit here and watch."

Auburn is counting on Jimmy Brumbaugh to hold back the Tide. Brumbaugh, a 285-pound defensive lineman, is one of Auburn's best defensive players. He sat out 1998 while recovering from a torn patella tendon in his knee. "It was hard for me—my first year of not playing football," he says. "But to see what the team went through was worse." The tendon has healed, and Brumbaugh is nearly through his fifth and final season at Auburn. "We've been working really hard. We want to put to rest everything that happened last year and move on." Brumbaugh, from Keystone Heights, Florida, was recruited by Florida State,

Auburn, and "a bunch of small schools." He chose Auburn because he figured he'd get more playing time than at FSU. When he was a college freshman, he weighed 245 pounds and could bench-press 320 pounds. After four years in college, he'd gained forty pounds and increased his bench-press to 400. "But I'm stronger in a lot of other areas," he says.

According to Brumbaugh, weightlifting is crucial to becoming a good football player, and there can be no sloughing off. "You have to lift and work out year-round, even if you're not in school. If you're not doing it, somebody else is. Even during Christmas break, you have to take it on yourself to work out. You have a few days off, but if you want to be good you have to lift year-round. Even the pros will tell you that."

Brumbaugh says that in the winter, after the season, the players work out for six weeks. The winter workouts start in February and conclude in March. There is a short break before the start of spring practice. On Monday, Wednesday, and Friday in the winter, the players do agility drills in Auburn's new indoor practice facility. On the other days (including Saturdays), they run and lift weights. "Whew, winter workouts are hard," says Brumbaugh.

After the winter and spring sessions, the players gird for the coming fall campaign. In August, when the team practices twice a day, Brumbaugh would get up at 4:30 A.M. and be on the field by 5:45—"in my line and ready to stretch. After stretching, it's drills—eighteen five-minute drills. Then we run. In the afternoon, we have meetings staring at 2:30, then we're back on the field at 3:30 or so, maybe later if it's hot. I don't get back in bed until 9 or 10 at night." The morning practice is an hour-and-a-half; in the evening, it's nearly twice as long.

Brumbaugh played as a freshman at Auburn, and called the experience "tough. I played against a lot of good offensive linemen—Reggie Green and Jason Odom at Florida, for example." Because he was light, he played "fast." Says Brumbraugh: "After you've been here a few years, you get smarter." Brumbaugh graduated with a degree in health and human performance.

Seventy percent of Auburn's players live in off-campus apartments. For Brumbaugh an apartment was a necessity: At age twenty-three, he is married and has two children. He married his wife, Kelly, when he was twenty and she was twenty-six. She has a child from a previous relationship. The couple now have a young boy of their own. Brumbaugh says that apartment living can be "good and bad. It's good if you know how to handle it. You don't have coaches walking in on you all the time. You've got a free reign, and it lets you be more of a student. Most of the guys can handle it, but some can't. You gotta know how to manage money, how to get up in the morning, how to be a grownup."

Brumbaugh is excited about playing for Tuberville. "I always dreamed of playing pro football, and he knows what it will take for me to get to the next level. He was down at Miami with Warren Sapp and Russell Maryland, and

I'm about the same size as those guys." Brumbaugh thinks Tuberville "will be good for Auburn." Of college football, he says, "it is tough, but fun. Everybody gets fired up for games. Our classmates talk about the games, and the teachers, too, sometimes."

10:00 P.M.

The traffic through downtown Auburn and around Toomer's Corner is bumper to bumper. Toomer's Corner is one of the great traditions in SEC football. Named after Toomer's Pharmacy, located where College Street intersects Magnolia Avenue, in the heart of the campus, Toomer's Corner is the gathering spot for Auburn victory celebrations. Merchants put out toilet paper, and Auburn students and fans use it to "roll" trees (and anything else that doesn't move). The area looks like a blizzard after a few hours of tree rolling. Little buds of toilet paper still hang in the trees from Auburn's victory over Georgia the previous Saturday. Samford Hall glows in the darkness. Abandoned cars are everywhere—on sidewalks and grassy areas—saving spots for tomorrow's tailgating. Two guys are playing frisbee on Samford Hall's lawn. Shouts of War Eagle pierce the air, but they are drowned out when a white Pathfinder cruises by blaring "Sweet Home Alabama," the Lynyrd Skynyrd song that is Alabama's unofficial anthem.

Perhaps the most disturbing recent scandal at Auburn did not directly involve the football program—but it did involve Lowder. In 1999, the editor of the Auburn student newspaper, the *Plainsman*, was nearly fired by the school's communications board, which oversees the paper. The editor, Lee Davidson, had screwed up enough courage to investigate Lowder and the board of trustees. In late 1998, Davidson published a *Plainsman* article on Lowder's role in the resignation of Bowden. According to Davidson, "A bunch of trustees told me that Lowder was responsible and micromanaged the board."

Her story detailed Lowder's financial ties to members of the board. According to Davidson, Lowder bought one board member out of bankruptcy, while another was a lobbyist and shared office space in Colonial Bank. The wife of another trustee was on the Colonial Bank board of directors." Davidson analyzed board voting records, which "showed a trend of the board voting in a block and following Mr. Lowder." Davidson noted that the Auburn alumni credit cards, issued by Colonial Bank, had not been up for bid since Lowder had joined the Auburn board in 1983. "It was a very fair, very unbiased, and very accurate story," asserts Davidson.

The Associated Press picked up Davidson's story and ran it regionally. Until then, nobody had ever outlined Lowder's control of the Auburn board. According to Davidson, the story received a lot of positive feedback from alumni and Auburn faculty. Davidson tried several times to interview Lowder, but he wouldn't talk to her. She pressed him. She went to a board meeting and tried to shake Lowder's hand. "I wanted to tell him that, professionally, this story was important to the paper." She asked that they set up a time and place to talk. Lowder rebuffed her. "He wouldn't shake my hand. He said that I had no manners, and he didn't want anything to do with me."

Davidson then ran a "negative space" article in the *Plainsman* that mocked Lowder for his refusal to talk. The headline read: SPEAK LOWDER, WE CAN'T HEAR YOU. There were a couple of Lowder quotes, but the rest of the article's space was left blank. Davidson next published an editorial, headlined BOBBY LOWDER, JUST GO AWAY, in which she called on the businessman to resign from the board. "We handled the story as professionally as I think we could have," says Davidson, who has since graduated and is now working as a journalist in Alabama.

In January 1999, the Auburn Communications Board reacted with Orwellian displeasure to the *Plainsman*'s coverage of Lowder. Grant Davis, the director of student affairs, ran the communications board. That position reports directly to the board of trustees. The communications board is composed of Auburn students, faculty members, and administration officials. David Housel, the athletic director and a former editor of the *Plainsman*, is on the communications board. By a vote of 5-4, the board voted to censure Davidson for her "reckless" coverage of Lowder, and it threatened to fire her if she kept after him.

Five male student members of the communications board—four of them members of the university's Student Government Association, and one a student who had run for SGA office—initiated the crackdown on the *Plainsman*, and voted against Davidson. Four faculty members cast votes in her favor. Will Stegall, then-president of the SGA, led the charge against Davidson. He himself had been criticized by the *Plainsman* in an earlier article. Stegall said that Davidson had acted irresponsibly toward Lowder—but he made it clear that he was not an impartial observer. "Mr. Lowder has been more than gracious to me," he said. "I can call him up on his cell phone at any time." Stegall and the male students on the board were members of a secret society at Auburn called Spades, which Davidson believes has ties to Lowder. Says Jerry Brown: "It was clear that Lowder was working through intermediaries on the Student Government Association."

Both Davis and Housel tried to wiggle out of the controversy. When asked for his vote, Davis said: "Pass." Housel was in a very ticklish position. Would he support Davidson, a fellow press person, in what was a basic first amendment matter? Or would he side with his boss? Like Davis, Housel opted not to vote at all. He left the meeting room before the vote was cast—ostensibly because he got a call on his cell phone and had to take care of some urgent business. Says Housel: "I had to leave; a lawyer called, and I had to meet with him." Housel suggests that he might have voted for Davidson. "The first amendment to the constitution is clear." But that's easy to say after the fact. Housel could have made a point to support Davidson and the newspaper that he once edited—but, perhaps more concerned about his job than principle, he chose not to do so.

Saturday, November 20—Game Day—11:05 A.M.

All is quiet on the Plains. It is an overcast morning, and the campus resembles a big industrial city with smoke billowing up from a thousand and one grills. The smell of hot dogs, onions, hamburgers, and ribs wafts through the air. Single-engine airplanes are warbling overhead, pulling display ads. Usually the planes only fly over the stadium, but on this morning they are criss-crossing the campus. (Is there an air-traffic control center in Opelika? One guy with a pair of binoculars and a bullhorn?) Chairs line curbs, saving parking places for friends. A young boy runs past, headed toward a car. Soon, he is racing back in the other direction, carrying his baby sister's stuffed bunny. Behind the Hill dormitories, the Auburn band is practicing the War Eagle fight song. The band members are dressed casually, in blue jeans and T-shirts. Students are lolling about, seemingly accustomed to the circus atmosphere of game day. Some congregate on the steps of Terrell cafeteria in their pajamas. Ticket scalpers are already standing on almost every corner. Many hold signs reading: "I need tickets." Others just hold up fingers indicating the number of tickets they have to sell. Good seats are priced from $125 to $200 each.

Noon

The War Eagle Wagon is parked in the "triangle" between Parker Hall and the cage where Auburn's real eagle lives. The Wagon looks like a pewter-colored U-Haul, but actually is a ten-foot smoker on wheels. Bill Haberstroh, an Auburn resident, owns the Wagon. On game weekends, he uses it to slow-cook meat for friends, family, neighbors, and anybody else with a carnivorous appetite. If there is room on the racks, he'll cook it. Inside the smoker are about eight racks of ribs—along with a few turkeys, hams, and chickens. "It's a group effort,"

Auburn vs. Itself (and Bama)

Haberstroh says. "Some of the meat is for us, and we have friends coming from Kentucky, Panama City, and Atlanta. We also share it [the smoker] with our neighboring tailgaters. It's all booked up today."

As he speaks, he turns a handle with his hand, which moves the meat in a circle around the fire. You can hear the meat sizzling 100 yards away. "I've brought this to five out of seven games this year," he says. "I brought it down on Monday." Haberstroh started cooking at 8:30 this morning. "That was late, compared to some people." A couple of men amble over and pitch a tent for him, so he can stay out of the rain that's begun to fall. Haberstroh graduated from Auburn with a degree in agronomy. "I got a degree in dirt." He's an Auburn fan, of course, but has only been tailgating since 1986. This makes him something of a novice among his friends, who haven't missed a home game since 1978. Haberstroh doesn't have long to chat, alas: he's responsible for a few hundred dollars worth of meat, and it's time to eat.

Across the street from Parker Hall, in what's known as the Quad, two fire trucks and a police car are blocking the road. Sirens are wailing—another fire truck is trying to reach the scene. A mass of abandoned cars are parked halfway up on the sidewalk. A fire alarm in Lupton Hall, a girls' dormitory, is wailing. If there is a fire, it's minor. About thirty girls are milling around outside—some still in their pajamas. Half a dozen have towels on their heads. Win or lose, fire or no fire, this will be a big night on the social calendar. But it must be approached smartly. As these girls fully understand, you don't get dressed and start partying too early—you'd be a howling wreck by the start of the game. No: you pace the day, conserve your energy, and then release it slowly—until the bands start cranking out the music at the fraternity houses after the game. That's when the hair comes down.

1:00 P.M.

Walking down the concourse, several people are handing out booklets about a movie, The Omega Code. "It's about the coming of the Lord," a representative for New Covenant Fellowship says. "Go check it out."

Though the sign on the concourse running beside Haley Center reads "No RVs or campers allowed," cars are a different story. They're packed into the concourse. It looks like 5:00 P.M. traffic in Atlanta.

Inside Haley Center, the bookstore is doing a booming business. It's packed with Auburn fans buying shirts, flags, stickers, and other items. According to the manager, ponchos are the best seller on a rainy day. A three-year-old boy walks out of the store with a sign around his neck. It reads: "We need two tickets. It's our first game."

BRAGGING RIGHTS

The Alabama Press Association (APA), headed by Bill Keller, came to the aid of Lee Davidson and the *Plainsman*. The APA offered legal and moral support. Dennis Bailey, the general counsel for the APA, wrote the communications board and told them that Davidson was a state employee and should not be threatened. Various newspapers, including the *Oskegee News*, also weighed in, criticizing the communications board for its actions. By a vote of 60 to 4, the Auburn All Faculty Senate passed a resolution calling for the communications board to rescind its resolution against Davidson. The senate praised Davidson and the *Plainsman* staff for their "exemplary independence, initiative, integrity and dedication to the service of the university."

Stegall was defiant, saying that the board would not rescind the resolution. He said he was happy that four faculty members agreed with his viewpoint. José Madrigal, a native of Cuba and chairman of Auburn's foreign language department, said that "in the thirty years I've been at Auburn, I don't think anybody has ever been censured. What a coincidence that it happened with Lowder. I'm originally from Cuba, and I know what censorship is. I think we should take a very strong position on what is going on."

Under pressure, the communications board backed down. The resolution censuring Davidson was softened. In the end, Davidson says, "they slapped me on the wrist and reminded me of my duties and responsibilities as editor."

Davidson says it has taken her a while to come to terms with the Lowder brouhaha. She is critical of Lowder, Muse, Housel, Davis, and the SGA students who voted against her. "We made the *Plainsman* a more serious and professional newspaper, and the SGA students weren't ready for that. They didn't appreciate a little reporting. They only wanted to see good news—blood drives and the like. They don't understand the fundamentals of journalism. Mr. Lowder wasn't the only person we pursued."

What's more, she believes the SGA leaders were biased against her because she was a female editor. Davidson attended Auburn trustee meetings, and she was surprised by what saw. "It was humbling to watch how our university officials conducted themselves. They were meek and cowering. That applies to Muse and Housel." Of Muse, she says: "He's scared, and we wrote that he's weak and needs to stand up [to Lowder], and the alums do, too. The big factor behind a lot of this is sports. Football reigns supreme in Alabama and at Auburn—and as long as your goal is not to get an education, but to see and win football games, you're going to have problems. Lowder has done a lot of good things for [Auburn] sports, but it hurts the university to have one man have undue influence."

It was hard to report on Lowder, says Davidson. "A lot of people like what he is doing," and therefore don't want to talk. Davidson said that some Alabama papers—chief among them the *Montgomery Advertiser*, in Lowder's hometown—refused to investigate the *Plainsman's* battle with the communications board. "They didn't do anything when they tried to take my job away, even though it was a first amendment issue." She adds: "I wasn't born to attend Auburn or Alabama, like so many people in this state. I didn't go to Auburn with preconceived notions. You have to look at Auburn as it is, not as what you want to see it. There is a big difference."

Last year Lee Davidson won a national award for her work at the *Plainsman* from the National Collegiate Press Association. The *Plainsman* itself also won an award—the Pacemaker, which is the collegiate equivalent of the Pulitzer prize.

Will Stegall? He works for Bobby Lowder at Colonial Bank.

Grant Davis? He tried to keep a low profile during the *Plainsman* debate. He's now executive secretary of the board of trustees.

2:00 P.M.

Two women standing outside of Haley Center are drawing a lot of attention—and laughs. They're dressed in crimson jogging pants and Alabama sweatshirts. One woman, Gail Relford of Glencoe, Alabama, has a pillow in her pants that makes her butt seem enormous. The other, Rhonda Adcock of Pell City, has stuffed a pillow under her shirt to create the illusion that she has a massive beer belly. Their hair is in pigtails tied in the back with . . . socks. Each wears mismatched shoes: one has on black and purple tennis shoes, while the other wears a sandal on one foot and a tennis shoe on the other. Their faces are painted with bright blue eyeshadow, freckles, warts, and bright pink lipstick. They've also got fake buck teeth. Some of the fake teeth are missing, making it hard for them to talk.

"My mama gave me this outfit," Adcock says. "It's just something fun we do. We've gotten a good response. Even a few Alabama people laughed."

"We're big Auburn fans, and we get a good laugh out of doing this," Relford adds. "We'll stay dressed like this until game time." Then they'll put on regular clothes.

On the concourse, a man in his eighties is standing like a citadel in orange pants and suspenders. Four Alabama fans try to walk past him. Auburn's version of Don Quixote, he sticks out his umbrella and refuses to let them past. "Get the hell out of here!" he shouts. The Bama fans detour around him.

In the Haley Center parking lot, across the street from the stadium, a Jeep Cherokee is displaying an Auburn flag on the passenger-side window and an

Alabama flag on the driver's side. The family—Merl and Debbie Haynes of Oxford, along with their twin sons and Debbie's mother—are eating food out of the back of the SUV. All but Merl are wearing Auburn attire. "It's four against one," Debbie says.

"I'm for Alabama and the rest are for Auburn," says Merl. "Our son goes to Auburn. My money goes to Auburn, but my heart is in Tuscaloosa."

Across the street from the stadium, on a small patch of grass in front of the Math Annex, four people are sitting under a blue tent. They're trying to chat up practically everyone walking past. A six-year-old girl passes by with her dad. Three of the tent people yell, "Roll Tide!" The little girl yells back confidently, "War Eagle!"

"The atmosphere is right here," says Phyllis Grant, one of the tent people, as she chatters with other passersby. She's with her son, Chris, along with co-workers Mary Jim and Dr. Bob Hamilton. All are from Montgomery.

"We are the frontier people sent to set up the lodge," says Phyllis. "We've just been sitting here eating, drinking, and visiting." Both Phyllis and Mary went to the University of Alabama. Mary has a daughter who is a student in Tuscaloosa. Chris, Phyllis's teenage son, also plans to attend Alabama. "I can go anywhere as long as it's Alabama," says Chris.

In this group, Bob Hamilton is a minority. He is an Auburn graduate. "We took him to an Alabama game, and he didn't know how to function," Mary quips. This was her and Phyllis's first visit to Auburn.

"I thought it was time to show them God's country," Hamilton says.

"We're having a wonderful time," Phyllis replies. "The folks are very hospitable, and it's a pretty campus."

They were cheering for different teams, but promised no hard feelings after the game. "Football and the SEC are about getting together and having fun," Phyllis says. "It doesn't matter who wins, as long as we have a great time."

"Cheers to that," Mary says as everyone raises their glasses.

You'd be hard-pressed to find anybody more scornful of Bobby Lowder and the Auburn trustees than Jerry Brown. He and Housel used to be friends, but circumstances have blown their relationship apart. Brown moved 2,000 miles away from Auburn, to Montana, partly because he simply needed a change of pace—and partly because he was fed up with what he perceived to be the provincial shenanigans at the university, where he taught for twenty years. He was disturbed by Lowder's power, disturbed by the attack on the *Plainsman*, disturbed that Auburn "was controlled by rich and cunning people who've exploited a corrupt political system and a sports-addicted public." He is disdainful of the trustees who have interlocking financial relationships with Lowder. He calls Lowder "the spider in the web," and says of the other trustees: "They are small men with big egos and not much real knowledge of how a university should be run. It makes me ashamed, angry, sad."

Brown grew up on a dirt road in Clarke County, Alabama. While most of his friends went to Alabama, he found Auburn a more comfortable fit. It was a school where "country boys with little money and less couth could be educated without clipping their roots," he wrote recently in a farewell column for the *Mobile Register*. "Parents like mine wanted their children to be educated so they wouldn't have to follow a mule, sling hash, or stack lumber at a sawmill, though that work was honorable." His father hoped he'd become a county agent so that they could fish in anybody's pond. In 1963, Brown's dad and his brother, Tollie, drove him to Auburn in the family's 1957 Chevy pickup. He graduated in 1967, and later took up a teaching career at his alma mater. He was dean of the journalism department for seven years.

Brown believes there are "schemes" to turn Auburn into a business-tech school. There are also plans to merge the journalism department with the communications department—a move the journalism faculty bitterly opposes. Brown and other Lowder critics are suspicious that the Auburn board has got a vendetta against the journalism department. "The trustees are essentially trying to destroy it because of its relationship to the *Plainsman*," he says. Ed Williams, current faculty adviser to the *Plainsman*, agrees. "The feeling is that the board of trustees is behind this [plan to downsize the journalism department], and that it's political."

Lowder told the *Mobile Register* that the idea wasn't his. "I don't have a dog in that fight," he said. "All this came up, and people are screaming at me. I haven't talked to anybody about that. Do you think merging journalism and communications would stop the *Plainsman* from what they want to write?" Liberal Arts Dean John Heilman and Provost William Walker have said that the university could save $50,000 annually by moving the journalism school into communications. That's a tiny fraction of the Auburn budget. According to Brown, Lowder recently wrote a letter to the *Chronicle of Higher Education* in which he made clear that Auburn was not going to be the Harvard of the South. People who didn't like that fact, he wrote, could find work somewhere else. "It was an attempt to defend his position for remaking the university," says Brown.

In his farewell column, Brown writes: "My idealistic and simplistic views [of Auburn] do not rule the day. Cold-eyed realists who see the university as a business or sports franchise dominate—and look at the disastrous results. To many across the country, Auburn is a laughingstock—the butt of his own joke. The university deserves better. . . . I know that President Muse has been too quiet for some, but I sense under his coolness a man with all the right values.

BRAGGING RIGHTS

And I know that there are off-campus alums who have watched what is happening with sadness and confusion, too civil to place blame and too cautious to get their hands soiled, but who will someday say, "Hold, enough!"

3:00 P.M.

A blue van is tailgating in the parking lot of Sewell Hall. There is a number 11 on the window. The owner is former Auburn quarterback Phil Gargis, from Homewood, who played from 1973 to 1976. "My son, Phillip Gargis, is a redshirt freshman for Auburn," he says. "He doesn't play because he is redshirted, but he gets to dress out and stand on the sidelines." Gargis spoke with a few Auburn players this morning, and he says they were nervous. "This is the one game that carries on for the rest of the year. It's really bigger than anyone can imagine."

When Gargis was playing for Auburn, the Tigers never beat Alabama. He remembers always feeling anxious about this game, because the outcome could make or break the season. And yet, he says, most of the hype surrounding the rivalry comes from the fans. "Many of the players have played against each other in high school and enjoy getting to play against them again."

Roy and Margaret Crow, along with Burke and Elaine Grace, hail from Eufaula, Alabama. Both couples have "mixed marriages." One spouse pulls for Auburn, the other for Alabama. Roy Crow attended Auburn and was a Sigma Nu. His wife, Margaret, attended Alabama. The Graces are just the opposite. Elaine Grace is an Auburn fan, while her husband, Burke, pulls for the Crimson Tide.

Years ago, for their first date, the Graces attended the Auburn-Alabama game. "She got the tickets," Burke says, "and I went."

Roy Crow is excited because Margaret has laryngitis and cannot holler tonight for Bama. Margaret seems to have another plan. "I can't talk, but I can still hit him," she says. Though Roy pulls for Auburn, he once wore crimson to the Alabama-Auburn game. His wife had tricked him. "Roy is colorblind, so one year I laid out his clothes to wear," Margaret says. "I put out a crimson sweater, and he didn't know the difference."

3:30 P.M.

The light rain, which has fallen steadily since noon, is beginning to let up.

Auburn vs. Itself (and Bama)

4:15 P.M.

The Tiger Walk begins. It's tradition for the Auburn football team to walk from Sewell Hall to the stadium. They walk down Donahue Street. Thousands of fans line the path to cheer the team as it passes. Children and photographers sit upon shoulders for a better view. The players wear suits and ties. They try not to smile as fans reach out to touch them. Often, they grin when they see a familiar face.

4:30 P.M.

People begin making their way to the stadium. A boy peddling football programs yells, "Get your twentieth-century programs!" The Auburn University band is playing on the lawn in front of the stadium. Many fans stand around to see the pregame show. There are lots of "I need tickets" signs, but little sales activity. Tickets are priced around $125 to $150 each. One man asks for $400 for two tickets.

5:20 P.M.

On a chilly evening, the student section is overflowing. Students are standing in the aisles. As at other universities, Auburn doesn't reserve seats for all of its students. Doing that would cut into football revenues. Many people are gazing up at the stadium's big video screen, where highlights of the Florida–Florida State game are being shown. Florida State beat Florida earlier in the day. Despite the intense fan rivalry, the Auburn and Alabama cheerleaders are mingling on the field, posing together for pictures.

"Culture Is the Problem"

Willford S. Bailey knows Auburn University, and Auburn sports, as well as anyone. Bailey, seventy-nine, grew up in poverty in north Alabama. When he was a kid, he picked cotton from 6 A.M. to 6 P.M., earning one dollar a day. His mother ran a boarding school so Bailey could attend Auburn. He went on to earn a doctorate from Johns Hopkins—and then spent fifty years at Auburn in

2 5 1

positions ranging from instructor to interim president in 1983–84. He was secretary of the Southeastern Conference for eight years, and worked for the National Institute of Health. He has written a book about corruption in intercollegiate athletics—and he has seen more than a little corruption at Auburn. "We are the only country in the world where big-time sports programs are part of our university system," he says.

In 1976, when Bailey was head of Auburn's athletic committee, "we had eighty allegations of [NCAA] violations [mostly in football and basketball]. I chaired the investigating committee, and we found that practically all of them were true. It was about the most traumatic experience I ever had. I faced the [NCAA] infractions committee for a day and a half in San Diego." He recalls Auburn getting a three-year penalty.

Later, says Bailey, "we had an athletic director who was also the football coach." He is referring to Pat Dye. "He was willing for his coaches to lie to try to protect him. He got real mad when I found out that one of his assistants had lied to avoid an NCAA violation." Bailey says that when he was interim president, he learned that the previous president had transferred $1 million from Auburn's library fund to the athletic department to fund scholarships—at a time when "the library was in deep financial trouble." Says Bailey: "I told Pat Dye that the athletic department would have to refund a quarter of a million dollars a year for four years to pay back the money, and they did."

Bailey says that in recent years, there have been "fewer major violations" in college athletics. "There has been improvement. But there are still institutions that break the rules. There are too many people—coaches and fans—who think that winning is the only thing. When I was a student here, sixty years ago, there were a few years when we didn't win a single ball game. But at that time there wasn't such a fanaticism on the part of fans making contributions to the athletic department." In his view, "Alabama's culture is part of the problem, and that's pretty much true throughout the South."

He is not a Lowder supporter. "Lowder is likable in some ways, but egotistical," says Bailey. "He wants to run this university, and he especially wants to run the athletic department. In my opinion, most of the conflicts at the school are a result of Bobby Lowder's efforts to control everything. He wants to manipulate everybody."

For all the warts he sees at Auburn, and in major-college athletics, Bailey remains something of a football fan. He sits with Muse in the president's box at Auburn home games. "I enjoy it," says Bailey, "but I'm not a fanatic. That is not in the best interests of intercollegiate athletics."

Auburn vs. Itself (and Bama)

6:30 P.M.

The game begins with a thunderous roar. Atop the stadium, Muse has settled in his box. Lowder is in his box. The trustees are in their box.

9:45 P.M.

Alabama has won, 28-17, beating Auburn for the first time in Auburn. The Crimson Tide, taking advantage of strong second-half running by Alexander and three questionable decisions by Tuberville, come from behind to win it. Auburn holds Alexander to 44 yards rushing in the first half, but he rambles for 144 in the second and scores the go-ahead touchdown.

Auburn might have won the game, but Tuberville gambled at some crucial spots—and came up a cropper on all of them. Early in the game, Tuberville called for a fake punt from deep in his own territory. That was gamble number one. The pass failed. Bama took over and kicked a field goal. The game turned in the third quarter. Leading 14-6, Auburn stopped Alexander on fourth down at its own 5-yard line. It was a huge defensive play. Auburn took over and (gamble number two) tried a pass on first down. Alabama defensive lineman Kindal Moorehead tackled Auburn quarterback Ben Leard in the end zone for a safety. Suddenly, the score was 14-8 and Bama had claimed the momentum.

That turned out to be the play of the game. Bama grabbed the ensuing kick and drove for the go-ahead touchdown, Alexander galloping into the end zone from the 8-yard line. Trailing by 8 points late in the game, Auburn had one last chance to tie. The Tigers drove to the Tide 18 yard line—but on fourth-and-eight Tuberville elected to kick a field goal (gamble number three), rather than go for the first down, touchdown and potentially tying two-point conversion. Auburn never got the ball back. Alexander, who carried the ball twenty-one times for 101 yards in the fourth quarter alone, scored again and the game was over. "He killed us," said Tuberville of Alexander. Auburn's players might have said the same thing about their coach. Alabama coach Mike DuBose called the victory "tremendous," and heaped praise on Alexander saying: "I don't know how the Heisman Trophy race stands, but there can't be a better player in this country than Shaun Alexander." Unfortunately, Alexander's Heisman chances had evaporated a few weeks earlier against Tennessee.

After the game, Auburn's senior defensive linemen were devastated. Marcus Washington and Quinton Reese embraced on the field and walked off together. "It

253

hurts a lot," said Washington. "This is the first time Alabama won down here. It will probably stick with us seniors for the rest of our lives. It hurts a lot." Jimmy Brumbaugh trailed just behind his two defensive teammates, wiping tears from his eyes as he left Jordan-Hare for the last time. For all three men, and five other starters on the Auburn defense, their college careers were over.

The home-team fans hurry out of the stadium to avoid the humiliating sight of an Alabama celebration. The Auburn band plays on. Shouts of "Gator Meat" and "Roll on out of here" can be heard coming from the Auburn sections. Some fans throw bottles at Alabama players on the field. The Auburn band breaks into a sweet a cappella rendition of the Alma Mater. A few Auburn fans exit the stadium chanting, "It's great . . . to be . . . an Auburn Tiger. I say . . . it's great . . . to be . . . an Auburn Tiger."

Outside the stadium, Bruce and Gini Hose of Montgomery are walking hand-in-hand. Bruce is wearing an Alabama hat and Gini an Auburn sweater. "We're not split at all," Bruce says. "We're still holding hands, aren't we?" Gini is not disappointed. "We played really well, and that's what matters."

Across campus, dozens of Alabama fans try to roll Toomer's Corner with red-and-white streamers. Scores of angry Auburn fans are ready to fight to prevent that from happening. "Get the fuck out of here," shouts a burly male Auburn student, his eyes bulging. A line of policemen stands between the two groups, preventing what could easily escalate into a riot. Many people are arrested for trying to cross the police line. Some Bama fans tear off pieces of shrubbery to keep as souvenirs.

I asked the former Auburn board member if college football has become too big, too powerful. He was emphatic: "Yes, there is too much emphasis on the game, and it has a detrimental effect on universities. Auburn is the worst example. Coaches are told to win at all costs—but don't cheat." The implication is clear: it really can't be done. He goes on: "College football has become a spectacle. It is glorified beyond reason. And there are a lot of people like Lowder who want to live in its reflected glory. They want to be known as the people in charge of this wonderful thing—the person to call if you want a new coach. Lowder thinks he's helping. But a lot of bad things are done by people who believe they're doing good."

SIXTEEN

IMPRESSIONS: AINSLEY BATTLES AND THE ART OF PLAYING SAFETY

Carl Battles was not pleased. His son, Ainsley, was a good athlete, but he was goofing off in his eighth-grade classes in Lilburn, Georgia, a suburb of Atlanta. He wasn't applying himself to school. So Dad, a doctor at the DeKalb County Corrections Center in Georgia, made a brass-tacks decision: he told Ainsley he would not be playing football his freshman year in high school. "It was a message to me that I had to put academics first," says Ainsley Battles.

And so he did. Four years later, eighteen-year-old Ainsley Battles graduated from Buckview High School with a B average. He wasn't valedictorian, to be sure, but for a kid who was seriously inclined toward sports, and who was one of the better high school football players in Georgia, it was a respectable achievement. Battles had learned his eighth-grade lesson. He didn't do so well with his SAT test (he scored a mediocre 880)—but never mind: Battles' solid grade point average, work ethic, and athletic skills made him an attractive scholarship prospect to several universities—among them, Mississippi State, Clemson, Georgia Tech, and even Vanderbilt.

Battles was a competitor and, thanks to his parents, a kid who had some understanding of the importance of school. So as he wrestled with his college decision, he asked himself three questions. The first was: what is the best football conference in America? "To me, the SEC is definitely the best, and I wanted to see if I could play against the best. Any competitor would want to." The second question was: Which school offered him the best opportunity to play? Battles felt like he could play at any of the schools soliciting his services. And then there was the last question. Battle's dad had always harped on academics, and on the notion that sports careers tend to be short. He was one injury away from football oblivion.

"That got me thinking about the big picture," said Battles. "So I said to myself, 'All right, what if I get a Mississippi State degree? Nothing wrong with it. A Clemson degree? A Vandy degree? Which degree will open more doors for me?'" His answer: Vanderbilt. "When I came to Nashville on my visit, I noticed the quality of the people here were a notch higher than anywhere else. Your friends in college will have a big influence on what you turn out to be. If you hang out with a bunch of people who aren't doing the right thing, more than likely you'll do the same. I didn't want that."

Ainsley seems to have done the right thing. He went to Vandy and largely fulfilled both his academic and athletic ambitions. He started for three years at strong safety—on highly regarded Vandy defenses. And he earned his degree, in human and organizational development—a very popular major among athletes at Vanderbilt, with courses in psychology, economics, and science. "It's a broad major," says Battles. "It can be summed up as the study of people and organizations and how they mesh together."

Battles was not a stellar student at Vandy, but he pushed past his weaknesses at a demanding institution. He carried a C average into his senior season in 1999, but he'd started slowly. As a freshman, he had lapsed into his old habit of concentrating more on football than academics. The football went well: he was Vandy's special teams Player of the Year in 1996. "I went home and gave the trophy to my dad, and he said, 'Whoa.' It was like all his hard work and sacrifice had paid off, too, in addition to mine." Battles was also the starting "nickle back" (fifth defensive back) the last eight games of the season. Asked what he remembers about his freshman season, he said: "Playing Florida, and making every tackle on kickoff coverage two games in a row."

When Vandy played Florida that year, the Gators were ranked number one in the country. But Vandy proved a stubborn opponent, losing 28-21. Woody Widenhofer, Vandy's head coach, was the team's defensive coordinator that year—and he showed opponents, as well as Vandy players, that he was a defensive wizard. Says Battles: "That year we introduced a nine-man [defensive front]. We put our corners on islands—by themselves against receivers, no help—and blitzed Florida, and watched what they could do." (Vandy had an outstanding cornerback that year, Corey Chavous, who is now playing in the NFL.) "It was the mentality of our defensive coordinator. He said, 'Nobody else in the country does this, so why not us. What are we going to do, lose?' We saw how much faith he had in us. It was like, whoa." Battles loves saying "whoa."

"Humbling Out"

But while his athletic career got off to an exciting start, Battle's freshman grades were, he says, "lackluster." Every freshman at Vandy must spend three hours a day at "study table." Every weekday, from 6:00 to 7:00 A.M, and from 7:00 to 9:00 at night, first-year students (and also students on probation) are required to attend study hall. Battle made the study table regularly, but he didn't study much. "I still had the old mentality of, well, I came here to play football and just hang out."

You don't "hang out" at Vandy, and Battles quickly found himself in a hole. He got chewed out again by his dad, and in response started using Vandy's academic-support services more regularly. "They have tutors, and I work with them a lot now," he said just before the start of the 1999 season. "I humbled out; instead of just writing a paper and turning it in, I get help. The thing about Vandy is that they treat you like an adult. They're not going to force-feed you. First year, you do have to go to study table. They do their best to get you started academically. What you do after that is up to you. They have all the resources, but it's up to you to take advantage of them."

When he was a freshman, Battles lived in Branscomb Hall, a dormitory. Of the roughly sixty students in the dorm, only three were athletes. Battles roomed with a regular student, Jeff Fabrikant. "Living with him was really interesting," says Battles. "He studied a whole lot more than I did. There was this contrast: he studied all the time, and I played [football] all the time. I said to him, 'Why are you doing this?' And he said to me, 'Why are you doing that?'" The two became friends, however.

For Battles, Vandy presented some cultural challenges. He says there are "definitely stuck-up, arrogant types" at Vandy, who seem preoccupied with family pedigrees and social status. "But on the flip side, I met a lot of people who were relatable and became my friends—more than I would have thought, really." At Vandy, he said, "there is daily interaction between the students and athletes. There is no line separating the two sides. A lot of the students like that, because it makes watching the games more personal. They say, 'I know that guy. We have classes together.' Instead of going to the games just for entertainment, they think of us as people. I know them, they know me."

Throttling Florida

Vanderbilt had a rather good 1999 season—by Vandy standards. The team won five games, lost six. With a little better play in some key spots, the Commodores would have beaten both Georgia and Florida (they were the better team in both games) and perhaps earned a rare trip to a bowl game. Though they lost to Florida by a score of 13-6, Vanderbilt embarrassed the Gators. Florida came into the game with a 7-1 record, leading the SEC in scoring (35 points per game) and total offense (449 yards per game). But they were shut down by Widenhofer & Co., who have become masters at throttling the SEC's most powerful offenses. The Gators could manage only 269 total yards against Vandy, and only 143 yards passing—both record lows for Florida in the Steve Spurrier era. Vandy outgained Florida by 100 yards for the game.

After the game, Florida quarterback Doug Johnson claimed that Vanderbilt's defensive players often knew what plays the Gators were running—having pilfered their audible signals. "It was a strange game," said Johnson. "They knew our offense better than we did. Every play we sent out, they knew where it was going—every play. When I see they're going to blitz and I check out to 'quick game,' and they begin pointing where the play is going, I know it's going to be a long night." Johnson added: "When one of our receivers couldn't hear [the play], their guys would tell him what [route] he was supposed to run. You think I'm being sarcastic, but I'm not." Spurrier called Johnson's comments "excuses," adding: "That's the most we've been outplayed and outcoached in a victory in the ten years I've been coach."

There was much talk after the game that Tim Olmstead, a former Florida quarterback who'd transferred to Vandy prior to the season, had helped the Commodores break down the Gator offense. Vandy coaches and players acknowledged that he was of some help—but they were indignant at the suggestion that crafty intelligence—rather than their own tape study, tactical intelligence, and good play—was behind their strong defensive performance. Several weeks before the Florida game, Battles offered convincing proof of just how savvy he and his defensive mates were on a football field. He absolutely went into *a stream of consciousness riff* on the art of "reading plays" from the defensive back position—and holding your own against top receivers.

Breaking Codes

Before one can intuit what play the offense is running, Battles says, many things must be considered in the precious moments between the time the opposing offensive players walk up to the line of scrimmage and the moment the ball is snapped. "First, based on your defensive schemes, you figure a receiver can run only A, B, and C routes; he cannot run other routes because [of his position on the field]—for example, he may be too close to the sideline. Then you consider other things: What is the down and distance? What formation is the offensive backfield in? Where is the tight end—on the line, off the line? Are there two receivers, three receivers, or a cluster? It all ties in.

"If you watch film, you can see things: okay, on first and ten, or second and seven yards plus, or second and five yards or less, the opponent likes [certain] plays. And from watching tape, I know what those plays are. I can almost tell you what they're going to run, who they're going to run, or where they'll be throwing the ball. And if you know the weakness of your own defensive scheme, you can anticipate where the defense is going to want to look. And you can try and bait the quarterback into doing something that you want him to do. He knows your weakness, *but you know it, too, and he doesn't know that you know what he might want to do.* That comes from watching a lot of tape and getting out on the field.

"The hardest part is not the memorization. You're out on the field, you see the down and distance, you see the formation, you do see the 60,000 people around you. Let's say it's second and three and they line up in an I formation: You say, 'Are they going to run play action, run off tackle, or a dive?' Your mind is racing. Then they run somebody in motion, and you think: 'During the year, when they've gone in motion they've done A, B, and C. Will they crack down on the linebacker? If so, I've got to support the run. If they crack and release, I've got to play the pass. What if I'm blitzing? Where's the back at? Should I peel [meaning abort a blitz and cover the back flaring out of the backfield]? Should I cover the tight end and let the linebacker blitz? Or should I blitz and let him cover the tight end?' You got to think about all those things." Whew!

Body Positions

Vandy defensive backs spend a lot of time not just studying the opponent's play-calling patterns, but also opposing players themselves—especially receivers and quarterbacks. Battles pays close attention to a receiver's body position and feet when he is running routes. Little things help him predict where the opponent is headed.

"A receiver's natural tendency is to run low, get up, and then settle back down." By "get up" he means that receivers tend to raise their bodies just before changing direction. When Battles sees a body rise, he knows a directional break is coming. When receivers are just flying down the field—running straight ahead as opposed to making a 90-degree or 45-degree break—they don't really change their body position. Beyond that, he adds, "all receivers run routes a little differently, and they are coached differently at different schools." He says that Florida's receivers "have the best feet off the line of scrimmage that I've seen, and they're coached that way. Some receivers are taught, when they're going to cut inside, to chop their feet and then go; some are taught to plant [the outside foot] and cut; and some round the routes."

Quarterbacks are also scrutinized on tape. Battles says that if he and his colleagues and coaches watch enough tape, they can decipher the hand signals that certain quarterbacks give to their receivers at the line of scrimmage when they want a flanker to, say, run a hitch route, or a curl or a fade. Much depends on the down and distance. In addition, Vandy will put a stopwatch to a tape to figure out how long, on average, a team takes to snap the ball. Says Battles: "You can time it: a quarterback will get down under the center, look left, look right, then look forward and down and the center will snap the ball. You need to know that stuff when you're blitzing. Sometimes, the QB will look left and then get back under center and try to throw your timing off. This is the behind-the-scenes stuff that people don't know about. This is all stuff that I learned here. The game is very complex, but very simple, too."

Battles says that Florida quarterbacks tend to audible a lot. "Sometimes they'll get a [play] signal from the sidelines. The quarterback will come to the line, look around, and then look at a coach on the sideline, who will give him some kind of signal—sometimes telling him what a defensive end is doing. During the course of a game, you can usually figure those out, too."

Asked to name his strength as a football player, Battles says, unsurprisingly, "my knowledge of the game. While I'm fast and can tackle, I like to get into the huddle and tell the other safety and corners what plays to look out for. Or when the quarterback comes up to the line and does his hand gestures, I yell at the corners what routes the receivers may run. It doesn't mean they're going to run it, but look out for it."

Battles has aspirations to play pro football. But if that doesn't work out, he told me he might also become a minister. He was a member of the Nashville branch of the International Churches of Christ. Last summer he went on a church-sponsored trip to London to attend religious classes. He said it was a life-changing experience. "It opened my eyes to the world, and showed me how good we have it in America. It makes me so grateful. I see how much I have, and how much I have to give. I can say of myself, 'Well, I have a drive for excellence, and I work hard. But where does my drive come from?' And if you trace life back far enough, you realize you're just a vehicle." He studied Christian history in England during his trip, and learned how Christians in that country in the 1500s suffered for their beliefs: "People were chained to the floor. It helped me see the big picture and realize what being a Christian is all about."

Soon, he'll get a first-hand look at what the National Football League is all about. Battles was not drafted, but he signed a free-agent contract with a team that Widenhofer knows well—the Pittsburgh Steelers. For the moment, Battles doesn't have to worry about balancing academics and athletics. With a Vandy degree in hand, and a professional tryout ahead, he can indulge his first love—football. But he's not likely to stray too far from the lesson he learned way back in the eighth grade, and again as a freshman in college: be smart, work hard, or be prepared to hear from the enforcer—Dad.

SEVENTEEN

THE COCKTAIL PARTY: GEORGIA VERSUS FLORIDA

I wouldn't call it hatred, but we definitely don't like each other.
—Travis Cummings, president of Georgia's Jacksonville
Booster Club, on the rivalry with Florida

October 30, 1999

Gentleman's Quarterly magazine once posted a list of the 100 things a man should do before the age of thirty-three. One of the recommendations: attend the world's largest outdoor cocktail party, which is also known as the Georgia-Florida football game. The two teams play annually in Jacksonville, Florida, which has been home to this Border War for more than fifty years. About sixty miles south of the Georgia state line, Jacksonville is considered a neutral site. The 73,000 seats in Alltel Stadium are divided up equally—half for the red and black worn by Georgia fans, half for the orange and blue worn by Florida loyalists. In fact, Jacksonville adds 10,000 temporary seats to the stadium for the Georgia-Florida game to help sate the demand for tickets. "It's quite a sight," says Georgia Athletic Director Vince Dooley. He would know: he was the Georgia football coach for twenty-five years. "The two teams go after each other pretty good."

Sensitive to the drinking issue, the Jacksonville Chamber of Commerce has lately been discouraging the media from describing the Georgia-Florida weekend as a "cocktail party." They fear it's not quite the right image for a college football game. It may not be the right image—but c'mon, it's the reality: when Georgia and Florida fans converge in Jacksonville, they are geared to paarrrr-tee—and to hell with anything else. You could tell this crowd that a meteor was scheduled to obliterate the Earth in two days: "Fine, pour me a bourbon, and Gooooo Dawgs! Sic 'em! Woof! Woof! Woof!" That would be the response of an average Georgia fan. Florida fans would extend their arms straight out, put one palm atop the other, and then open and close their arms in imitation of an alligator's mouth. It's the

261

BRAGGING RIGHTS

Gator Chomp: get out of the way! This is an event, a happening—a long weekend of celebration for two universities and two states. It's a grudge game, a block party, a kegger, a carnival, a sports festival—all rolled into one.

The weekend is so big that last year, a University of Georgia student government candidate proposed that the university officially cancel all classes on Florida Friday, the day before the game. That way, students would feel less guilty streaming south out of Athens with their cars stuffed with beer coolers when they should otherwise be in, say, biology lab. The proposal never made it on the books, but it's a holiday nonetheless. Classes in Athens and Gainesville are empty of students, and the professors are not surprised. Jacksonville hotel rooms are booked months, sometimes years, in advance.

Before the game is ever fought on the field, the students wage a freeway battle of sorts with shaving cream and car stickers. Both armies are visible on Interstate 10, where Georgia fans heading south meet Florida fans driving east. HONK IF YOU'RE A DAWG! reads one. WE REMEMBER 37-17 says another—a reference to the score of the 1997 game when Georgia upset Florida, the Bulldogs' only victory over the Gators in the 1990s. Another sticker reads: FLARDA SUX. The misspelling is intended to imply that the other school is populated by idiot rednecks. (And you are. . . ?) Florida cars mount a counterattack: GO GATORS: A DECADE OF DOMINANCE—a reference to the eight victories racked up by Florida in its last nine games with Georiga. Another sticker reads: TURN THE DAWGS INTO PUPPIES.

Doug Gillett, a 1999 Georgia graduate, put this game into perspective. "There may be bigger college football rivalries in the country, like Florida–Florida State or Michigan–Ohio State. But I can't think of any like Georgia-Florida, which takes over a city. It's just big—the atmosphere is like a bowl game. It's more or less accepted that if you're in Jacksonville and you're not involved in the world's largest outdoor cocktail party, you might has well just leave the city for the weekend." Alums are just as obsessed as the students: many spend the Thursday and Friday before the game playing golf in northern Florida or relaxing at the beach with friends.

Nowadays, Florida's biggest games are against Florida State and Tennessee. But any Gator fan over age thirty can tell you horror stories about playing the Dawgs. In the 1970s and 1980s, Georgia absolutely tormented the Gators— beating them often and, many times, stealing victories from Florida in the waning minutes of games. In 1983, Bulldog quarterback John Lastinger led Georgia on a 99-yard, second-half drive that took nearly 7 minutes and 30 seconds off the clock and culminated with Barry Young plunging into the end zone. Georgia won, 10-9. In 1985 Florida was ranked number one coming into this game. Georgia stunned the Gators, 24-3. The most memorable victory in Georgia's history came over the Gators in 1980. With just over a minute to go in the game, Florida was leading 21-19 and seemingly poised to win not only this game, but the SEC title. Georgia was in a nearly impossible situation: facing a third down from its own *7-yard line*. Georgia quarterback Buck Belue stepped to the line of scrimmage. Bulldog radio announcer Larry Munson then described the ensuing play:

> *Florida in a stand-up five . . . they may or may not blitz . . . they won't. Buck*
> *back [to throw] . . . third down on the eight . . . in trouble . . . got a block*
> *behind him . . . gonna throw on the run...complete to the 25, to the 30,*
> *Lindsay Scott 35, 40, Lindsay Scott, 45, 50, 45, 40 . . . Run Lindsay . . . 25,*
> *20, 15, 10, 5 . . . LINDSAY SCOTT! LINDSAY SCOTT! LINDSAY SCOTT!*

That miraculous 93-yard touchdown catch and run by Scott not only beat Florida, it propelled Georgia to the national title. When Scott ran into the end zone, gleeful Dawg fans jumped to their feet in the stadium, sending bourbon and coke flying out of plastic cups in all directions. A 1952 Florida grad recently recalled listening to the 1980 game on the radio. When it was over, he wrote, and Florida had lost, "I went outside my home and threw all the patio furniture into the pool." Winning matters.

Jim Donnan, the Georgia football coach, looks a lot like the actor Ned Beatty. He's chunky, with thinning hair and a round face. He played quarterback in college, at N.C. State, but he looks more like a former fullback now. His eyes can twinkle mischievously. But he's got a fiery side. After two Georgia managers, Carter McKinnis and Jared Jones, were kind enough to give me a quick primer on offensive formations during a Georgia practice last year, Donnan came up to me later and muttered menacingly: "Didya git you some good plays?" He then walked off. During that same practice, an offensive lineman jumped offside during a team drill. That sparked Donnan's ire.

"You don't jump offside at Georgia," he screamed at the offending lineman. "This is a *college football team*, not a high school team. . . . Hey, why don't *all of you* jump offside! Go ahead, the whole damn team jump offside!" As he said that, Donnan ran down the line of scrimmage and gave each of Georgia's five offensive linemen a slight shove in the back, one after another. "Now huddle up!"

Donnan was hired in 1996, after Ray Goff had been fired, and two years later he vowed to "shock the world." It was a bold statement from a brash coach. Donnan has a good offensive mind. In the late 1980s he was the offensive coordinator for Oklahoma, which won the national championship in 1985. He later became the head coach at Marshall, where he coached for six years and (in 1992) won the 1AA national championship. Georgia Athletic Director Vince Dooley brought Donnan in for a simple reason: to get the Bulldogs over the hump. The hump is the SEC championship. Georgia hasn't won it, amazingly, since 1982, when Herschel Walker was a junior. That's because the hump is guarded by two imposing sentinels, named Tennessee and Florida. Georgia has been their whipping boy in the the 1990s.

Donnan has done a lot, and done a little. He's recruited reasonably well. His biggest catch has been quarterback Quincy Carter, a former professional baseball player who'd originally signed with Georgia Tech. Big, strong, and mobile, Carter is an excellent rollout passer. But like most everybody on Georgia's team, Carter was young. Though only a sophomore in 1999, he was one of the Bulldogs' most experienced players. Georgia's receiving corps lacked big-play ability; the tight ends were the most consistent threat. On defense, the same problem was evident: there was talent—linebackers Boss Bailey and Will Witherspoon were athletic "comers"—but it was young and inconsistent. Defense linemen Marcus Stroud and Richard Seymour were dependable up front.

Georgia had built some momentum the previous two years. Donnan won nine games in 1997 and ten in 1998 (both seasons culminating with bowl wins and top-twenty rankings). What he hadn't been able to do is get over that hump. The reason? Coming into the 1999 Florida game, he was a combined 1-6 against Phillip Fulmer and Steve Spurrier—the lone victory coming over Florida in 1997. Heck, Georgia has never played in the SEC championship game, which started in 1992. "I feel like our talent level approximates [Tennessee's and Florida's]," Donnan said just before the 1999 season. "But whatever I say, people will ask, 'What's your record against them?' And it's not very good. For us to compare to them, we've got to be one of the top five teams in the country, and I'd say we're in the realm of number five through fifteen, probably. There is no need to keep talking about it. We've just got to go out and win."

Because Georgia has played in the shadows of its two conference rivals for several years, it's easy to forget what a solid football tradition the Bulldogs have. Glenn "Pop" Warner, one of college football's most successful coaches, started his career at Georgia. Wallace Butts, who coached Georgia from 1939 to 1960, won four SEC championships and, in 1942, a consensus national championship. And more than a few great players have passed through Athens. In fact, Georgia arguably boasts the SEC's best running back tradition. Everybody knows Herschel Walker, of course, but Terrell Davis, Rodney Hampton, Robert Edwards, and Garrison Hearst all played running back for the Dawgs.

Losing Fizz?

Edwards certainly helped Georgia beat Florida in 1997, but individual performances are seldom enough to win SEC slugfests. It's a team game, and Georgia's depth seldom matched Florida's in the 1990s. In fact, there have been rumblings among Georgia fans that the cocktail party is losing fizz. Some alums are beginning to think that Jacksonville is not such a neutral site after all. According to Dooley, there is a block of alumni who would like to stop playing the Florida game in Jacksonville and return it to a more traditional home-and-home format, as nearly all other conference games are played.

The two teams renew their contract with the city of Jacksonville every eight years, and Dooley says that "within a year we'll start looking at the issue seriously. Our fans are now almost split" on whether the game should stay in Jacksonville or not. "When you get beat quite a bit it almost becomes a Florida home game every year. We used to consider it almost a southern Georgia game. You have to do what your constituents want to do." Dooley says that there used to be a lot of fights at the game, when it was held at the old Gator Bowl stadium, and there were various management problems. And he asserts that because Jacksonville now has a pro football team (the Jaguars), the game "has lost a little bit."

Travis Cummings would not agree. He's the president of the Jacksonville Bulldog Club, which has nearly 700 members and acts as official host for the Bulldog nation on Florida weekend. The club greets the football team at the airport, when the Dawgs fly in, and stakes signs along the road to the hotel: THE JACKSONVILLE BULLDOG CLUB WELCOMES THE DAWGS!

Cummings, who is twenty-eight, is a native of Jacksonville. His grandmother's family is from south Georgia, and he graduated from Valdosta State—a south Georgia college. He's been going to this game since he was a tot. His grandmother used to take him to the airport to watch the Bulldogs arrive—a tradition he carried over with the Jacksonville club. She also took him to Athens in 1980 to soak up a little atmosphere—right after Georgia won the national championship. "We went straight to the bookstore and loaded up on souvenir stuff," he said. "I was like a kid in a candy store." On the way they stopped in Wrightsville, Georgia—Walker's hometown. (Everything about Georgia football eventually comes 'round to Herschel.) "My brothers and other relatives were big Dawg fans, and it just got hold of me at an early age. It was a given. And it sticks with you. Georgia folks are good fans and good people. We go up to all the games."

The Florida game is important to the Jacksonville Bulldog Club. It sponsors four academic scholarships a year to Georgia—and counts on the Jacksonville bash to raise the lion's share of the $12,000 needed annually to fund the scholarships. "It is really a commitment," Cummings says. "If the team is having a lean year, it can be tough raising the money. But we've done it every year." The club holds a massive barbecue lunch every year before the game, selling two meals and a stadium parking pass for $40. "We'll feed about 2,000 to 2,500 at the barbecue," Cummings said the day before the game. The lunch is held at Metropolitan Park, a pavilion on St. John's River next to Alltel Stadium. Cummings had just returned from a tour of the stadium area, where he said he saw "a sea of RVs." The club hires a country music band, and "looks after" (meaning treats to a lunch) the Georgia cheerleaders and the coaches' wives. Cummings says that if expenses are kept under control, "we'll make anywhere from $7,000 to $8,000." He himself hangs out with about sixty friends. "We get about fifteen parking places and tailgate and have a good time. I've had people calling me for two months, saying: 'Hey, what's going on for the weekend?' It's a hot ticket." In fact, outside of the state fair, which is curiously held the same weekend, the Georgia-Florida game is the biggest event all year in Jacksonville. "Parking is just a nightmare," says Cummings. "Everybody would rather that they didn't have the fair at the same time."

Years ago, says Cummings, beer was sold at the Gator Bowl. There is no alcohol on sale inside the stadium anymore, but "it gets in there somehow. People are drinking all day, and the game gets pretty emotional." Flasks are passé—better suited to Princeton grads wearing bow ties. This is the southeast, and for those wanting to nip during the game, the preferred liquor-smuggling method is the plastic Ziploc bag. So malleable. So perfect. "A bag is more compact and easier to get in," explains Cummings. "Usually every tailgate has some Ziplocs handy before the walk-in; you can stick 'em in your socks or in a purse." Asked about the attitude of the rival crowds to one another, Cummings says: "I wouldn't say there is hatred, but we definitely don't like each other come game day." Florida fans, in fact, are PO'd at Georgia's Jacksonville Club. Reason: the club's logo shows a bulldog with an alligator in its mouth. "We changed the logo back in the late 1970s; we were looking for something more than just the Bulldog head. I'm sure Florida fans love that," says Cummings. It seems innocent fun, but Gator fans complained about that logo on the Internet in the days leading up to the game.

The Landing

The epicenter for the Georgia-Florida weekend is The Jacksonville Landing, which is an enormous indoor-outdoor complex along the St. John's River. It's a collection of restaurants and shops, along with an open area for concerts. But that implies a complexity that the Landing really lacks when the Gators and Dawgs are in town. On the Friday before the game, the Landing functions in two simple ways: places to buy beer, and places to drink beer. Restaurants—

Georgia vs. Florida

Chinese, Mexican, U.S. chains—hang handwritten signs in their windows touting BEER! And they sell it in disposable cups and hollowed out footballs that are as big as heads. The Friday night crowd is unmistakably young—easily 90 percent college students who are fresh-faced, casually dressed. Their goals are basic: drink beer, laugh with friends, drink beer, make fun of the other team's fans, drink beer, meet girls, drink beer, eat, drink beer, meet guys, drink beer, dance, get obnoxious, drink beer. If, by a twist of cosmic fate, a few guys and gals hit it off for a night and are pleased to satisfy the hormonal imperative, so much the better. But the weekend is mostly about beer and football. Some students stay inside the multistory complex, claiming hard-to-find tables and booths, but most congregate either in the spacious common area or on balconies overlooking the scene. The staircases are so jammed they are almost unnavigable.

The entertainment last year was the Beach Boys, who played on Friday night. Having a wheezy band play for Generation Y seemed odd—but it didn't really matter. You could barely hear those high-pitched California harmonies above the noise. Actually, the Landing was not really noisy; it just *buzzes*. It's the collective thrum of a thousand kids laughing and shouting simultaneously. Or maybe it's just a boozy cacophony. Whatever. The female students certainly seem well practiced at shrieking in wide-eyed disbelief as they recognize friends and sorority sisters who (surprisingly?) made the trip. *Everybody* makes the trip. Occasionally, a gutsy frat man from Gainesville will shout "Georgia sucks!" Georgia fans respond by singing: "It's great . . . to be . . . a Gator hater! I say . . . it's great . . . to be . . . a Gator hater!" Everybody laughs—and then quickly checks the level of beer in their cups. The Beach Boys keep singing, but the buzz prevails.

The Game, in the Rain

Georgia came into the game ranked fourteenth in the nation, and sporting a 6-1 record. Their only loss was to nemesis number one, Tennessee. The previous week, Georgia had lost five turnovers but still whomped Kentucky, scoring 49 points. Florida was also 6-1, having beaten Tennessee but lost to Alabama.

Coming into the game, the Bulldogs wanted to run the football, put pressure on Florida quarterback Doug Johnson, and force some turnovers. They did all those things—and still lost. The Dogs rushed for 188 yards and intercepted Johnson twice. But at key junctions in the game, Florida's defense was dominant—forcing two huge second-half turnovers. One Georgia fumble prevented the Bulldogs from taking the lead in the second half, the other positioned the Gators for an easy second-half score. Together, those plays killed Georgia's chances—and ensured that the Dawgs would lose for the ninth time in ten years to the Gators.

The first half was evenly played, and fairly well-played—despite a steady rainfall. Quincy Carter sliced through Florida's defense on option plays and scored two touchdowns. Georgia fans were happy. But Florida's offense was in rhythm: quarterback Doug Johnson threw for 234 yards in the first half, connecting mainly with receiver Darrell Jackson. He would finish the game with six receptions for 141 yards—his sixth-straight 100-yard receiving game. Johnson led the Gators on a ten-play, 72-yard touchdown drive late in the second quarter. When the half ended, the Gators were leading 16-14. Georgia fans were sad.

The game turned decisively in Florida's favor in the second half. Poised to take the lead, Georgia running back Jasper Sanks fumbled the ball at the Florida 10-yard line after being popped by Gator linebacker Keith Kelsey. Soon after, Gator running back Bo Carroll darted through the Georgia line and ran 30 yards for a touchdown that gave Florida a commanding 23-14 lead. On Georgia's next drive, Florida defensive end Alex Brown sacked Carter and forced him to fumble—at the Georgia two-yard line. Johnson ran the ball into the end zone and the game was effectively over.

Brown had played a monster game against Tennessee early in the season, but was lackluster in subsequent games. But the talented pass rusher found himself against Georgia—thanks partly to the fact that Florida defensive tackle Gerard Warren, who is an unmovable object in the middle, was drawing two Georgia blockers. For the game Brown recorded eight tackles, two sacks, caused a fumble, and intercepted a Carter pass. "Alex decided he wanted to play," said Florida defensive coordinator Jon Hoke. "It's frustrating that he doesn't do it [more consistently]."

As it had against Tennessee, the Florida defense won this game. Carter finished with just 76 yards passing on six completions. He spent much of the second half running for his life. Georgia was hurt badly when offensive lineman Jonas Jennings injured his ankle in the third quarter and could not return. Without him the Bulldog running game disappeared. "We did a good job of outrushing them in the first half," said Georgia running back Patrick Pass. "But when Jonas went out, it was hard to put it in the end zone."

The final score was 30-14, Florida. Carroll led all rushers with 118 yards on only 13 carries. "We just had to pay attention and play hard in the rain," the speedster said. Florida coach Steve Spurrier credited his defense with the win, saying "they played spectacularly." Linebacker Kelsey sympathized with Carter, who was under intense pressure from Brown & Co. most of the day.

"He is a tough guy but we shook him up a little. He's a fighter."

After the game, a subdued Jim Donnan said: "Everybody's [emotionally] depleted right now." That was understandable. The Dawgs had again lost to both Florida and Tennessee, and again come up short in their by-now generational quest to win another SEC title. "We're down because we were in the game and we know we could have won," added Donnan. "But we're gonna have as good a year as we can."

Georgia defensive end Charles Grant—one of the most promising defensive players in the SEC—did not mince words, or heap praise on the Gators. "The best team did not win," he asserted. Grant, who's 6'4" and weighs 260 pounds, had played much of the game against Florida's best offensive lineman, Kenyatta Walker, who like Grant, is a first-rate trash talker. "Number 78 [Walker] is good, but he did not show me much," said Grant. He expressed frustration with the officials, who he believes blew a call on the crucial Sanks fumble. "Jaspar was down, but they still called it a fumble."

For Georgia, the bottom line was unforgiving: there would be no SEC championship in 1999. But as Donnan pointed out, there were still some big games ahead for his team, including the annual clash with in-state rival Georgia Tech. Georgia fans were already foaming about that bitter contest. Here is how a Bulldog booster expressed his prediction for the game against the Georgia Tech Yellow Jackets: "It was as if a huge white paw slapped the stinger right off the ass of that damned bee, driving the stinger into the face of the dreaded insect, killing it." Okaaaaay.

After the game, everybody is wet and chilled—and back at the Landing. The beer drinking has resumed. A change of clothes? A waste of time. After the Florida win, drunken Gators fans are bellowing obnoxiously, in that great postgame college tradition. One Georgia fan is injured when he is struck in the eye by a beer-filled plastic football hurled from the upper level into the crowd below.

Outside, Daniel Wells, a UGA junior, is standing beside a double-decker RV. Hip-hop music is blaring from the sound system. Half a dozen delirious Georgia students and alums are on top of the vehicle, dancing and swaying. The contraption looks ready to collapse. Wells, his face painted red and black, stares up at the dancers in amazement. After three straight trips to Jacksonville, he said, nothing much surprised him anymore. "I've seen some pretty wild stuff down here. You put alcohol with all these crazy fans, and this is what you get. But everybody loves it. I do."

Wells and four friends packed into a Honda Civic and made the trip a day earlier. They wanted to stay in a hotel, but they were all booked. So the five young men wound up sleeping on the floor of a local apartment. Nobody even knew the Georgia graduate who lived there—he was a friend of a friend of

BRAGGING RIGHTS

Wells's. But big parties call for drastic measures. "I'd do just about anything to get down to Jacksonville," said Wells. "Ride with anyone, stay anywhere. All you have to do is look around at the Landing. Look at all the people, and you know it's worth it. I wouldn't miss it for anything. You know?" Yes, we know.

Tomorrow, he and the rest of the Georgia students would be going back:

> *Going back, going back*
> *Going back to Athens town*
> *Going back, going back*
> *To the best old place around.*
> *Going back, going back*
> *To hear that grand old sound*
> *Of a chapel bell and a Georgia yell*
> *Going back to Athens town.*

EIGHTEEN

THE LOST BOYS

Barrett Askew grew up in Lanett, Alabama—fifteen minutes from the campus of Auburn University. In 1995, he was considered the top high school linebacker prospect in Alabama, and one of the top defensive prospects in the Southeast. He was recruited by practically everybody, he says—Florida, Tennessee, Georgia, Georgia Tech, Ole Miss, Misssissippi State, and Miami. He signed with the school next door—Auburn. He was happy; his parents and high school coach were proud. The world was his oyster. Expectations were high. They always are with SEC prospects.

Askew, who is a 230-pound outside linebacker, says his first year on the Plains went well. "It was fun. It was straight." He made friends, played hard on the football field. All players are allowed four years of athletic eligibility—and all are given an extra, so-called redshirt year to refine their skills, to recover from an injury, or to simply adjust to college life—if the coaches deem it worthwhile. Many players *are* redshirted their first year, and that is what happened to Askew. He was held out of games to build up his strength, speed, and linebacker skills. That still left him with a full four years to play football at Auburn.

But Askew's Auburn career soured his second year. "We had a lot of defensive changes," he said. Worse, Askew and Bill Oliver, Auburn's defensive coordinator, at that time, did not get along. According to Askew, Oliver didn't like him personally or as a football player. "He was on me all the time. He told me that I probably wouldn't be able to play at Auburn. He said I looked slow on film. He just didn't like me. When they bring in freshmen and put them in front of you, you know you're not going to play."

BRAGGING RIGHTS

That is life in the SEC: every year twenty to thirty high school prospects are signed amid much fanfare. Fans optimistically predict great things for the new-comers. The first-year players feel the same way. They arrive on campus with confidence and dreams of collegiate glory. But it doesn't often turn out that way. For many, things go bad in a hurry. The SEC's dirty little secret is that its foot-ball teams have a high attrition rate. Kids fall out of programs in alarming num-bers. Some simply get homesick and leave. Greg Barnum, a promising center at Tennessee, decided after his freshman season that he wanted to return to his native Texas. Some players have family problems. Some flunk drug tests or break the law. Some get injured. Some can't or won't do the classwork. Many get discouraged with their prospects for playing time and then transfer.

That's what Askew did. He transferred to the University of Tennessee at Chattanooga, where he was the starting linebacker last year. He said the deci-sion was easy. "I wish I could have stayed in the SEC," says Askew. "I miss it. But some things you just have to go through." He said that he "loves" UTC. "I'm enjoying it. It's fine. Two players that I graduated from high school with came here. They talked me into coming." He still has aspirations of playing pro foot-ball, but he's realistic. "It will be tough." There were twenty-three players in Askew's 1995 signing class at Auburn. After the 1999 season, the last for the group, only eleven players had completed their eligibility. And only three had graduated. The rest were, as they say in Latin America, disappeared.

But that's nothing compared to the 1995 Ole Miss class. Of the twenty-six players signed to scholarships, last year only *four*—I repeat, *four*—were still on the team. Langston Rodgers, the Ole Miss sports information director, is not quite sure what happened to all those players. "Some may not have made their grades," he says. "Some may not have qualified (for admission). We didn't run anybody off."

Actually, he does know what happened to a few of the 1995 signees, and tells me. One kid, Joey Embry, drowned; another (Matt Luke) graduated; one signee (Jason Clinsan) was married, had a child, and needed money. So he quit to go to work. "Another pair, Bo Bennett and Sam Owen, were so-called legacy signees. Their dads had played for Ole Miss. For reasons unknown, says Rodgers, both decided to quit. Paul Carillo, a quarterback from California, transferred.

After telling me this, Rodgers then reveals that not all of the twenty-six play-ers were actually given scholarships. Twelve of the twenty-six scholarship signees were, in fact, "walk-ons"—kids who play football but are *not* on schol-arship. Tommy Tuberville was the Ole Miss coach in 1995, and the school was on probation. The school was allowed only thirteen scholarships that year. Nevertheless, twenty-six players signed "letters of intent" to play for Mississippi. Letters of intent bind players to a particular school, but they are not actual scholarship papers; they become null and void if the actual followup scholarship papers are not signed within two weeks. The twelve walk-ons never signed the second document, the actual scholarship papers. According to Rodgers, "Tuberville never told us which players were walk-ons and which were actual scholarship players." Why this charade? Rodgers is not sure, but surely public relations had lots to do with it. First, Tuberville probably did not want to reinforce the fact that Mississippi had been sanctioned by the NCAA. So he created the impression that Ole Miss had signed a normal class. Second, putting the names of walk-ons on the scholarship list "makes mammas and daddies feel good," says Rodgers. The NCAA has since prohibited this sleight of hand. Now, schools can only announce a scholarship signee if he has signed both the initial letter of intent and, after that, the actual scholarship document.

Doug Dickey, the Tennessee athletic director, is sanguine about the attrition issue. He chalks up team turnover to "the normal problems of life," adding: "I don't think the attrition problem is severe." Well, in addition to Barnum, Tennessee in just a few short months lost Onterrio Smith (drug test failures), linebacker Devon Davis (no playing time), lineman Tim Hodges (no playing time), and linebacker Austin Kemp (back injury), among others. At Florida, former starting strong safety Rod Graddy was kicked off the team last year after being suspended three times in three years. The last straw for him came when two occupants of a car he was driving were arrested—one for robbery and assault and the other for accessory to theft. Such incidents are not common in major-college football, but they aren't exactly rare either.

Oddly, given that so many kids transfer because of a lack of playing time, coaches and athletic directors fret about the NCAA limit on scholarships. Most are reasonably comfortable with the eighty-five-scholarship limit, but they'd prefer a few more. Both Dickey and Vince Dooley, the Georgia athletic director, say the eighty-five limit barely provides them with enough players for spring practice (typically sixty to seventy, after the seniors have left and before the freshmen have arrived). But I don't see the logic in raising the scholarship total. Adding scholarship players is not going to make room for more kids to play; it would probably just result in more transfers. What's the point of that? Kids come to the SEC to play—and soon learn the competition is tough. When they see no playing time ahead, they often leave.

Dickey says that when he was a player, in the 1960s, "there were 100 guys on my *freshman* team"—more than the total number of scholarships allowed now. Many would get run off because they weren't good enough to play, or because there was no room. Now, with the lower scholarship limit, he insists that "coaches work hard to recruit kids who can make it. We're recruiting kids to succeed." While Dickey suggests that about two players fall out of football programs every year, in reality the number is closer to four or five. One day, the kids are budding stars—the toast of their hometowns. And then, suddenly, they are gone. Poof. Here's the breakdown of the 1995 signing classes at LSU and Auburn.

LSU's 1995 Football Signees

1. Kevin Faulk, running back
   Carencro, Louisiana

   Four-year letterman; graduated; New England Patriots

2. Larry Foster, wide receiver
   Harvey, Louisiana

   Three-year letterman; kicked off team

3. Benaderyl Franklin
   Moss Point, Mississippi

   Left team

4. Monte Gatlin, linebacker
   Magnolia, Mississippi

   One-year letterman; transferred to Jackson State

5. Ryan Hebert, lineman
   Baton Rouge, Louisiana

   One-year letterman; graduated

6. Greg Hill, back
   Mansfield, Louisiana

   Two-year letterman; transferred to Northwestern State (LA)

7. Lloyd Jones, defensive back
   Hitchcock, Texas

   Never enrolled

8. Roshaun Mathews, linebacker
   Baton Rouge, Louisiana

   Letterman; graduated; transferred to Southern University

9. Todd McClure, lineman
   Baton Rouge, Louisiana

   Four-year letterman; graduated; Atlanta Falcons

10. Anthony McFarland, def. tackle
    Winnsboro, Louisiana

    Completed eligibility; graduated; Tampa Bay

11. Nashaell Menard, lineman
    Marrero, Louisiana

    Deceased

12. Arnold Miller, defensive end
    New Orleans, Louisiana

    Completed eligiblity; graduated; Cleveland Browns

13. Jamal Pack, tight end
    Marrero, Louisiana

    Three-year letterman; graduated

14. Nicky Savoie, quarterback
    Cut Off, Louisiana

    Two-year letterman

15. Anthony Skinner, back
    Patterson, Louisiana

    One-year letterman; left team

The Lost Boys

16. Charles Smith, linebacker
New Orleans, Louisiana
Completed eligibility after 1999; four-year letterman

17. Markeith Spears, linebacker
Zachery, Louisiana
Four-year letterman; graduated

18. Ryan Thomassie, off. lineman
Galliano, Louisiana
Four-year letterman; graduated; playing in NFL–Europe

19. Damien Tullier, def. tackle
New Orleans, Louisiana
Retired for medical reasons; one-year letterman; graduated

20. Herbert Tyler, quarterback
New Orleans, Louisiana
Four-year letterman; graduated; entering law school

21. Joseph Wesley, linebacker
Brookhaven, Mississippi
Four-year starter; graduated; San Francisco 49ers

22. Clifton White, quarterback
Hahnville, Louisiana
Retired for medical reasons; one-year letterman; graduated

23. Jeremy Whitten, wide reciever
Louisville, Kentucky
Completed eligibility

24. Rondell Mealey, running back
Destrehan, Louisiana
Four-year letterman; graduated; drafted by Green Bay Packers

25. Marcus Taylor
Never enrolled

Auburn's 1995 Football Signees

1. Barrett Askew, linebacker
Lanett, Alabama
Transferred to Tennessee-Chattanooga

2. Robert Baker, wide receiver
Gainsesville, Florida
Played two years; academically ineligible third year; convicted of selling selling drugs, kicked off team

3. Stan Bellamy, linebacker
Columbus, Georgia
Medical scholarship; graduated

4. Jayson Bray, defensive back
LaGrange, Georgia
Completed eligibility after 1998 season; signed as an NFL free agent

5. Jimmy Brumbaugh, def. line
Keystone Heights, Florida
Completed eligibility after 1999 season; signed as an NFL free agent

6. Tucker Dearth, linebacker
Birmingham, Alabama
Quit team to play baseball; graduated

BRAGGING RIGHTS

7. T. J. Dunigan, defensive tackle   Started at center in 1997; quit before 1998
    Coffeeville, Alabama   season

8. Ben Elliot, offensive tackle   Medical scholarship; still in school
    Poplarville, Mississippi

9. Dan Evans, defensive back   Transferred to Youngstown State
    Lauderdale Lakes, Florida

10. Martavious Houston, def. back   Dismissed from team in the spring of 1998
    Lauderdale Lakes, Florida

11. Jeno James, offensive tackle   Completed eligibility after 1999; drafted by
    Montgomery, Alabama   Carolina Panthers

12. Errick Lowe, wide receivers   Completed eligibility
    Lake Worth , Florida

13. Michael Mallard, def. tackle   Academic casualty; left team
    Luverne, Alabama

14. T. J. Meers, offensive lineman   Entering senior season
    Atlanta, Georgia

15. Cencade Pennington, r. back   Completed eligibility after 1999 season;
    Troy, Alabama   graduated

16. Quinton Reese, linebacker   Completed eligibility after 1999 season;
    Birmingham, Alabama   drafted by the Detroit Lions

17. Norris Sealey, wide receiver   Quit team after one season
    Miami, Florida

18. Rick Sealey, linebkr–def. end   Quit team after one season
    Miami, Florida

19. Mark Smith, defensive line   Completed eligibility after 1998 season;
    Vicksburg, Mississippi   playing in the NFL

20. Takeo Spikes, linebacker   Completed eligibility after 1998; playing in
    Sandersville, Georgia   NFL

21. Marion Taylor, cornerback   Transferred to Grambling
    Smiths Station, Alabama

22. Ryan Taylor, linebacker   Completed eligibility after 1998; signed as an
    Dublin, Georgia   NFL free agent

23. Rusty Williams, running back   Completed eligibility after 1999 season
    Moncks Corner, South Carolina

NINETEEN

A MATTER OF DEGREES: GRADUATION RATES

The graduation rates for college football teams are always a hot topic of conversation. To separate fact from fiction, here are the latest SEC graduation numbers from the National Collegiate Athletic Association (NCAA). There are two sets of numbers for both SEC football teams and the overall student body at SEC schools. The 1992/93 number shows the graduation rate for, first, freshmen football players starting school that year, and then regular students who entered college as freshmen that year. The "four-year" rate is the average graduation rate for four classes—beginning with the 1988/89 freshman class and including the next three classes. Yes, the numbers seem old—but NCAA graduation rates are based on the number of students from a class that graduate within *six* years. So the students, and programs, are getting a one-year grace period, so to speak, if you consider that many incoming athletes are "redshirted" their freshman year and thus remain in college for at least five years.

As every major-college football coach and athletic director is quick to point out, the football graduation rates are affected by student-athletes who leave school early to play professional football. If the pro player returns to school during his off-season and completes the courses necessary to obtain his degree, he is counted as a graduate if the course requirements are finished within six years from the time when he started school. If a player takes longer than six years to earn his degree, he is *not* counted as a graduate. Note that at some schools (notably Mississippi and Mississippi State), the graduation rate for football players is higher than the regular student body. One reason, obviously, is that Mississippi is a poor state—and the football players are getting their education for free.

Using the four-year average for football players, which is the most representative sample, I have placed SEC schools in order from best (top) to worst (bottom). Vanderbilt football players have, by far, the best four-year average graduation rate; Arkansas, the worst. The worst number is the four-year average graduation rate for *all students* at Arkansas. Why are these numbers important? According to the 1999 Statistical Abstract of the United States, there were 54,000 players on college football teams last year. Of that number, about 340 coming out of school made a professional roster. And the number of players who will last four or more seasons in the NFL? 150.

Percent of Graduating Students: SEC

	1992/93	Four-year Average
Vanderbilt		
Football players	76	81
All students	82	82
Mississippi		
Football players	68	57
All students	48	48
Mississippi State		
Football players	50	57
All students	49	48
Kentucky		
Football players	65	53
All students	51	50
Florida		
Football players	74	52
All students	67	64
Auburn		
Football players	42	46
All students	66	66
Georgia		
Football players	56	44
All students	66	62
Alabama		
Football players	63	45
All students	59	57

Graduation Rates

	1992/93	Four-year Average
LSU		
Football players	41	40
All students	48	47
South Carolina		
Football players	53	38
All students	56	59
Tennessee		
Football players	57	34
All students	56	55
Arkansas		
Football players	34	28
All students	20	18

Other Universities with Major Football Programs

	1992/93	Four-year Average
Florida State		
Football players	67	60
All students	64	64
Penn State		
Football players	84	78
All students	80	79
Michigan		
Football players	50	52
All students	83	83
Arizona		
Football players	69	55
All students	54	51
Ohio State		
Football players	33	36
All students	56	57

TWENTY

INVITATION TO A BEHEADING: THE FALL OF GERRY DINARDO

Gerry DiNardo is part-owner of an Italian restaurant in Baton Rouge, Louisiana. Pasta seems a little out of place in the land of po'boys and jambalaya. But then so is DiNardo. Born and raised in Brooklyn, New York, he is a proud Italian—and looks the part: stocky build, Mediterranean skin, dark, receding hairline, back-slapping personality.

DiNardo (the coach) opened DiNardo's (the restaurant) in 1998. As a galoot might say, it's a classy joint: Sinatra on the sound system, Chianti for sale at the front desk ($15). The restaurant offered DiNardo two obvious benefits. First, it seemed a promising investment—a way to leverage his celebrity status as the football coach of Louisiana State University. Second, it gave him a chance to indulge his love of Italian culture.

Maybe there was another motivation, too: it might prove a nice diversion from LSU football. 1998 was a bad year for the football team, and who knew what the future would bring? What better way to take your mind off of grim gridiron business? The restaurant's red sauce comes courtesy of DiNardo's mother, Mary, who lives in Florida. "It's been tweaked for the Cajun palette," says a manager. "New Yorkers think it's a little strong."

Last fall I asked Herb Vincent, LSU's sports information director, if I could meet DiNardo at his restaurant. Herb made the call, and the coach agreed. The restaurant is located on Highland Road in south Baton Rouge, about a twenty-minute drive from the LSU campus. When I got off Interstate 10 and turned left onto Highland, the first thing I noticed was a small roller coaster ride, sitting on one corner of the intersection. Here is symbolism, I thought. Ever since the redoubtable Charlie McClendon was forced to retire as LSU

The Fall of Gerry DiNardo

football coach in 1979, after eighteen years with the program, LSU has been on a wild ride. The football program has been a model of *inconsistency*—and that is a charitable view. Sam King, a columnist for the *Baton Rouge Advocate*, recently summed up LSU football thusly: "Baton Rouge, it seems, is a lot like New Orleans: a drinking city with a football problem." There have been a few "up" years—mainly in the mid-1980s, when Bill Arnsparger (famous for coaching the Miami Dolphins' "no name" defense) was coach—but more often than not, LSU football has been *down*. LSU had six straight losing seasons between 1990 and 1995. Then DiNardo was hired away from Vanderbilt to do what his predecessors—Curley Hallman and Mike Archer—could not do: bring back the magic to LSU football. DiNardo, in fact, used those exact words: "I want to bring back the magic."

DiNardo wasn't LSU's first choice for the job. Former Texas Tech coach Pat Sullivan was, but he couldn't get out of his contract. But the burly Italian had impressed people with his work at Vanderbilt which, with its academic rigors, is a tough place to win. His four-year record with Vanderbilt was 18-26. DiNardo had played offensive line for Notre Dame in the 1970s, when Ara Parseghian was the Irish coach. He was the offensive coordinator at Colorado in 1990 when the Buffaloes won a share of the national title. He then took over at Vandy. DiNardo's last game at Vandy raised a few eyebrows in Baton Rouge—the Commodores were destroyed, 65-0—but most LSU fans gave him the benefit of the doubt. They had no choice, of course.

DiNardo got off to a good start with the Tigers. He cobbled together three winning seasons; won three (minor) bowl games. His cumulative record was a very respectable 26-9-1. The teams weren't great—none even reached the SEC championship game, but like some Discovery-channel adventurer, he had raised a sunken ship. The fans were happy. In fact, many worried that DiNardo would be hired away by Notre Dame or the Dallas Cowboys. "People told me I could run for governor," the coach told me at his restaurant. "I told them a less political job would be a relief." But, alas, the good times didn't last—and neither did DiNardo. After three years, his coaster ride had already reached its zenith. Soon, several factors would combine to push the program over the edge. By the time the football team reached the end of its high-speed descent, near the end of the 1999 season, DiNardo had been thrown over the side.

"Fabric of the Culture"

Like so many other schools in the SEC, LSU football has a powerful hold on the people of Louisiana. "No subject in this state is embraced more passionately," says Charlie Weems, a New Orleans attorney who is chairman of the university's board of supervisors. "LSU football is as embedded in the fabric of our culture as alligators in the bayou and Community Coffee." One reason is that Louisiana is loaded with good athletes. Few states in the country produce as many good high school football players. Though some go to Southern University and Grambling, LSU tends to get the pick of the litter. Charles Alexander, Y. A. Tittle, Jim Taylor, Bert Jones, Steve Van Buren, Bill Cannon, Jerry Stovall, Tommy Cassanova: all played for LSU.

The Tigers have won seven SEC titles (their last in 1988) and one national championship (in 1958). Tiger Stadium—which holds 80,000 fans now but is being expanded to 91,000 (the fourth-largest stadium in the country)—has long been one of the most fearsome venues in the nation for visiting football teams. Not for nothing is it called Death Valley. The stadium takes on an eerie glow at dusk, when the sun sets and the fog rolls in off the Mississippi River, and the crowd—stoked up on spicy crayfish and southern whiskey—starts yelping and getting rowdy.

Louisianans like to have fun, and Saturday night football games in Red Stick (the English translation of Baton Rouge) are notoriously raucous. When the band breaks into "Tiger Rag"—its classic fight song—and makes a four-corner salute to the crowd, the place goes wild. And then comes the big act: the LSU mascot, a 550-pound Bengal tiger named Mike, is trundled across the field in his steel cage. Blonde cheerleaders, all flashing million-dollar smiles, ride atop the cage with the élan of beauty queens riding in a convertible. After Mike is introduced, LSU officials move him to a spot just outside the visiting team's locker room, so they can hear his jungle roar moments before taking the field. It's a confidence killer—or used to be.

Bear Bryant once said that "Baton Rouge happens to be the worst place in the world to be a visiting team. It's like being inside a drum." Late in a 1988 contest against Auburn, quarterback Tommy Hodsen threw a touchdown pass to Eddie Fuller to win the game. The crowd roar was so loud that it registered as a small earthquake on a seismograph in the university's geology department. When LSU beat Florida in 1997—the team's last big win—a female fan named Margaret was quoted after the game as saying: "The only thing I remember is the smell of Jim Beam in the air." The quote is stuck to a bulletin board in the university's sports information office. There are some stunning pictures in the LSU football office of the crowd after that Florida victory: more than a few fans can be seen stumbling around in a near-delirious stupor.

Oh, where have those days gone? LSU fans still like to party, but nowadays they're generally done cheering for the football team by halftime. As Austin Powers might put it, there is a lot of bad mojo at LSU. The football program—rocked by politics, bad hires, weak coaching, and player problems—is in terrible shape. Tiger Stadium has so lost its aura of invincibility that one half expects to see a purring cat inside the mascot cage, not a ferocious tiger. Nobody quite underscores the promise and peril that is LSU football more than Cecil Collins. A running back from Leesville, Lousiana, Collins was the state's Mr. Football in 1995, when he was a high school senior. He signed a scholarship with LSU. Collins, nearly everyone agrees, was one of the most talented running backs ever to wear LSU's purple and gold colors. But like a lot of lightly educated Louisiana kids, Collins had behavioral problems.

In his nearly three years at the school, Collins spent as much time in police custody as he did on the football field. When he played, he was virtually unstoppable. But he played in only three games! He was arrested twice in less than three years for illegal entry into apartments where women lived. Once inside, he made dangerous and unwelcome advances. After his second arrest, in June 1998, he was charged with two felony counts of unauthorized entry into an inhabited dwelling, and two misdemeanor counts of simple battery. He was kicked off the team. According to an LSU Web site, while Collins was in school he led what Bo Bahnsen, an NCAA compliance officer at the university, called "a fast life." Friends said that despite coming from a family of modest means—his father is a prison guard in Houston—Collins wore flashy clothes and drove *two* Cadillacs as a freshman—a 1982 Fleetwood and a 1991 Seville. Collins reportedly told his friends that he had money to pay for the cars because his mom had won the lottery—twice.

In fact, Beverly Collins apparently was a one-time winner of a $100,000 state jackpot. When Collins's father, James, was asked about his son's lavish lifestyle, he replied: "Cecil never mentioned any of this stuff to me." (Collins was friends with a Baton Rouge–based rap-music producer who calls himself Master P. He runs a record company, and also started a sports management group that he has since sold.) Collins transferred to McNeese State, but he was kicked off that team, too, for failing a drug test. He was drafted by the Miami Dolphins, and showed professional potential. But he was arrested again for breaking into a house. Cecil Collins now sits in jail. "He's a tremendous talent, and he had a great personality, but he's got demons," says Greg LaRose, the executive editor of *Tiger Rag*, a Baton Rouge sports paper that follows LSU athletics.

Misty Demons

There are plenty of demons in Louisiana, and they have a tendency to drag down the football program. With its history of corruption, progressive politics, and abject poverty, the state is something of a U.S. version of Argentina.

BRAGGING RIGHTS

(Former governor Edwin Edwards was convicted of accepting bribes for a New Orleans casino license last spring.) The only things missing are the generals and Eva Peron. Baton Rouge, which is located about an hour's drive from New Orleans, is the capital of Louisiana. That gives state politicians plenty of opportunities to meddle with the football team. Actually, Huey Long, the state's famously dictatorial governor, played the role of general quite nicely in the 1930s. The Kingfish, as he was called, was obsessed with LSU football—so much so that two fine coaches quit because they could not tolerate his interference. On one occasion, he got word that the Barnum & Bailey Circus, which was coming to town, had been siphoning ticket sales to a home football game. That wouldn't do. Long invoked an obscure law mandating that all animals being brought into the state must be given an antibacterial "dip." That delayed the circus visit, and the football game was a sellout.

Long was also strangely preoccupied with improving the LSU band. When he wasn't trying to coach the team, he'd strike up the band on the field before games. There are pictures of him, in a white suit and Panama hat, standing beside the drum major and holding the baton. Long hired orchestra leader Castro Carazo away from a New Orleans hotel to direct the band. Later, Carazo and the guv'nor together wrote "Touchdown for LSU," one of the school's most popular fight songs.

LSU's most glorious football moment came in 1959, on a misty Halloween night. LSU, ranked number one in the nation, was hosting third-ranked Mississippi, its most-hated rival. In the fourth quarter, Mississippi was nursing a 3-0 lead when LSU's Billy Cannon picked up a bouncing punt and ran 89 yards for the winning touchdown, breaking several tackles along the way. The radio announcer, J. C. Politz, was describing the play as it unfolded. Tens of thousands of fans across the state were sitting in front of their radios, listening raptly. Suddenly, a technician in the broadcast booth reached forward and started turning a knob. He wanted to amplify Politz's voice as Cannon chugged down the field—but instead he turned *down* the volume, ruining the radio call of LSU's most famous football play.

There are plenty of other oddities in LSU's football history. After Charlie McClendon stepped down as coach, LSU hired Bo Rein, the thirty-four-year-old coach at N.C. State, to replace him. But he died forty-two days after accepting the job, in early 1980. Rein was making a short flight across Louisiana when he and the pilot were apparently incapacitated by fumes. The plane flew all the way to the Atlantic Ocean, ran out of fuel, and crashed. Quarterback Y. A. Tittle, who went on to have a Hall of Fame pro football career, also played defensive back for LSU. In a 1947 game against Ole Miss, he intercepted a pass and started running the other way. But his belt buckle broke and his pants started falling down. Hugging the football with one hand

and his pants with the other, Tittle managed to amble 47 yards before he and his pants collapsed. Tittle became nearly as famous for his bald head as his passing skills; he started losing his hair as a young man. When later asked about his hair loss, he blamed the helmet he wore at LSU—and also the fact that he'd been forced to shave his head as a freshman. "I'm not sure it didn't stunt my hair growth," he said, "because it sure never grew back the right way."

In 1952 Jim Corbett, LSU's sports publicity director, devised a new numbering system for the team's uniform. He decided to mix letters and numbers to identify the players. Ends, guards, and tackles were ID'd by the letters E, G, and T, respectively, followed by a number. Quarterbacks, centers, left halfbacks, and right halfbacks were Q, C, L, and R, followed by numbers. It was a hair-brained idea that lasted one year. Most LSU fans have long since forgotten about it—but not the unfortunate players on that '52 squad. They can be seen in team photos wearing LSU jerseys emblazoned with G4, Q2, and E4 symbols. None of them is smiling.

LSU is the only college football team to play a game in Cuba. The Bengal Tigers played the University of Havana in 1907. During warmups before the game, the LSU coaches noticed the Cubans drinking red wine on the sidelines. Glasses full of vino were lined up on the bench! Havana's biggest player, 300-pound A. C. Infante-Garcia, was drinking conspicuously. W. M. Lyles, who at 200 pounds was one of LSU's biggest players, was responsible for taking on the mammoth, mean-spirited Cuban lineman. He was not looking forward to it. An LSU teammate, G. E. "Doc" Fenton, noticed Infante-Garcia's drinking habit, and suggested to Lyles that if he popped his hulking opponent in the midsection, the results might be favorable (if a little messy). Lyle took his friend's advice. Soon after the game commenced, he rammed his head into Infante-Garcia's stomach. According to Fenton, "The big guy spouted like an artesian well. I give you my word: we had to swim out of there." LSU won the game 56-0.

LSU's current athletic director, Joe Dean, tends to spout off once in a while himself. A former star basketball player at LSU, Dean was a well-known basketball TV personality before becoming the school's AD in 1987. Dean is a colorful character. As a TV commentator for basketball games, he coined a fabulous expression. After a player swished a shot, Dean would often say: "String music." But remarks he has since made as LSU's athletic director have not been so well received. Dean allegedly said that LSU's first women's softball team was disbanded because of the sexual preference of the players. He also allegedly quipped that if he had to start one women's sport at LSU, he'd prefer women's soccer because the players "look cute in their shorts."

Such a sexist (though surely innocent) remark might shed light on why five female athletes filed a lawsuit against LSU, claiming that it discriminated against women athletes. A lower-court decision described LSU's attitude toward female athletes as "archaic"—but nevertheless asserted that the school did *not* intend to violate Title IX, the federal law requiring equal athletic opportunities at schools that accept federal funding. Last January a federal appeals court overturned that ruling, however—and concluded that LSU *had intentionally discriminated* against female athletes. The appeals panel said that LSU's views toward women athletes was "motivated by chauvinist notions," and the judges singled Dean out for criticism. Dean didn't help the cause by allegedly describing the plaintiffs as "honey," "sweetie," and "cutie." LSU is appealing the latest decision, and the case could wind up before the Supreme Court.

"Emotional Meeting"

What accounts for all the bad karma in Baton Rouge? I hoped to find out at DiNardo's restaurant—or at least have some decent pasta. I got there in mid-November, late in the season. The Tigers had just gotten whipped by Houston. There was only one game remaining—but Gerry DiNardo would not be coaching in it. He'd been fired two days earlier during a meeting with Dean and LSU Chancellor Mark Emmert. DiNardo was given the option of coaching the last game, but he declined. Dean described the meeting at which DiNardo was sacked as "emotional. Gerry was emotional. I was emotional. Dr. Emmert was emotional. These things aren't easy. We liked him a lot. I was a big fan of his. Gerry has great integrity. He is a quality human being."

All true. But while personality and integrity are important in a coach, a team's win-loss record is where the rubber meets the road. DiNardo did not win. His five-year record was 32-24-1. Most of the wins came early in his tenure; most of the losses, late. At the time of his dismissal, LSU had lost fourteen of its last fifteen SEC games. He had two lousy seasons in a row—a bad season in 1998, followed by a horrendous one last year. That will get you fired in the SEC. By midseason, after several consecutive losses, fans who had been toasting DiNardo after 1997 were writing nasty letters to Dean, influential boosters, and the media, demanding the coach's head. A few took to wearing paper bags over their heads at Tiger Stadium—a sure sign of trouble. Contributions to the Tiger Athletic Fund were falling—which in college athletics is the equivalent of a six-alarm fire. Local merchants, who depend heavily on the LSU fans, were suffering. Three games into the 1999 season, the Garden District Nursery in Baton Rouge, which sells a lot of LSU paraphernalia, was holding a DiNardo SALE: 70 PERCENT OFF ALL LSU MERCHANDISE.

The Fall of Gerry DiNardo

Fans were giving away their tickets. Hotels had vacant rooms on football weekends. "After the team started losing, we had a lot of cancellations," said Julie Perschall, a guest services representative for a Hampton Inn in Red Stick. "We sold out for the big games—Florida, Ole Miss, Auburn—but since then it's been pretty bad." Said Hampton Inn employee Melissa Albert: "My dad has season tickets, but he sold them for the Ole Miss and Houston games."

It was, in short, another dark moment for LSU football. Given that, I expected DiNardo's restaurant to be quiet, forlorn, short of customers. That wasn't the case. The parking lot outside the low-slung, shingled restaurant was nearly full. And inside, there was a nice crowd. DiNardo was entertaining a large group of people—his wife, Terri, a couple of former players, two people from the LSU football TV show. He seemed in decent spirits, given the circumstances, and there was plenty of laughter at his table. DiNardo was wearing an open-collared paisley silk shirt when we met. We shook hands and moved to a table in the back, where over a glass of wine the coach attempted to deconstruct his downfall. One wag had recently described LSU's 1999 season as "designed by Joseph Mengele."

DiNardo was friendly—not upbeat, but hardly morose, either. He had lobbied hard for his job and lost the campaign. But I perceived a slight sense of relief in his demeanor: after being publicly ostracized for months, getting sacked isn't always a bad thing. It puts an end to the misery. The last few weeks had been ugly. His tenuous job status was a staple of conversation in Baton Rouge—on radio talk shows, on the Internet, and in the newspapers. Many in the intelligentsia were practically *insisting* that he be fired. LSU Web sites were buzzing with speculation about who the next coach would be. Not *everyone* was against him; there were a few blessed souls who argued that DiNardo should stay on in the interest of stability. They argued that LSU had a tendency to dismiss its coaches too quickly—which only exacerbated the problems. But as the 1999 season unfolded, DiNardo's supporters became increasingly scarce. His LSU career began to conjure images of the ghostly landscape (ancient tree stumps poking out of the swamp) one sees on the drive from New Orleans to Baton Rouge.

DiNardo handled his dismissal admirably. Just before he was fired, he said: "I've still got it better than 99 percent of the people on the planet." A day after the ax fell, he met with a group of local reporters and chatted amiably. He praised Dean as "the best boss I've ever had." And he had called Chancellor Emmert "terrific." He was open, accessible.

But according to sources in Baton Rouge, that was a far cry from the way he'd been during the season. Weems said DiNardo's personality changed after the 1998 season. The coach began to develop what Weems called a "bunker

2 8 7

mentality." Said Weems: "He was stung by the public reaction to his losing seven of his last eight games. He became kind of withdrawn and uncommunicative, and it continued throughout the spring and summer of 1999. I think he resented the criticism." Scott McKay, the publisher and editor of an independent LSU sports tabloid named *Purple & Gold*, was one of the first local writers to call for DiNardo's resignation. Sitting in Ivars, a popular bar in Baton Rouge, McKay described DiNardo as "difficult"and "a tightass," adding: "He's not that good with the media." McKay doesn't dislike DiNardo personally, but felt he was wrong for the job. And wrong for his publication, too. "I was the first to call for his head," said McKay, "but he exacted his revenge. Our subscription sales have fallen the last two years because he's lost nearly every game."

Maybe losing your job can be liberating. Certainly, DiNardo was ready to talk when I met with him. "The last two years have been real tough," he said. "We were on such a roll at first. But once it goes bad—not only in the South, but anywhere—it's hard to stop. Problems become magnified. We've had a heckuva time trying to stop the downward spiral."

DiNardo maintained that he was not bitter about his dismissal, but he was clearly bothered. (Is there a distinction?) "If the LSU administration had come out two weeks ago and said, 'DiNardo is our coach, and we're going to stay with him,' we would have had a chance to turn things around. It doesn't mean we would have, but that was our only chance to stop the slide." Should he have been given more time? His response is ambivalent. "Not necessarily," he said, acknowledging that LSU football was in pretty tough shape. "But I strongly believe that if you look at any school, if they want to change their history, they have to make some drastic, extraordinary changes. And part of that is keeping a coach a little bit longer. It doesn't have to be me—I don't want to sound like a coach complaining about being fired. But I'm the only coach at LSU since Charlie Mac who's lasted longer than four years, and he's been gone for nineteen years." That is an interesting point.

Raised Expectations

DiNardo said that after his first season at Vanderbilt, when the Commodores were 5-6, he called Lou Holtz (then the Notre Dame coach) and asked him for advice. "I used to call Lou a lot. I asked him, 'What can you tell me about the second year?' And Lou said, 'Expectations are raised. And when expectations are raised, you'd better win the close games.' He was a prophet." More than a few things hurt DiNardo, but at the top of the list was his inability to win close games. Over the last two years, LSU played nine games that were decided by six points or less. The Tigers lost *all* of them. The biggest, said DiNardo, was the first close game—against Georgia in 1998. The Tigers were 3-0 at the time, ranked sixth in the country. Late in the game, LSU was trailing by four points but driving to win the game. "We had to score a touchdown," said DiNardo. "We were in the red zone and starting to take over the line of scrimmage." Then LSU jumped offsides, got backed up, and eventually was forced to try a field goal. It was no good, and LSU lost the game. "From that point on," said the coach, "it's been downhill. We've just really struggled."

DiNardo's firing is a cautionary tale for all coaches, for it shows how quickly they can fall out of favor and lose their jobs—a hero one year, a pariah the next. The coach's tumble also opened a window on the inner workings of a university athletic system—the behind-the scenes process by which coaches are hired and fired. Joe Dean was Gerry DiNardo's immediate boss. He is the guy charged with running the LSU athletic department. One might assume that as the 1999 season unfolded, DiNardo's fate would be in Dean's hands. It wasn't. Athletic directors have clout, but their power is also limited. Hiring or firing decisions are often group efforts involving the university president, chancellor, athletic director, major financial contributors, and, in LSU's case, the board of supervisors. And, of course, there are group dynamics—power plays—that influence the discussions.

Dean is a close friend of DiNardo, and even as the 1999 season spiraled into oblivion, he resisted the idea of firing the embattled coach. Loyalty was one reason why. But there was another. Dean had already been burned by his disastrous decision to hire Curley Hallman in 1991. Even before he officially fired Mike Archer (Hallman's predecessor), Dean had hired a consulting firm—a subsidiary of a TV broadcasting company—to find a new coach for LSU. Archer—whom the LSU administration had hired, amazingly, because he was well-liked by the players—seemed over his head after two years on the job. A new savior was needed.

The consulting company suggested several candidates for the job, and Hallman, the coach at Southern Mississippi University, was one of them. During his three years at Southern Miss, Hallman was best known for slaying dragons. His small-time teams beat some big-name programs—Florida State, Alabama, and Auburn, to name three. Dean was impressed, and so apparently was Gil Brandt, the former Dallas Cowboys' personnel guru. According to Dean, "Gil Brandt told me to hire Curley Hallman . . . and don't look back."

Dean did just that. Unfortunately, what Dean and others didn't realize at the time was that Hallman's success at Southern Miss owed much to his quarterback—Brett Favre. Hallman didn't have much Favre-like talent at LSU, and he floundered. He had four straight losing seasons; his best record was 5-6.

Though he has done many good things at LSU, Dean has been haunted by the Hallman fiasco. The athletic director did not want a second blot on his ledger, and so tried to hang onto DiNardo even as the losses mounted. "Dean was going to give DiNardo every chance in the world," says LaRose. Dean said much the same to a Baton Rouge newspaper columnist (the LSU athletic director would not talk to me): "It's very difficult changing coaches. Hiring the right person is not easy. We've gone through that. I didn't want to go through it again, so I kept hoping that the team would come together and we'd begin to win some games. That just didn't happen."

Dean, who's seventy and near retirement, was DiNardo's only hope for survival. But he was a thin reed. The athletic director was out of favor with the bosses—and thus relegated to a supporting actor in the DiNardo drama. The two main players became Emmert and Weems. Emmert had spent a few years as an administrator at the University of Colorado, where DiNardo had been an assistant football coach, and then became chancellor at the University of Connecticut. But by the time he got to LSU, in 1999, he'd still never participated in any major hiring or firing decisions. He would ultimately decide DiNardo's fate—with the advice of Weems and a few other movers and shakers who had their fingers on the fading pulse of LSU football.

Unlike administrators, board members and boosters are not always close to the coaches. They tend to be businessmen, and businessmen are paid to be decisive. So when things go badly, they're inclined to cut losses and move on. That is especially true at LSU, which seems to have as little patience with its football coaches as a diva with her hairdresser. "There has been a revolving door since 1979," says columnist King. Jerry Stovall, Bo Rein, Bill Arnsbarger, Mike Archer, Curly Hallman, Gerry DiNardo: six coaches have come and gone. Not all were bad hires. Arnsbarger was an excellent choice, but after three outstanding years he quit to become the athletic director at Florida. His replacement, Archer, won eighteen games in two seasons. But he got sidetracked when a local leader accused his staff of racism. The charge was preposterous, but it affected recruiting in Louisiana. Archer never really recovered.

Power Shift

When DiNardo first arrived at LSU, Charlie Cusimano, who's from Metairie, was chairman of the board of supervisors. "He was in my corner," said DiNardo. "He and I are very good friends." But when Louisiana elected a new governor, the membership of the board changed. And so did the leadership. Cusimano remained on the board but "lost his power," said DiNardo. Weems

The Fall of Gerry DiNardo

took over as chairman. Weems is an attorney, a partner with Gold, Weems, Bruser, Sues & Rundell in New Orleans. Both Weems and DiNardo described their relationship with each other as cordial; they weren't best friends, but there was no overt hostility either. "He's been fair," says DiNardo of Weems. "He never did anything to me—but he concluded I was no longer effective as the head football coach. He wanted a change." Did the two men talk about the program? "Oh, yeah. Absolutely. But he decided that they'd be better off without me. He's a businessman, and I respect that."

DiNardo's troubles, in fact, began a year before his dismissal. The 1998 team had some talented players—including Marshall Faulk at running back—and was expected to win the SEC West Division. Fan expectations were high. The offense performed reasonably well, but the Tigers defense was a sieve—the worst in the school's history, as it turned out. The team limped home with a 4-7 record.

There were two or three agonizingly close losses. Stanley Jacobs, who heads the board of supervisors athletic committee, points to the 1998 Alabama game as an example of the team's disastrous run of bad luck. In the second half of that game, LSU quarterback Herb Tyler passed to Abram Booty in the end zone for an apparent touchdown, which would have given LSU an insurmountable lead. But a Bama defensive back stripped the ball from Booty and ran the ball out of the end zone. Alabama dodged a bullet, and went on to score. The Crimson Tide tried an onside kick, recovered the ball, and scored again! Instead of winning easily, as it appeared they would, LSU lost the game by one point.

Despite the team's poor record in 1998, Dean extended DiNardo's contract after the season. As the athletic director said later, he didn't want anyone—including potential recruits—to think he'd lost confidence in the coach. But DiNardo found himself in a sticky wicket. He'd squandered a year when his team was talented and experienced in key positions—and should have posted a solid record. Now, entering 1999, there was considerable pressure from the fans for a bounce-back season. The problem was, LSU had less talent and experience in 1999 than the year before.

LSU did not bounce back, of course. Even before the season started, there were difficulties. In February 1999, twenty-seven high school players signed papers pledging to play football for LSU—but nine of those players never even made it to campus. Most of these nine failed to qualify academically; another pair opted to play professional baseball. To have lost that many players before school even started was not only an embarrassment for the school, it adversely affected the football team. Because a school can only sign twenty-five players a year, those lost scholarships—lost players—would hurt the team's depth down the road. And, in fact, during the 1999 season LSU at one time had only sixty-six scholarship players, nearly twenty under the limit.

Eligibility and sundry off-the-field problems were a recurring nightmare for DiNardo. The program's attrition rate has been atrocious. Over the last four years DiNardo has lost, on average, about one third of his annual recruiting classes by the end of the first year. That means that out of, say, twenty-five high school players signed, roughly seven or eight were out of the program in twelve months. Some didn't get into school in the first place, some quit, some transferred, some got kicked off the squad.

During our talk, DiNardo took some responsibility for the academic and behavior problems that afflicted his program—but he heaped a lot of the blame on social issues in the state of Louisiana. After playing at Notre Dame and coaching at Vanderbilt, which are very careful about their scholarship offers, DiNardo says that "we went overboard with recruiting when we got here. We were like kids in a candy store. We could recruit anybody. Some kid has got a third-grade reading level? 'It doesn't matter,' we said, 'we'll get him in.' If I could do that part over again, I would."

A Caste System

In DiNardo's view, it's almost impossible to avoid player problems in Louisiana. "LSU recruits kids from the worst school systems in America—the worst in America. New Orleans is the only city in America that has more students in private schools than public schools." At the same time, he adds, LSU has been trying to boost its academic reputation. The school's admissions standards have been rising.

In the past, said DiNardo, when LSU was predominately white and had an open-enrollment policy, nearly anybody with a Louisiana high school degree was admitted to the Baton Rouge campus. That is not the case anymore. Now, says DiNardo, there is a "caste system" at LSU—a great gap between the average student and the football players. He maintains that "LSU doesn't have a degree program where a lot of our [football players] can succeed." And so many fail—flunk out. "That is an institutional problem that can't be solved by a coach or athletic director. They have to address that." He asserts that the academic history of LSU's football program is "terrible," and that if the school aims to change it, it will have to make some drastic changes.

It's hard to refute what DiNardo says about Louisiana's demographics and public school system. But McKay, *Purple & Gold* editor and publisher, doesn't let the former coach off the hook. "DiNardo says that part of the problem is that Louisiana is a poor state? Well, nobody wants to hear that. Louisiana has been a poor state for a long time, and over our history we've had coaches that have gotten a lot out of their players. And the players have improved year after year. If you want to blame the state, cut your losses and just say that you weren't a good fit here." And that's essentially what McKay says doomed the coach: "He wasn't a good fit. He and his staff weren't able to reach the kids. That's the long and the short of it. You had a staff on the cusp of taking the next step and becoming a championship-quality team, and instead it went straight south on them."

McKay argues that DiNardo made a lot of bad decisions—bad staff decisions, bad recruiting decisions. Here is one example. Last year, says McKay, LSU recruited a kid named Ranny Davis out of H. L. Bougeois High School in Houma, Louisiana. Houma is down in the bayou country, near the Gulf of Mexico. Davis was a 6'3", 230-pound linebacker prospect—"a very, very good player, super athlete," said McKay. "But he had no hope of making his grades. But they give him a scholarship anyway, and end up placing him in Hinds Junior College in Mississippi."

Meantime, there is another linebacker in New Orleans, named Ryan O'Neal, who is eager to play football for LSU. O'Neal was an excellent student at Jesuit High School—a national merit semifinalist—and a good football player. A 6'1", 220-pound linebacker, he made 180 tackles his senior year and was named the metro–New Orleans Player of the Year by the *Times Picayune* newspaper. "He wasn't the highest-ranked recruit in the world," said McKay, "but neither was Davis." O'Neal got scholarship offers from Tulane, Ole Miss, and others—but not LSU. "By the grace of God," says McKay, "DiNardo persuades O'Neal to walk on at LSU through some state program that helped pay for his books and tuition. But the kid wanted to come here on a full athletic scholarship; he felt he was good enough."

McKay suggests that DiNardo didn't give O'Neal an athletic scholarship because he knew the kid would get financial aid through other means, enabling him to use O'Neal's scholarship on another player. If that was DiNardo's thinking, he wouldn't be the first coach to try such a ploy to expand his team's talent base. But he didn't need to do it because, as things turned out, only eighteen of the twenty-seven players who signed to play for LSU that year actually enrolled in school. McKay believes DiNardo was wrong not to offer O'Neal a scholarship because "he knew Davis and others weren't going to qualify."

Those who do qualify at LSU often end up on the wrong end of the law. With the 1999 season only two games old, starting wide receiver Larry Foster was arrested for stealing a student's purse. He was one of LSU's team captains—a leader. Foster supposedly had a bad hamstring at the time of the theft, but apparently had no trouble running away from the scene before he was caught.

He was kicked off the team. Two other starters—Mark Roman, a cornerback, and Clarence LeBlanc, a safety—were also booted for having illegal contact with a "runner" representing a professional agent. Those incidents followed another scandal in which a group of football players had been caught using long-distance phone-access cards fraudulently.

Reacting to these and several other incidents, the football coach at Evangel Christian Academy, a prominent private school in the state, publicly denigrated LSU. The Evangel coach, Dennis Dunn, said that LSU was not a school where he wanted to send his kids either to get an education or to play football. What made Dunn's comment newsworthy was that Evengel has one of the best high school football programs in the United States. The nation's top recruit, quarterback Brock Berlin, played for Evangel—and he had already decided to play football at Florida.

As troubling as all of the disciplinary problems were, they might have been forgotten had the team played good football. It didn't. By mid-November, LSU's season had disintegrated. After winning its first two games against small, nonconference opponents, LSU lost seven straight. The year before, the LSU defense had been horrendous. But this year the opposite was true. The defense played adequately, but the offense sputtered. The offensive line was decimated by injuries, and there was a costly quarterback controversy.

Josh Booty, a legendary high school quarterback in Louisiana, had ditched his professional baseball career after five years so that he could attend LSU and fulfill his football destiny. He was a twenty-four-year-old freshman. Booty was not the only QB on the team; there were two others, Craig Nall and Rohan Davey. Like Booty, both Nall and Davey possessed some raw talent, and both had something that Booty didn't have, a little experience. Nall had played some in 1998, and even started the last game of the season. Davey was third string the previous year, but he'd been in the system—taking snaps on the LSU practice field while Booty was struggling to hit a curve ball.

DiNardo and his offensive coordinator, Bob McConnell, gave all three QB contenders a chance to shine during fall practice. None of them did so. So DiNardo started Nall in the first game against San Jose State. LSU won, but Nall did not play well. He was benched and did not play much more the rest of the year. In the second game, against North Texas State, Davey played the first half and Booty the second. Davey played very well against North Texas, and seemed ready to grab the starting job. He started game three, against Auburn— and that's really where the 1999 season began to crumble—for Davey, for LSU, and for DiNardo.

Auburn was a game that LSU expected to win. Auburn had just experienced a couple of rocky years itself. Terry Bowden had quit midway through 1998 season. Like DiNardo, Bowden was under fire for losing games and recruiting too many bad apples. If there was a program in worse shape than LSU, it seemed to be Auburn. Tommy Tuberville had taken the reins (jumping to Auburn from Mississippi), and though he is a talented coach, the War Eagles seemed bereft of offensive talent heading into the 1999 season. Turns out they had more than LSU. Auburn walloped LSU, 41-7. The game was over at the half. Disgruntled LSU fans left in droves. "I don't even think my mother was left after the first half," said LSU linebacker Thomas Dunson.

Crucial Decisions

DiNardo had made two important staff decisions over the previous two years. In 1998 his longtime defensive coordinator, Carl Reese, was hired away by Texas. DiNardo replaced him with an experienced coach, Lou Tepper, who had been the head coach at Illinois. But Tepper's defense in 1998 was pathetic, could not stop anybody. Come 1999, there was another vital staff vacancy. DiNardo's offensive coordinator, Morris Watts, left LSU and took the same job at Michigan State University, where he'd coached previously. Rather than hire an experienced offensive coach to replace Watts—somebody who might help tutor the three young quarterbacks—DiNardo chose to elevate Bob McConnell to the offensive coordinator position. McConnell had been the team's wide receiver coach. He had some experience running an offense and coaching quarterbacks—but at the University of Massachusetts Amherst, a smaller school, and that was ten years earlier. McConnell had been an offensive lineman in college.

I compared LSU's 1999 staff with others in the SEC, and one of the things that jumped out at me was that several of DiNardo's group came from small colleges. There is nothing wrong with that, but at Florida, Tennessee, and Alabama, the assistant coaches seemed to have more high-level college football coaching experience. And most of the offensive coordinators had played quarterback themselves while in college. In a dog-eat-dog conference, little things mean a lot.

In any case, the Auburn game was a bad omen—and set in motion a process that would culminate in DiNardo's sacking. McKay said that he was approached after the Auburn game by a prominent member of the LSU board of supervisors, who said: "You know what, we will never beat Auburn again. Because Tuberville is at Auburn, and DiNardo can't beat Tuberville." He had a point. Before taking the Auburn job, Tuberville was the coach at Ole Miss—an SEC school with ambitions but with fewer resources and fewer good football players than LSU. Nevertheless, Tuberville beat DiNardo the last two years he was in Oxford. "He had no business doing that," said McKay. "And if you can't beat Auburn—and you've got to play Florida and Alabama every year, too—well, you aren't going to win the SEC West Division, much less the conference championship."

Charlie Weems, the board of supervisors chairman, was also disturbed by the Auburn loss. By the fourth quarter of that game, Weems had left his box atop Tiger Stadium and paid a visit to Dean in the press box. "I found Joe and said to him: 'I don't know what's happening, and neither do you. But if we have to make a change down the line, is that something that you'd have a problem with? And what is the status of DiNardo's contract?'" According to Weems, Dean said he wouldn't have a problem cutting DiNardo loose. "If that's what we had to do, he was prepared to do it," said Weems. "And Joe said that money wasn't an issue. My general philosophy is to try and anticipate things; I don't like to do things hastily."

After the Auburn game, things only got worse for DiNardo. The Tigers played respectably at times, but could not catch a break. They lost close games, and in one instance, got robbed by the officials. The next game, against Georgia, went into overtime. The Bulldogs kicked a field goal to win. Next, Florida beat LSU easily. Then came a trip to Kentucky. In years past, Kentucky was a sure win for LSU. But the Wildcats had beaten LSU the year before, and they whipped the Tigers again in 1999, 31-5. Rumors began to spread that DiNardo would be canned. "If you've ever been around one of those situations," says Weems, "it takes on a life of its own. This was a season that everybody came into with high expectations, but things didn't fall into place. There were weeks when we got close to winning, and weeks when we weren't even competitive. That's football. We [the board of supervisors] got an unbelievable amount of mail from people around the state. I certainly did. It seemed there were serious problems with the program. Not all were Jerry's fault, but when you're losing there is a natural inclination to point fingers."

By the end of game three, DiNardo had decided to give Booty the starting quarterback job. He kept it for nearly all of the season. It was a popular decision—Booty as returning hero—but it backfired. Booty threw an LSU-record nineteen interceptions—and displayed something of a petulant, snotty attitude besides. He criticized the team during the season, and refused at times to talk to the media. "I don't think any coach would yield to pressure to give a guy a start," says LaRose, "but it was unreal how much the fans clamored for the return of Josh Booty. It was a giant story in January 1999."

The fans thought Booty was a star in waiting, but he wasn't impressive. And surely too much was expected of him: he hadn't played football in five years! He was a freshman—an old freshman, to be sure—but a freshman. LaRose, who says he watched nearly every practice in the spring and fall, contends that

The Fall of Gerry DiNardo

Davey should have been the quarterback. "I thought he was the guy who seemed to have leadership qualities. Davey seemed to put it all together." Others agree, but DiNardo and McConnell gave up on him after the Auburn debacle.

LaRose also suggests that DiNardo may have driven Reese and Watts from the program by his tendency to micromanage when things weren't going well. "When he had the least bit of trouble, he tended to take over for the coordinator. I think they left not because of personal differences with DiNardo but professional differences: not being able to execute plans they drew up."

DiNardo disagrees with the criticism that he is hard to get along with, or that his staff was conspicuously weak. He points out that the average stay for any assistant coach at any one school is 3.1 years. "Carl Reese left because Texas offered him a better financial package. He and I had been together for seven or eight years, which was the longest time he'd ever worked with one person, and I think he just wanted to move. Morris Watts had been at Michigan State for eight years previously, and they promised him . . . lifetime health insurance, which was important to him. Plus he really liked Michigan State, even though he'd been fired there at one point." Jacobs, the chairman of the board of supervisors athletic committee, believes that staff issues did, in fact, hurt DiNardo. "When Gerry came here five years ago," said Jacobs, "I thought he had a really good staff. But it seemed to get weaker. And his way of compensating was to say: 'I'll work harder.' Instead of working 6 A.M. to 8 P.M., he worked from 5 A.M. to 10 P.M. He worked harder and harder, and the team became less and less productive. Why did he do that? Gerry is not an insecure person. I think he thought that he could just make up the difference himself—that he could make it happen. But it is a monster job. At some point in time, you just have to work smart."

Bad Breaks

DiNardo may not have been smart. But he was certainly not lucky. Two losses, in particular, ruined any chance he had of saving his job. LSU played well against two of the better teams in the SEC, Mississippi State and Alabama, but lost both games by inches. Against Mississippi State, LSU led for most of the game. But trailing by a score of 16-11, the Bulldogs drove down the LSU one-yard line with time running out. On fourth down, Jackie Sherrill opted to go for the winning touchdown with a running play. TV replays clearly showed his running back falling to the ground short of the goal line—but in the tangle of bodies the runner crawled over the white line. After a delay, and clearly unable to see, the linesmen threw up their arms: touchdown, Mississippi State. It was a terrible call, but nothing would change it: LSU had lost again.

The Tigers also played a strong game against Alabama, who would go on to win the SEC championship. This time LSU was trailing, 23-17, with less than a minute to go in the game. The Tigers had the ball on the Alabama one-yard line. A touchdown and extra point would win the game. The Tigers called a quarterback rollout, giving Booty the option to run or pass. Though there were receivers open in the end zone, Booty elected to try and score himself. He didn't make it; he was tackled just short of the end zone. Before LSU could get off another play, time expired. LSU had lost another heartbreaker. Said Booty of his decision on the last play: "I probably should have thrown it."

By late October 1999, at the halfway point in the season, DiNardo's team was imploding. After four straight losses, the team's record was 2-4. Pressure was mounting—on DiNardo, on Dean, on the boosters—who are by now hearing it from fans. Dean sets up a meeting between the coach and the mandarins of LSU football at the chancellor's house. In addition to Dean, DiNardo, and Emmert, Weems was in attendance, along with Jacobs and Richard Gill—the past president of the Tiger Athletic Fund, the athletic department's booster club. The meeting was on a Friday, one day before LSU played its archrival, Ole Miss. According to Weems, "We had a long and involved talk with Gerry about the state of the program: where it was, what he saw as the problems, how they could be addressed."

It was clearly a do-or-die time for the coach, but Weems says the coach did not seem uncomfortable during the roughly three-hour conclave. "Gerry knows us all, and we're all very fond of him. We think he's a good man. He was comfortable and open and honest. Gerry is a persuasive salesman; he'd done a lot of work for the meeting. He had a lot of documents with him." The boosters asked about the staff, recruiting, player problems. "I don't think any of us would try to second-guess the coach, but we were concerned about Gerry. I felt like a guy in his situation needed to reach out and keep all the goodwill he could—but that wasn't his focus. His view was, if you win you stay; if you lose, you get fired."

According to Weems, DiNardo acknowledged taking some recruiting risks that, in hindsight, he wished he hadn't taken. He complained about the educational problems in Louisiana. He acknowledged that he'd made some mistakes with his staff. "He did acknowledge that mistakes had been made," said the board of supervisors chairman. And the coach laid out his agenda for turning things around. The meeting was beneficial. The air was cleared, and according to Weems, "Gerry felt real good after the meeting. It gave him an opportunity to make his case."

Desperately needing a win, the Tigers instead got their heads handed to them by Ole Miss. Then came the tough Alabama loss. At that point, Weems canvassed most of the eighteen board members to ascertain their views on the coach. The response was clear: it was time to hoist the French razor. "I won't say the die was cast, but in our informal conversations a strong consensus had developed. There were some people who wanted to stick with Gerry, but the overall feeling among the board members and the LSU faithful was that short of divine intervention, [DiNardo's firing] was looking inevitable. But our intention was always to wait until the season was over." With a 2-7 record and two games left, the coach still had an outside shot at survival. But he'd have to beat both Houston and Arkansas impressively.

Both games were in Baton Rouge. Houston was a middling team. Like Ole Miss, Kentucky, and Auburn, this was a game that LSU fans expected to chalk up in the win column. "There was great anxiety," said Weems. "Gerry was being beaten to death in the media. The Houston game was played on November 12. Some LSU fans wore T-shirts proclaiming (with Cajun spellings) that DINARDEAUX MUST GEAUX.

That was surely the prevailing sentiment after the game. LSU played poorly and lost, 20-7. "Houston shouldn't be able to play with us, but they pretty much manhandled us," said Weems. "They pushed us around. It was ugly." Midway through the fourth quarter, Tiger Stadium was half-full. At game's end the fans jeered both DiNardo and the LSU players as they walked off the field. Dean was also booed. He left the field with his arms raised in a gesture that the *Tiger Rag* described as "mock triumph." A fan grabbed a cheerleader's megaphone and let loose a tirade at the beleaguered athletic director: "ONE MORE YEAR, JOE DEAN! ONE MORE YEAR, JOE DEAN!" The LSU AD and another angry LSU fan started trading insults. Said Jacobs: "There was complete apathy in the stadium, and that's when we knew we had hit rock bottom."

The End Game

The next morning, November 14, Emmert gave Weems a call. The chancellor asked the board of supervisors chairman to come by his house. Weems played a round of golf, and then drove to the chancellor's house. Said Weems: "We spent the afternoon talking about the situation. We chewed it over and ultimately decided it was time to pull the trigger." Weems called Dean and Jacobs to make sure everybody was comfortable with the decision. By then, DiNardo's few remaining supporters were in full retreat. Emmert met with DiNardo the next day and fired him. It was over.

No coach goes away empty-handed these days. DiNardo had four years left on his contract, so the three men negotiated a buyout: DiNardo would be paid $150,000 for each year, meaning his dismissal will cost the university $600,000. Last July DiNardo was named the first coach of the Birmingham franchise of the new XFL professional football league. "He really likes the South, he loved being in Baton Rouge, and he really thought a lot of Birmingham," said Dean.

Weems was pleased by Emmert's decisiveness. "He is a quick study," the lawyer said of the chancellor. "He had been watching this situation all year, and there wasn't any hesitation." Had DiNardo not been fired, said Weems, "the last two weeks [of the season] would have been brutal."

In December 1999, LSU held a press conference and announced that Lou Saban had been named the university's new football coach. McKay argues that LSU desperately needed a "rainmaker" to change its luck, and Saban fits that description. Saban had been the coach at Michigan State, where he'd gradually built the program to a point where it was competitive with the Big Ten's most powerful teams—Michigan, Ohio State, and Penn State. He's got the same challenge ahead of him at LSU—bring the Tiger program to a position of at least close parity with the SEC's best teams.

Saban is considered a good recruiter, but finding talent is seldom a problem at LSU. Louisiana has lots of talent. The challenge for Saban will be to get prospects in school, keep them in school, and keep them out of trouble. He must also maintain a staff that can get the most out of the players. LSU followers are happy to get Saban. Rainmakers don't come cheap—the school is paying Saban about $1 million a year. After being named to his new job, Saban put together a coaching staff that did not include a single asssistant from Michigan State. That's unusual—typically, a few assistants follow the head man to his new position—and did not go unnoticed in Baton Rouge. Was it a sign that Saban was not popular with his previous coaches? Would the new staff be compatible? Would Saban fit in on the bayou? Would the mojo ever turn? In a place called Death Valley, it's never too soon to start worrying.

TWENTY-ONE

BELLY OF THE BEAST: THREE LSU PLAYERS TALK FOOTBALL, AGENTS, INJURIES, AND COACHES

Tommy Banks, Fred Booker, and Joe Domingeaux were a little shell-shocked with one game remaining in the 1999 season. Who could blame them? The LSU football season had imploded. LSU had won its first two games, against easy nonconference opponents, but after that . . . disaster. The team lost seven straight games. Worse, Gerry DiNardo, the Tigers' head coach, had just been fired. Banks, Booker, and Domingeaux are all Louisiana boys, and all had high hopes when they signed with LSU. They are a talented trio: all started for LSU last year. Banks was a junior fullback; Booker, a junior cornerback; and Domingeaux, a sophomore tight end.

They all spoke candidly about the beleaguered LSU program and the rigors of playing major-college football. LSU didn't merely have a bad football season; the team was buffeted by a nightmarish array of personnel problems. At least three promising players quit the team because they were unhappy about their lack of playing time. Two starting defensive backs, Mark Roman and Clarence LeBlanc, were kicked off the squad for having illegal contact with an agent. Larry Foster, a starting wide receiver and team captain, was arrested for theft and booted off the squad. In addition, there was a phone-card scandal involving a few football players. That, too, resulted in suspensions. If those weren't enough, LSU was hobbled by numerous injuries. It was all too much for a team that, even under the most favorable circumstances, was young and trying to regain its equilibrium after a terrible 1998 season.

Booker, who is from Hammond, Louisiana, about thirty miles west of Baton Rouge, plays right cornerback for the Tigers. For him playing football

301

for LSU was a longtime goal. In Hammond, he says, "everybody loves LSU. If you go to LSU, it's a big-time thing." Hammond High School is a big, 5A school, and like many communities in Louisiana, heavily into football. Booker says that when he was a senior, several teammates earned football scholarships to Division 1 colleges. Two signed with Notre Dame. Booker was a blue-chip player himself, "but I didn't give anybody but LSU a chance. I was recruited by a lot of schools, but I told them straight out I was going to Baton Rouge. Once I had the opportunity to come here, I jumped on it. That's what I was looking for." At LSU, he lived with Mark Roman, who was the team's other starting cornerback before getting booted from the team for contact with an agent. (Roman, an exceptional athlete, was taken in the second round of the most recent NFL draft.)

Bright-eyed and personable, Booker credits his parents for keeping him even-keeled. His mom works with mentally handicapped kids—"she really likes kids and tries to help them," he says. His dad is a firefighter. "I've been riding in fire trucks since I was small. I was in every Hammond parade, sitting on a truck and blowing a horn. I slid down the pole, played with the fire hoses. Those were pretty big things with me." Booker says he comes from a big family. "Hammond is not that big, but it seems like I'm kin in some kind of way to everybody in town."

Banks is a burly fullback from West Monroe, Louisiana, which is a hotbed of high school football. Banks was a star running back at West Monroe High School, which has 2,000 students and won the last three state 5A football championships in Louisiana. He carried the ball twenty to twenty-five times a game at West Monroe, but at LSU he's been purely a blocker. Going into the last game of 1999, he had a measly two carries. As one might expect, Banks has got Mack truck physique—bulging forearms, a thick neck, close-cropped red hair. He's 6'1", weighs 250 pounds, talks with a little bit of a cowboy lilt. He seems a forthright young man, with a dependable toughness of character.

At the end of a college football season, the players are tired and banged up. Everybody's got aches and pains; many players are nursing injuries. Booker's feet were painfully sore—from months of having receivers running over them; Domingeaux had calcium deposits in a heel that were rubbing up against his Achilles tendon. He was anticipating off-season surgery to correct the problem. Banks played the entire 1999 season with a broken wrist. He hurt it during preseason two-a-day practices. "I thought I just jammed it up, so I never did anything about it. I taped it up and kept playing." He, too, was going under the knife prior to the 2000 season.

Banks is as smart as he is tough: he's a microbiology major with a 3.5 grade point average. His dad is a laborer for a paper mill; his mom is an elementary school teacher. "They are the big reason I am where I am now," he says.

Three Tigers Talk Football

"They've instilled in me the value of hard work. My mom went back to school a few years ago to become a teacher, I guess because we needed a little financial help. Dad has had to work hard all his life. Growing up, he was always my coach in every sport I played. He's a big football guy. I don't know if I've ever had a conversation with him since I got to LSU that wasn't about football. That's unreal. Growing up, he was hoping I could get a scholarship to some small school, just to play. That I ended up here, at a big SEC school, was not in his wildest dreams. He does shift work (driving tractors) and misses a lot of games. It hurts him when that happens."

Domingeaux, whose name is pronounced "Dimaggio" (like the New York Yankee baseball great) is from Crowley, Louisiana, a town (population: 20,000) twenty-five miles west of Lafayette, and seventy-five miles west of Baton Rouge. Tall, lanky, and laid-back, Domingeaux is wearing sweatpants, a T-shirt, and flip-flops—the last a favorite with athletes and coaches when they hang out in the athletic complex.

After sitting down, Domingeaux puts one hand on his head and the other on his chin and snaps his jaw up toward the ceiling. I hear his neck crack. He then switches hands and jerks his jaw up in the other direction. Again, a neck crack. I cringe. "Just getting ready for practice," he says. His father, a truck driver, lives in Oakland, California. Domingeaux's parents have been separated for eleven years. His mom works for a Wal-Mart in Crowley. Domingeaux still talks to his dad, and says of the divorce, "It's not a problem." He's got an older brother and a younger sister. Domingeaux, who is a kinesiology major, started for LSU as a true freshman, in 1997, then tore a knee ligament the following spring. He had surgery and missed the entire 1998 season while rehabilitating the knee.

All three players seem a little melancholy and fatigued. In every way, it had been a bruising season. "The body's tired, everybody's tired," says Domingeaux. "We've backed off [the contact] these last two weeks just to see what we've got left in our bodies." But the LSU kids also show ample evidence of the one quality that one expects in young people, and especially young football players: resilience. They are beat up, physically and psychologically, but still determined to end a dismal season with a victory—a trumpet blast at the end of a fugue, if you will. And they did. In the 1999 season finale, the Tigers whipped Arkansas. I spoke with Banks, Booker, and Domingeaux just before that game.

Question: *There's no sugarcoating this year, is there?*

Banks: It's been real tough. We worked hard in the off-season and during the spring and summer. We got a new strength-and-conditioning coach, and he did a good job of getting us ready. And the fall camp was the hardest we've had since DiNardo got here. We figured all the hard work would turn into some wins, but it hasn't turned out that way. It's been disappointing—a lot of off-the-field problems and things we can't help. It's just been a real disappointing year.

Question: *Has the team been down in recent weeks?*

Banks: I think so. Different people take things different ways, but I think as far as the whole team, morale has been going down. You can't do much about it now.

Question: *How did Coach DiNardo react to all the talk about his possible dismissal?*

Banks: The last few games, when it really started getting bad, he took a different approach to coaching. He seemed a lot happier on the practice field and on the sidelines—a lot more excited. He started doing things differently. He still worked us hard in practice and on the field—watching tape and getting the game-plan ready. But the last few games, he lightened up.

Question: *What is Coach DiNardo like as a coach?*

Banks: This past year he was more hands-on than in past years—especially with the offense. He stayed with the offense a lot during practice, and he really coached. He's not just a head coach who walks around checking on what everybody is doing. He really got into the offense this year. He's a big disciplinarian. He makes sure you go to class and stay out of trouble; he's real big on the academic side of the sport. His big deal is that everybody graduates. I think he has his good qualities.

Question: *Sorry to see him go?*

Banks: [Pause] I feel bad for him; this was his job. You've got to feel bad for him. I'm not saying that he was the cause of our downfall, but maybe bringing in somebody new will turn things around and give us a new outlook.

Domingeaux: He and I had a really good relationship. He told me after my freshman year that he really respected me for staying out of trouble and handling my schoolwork. So we were pretty cool. He was hard—really strict, a tough guy. That's his philosophy. But he's a good person. I'm sorry to see him go. That's just this business, though: you've got win football games to keep your job.

Three Tigers Talk Football

Question: *Fred, why were there so many disciplinary problems?*

Booker: I think things just happen. We're very close as a team. Because Coach DiNardo was a disciplinarian, we all tried to look out for each other, encourage each other to go to class, and make sure we didn't get into too much trouble. Sometimes people just make bad decisions, and it's spotlighted because you're an athlete. Everybody makes mistakes at times. I know a lot of people who have done things like our players have—but when you're an athlete, it stands out.

Question: *What went wrong with the football team?*

Booker: Everything. I mean, anything that could go wrong has gone wrong. And it's not getting any better. No matter how hard we play, we can't come up with a win. We're always coming up short at the end.

Question: *That last-second loss to Mississippi State, when the officials seemed to mistakenly award your opponent the winning touchdown, must have really hurt.* [In the closing seconds of that game, the officials ruled that a Mississippi State running back had scored a touchdown on fourth down, when TV replays showed that he, in fact, had crawled into the end zone.]

Booker: That's how it's been going for us these past two years. We just can't get a break. We're hoping for a spark this last game so we can get rolling again next year.

Banks: The last two years, we've got beat—really beat—four or five times. The rest of the games have been close. If they weren't one-point games, we had the ball at the end, trying to drive the ball for the win. It just hasn't happened. It's a game of inches, and we haven't been getting those inches.

Question: *You've had a lot of injuries, and this was a rebuilding year anyway, wasn't it?*

Banks: We lost Herb Tyler, our quarterback from last year's team, which was a big loss. Kevin Faulk, a good running back, was another big loss. We lost a couple of starting offensive linemen from last year's team—Todd McClure and Ryan Thomassie. This year, the third game of the season we lost Larry Foster, a starting wide receiver, who was a big part of our offense. [Offensive lineman] Trey Langley has been out pretty much the whole year. Brandon Winey [another offensive lineman] has missed some games. At one point we were playing with our fourth-string center—that's how bad it got. It should help us next year [in 2000], because a lot of these young guys have gotten playing experience. So we should have more depth.

Question: *Fred, what are your thoughts on the firing of DiNardo?*

Booker: Naturally, everybody is going to blame the head coach. But he can't make us play; he can't go out there and play the game for us. It's up to him to get us ready and provide discipline, and up to us to play well and win games. But around town everybody was going after his head, and they're happy now that he's been fired. That's what everybody's been talking about for two years. When I first got here, I was a little wild, a little out of hand. Coach DiNardo tamed me, and eventually we developed a relationship that was kind of close. I'm sorry to see him go. But maybe that's what we need to get things going around here.

Question: *What did you think about the suspensions of Roman and LeBlanc?* [They allegedly asked for or received favors from Banks Menard, a "runner" representing a New Orleans–based professional agent named Tank Black. A runner's job is to curry favor with college athletes and then persuade them to sign with his agent-employer. Black, who has represented several former University of Florida players now in the NFL, was recently arrested and charged with allegedly bilking money from some of his clients.]

Booker: I didn't know what was going on. I was surprised they got suspended. I know them both closely, and from what I know neither one has any money [meaning he doesn't think they were getting money from Black]. The other day our apartment lights were turned off, so we don't have any money. Roman's my roommate, and I'm sure he hasn't been taking anything personally. Now, if someone in his family did, I don't know anything about that.

Question: *And LeBlanc allegedly asked an agent for a car, or received one from Black or Banks Menard?*

Booker: Clarence hasn't had a car since he's been here. As far as I can tell, the charges are not true. And I think the rules are really unfair: it should be assumed that they are not guilty, and they should have stayed on the team until it's proven otherwise.

Question: *What was the players' reaction to being kicked off the team?* [DiNardo told me that Roman and LeBlanc were caught on tape by police talking to Menard or Black about gifts.]

Three Tigers Talk Football

Booker: They were shocked. Both of them said the same thing: we don't have anything—no money or nothing. How could they make up something like that? Then they got Brandon Winey. He is well taken care of by his parents; they are well-off. I can't see him ever taking anything. But they said he took money. It's just a bunch of rumors that come along with a losing season.

Question: *Do you know this agent's runner, Banks Menard?*

Booker: Yeah, I know him. Everybody knows him. Everybody knows those type of guys are around. If you're from Louisiana and played high school football in this area, you know him. I guess you could say that he's a pal with some players, especially guys from around this area. He was just like an uncle to Kevin Faulk. [Tank Black gave money and gifts to Faulk while he was at LSU.]

Question: *Do the coaches warn you about agents?*

Booker: They tell us to stay away from them. This past summer [1999], it was a big deal because one of our assistant coaches was approached. Tank Black or Banks Menard apparently offered him money to get some of our players. [The coach turned down the offer and reported it to the police.] So it's been a big deal. We get information, and they tell us to see the coaches if we have questions. They warn us about agents every year. DiNardo did a good job of making us aware of the situation. He took pride in being protective; he didn't want us getting caught with an agent and losing our senior year. That's terrible, especially if you're trying to get to the next level.

Question: *Has Menard ever offered you cash or gifts?*

Booker: I've seen him around, I've talked to him, but he's never offered me anything. I know who he is, but I keep my head. I don't need any money. If I do, I'll come to the school and try to get a grant or something. I don't want to lose my eligibility, because I love playing football. The SEC might be the closest I get to the NFL, so I want to take pride in playing here and have a good college career.

Domingeaux: I've never seen him, but I think that goes on everywhere. You just have to be smart about what you're doing. If you're getting looked at by agents, you just have to wait. Your money will come to you if you're getting looked at. You just have to be smart about the decisions you make.

BRAGGING RIGHTS

Question: *Is LSU getting a bad reputation?*

Booker: I don't think so. I think we're getting a bad rap, because things like this happen to every program. As a matter of fact, I know they do because I have a lot of friends all over the place at D1 colleges. And a lot of things go on. It's all how the media plays the situation.

Question: *You have had a few guys quit the team this year. Why?*

Booker: We had three receivers leave this year: Mike Hayes, N. Bates, and Michael Stamps, who was another guy who got suspended. We never found out why. Hayes and Bates transferred to Southern [University] this year, and it hurt us. At one point we were down to scout-team receivers. I guess Hayes and Bates were unhappy with their situation, because at the time we had a lot of depth at receiver. If they'd stuck around, they would have got their chance. Mike Hayes is the leading receiver for Southern right now, so things are going good for him. Bates broke his leg early in the season.

Question: *What's the mood been on campus?*

Booker: It's tough on the students, too. Most of the people around here have been living LSU football since they were born. That's just the way it is. It's a football town; it's a football state, really. It's a big part of everyone's lives. A lot of students come here strictly for LSU football—that's the way it is. They love it. And I can understand them being disappointed. I would be, too, if I'd been rooting for a team all my life. But it's tough on us, too. The students don't understand what we go through. They go to class for a couple of hours, then go home and sleep or watch TV or whatever. We have to go outside and practice for four hours. They don't understand all the hard work we do, but I can still understand their being a little disappointed in us.

Question: *What are you majoring in, Fred?*

Booker: I'm majoring in general studies, with a minor in business and political science. General studies gives you a broad range of classes. I'm getting a minor in business just in case I want to fall back on it. I started to major in business, but it got a little hard, so I changed.

Question: *Do you have ambitions outside of football?*

Three Tigers Talk Football

Booker: I don't know. I haven't thought about it much, but I better get it together because I only have a [few] semesters left. I'm on track to graduate in the spring [of 2000]. I like school—but I'd really just like to come back and go to school for one semester without football, so I can see what college life is about. You don't really get a chance to enjoy it when you're an athlete. All your time is spent out on the field or in meetings.

Question: *Is playing major-college football like having a job?*

Domingeaux: Oh, yeah. It's like football is 50 percent of your day. I mean, from about noon to six or seven P.M., it's football. Either you're getting ready to practice, practicing, getting treatment after practice, or going to meetings. It's hard, because by the time you get through with practice you're tired and try to put your school work off till later on. And then you don't end up doing it. I'm always doing stuff at the last minute, the day before it's due.

Banks: They have practice limits of twenty hours a week—but that's in name only.

Booker: We know it's more than that.

Banks: Exactly. Things get stretched out. Five-minute practice periods become six- and seven-minute periods, and sometimes coaches will hold them for ten minutes. It's a long day.

Question: *A lot of meetings?*

Booker: A *lot* of meetings. That was a big transition for me coming in as a freshman. In high school I was used to practicing and then going home and having fun. Once I got here and they told me about meetings, I said: "What? A meeting?" We have all these meetings, and I'm looking at my watch and thinking: "When do we get to go home?" [He laughs.] That's a big thing coming in as a freshman: you've got to have your mind right. It's like a business. . . .

Question: *Too much football, do you think?*

Domingeaux: I think this year we did kind of have too much football. It's a seven-day-a-week thing for us. We practice Monday through Thursday and play the game on Saturday. We have meetings on Sundays. Friday is supposed to be an off day, but we have to travel to the hotel and take our position test. It's seven days a week. You really don't have a social life—well, you have one, but it feels timed or something. . . . It's almost like having a wife. [Laughter.]

BRAGGING RIGHTS

Question: *Is playing football fun?*

Banks: Losing takes a lot of the fun out of the game. It's a lot of hard work. The most fun comes toward the end of the season, when you've won and you see the hard work has paid off. During the season, you have fun during games, but it is so much hard work, so much time spent. Then, as the season moves toward the end, or after it's over, you look back and say, "I had a good time." But it's hard to sit there during the season and think about how much fun you're having.

Domingeaux: You're around a lot of people that you care about. You develop certain relationships with people going through all the practices and sweating blood and tears with all the guys. You develop a certain kind of bond with the players being around each other. It's pretty fun.

Question: *Are you beat up physically by this point in the season?*

Booker: I woke up this morning and I could barely walk—the tops of my feet hurt so badly. Oh, yes, the top of my feet hurt. It's from receivers running up on you and stepping on your feet. It gets old; you get bruised and worn out. In fact, I'm going to wear some pads in my shoes this week to save myself, so I can walk after the game. By this time in the season, you're beat up and tired. I haven't had a major injury this season, thankfully, just a lot of aches and pains. I've been here three seasons, and I've had two shoulder surgeries—each shoulder has been under the knife. It's from the tackling I do—that's it. You know, we have big backs in the SEC, and they run hard. Look at Tommy, as a matter of fact. I run into him all day in practice. [Laughter.]

Banks: I've been playing all year with a broken wrist. I taped it up and kept playing. But it kept hurting, so finally three weeks ago I had it X-rayed and found out it was fractured and there's a cyst growing on it. So I have to have surgery on that after the season. So I'm ready for that to heal up a little bit. The pain wasn't consistent, but it would hurt pretty badly every time I took a good shot or jammed somebody up.

Question: *What's the toughest defense you played against this year?*

Banks: I don't know if it was just that they were ready for our game, but probably Auburn. They have a good defense. They have a couple of standout guys, but against us they were all playing hard and hitting hard. I've played against a lot of great defenses this year. Mississippi State had a great defense—

Three Tigers Talk Football

I think at one time [they were] number one in the nation. Pretty much every SEC team we play has a good defense. I don't know if I'll ever play a defense as good as the [1998] Florida defense—their front seven was unbelievable. That was an NFL front seven. I've had good competition out there.

Question: *The offense has struggled this year?*

Banks: It's hard. Kind of like the defense did last year, we've had to change our offense around. . . . We haven't been running the ball as well as we have in the past. A lot of that has to do with injuries, and opponents are putting eight guys in the box and trying to stop the run. With Herb [Tyler] we could do a lot more things at quarterback because he was mobile and could roll out. He was like having another running back. Now we have Josh [Booty], who is a dropback passer, and so we've had to make some adjustments with that. Josh started the fourth game of the season, which was the first time we had an official starter. A lot of people don't realize how much that affects a team, waiting that long to find a starter, and having two totally different types of quarterback from season to season. It gets tough sometimes.

Question: *What is your major, Tommy?*

Banks: Microbiology. It's real tough. Hopefully, if the football doesn't work out, I can get into medical school and become a doctor. Right now my GPA is around 3.5 or 3.6, so I'm hoping to keep it above 3.5 and it will help me get into med school. I'll graduate in four years. This fall I'm taking just thirteen hours of class; this spring I'll take sixteen. With microbiology you have to take a lot of labs: they're three-hour classes, but you only get one hour of credit. So this semester [fall of 1999], I'm really going to class seventeen hours, but only getting thirteen hours credit. And next semester [spring of 2000], I'll be going to class for about twenty-four hours a week and only getting sixteen hours of credit. It gets tough.

Question: *And your major, Joe?*

Domingeaux: Kinesiology. I'll probably go into sports studies. It's mostly classes that I like. I can go into coaching with it. That's something I want to do after school—to coach and stay around sports.

Question: *What's your GPA, Joe?*

Domingeaux: I've got a 2.5. No complaints about school, although I don't like night classes. I've got two night classes a week, and they're each three hours long. One is biology and the other is kinesiology, the prevention of injury. I'm taking seventeen hours [in the fall], which is a pretty good load, but it's spaced out so I don't have six classes in a row.

Banks: Athletes can schedule classes before other students, so we can kind of schedule around practice.

Question: *How were your grades in high school, Joe?*

Domingeaux: I had a 2.8 GPA, and an ACT test composite of 19. I had to take the test three times, though. That's a hard test.

Question: *Do professors treat you differently because you're an athlete?*

Domingeaux: Naw. You're just a regular student. You might have some teachers who follow the sport and know you by name and try to help explain things to you more. When a professor knows you by name, you know you're either going to get lots of help or you're in big trouble [because they don't like sports].

Question: *I've always been curious about the grades players get after games from the coaches. Were the grades bad after the Houston game?*

Booker: Bad grades? Naw, the secondary really had pretty good grades. They didn't come out and throw the ball. They tried to play smash-mouth football. The biggest things they graded us on were our alignment and pursuit to the ball, because we didn't have to defend the pass that much. We get graded on [positional] alignment, adjustments, and pursuit to the ball. The coaches preach pursuit—everybody flying to the ball. That's the biggest thing they grade on. If you don't pursue, they are not going to play you. I think I graded 85 percent for the Houston game; my pursuit grade was 97—that's just one pursuit error, one time I didn't pursue or got a little lackadaisical. An 85 is pretty good, but I can grade 85 percent and give up two touchdowns. That could be just two bad plays, two turning points. I don't think grades really reflect how good you played in a game.

Banks: My highest grades have been around 92—I've made a couple of those. Fullbacks get graded on blocking technique, making sure I hit the [defender's] correct shoulder, and making sure I get beneath the defender's pads. When you're blocking somebody, it's not just going and hitting somebody; you gotta make sure you get the correct side, because the running back will be cutting a certain way. And we also have to make sure to have the right assignment—hit the correct guy. It's a lot of stuff to learn. People don't understand everything that goes into the game.

I think anywhere in the mid-80s is a good grade. I've had some grades below that and some above. But like Fred said, a lot of times grades don't really matter. My freshman year we beat Florida, then came back and lost to Ole Miss. But I had one of my highest grades ever in the Ole Miss game, a 93.

Question: *Where do you live, on campus or off?*

Domingeaux: I live on campus, in a campus apartment. And mostly with regular students.

Booker: Tommy and I live off-campus in apartments that are right down the street from each other. We're close to the [athletic] complex. I have two players as roommates.

Question: *What do you guys do on Fridays before a game? What's the routine?*

Domingeaux: The tight ends and receivers take a position test every Friday afternoon. It's a written test, and it takes about an hour to finish. If we have to leave for the hotel at six P.M., then we have to be at the meeting room by four and do the test. Then we go play catch for thirty minutes or so right outside the locker room. After that we go to the faculty club and eat a meal together as a team. Then we load up the bus and go to the locker room and get a ten-minute meeting in. Then we go to a movie. It's fun, if it's a good movie. Then we go to the hotel [a nearby Holiday Inn]. We have a little snack—peanut butter and jelly sandwiches, ice cream sandwiches, or whatever. After that we go to our room and go to sleep. Coaches do room checks. Then we wake up the next morning and have our itinerary for the day—more meetings, special teams, and all that. What we do depends on the time of the game. If it's a night game, we have a lot of meetings during the day; but if it's a day game, we just have [team] offense and defense meetings and punt/punt returns and other special teams.

Question: *What's the mood on game day?*

Domingeaux: We're pretty laid back. You just try to relax any way you can; you don't even walk around. You sit down to get off your legs. The sense of humor and everything else is the same. Then, once we have the last meeting before getting on the bus, everybody's mood kind of changes and gets more serious.

BRAGGING RIGHTS

Question: *What do you guys do for fun?*

Domingeaux: Video games. Play some PlayStation or Dreamcast. That's more competition than on the field. That's what we do a lot.

Question: *What comes next on the football agenda after the fall season?*

Banks: The strength coach said that working out [lifting weights] the last couple of weeks of school, in December, would be optional. We can come in and work out if we want, to get a hard start. Then we get a month off in January. We come back the beginning of February and start up pretty hard and heavy. Most people take advantage of the break because we don't get many of them.

Question: *Do you have girlfriends, or have they left you after this season?* [Laughter]

Booker: It's rough, believe me. When you're losing, it's hard to hold on to them!

Question: *What's playing in the SEC like?*

Booker: Whew! It's a tough conference. No matter who you play, they are going to be good. I mean, people can look at us and say, "That's a terrible team." But we play hard and we've got a lot of guys with talent. You've got to get up every week to play. There are no easy games; every time you play an SEC team, you're in for a fight.

Question: *Are you looking forward to next year?*

Domingeaux: We have a ton of talent; we're just loaded. We were young this year. Right now, the mood is let's have fun and then rebuild. We'll have to start over from scratch.

TWENTY-TWO

SHOWDOWN: THE SEC CHAMPIONSHIP— ALABAMA VERSUS FLORIDA

December 4, 1999

There were doubts, at first, about the SEC championship game. When it was first played, at Birmingham's Legion Field in 1992, there was no shortage of skeptics. Critics worried that adding a twelfth game to the conference schedule—a season-ending finale pitting the SEC's eastern division winner against the western division winner—would hurt the SEC's chances of winning the national championship. What if the SEC team with the higher national ranking were to lose the championship game? Others complained that an additional game would probably wear out the players—and keep them away from school for another couple of days near the end of the term. What's more, there was serious concern that fans and the media might not get excited about the championship game if it were a rematch—if it featured two teams who had played each other earlier in the year. And low TV ratings might embarrass the conference.

Well, the nattering nabobs of negativism have been routed. The SEC Championship has been a rousing success. "If you measure by attendance and TV ratings, the championship game has been very successful," SEC Commissioner Roy Kramer told me just before Alabama and Florida squared off in the Georgia Dome for the 1999 title. "It's been the highest-rated regular season [college football] game in each of the last six years." Roughly fifteen million people watched the 1998 championship game on TV. The Georgia Dome, located in Atlanta, seats 71,000—and it's always a sellout. In one respect, the SEC has been a little lucky: the championship game has yet to scuttle the title chances of the SEC's strongest team coming into the game. There have been three teams in a position to win a national title coming into the SEC championship game—Alabama in 1992, Florida in 1996, and Tennessee in 1998. All won and went on to be ranked number one. But the risk still remains: sooner or later a very highly ranked SEC team will be upset by its division rival in Atlanta, and lose its shot at the national crown. But it won't matter: the genie is out of the bottle. The SEC game already has proved itself a fitting and popular climax to the regular season.

And now that we think about it, with the blissful luxury of hindsight, how could the SEC Championship *not* have succeeded? Simply put, it's another SEC game! In a region that loves college football, that fact alone is enough to please a great many fans. That it's a *showdown* game only adds to the enjoyment. It's the perfect opportunity for the conference's two best teams to decide, man to man, who is the conference king. It's the perfect setting for fans to beat their chests one last time—to bellow boisterously about their football boys; the perfect time for state citizens to swell with anticipation and pride one last time—especially if (or when) the state team gives those pretenders next door a good ol'-fashioned butt-whippin'. And, of course, it's the perfect way for the conference to fill its coffers.

The game itself generates about $7.5 million in revenue—and much more than that in publicity. The two participating schools each receive $550,000 from the game (above their expenses, which are paid by the SEC), and the rest is divvied up among the remaining conference members. The SEC doesn't just sponsor a game, of course: it markets itself during an extravagant championship weekend. There is a coaches' luncheon on the Friday preceding the game. Last year 850 people attended, paying $25 a head to listen to the two gladiators, Mike DuBose and Steve Spurrier, answer questions from the crowd for an hour-and-a-half. On Friday night there is a dressy "legends dinner." Each SEC school brings one of their football greats to Atlanta, and each is honored with a little speech. The honorees last year were Mississippi State's D. D. Lewis, Georgia's Herschel Walker, Tennessee's Steve Kiner, Vanderbilt's Bob Werckle, Florida's Kerwin Bell, Alabama's Johnny Musso, Arkansas's Bill Montgomery, Kentucky's Steve Meilinger, LSU's Jerry Stovall, South Carolina's Rick Sanford, and Auburn's Jackie Burkett. Nearly 600 people attended the dinner, paying $85 each to munch with, and cheer, their SEC heroes. Walker got the loudest ovation.

On Saturday, there is a massive "fan fair" at the Georgia Conference Center. "It's modeled somewhat on the NFL experience that's grown in popularity every year," says Kramer. Kids throw and kick footballs (winning prizes, in some cases), watch SEC videos, get autographs from Herschel and the rest of the legends. The Alabama and Florida bands were on hand, and their brass sections were blaring. The cheerleaders were jumping for joy (arms and legs akimbo) and shaking their pom-poms. As Kramer says, "It's a festive-type event all day Saturday, right up until the game." More than 50,000 people attended.

It's all a happy prelude to a football game. And last year's championship game was intriguing. For one thing, it offered Alabama the chance to win its first SEC title since 1992, when the Crimson Tide beat Florida in the inaugural conference championship game. (The following year, Florida beat Alabama.) What's more, the 1999 game was a rematch. Earlier in the season, the Pachyderms had shocked Florida, dominating the time of possession and *outscoring* the Gators in a shootout, 40-39. That proved a watershed game for both teams—sending Alabama on its way toward the SEC Western Division title, and sending Florida into what I might call a *victorious tailspin*.

After that midseason loss to Alabama, Florida would lose only one more game—to archrival and number one–ranked Florida State, in the regular season. But the Gators struggled offensively down the stretch. In particular, the Florida passing game was shockingly inconsistent during the second half of the season—so much so that, in games against Georgia and Vanderbilt, Florida had to run the ball to win. Spurrier moaned about "dumb" plays, "stupid penalties," and his own poor coaching. Doug Johnson played the best game of his collegiate career in the loss to Alabama, completing 22 of 31 passes for 309 yards and 4 touchdowns. But he developed arm problems late in the season, and with the exception of the Florida State game, his play deteriorated.

The play of Florida's vaunted receiving corps—chiefly Travis Taylor and Darrell Jackson, among others—was spotty. Taylor badly twisted his ankle in the Tennessee game and was never quite the threat everyone expected him to be. Florida's defense, offensive line, and runners (led by redshirt freshman Earnest Graham) had played well—but a Florida team that can't throw is a bird without wings. Spurrier is a bird: he likes to throw, wants to throw, needs to throw. He will run to win, and smartly did so when necessary—but he'll always *try* to throw.

Spurrier, in fact, made what may have been the worst decision of his Florida career in 1999. Though never hugely confident in Johnson as a quarterback, The Head Ball Coach nevertheless decided to ride him all the way through the season. Spurrier had another skilled and experienced quarterback on his team, junior Jesse Palmer. But Spurrier tried to "redshirt" him last year, keep him out of action. By doing so Spurrier could save his backup QB a year of eligibility, leaving Palmer with two full years to play, rather than one. It was a risky decision, and would come back to haunt Spurrier and the Gators in this game—the most important of the season.

Alabama, meanwhile, was stealing a march on Florida's offense. Imagine that! For years Alabama's offense was a dowager—dignified, successful, but slow-moving. The Tide was old-school; it stubbornly insisted on playing grind-it-out offensive football, along with good defense. That formula had served Alabama well for many years—but not lately. Alabama's chief rivals, Tennessee and Florida, were recruiting skilled passers and receivers. During the 1990s the Gators and Vols moved up and down the football field like sports cars. Alabama, meanwhile, trundled along like a tank. Who can even remember the last truly skilled Alabama quarterback? But in 1999, Alabama got religion: the Tide installed an offense that seemed to resemble Florida's old "Fun-and-Gun." In Andrew Zow, Bama had found a strong quarterback who could stand in the pocket and throw—accurately. He had tossed for 336 yards in the Tide's first meeting against Florida, and played solidly (if not spectacularly) throughout the year. In addition, Alabama found a playmaker named Freddie Milons, a jitterbug who terrified opposing defenses with his quick feet and elusiveness. Shaun Alexander, the All-America running back, was Alabama's first (and maybe even second) option. But Milons gave Alabama an additional offensive dimension, a second threat, and that proved all the difference.

But the man who arguably deserves the most credit for Alabama's offensive transformation was Charlie Stubbs. He calls the plays, he spreads the field, and he is creative. That's a word that hasn't been heard much in Tuscaloosa since the brilliant Homer Smith left town. Stubbs not only ran Alexander, but sent him downfield on pass patterns. He threw all manner of screen passes—so-called middle screens, slip screens—to Milons, giving him frequent opportunities to run. Stubbs even put Milons under center occasionally—something Alabama liked to do with David Palmer in the mid-1990s. "We've got pretty good passing schemes," Stubbs said during the season.

So Alabama could move the ball. The question was, could the Tide stop Florida's offense? It seemed unlikely. Bama's defense was solid, but not exceptional—and it had lost two starters late in the year, tackle Kenny Smith and middle linebacker Marvin Constant. The Tide still had some run stoppers—including tackles Reggie Grimes and Cornelius Griffin—but there would be pressure on the team's young defensive backs in this game—Reggie Myles, Milo Lewis, Kecalf Bailey, and Gerald Dixon. Everybody knew the Gators would chuck the ball. Those guys would have to limit the damage from the Gator air attack.

The Title Game

As things turned out, Florida didn't really have an air attack in the 1999 championship game. The Gators had damaged themselves—shot themselves in the foot. Because of his arm troubles, quarterback Doug Johnson was unable to start for Florida in the SEC Championship. His arm was so floppy he could barely throw a football. So backup Palmer, who'd hardly played all year, was handed the task of winning the SEC title. He has talent, but he wasn't up to the task. Palmer had started the last game of the season, a win against lowly South Carolina—but to say he was rusty was an understatement. There is no substitute for game experience. Not much was made of it afterwards by the press, but by not playing Palmer more during the season Spurrier had effec-

The SEC Championship

tively hoisted himself by his own petard, as the saying goes. Spurrier is a coach who prides himself on pulling starters if they are not playing well. But he left himself without that option for most of the 1999 season. Palmer finally played—but only after it had become evident that something was wrong with Johnson's arm and the Florida passing game. But by then it was too late.

Still, the Gators started strongly. They took the opening kickoff and in less than two minutes drove fifty-five yards for a touchdown. Spurrier crossed up the Tide when he had tailback Graham throw a three-yard scoring pass to tight end Erron Kinney. Florida took the early lead, 7-0. Alabama then went backwards on its first possession. The Tide lost nine yards on three plays and was forced to punt. Florida seemed poised to take early command of the game. But after their quick opening score, Florida's offense petered out. The Gators didn't just struggle to score; they struggled to make first downs. Palmer and the Florida receivers were completely out of synch. The Gators could not complete simple five- or ten-yard out patterns. The running game was equally inept. How bad was it? Florida did not convert a single third-down opportunity in the game—not one. They were 0-9.

Alabama took advantage of Florida's offensive problems. Stubbs mixed up his plays beautifully, running Alexander, then throwing quick passes to both Milons and end Antonio Carter, who is another scatback. Milons lined up all over the field, and there wasn't much of it that his feet didn't touch during the course of the game. Alabama did what Florida could not do: make key third-down plays. In the second quarter, Zow hit Jason McAddley with a 27-yard touchdown pass on third-and-sixteen. With that crucial score Alabama took the lead—and from there the Tide would, ahem, roll. At the end of the first half, Alabama had piled up 231 yards of offense compared to a meager 70 for Florida. And they had held the ball for nearly eight minutes longer than the Gators. Still, Bama's lead was slight—12-7.

That cushion would prove big enough in this game, however. As bad as Florida's offense was in the first half, it was worse in the second. After their first drive, Florida could manage only four first downs and sixty-seven yards of offense *for the rest of the game.* The Gators were hapless. They looked more like the Citadel than the team whose deft passing had terrorized SEC defenses for years. The only people Florida scared in this game were its fans.

And yet, for all their problems, the Gators were only trailing by 15-7 when the fourth quarter began. And then came the biggest series of the game. Alabama was facing a third-and-eleven from its own seven-yard line. A stop here, and Florida still had a chance. Bama quarterback Tyler Watts dropped into the end zone to pass. Seeing no open receiver, Watts took off running up the middle. Before he was tackled, he'd managed to scramble for fourteen yards and a huge first down. That play really defined the game: Bama made big plays when it counted, and Florida could not. Moments later, receiver Milons lined up at quarterback, took the snap and weaved seventy-seven yards past Florida's befuddled defenders for a game-clinching touchdown. After that, the game got ugly. Grimes intercepted a Palmer pass and returned it for a touchdown. Ryan Pflugner kicked three field goals, and when it was over, Alabama had routed Florida 34-7, winning its first SEC Championship in seven years. Bama had racked up four times as much yardage as Florida—and, as they had in the first game, dominated the "time of ball possession" statistic. Alabama held the ball for more than forty minutes, compared to less than twenty minutes for the Gators.

"We Were More Physical"

It was an impressive win by Alabama, especially given that the Tide had beaten Spurrier at his own game—slicing up the Florida defense with wacky plays. After the game, one writer joked that standing forlornly on the sideline, Spurrier "looked like somebody had shot his dog." After Grimes returned the Palmer interception for a touchdown, Spurrier flipped his earphones off his head in disbelief and frustration. They fell to the turf like so many errant Florida passes. Coach Mike DuBose said that "we were more physical than they were, and I think that was the difference." Spurrier called it a "thorough beating. Alabama had more fire. They wanted it more than we did. They were the better team, they were the better coaches. They played like champions."

All true, but this game was *clearly* defined by Florida's offensive incompetence. Florida set four Spurrier-era records in this game—all of them bad: fewest first downs (6), fewest pass completions (8), fewest passing yards (83) and fewest total yards (114). The Bama defense played well—but against a team that suffered through its worst offensive showing in a decade. For the game, Palmer completed seven of twenty passes for eighty yards and three interceptions. Kevin McKinnon relieved him at one point, but his only pass was intercepted. Doug Johnson also made a brief appearance; in the third quarter. He short-armed two passes—both incompletions.

And so it went. "Our offense is about the worst we've ever had at Florida right now," Spurrier said. "I was surprised we couldn't get anything going the whole game." Asked why, he had no explanation. "I don't know what to do. Our players have not been playing very lively. It has been a different group since the middle of the season. We've got to find some people who want to play." Florida defensive end Alex Brown actually ripped his offensive teammates after the game, saying: "The defense is pissed at the offense. We had, what, seventy yards at halftime? That's awful. Somebody needs to make a play. Something is wrong. We need to watch film and fix something." In particular,

The SEC Championship

Brown took verbal potshots at the team's highly recruited receivers—Taylor, Jackson, Reche Caldwell, and Brian Haugabrook. "These receivers came here and were compared to Reidel [Anthony] and Ike [Hilliard]. Well, they need to come out and play. Reidel and Ike were great athletes who made plays. These guys are great athletes who don't make plays." Tough words, those.

Alabama offensive tackle Chris Samuels, who didn't give up a sack all year, had some words, too. But they were kind ones, for the players on Alabama's 2000 football team. Samuels, a senior, had endured some rough times at Bama—especially a 4-7 record in 1997 that was the team's worst season in forty years. But with the Tide no longer on probation, and with another SEC title under its belt, he saw even better times ahead. "I think we're all the way back," he said. "I'm expecting these guys to win the national championship next year."

Out of the Ashes

Certainly, 1999 was a triumph for Mike DuBose. He had slouched into the season, an embattled coach leading a program that had lost its lustre. His job was hanging by a thread, especially after Alabama lost to lowly Louisiana Tech on September 18. He was surely a couple of defeats away from the coaching graveyard. But he pulled himself out of the ashes—thanks mostly to the stunning Bama win over Florida in Gainesville. The Tide survived a couple of scares after that, especially against LSU, and showed just enough to win the SEC West. A few days before the SEC Championship, DuBose told a Mobile, Alabama, group how his life had changed. "A few years ago, when we had a 4-7 losing season, everywhere I went to speak people wanted to give me books on motivating people. Now that we're 9-2, people want to give me books on dieting."

DuBose absolutely reflects the contradictions in sports—and in human beings. Before the season started, we spoke on the phone. He sounded like an absolutely stand-up guy—he probably *is* a stand-up guy. "If your only focus is on winning," he said in his fine, flat Alabama accent, "then you compromise on some things." He would not compromise on academics, he said—making sure his players earn their degrees is vital. So is making his players "better people." He added: "My number one responsibility is to help the players become better people. Players now are smarter than they've ever been. You have to care about them, and you want them to be better people twenty years from now because of the discipline they learned here."

DuBose comes from, as they say in the South, "good people." He is from Opp, Alabama (population: 6,000). His father, Ray, worked for a Pepsi factory; his mom, Una, for a textile mill. He played linebacker for the Bear in the 1970s. He won a national championship. The Bear gave him the number worn by Alabama

3 2 1

legend Lee Roy Jordan, who was his hero. That is a high honor in Tuscaloosa. DuBose once made twenty tackles in a game against Tennessee. I asked him what quality he'd learned from the Bear. "Honesty," he replied. "Your word is your bond." Early in his coaching career, he accepted a job at Southern Miss. Hours after taking the position, Bryant called and offered him a job at Alabama. DuBose dearly wanted to work with the Bear—but he'd given his word to the Southern Miss coach, and he kept it. He reluctantly refused Bryant's offer. (DuBose coached at Southern Miss for a year and *then* joined the Bama staff.)

But less than a month after we talked, he was embroiled in a major scandal. He had lied about a longtime affair that he'd had with his secretary. It's not that DuBose wasn't—isn't—honest. He's like most people: his honesty is relative to circumstance. But with an SEC title under his belt, there will be no more talk (in the Alabama "family," anyway) of that messy episode. DuBose had fallen, yes, but he'd suffered, he'd made amends—and then pulled himself back up. And now, having found redemption inside a brightly lit domed stadium in Atlanta, he began to seem like the SEC's own Bill Clinton, without the gray hair and quivering lower lip. Somewhere, a southern gospel choir was singing "Hallelujah!"

Aside from all the personal baggage, DuBose deserves credit for reviving Alabama. He's admitted that his first two years as Alabama's coach were "overwhelming" and a "learning experience." The position "puts tremendous demands on your time," he says, "and I realized that I wasn't coaching and doing the things needed to get this program back to national prominence." So he learned to prioritize and "do what's best for the football team."

If that meant offending individual players, or even coaches, so be it. "I made some difficult decisions about staffing. I learned that it was wrong to assume that every assistant coach knew more about his position than I did. Ultimately, I'm the one accountable." He hired Ronnie Cottrell and "decided to build the program from the ground up with recruiting." It all worked—as anyone who'd watched the SEC championship game could attest. DuBose has been clamoring for more unity at Alabama. In the sixteen years since Bryant stepped down as coach and athletic director, the school has had six different athletic directors (the last three of whom were fired) and five football coaches. "There are too many factions out there with their own agendas," the coach said last September. "People may not want to hear this, but it's been a problem. It's time for people to start supporting whoever is in charge, whether it's the board of trustees, the president, the athletic director, the head coach. It's time to come together and support this university." Will it happen? "It's probably not realistic," he concluded—but that was before Bama won the SEC title. Winning solves problems.

For the SEC's top teams, there would be no national title chances as the New Year's bowl season approached. Alabama, Tennessee, and Florida were all picked to play in big bowls—but none was at the top of the Bowl

The SEC Championship

Championship Series points standings. Florida State and Virginia Tech battled in the Sugar Bowl for the national championship, and—of course—the Seminoles won it. Surprisingly, the SEC's top teams all lost their bowl games. SEC teams routinely lose bowl games—but it is rare for the conference's heavyweights to *all* lose their last game. But that's what happened. Tennessee was humbled by that midwestern battering ram known as Nebraska; Florida was nipped by Michigan State in the Citrus Bowl, and Alabama lost to Michigan, by one point in overtime, in the Orange Bowl. The season was over.

Individual statistics (Final)
Florida vs. Alabama (December 4, 1999 at Atlanta, Georgia)
Florida

Rushing	No	Gain	Loss	Net	TD	Long	Avg
Earnest Graham	9	31	4	27	0	12	3.0
John Capel	2	7	0	7	0	5	3.5
R. Gillespie	2	12	5	7	0	12	3.5
Chuck Marks	4	4	6	-2	0	3	-0.5
Shaun Bohanon	2	32	0	32	0	21	16.0
Jesse Palmer	3	5	13	-8	0	4	-2.7
Totals. . .	20	59	28	31	0	—	—

Passing	Att-Cmp-Int	Yds	TD	Long	Sck
Jesse Palmer	20-7-3	80	0	32	1
Doug Johnson	2-0-0	0	0	0	0
Earnest Graham	1-1-0	3	1	3	0
Kevin McKinnon	1-0-1	0	0	0	0
Totals. . .	24-8-4	83	1	—	1

Receiving	No	Yds	TD	Long
Darrell Jackson	3	49	0	32
Travis Taylor	2	22	0	14
Earnest Graham	2	9	0	9
Erron Kinney	1	3	1	3
Totals. . .	8	83	1	—

Punting	No	Yds	Avg	Long
Alan Rhine	8	324	40.5	57
Total. . .	8	324	40.5	—

All Returns	Punts			Kickoffs			Intercept		
	No	Yds	Lg	No	Yds	Lg	No	Yds	Lg
Chuck Marks	0	0	0	1	5	5	0	0	0
Lito Sheppard	0	0	0	1	3	3	0	0	0
Daryl Dixon	0	0	0	0	0	0	1	29	29
Bo Carroll	0	0	0	5	108	37	0	0	0
Totals. . .	0	0	—	7	116	—	1	29	—

Field Goal Attempts
—

BRAGGING RIGHTS

Alabama

Rushing

Rushing	No	Gain	Loss	Net	TD	Lg	Avg
Freddie Milons	6	116	0	116	1	77	19.3
Shaun Alexander	30	121	24	97	1	21	3.2
D. McClintock	4	48	0	48	0	37	12.0
Tyler Watts	4	24	6	18	0	14	4.5
Marvin Brown	1	0	0	0	0	0	0.0
Andrew Zow	1	0	5	-5	0	0	-5.0
TEAM	1	0	6	-6	0	0	-6
Totals. . .	49	341	41	300	2	—	—

Passing

Passing	Att-Cmp-Int	Yds	TD	Long	Sck
Andrew Zow	17-10-0	134	1	52	1
Tyler Watts	7-3-1	21	0	10	1
Freddie Mions	1-1-0	7	0	7	0
Totals. . .	25-14-1	162	1	—	2

Receiving

Receiving	No	Yds	TD	Long
Antonio Carter	5	71	0	52
Jason McAddley	4	46	1	27
Terry Jones, Jr.	1	19	0	19
D. McClintock	1	15	0	15
Tim Bowens	1	11	0	11
Shaun Alexander	1	1	0	1
Freddie Mions	1	-1	0	0
Totals. . .	14	162	1	—

Punting

Punting	No	Yds	Avg	Long
Patrick Morgan	3	120	40.0	45
Totals	3	120	—	—

All Returns

All Returns	Punts No	Yds	Lg	Kickoffs No	Yds	Lg	Intercept No	Yds	Lg
Freddie Milons	0	0	0	1	10	10	0	0	0
Milo Lewis	0	0	0	0	0	0	1	6	6
Marcus Spencer	0	0	0	0	0	0	2	53	
Arvin Richard	0	0	0	1	18	18	0	0	0
Reggie Grimes	0	0	0	0	0	0	1	38	38
Totals. . .	0	0	—	2	28	—	4	97	—

Field goal attempts

Ryan Pflugner	1st	02:12	42 yds—Missed
Ryan Pflugner	2nd	11:03	29 yds—Good
Ryan Pflugner	2nd	02:03	48 yds—Good
Ryan Pflugner	3rd	03:12	49 yds—Good
Ryan Pflugner	4th	05:31	36 yds—Missed

1999 SEC FOOTBALL

EASTERN DIVISION

	SEC	Pct	PF	PA	Overall	Pct	PF	PA	Home	Away	Neutral	vs Div	Streak
Florida	7-1	.875	226	118	9-4	.692	403	272	4-2	4-0	1-2	5-0	L 3
Tennessee	6-2	.750	251	116	9-3	.750	369	194	7-0	2-2	0-1	4-1	L 1
Georgia	5-3	.625	198	204	8-4	.667	339	307	5-1	2-2	1-1	3-2	W 1
Kentucky	4-4	.500	198	218	6-6	.500	328	343	3-3	3-2	0-1	2-3	L 2
Vanderbilt	2-6	.250	129	211	5-6	.455	252	256	2-4	3-2	0-0	1-4	L 3
S. Carolina	0-8	.000	63	216	0-11	.000	87	278	0-6	0-5	0-0	0-5	L 11

WESTERN DIVISION

	SEC	Pct	PF	PA	Overall	Pct	PF	PA	Home	Away	Neutral	vs Div	Streak
Alabama	7-1	.875	210	170	10-3	.769	378	265	5-2	4-0	1-1	5-0	L 1
Mississippi	6-2	.750	156	121	10-2	.833	255	156	7-0	2-2	1-0	3-2	W 2
Ole Miss	4-4	.500	235	176	8-4	.667	323	228	3-3	4-1	1-0	3-2	W 1
Arkansas	4-4	.500	198	196	8-4	.667	353	214	6-0	1-4	1-0	2-3	W 1
Auburn	2-6	.250	153	188	5-6	.455	233	236	3-4	2-2	0-0	1-4	L 1
LSU	1-7	.125	135	218	3-8	.273	223	259	3-4	0-4	0-0	1-4	W 1

1999–2000 SEC BOWL RESULTS

TOSTITOS FIESTA BOWL
Nebraska 91, Tennessee 21
Jan. 2 • Sun Devil Stadium • 71,526 • Tempe, Arizona

FEDEX ORANGE BOWL
Michigan 95, Alabama 34 [OT]
Jan. 1 • Pro Player Stadium • 70,461 • Miami, Florida

OURHOUSE.COM FLORIDA CITRUS BOWL
Michigan State 37, Florida 34
Jan. 1 • Florida Citrus Bowl • 62,011 • Orlando, Florida

SOUTHWESTERN BELL COTTON BALL
Arkansas 27, Texas 6
Jan 1 • Cotton Bowl • 72,723 • Dallas, Texas

OUTBACK BOWL
Georgia 28, Purdue 25 [OT]
Jan 1 • Raymond James Stadium • 54,059 • Tampa, Florida

SANFORD INDEPENDENCE BOWL
Ole Miss 27, Okalahoma 25
Dec. 31 • Independence Stadium • 49,873 • Shreveport, Louisiana

CHICK-FIL-A PEACH BOWL
Mississippi State 17, Clemson 7
Dec. 30 • Georgia Dome • 79,915 • Atlanta, Georgia

HOMEPOINT.COM MUSIC CITY BOWL
Syracuse 20, Kentucky 13
Dec. 29 • Adelphia Stadium • 59,221 • Nashville, Tennessee

BRAGGING RIGHTS

SEC NOTES

- The SEC finished the 1999–2000 bowl season with a 4-4 record, marking the fourth straight year that the league has won at least half of its bowl games. During the decade of the 1990s, the SEC has posted only two seasons with losing bowl records—1991 (2-3) and 1995 (2-4).

- Two SEC bowl games went into overtime while two others were decided on the last play of regulation. Michigan's 95-34 win over Alabama in the FedEx Orange Bowl and Georgia's 28-25 win over Purdue in the Outback Bowl were decided in overtime. Michigan State defeated Oklahoma, 27-25 in the Sanford Independence Bowl on last second field goals.

- For the second season, the SEC sent eight teams to post-season bowl games, which is a record for collegiate conferences. The Big Ten Conference sent seven teams to post-season bowls in 1999–2000.

- Georgia rallied from a 25-0 deficit to defeat Purdue, 28-25, in overtime at the Outback Bowl. The comeback was the largest ever in a bowl game, surpassing 22-point comebacks by BYU in the 1980 Holiday Bowl (46-45 over SMU) and Notre Dame in the 1979 Cotton Bowl (35-34 over Houston).

1999 SEC CHAMPIONSHIP GAME

ALABAMA 34, FLORIDA 7
Saturday, Dec. 4 • Atlanta, Georgia • Georgia Dome
Attendance: 74,309
MVP: Freddie Milons, Alabama

SEC CHAMPION COACHES

Paul Bryant (14) – Kentucky (1) 1950; Alabama (13) 1961-64-65-66-71-72-73-74-75-77-78-79-81
Vince Dooley (6) – Georgia 1966-68-76-80-81-82
Johnny Vaught (6) – Ole Miss 1947-54-55-60-62-63
Bob Neyland (5) – Tennessee 1938-39-49-46-51
Steve Spurrier (5) – Florida 1991-93-94-95-96
Wally Butts (4) – Georgia 1941-46-48-59
Pat Dye (4) – Auburn 1983-87-88-89
Frank Thomas (4) – Alabama 1933-34-37-45
Bill Alexander (3) – Georgia Tech 1939-43-44
Johnny Majors (3) – Tennessee 1985-89-90
Doug Dickey (2) – Tennessee 1967-69
Paul Dietzel (2) – LSU 1958-61
Bobby Dodd (2) – Georgia Tech 1951-52
Bernie Moore (2) – LSU 1935-36
Mike Archer (1) – LSU 1988

Bill Arnsparger (1) – LSU 1986
Ted Cox (1) – Tulane 1934
Fran Curci (1) – Kentucky 1976
Bill Curry (1) – Alabama 1989
Red Dawson (1) – Tulane 1939
Red Drew (1) – Alabama 1953
Henry Frnke (1) – Tulane 1949
Phil Fulmer (2) – Tennessee 1997-98
Ralph Jordan (1) – Auburn 1957
Charlie McClendon (1) – LSU 1970
Allyn McKeen (1) – Mississippi State 1941
Gene Stallings (1) – Alabama 1992
Bowden Wyatt (1) – Tennessee 1956
Mike DuBose (1) – Alabama 1999

CHAMPIONSHIPS BY SCHOOLS

Alabama: 21 (1933-34t-37-45-53-61t-64-65-66t-71-72-73-74-75-77-78-79-81t-89t-92-99)
Tennessee: 13 ((1938-39t-40-46t-51t-56-67-69-85-89t-90-97-98)
Georgia: 10 (1942-46t-48-59-66t-68-76t-80t-81t-82)
LSU: 7 (1935-36-58-61t-70-86-88t)
Ole Miss: 6 (1947-54-55-60-62-63)
Auburn: 5 (1957-83-87-88t-89t)
Florida: 5 (1991-93-94-95-96)
*Georgia Tech: 5 (1939t-43-44-51t-52)
*Tulane: 3 (1934-39t-49)
Kentucky: 2 (1950-76t)
Mississippi State: 1 (1941)

*Denotes former member of the SEC

(All stats courtesy the Southeastern Conference)

TWENTY-THREE

A SUMMING UP

Collège football matters in the South. The sport's roots are sunk dandelion-deep in the region. Historians Francis Butler Simkins and Charles Rolands, in their book *A History of the South* (1972) describe how college football came to grow so popular south of the Mason-Dixon line. "Pride in the strength of the sectional football teams took its place along with pride in the valor of the Confederate army as a major source of Southern chauvinism. Athletes became glamorous new Southern heroes, and their coach the best-known university figure to the general populace."

Much has changed, of course. Racial integration began in 1966—and since then the sport has grown tremendously, powered by television, passionate fans—and money. College football is very much rules-based nowadays, and that's not a bad thing. Lots of people mindlessly bash the NCAA—just as they belittle "big government"—but in my view the NCAA does a reasonably good job of walking the tightrope between offering the opportunity for higher education to a very broad group of student-athletes—many of them borderline students—and trying to ensure that they don't compromise the integrity of the universities that admit them. That is a tough juggling act in a country with a weak public schools system, a fragmented family structure—and a yowling obsession with sports.

And yet, much about college football remains just the way Simkins and Rolands described it. There is much glamour and pride in this game—maybe too much. When I started this book, I intended to balance my enthusiasm for big-time college football with a hard-eyed look at what goes on behind the scenes. The sport is a lot like a pretty woman (or handsome man)—nice to look at, but with a complicated personality. Yes, the Saturday games are a thrill. Who doesn't enjoy the color and the pageantry? Who doesn't lean forward in their stadium seat (or TV armchair) at the sight of a long, arcing spiral or a teeth-rattling tackle? Who doesn't marvel at the speed, the grace, the talent, the touchdowns? Who can ignore the human stories—the kids themselves, many of whom push through family or personal hardships to pursue their dreams?

John Henderson, a Nashville native, is one such kid. A junior defensive tackle at Tennessee, he's a mountain with legs—6'7" and 300 pounds, with Godzilla-size hands and strength to match. Ask him what he likes most about football, and he smiles bashfully and says: "The hitting." Henderson is a terror on the field. But off it, he is earnest, thoughtful, innocent. His mom and dad are divorced, but he talks to one of them almost every day. "He's one of the best kids you'll ever meet," says Maurice Fitzgerald, the football coach at Pearl-Cohn High School in Nashville, where Henderson was a star player. "He's probably got the cleanest room on the Tennessee campus. He enjoys blending in and being a regular student."

That's not easy for a guy with Henderson's athletic background. He came out of high school as the top defensive-line prospect in America. According to Fitzgerald, Henderson had thirty-five sacks as a senior. He was said to be "unblockable." Tennessee football fans waited breathlessly for his arrival in Knoxville.

But they had to wait a little longer than expected. Big John didn't qualify to play football as a freshman in 1998. He took his standardized ACT test four times—and fell tantalizingly short of the sum score needed to become a full college qualifier, under NCAA rules, and thus eligible to play as a freshman. Henderson had a commendable 2.8 grade point average in high school. That meant that, on the NCAA's sliding initial-eligibility scale, he needed a sum ACT score of 68 to gain full admission. He scored a 67—and, despite repeated attempts, he could not improve his result. "John had a lot of tutoring," said Fitzgerald, "and the tutors said he was prepared. But he told us several times that he was frightened [of the test]. He had anxiety attacks." Henderson and his mom opened the final test score together. To fully qualify, he needed to boost one of his composite marks (in math, science, social studies, or science) from a 16 to a 17. "When we saw the score was a 16, there was all this sadness in the house," said Henderson. "Oh, it was frustrating."

But Big John persevered. He went to UT as a "partial qualifier," which meant that he could practice but not play in games. It might have been the best thing that ever happened to him. Why? Because he made excellent use of his first year. He studied. "I knew I couldn't play, so I beared down on the books," he said. "I went to class the whole year." He took geology, botany,

English, and math. He ended his freshman year with a 3.0 grade point average and was named an SEC scholar athlete. He's more proud of that (but just barely) than the old Cadillac he drives—and labors to shine every weekend. Henderson likes English class. "Teachers have different ways of communicating," he said. "It's good to listen to how they think . . . it's good."

Last fall, just before the start of his sophomore year, he was planning to take thirteen or fourteen hours of classes. He was excited because—after sitting out a year—he was about to pull on the Vols' orange-and-white uniform for the first time and go out and hit people. Asked what his goals were entering the 1999 season, he said in his baritone voice: "I just want to go out there and help the team. I'm kinda itchy about playing. I'm excited." And he wanted to keep "bearing down" on his academics. "I want to get that 3.0 again," he said. "I'd like to do that." Says Carmen Tegeno, Tennessee's associate athletic director for student life, "John is great. He's worked hard [academically]. He goes to class every day. John meets his tutor every day. John takes [school] seriously, very seriously." One reason, say both Tegano and Fitzgerald, is that he's got a very strong family structure. He is close to his parents, as well as one of his uncles.

John Henderson (and other players like him) redeems major-college football for me. One can easily be cynical about this sport. Like so much of life, college football can be messy. Nothing defines SEC football so much as the pure, raw competitiveness of the football programs. These primal rivalries sometimes breed excess—and an inherent tendency (among alumni, college towns, and even the universities themselves) to overlook the excess, in just the way that Indiana has overlooked the excessive personality (to put it politely) of its basketball coach, Bob Knight.

Why? Because Florida football and Tennessee football and Alabama football are sacred cows. Their winning traditions are part and parcel of the very self-image of those states—and of all the people who live in those states. And those football programs are counted on to make money. Florida raised $19 million from individual donors in 1998 alone. People don't like throwing money at losers. "We raise money for two purposes," says John James, executive director of Gator Boosters, "to provide an education for our student-athletes, and to build facilities. The state does not help us with funding. We must do it on our own." Florida has 13,500 individual donors. More than 1,400 contribute $4,000 or more to the school's athletic association every year.

When you are accustomed to winning, and raking in money, it becomes important to keep on winning. Apply that principle to a dozen ultracompetitive SEC programs, or any major-college program, and you get the high-pressure, high-stakes entertainment industry that is college football. And, sometimes, the ethical envelope gets pushed. In 1998, a couple in Auburn, Alabama, confronted the Auburn coach at that time, Terry Bowden. Veronica and Glen Folds told the coach that they suspected some of his football players had broken into their house and stolen $10,000 in cash and $45,000 in jewelry. Bowden reportedly challenged the couple, gave them short shrift, was *not* sympathetic.

According to Veronica Folds, "Bowden asked if we had anything better to do than stir up trouble. I felt we couldn't compete with him, and that [the players] were going to get away with it." Bowden later described the incident as a "very serious thing." Asked about his initial reaction to the couple's charge, Bowden said: "I didn't know what to do. If [the players] stole that money, they should go to jail. But if they say they didn't do it, I gotta believe them."

When Tommy Tuberville replaced Bowden, practically the first thing he did was kick six players off scholarship because he didn't think they were good football players. My bet is that some of those kids will drop out of Auburn, exacerbating the game's high attrition rate.

Both incidents speak volumes about the South's hard-core football culture. Tuberville's move was a cause célèbre at other SEC schools: rival fans were appalled, *appalled*, by his callous and cruel decision. But they conveniently overlook the fact that their own coaches do the same thing. There wasn't much handwringing in Auburn, however. Why? Because while it was surely *unfortunate* that those kids lost their scholarships—well, football *is* a business, and scholarships *aren't* guaranteed for four years, and well, we *do* have to whip Alabama next year—and those players *weren't* going to help us do it, now were they?

Whistleblower

Last spring Linda Bensel-Meyers, a Tennessee English professor, blew the whistle on the Vols' student-athlete tutoring program, which is managed by Carmen Tegano, UT's associate athletic director for student life. Bensel-Meyers charged that English papers turned in by football players in past years had been plagiarized. She also asserted that grades had been altered, and football players funneled into soft majors, to keep them eligibile for competition. Tegeno and Tennessee officials dispute the allegations—and some of the professor's evidence seems old or flimsy. "Do you think I'd still be sitting here if tutors were writing papers?" asked Tegeno. "It's a safe bet that would not be the case. There is no paper writing, and the faculty senate talked to twenty-four tutors. The general counsel talked to fifteen tutors."

Tennessee investigated itself and declared that there had been no NCAA violations. It's not clear what, if anything, will come of the matter. But the central argument that Bensel-Meyers makes—that the UT athletic department should *not* be administering the tutoring program—is valid. Beneath all the heartfelt talk about the importance of education, major-college football teams have a strong interest in keeping their best athletes eligible to play football. That indisputable fact creates an obvious conflict of interest when the athletic department manages the tutoring program—and not just at Tennessee. Nearly all SEC athletic departments do the same thing—administer their student-athlete tutoring programs. Why? I put that question to Tegano, and he had no ready answer. "It's a philosophical question that merits discussion," he said. "If you have credible tutors, does it make any difference who manages them?" My answer is, yes.

Bensel-Meyers pointed out that a large number of UT football players major in urban studies, and she suggested that it is an easy major, of little long-term benefit to the student-athletes. Is it? Tegano says that 31 grades were recently given to UT athletes in eight different urban-studies courses—3 Bs, 16 Cs, 5 Ds and 7 Fs. "Put them all together," he says, "and the average is 2.1—a C. So how easy is that? Urban studies is a much more viable degree major than other degrees in the conference."

He may have a point. Certainly, urban studies seems a relevant major for African American student-athletes, who often come from big cities. At Florida, a sizeable number of football players major in "leisure management." At Alabama, most football players major in "human performance," "sports fitness," "consumer science," "general health studies," or "physical education." Those majors certainly don't sound very demanding—and will *never* be confused with engineering or economics. No doubt, Alabama officials will argue that human performance, sports fitness, and consumer science are actually grueling tests of academic prowess. Keith Carodine, director of academic affairs for the Florida athletic department, explained the leisure-managemeent curriculum to me, and it sounded reasonably rigorous.

The argument Bensel-Meyers makes is that were football not such a consuming sideline for the student-athletes, they might pursue more conventional degrees, of more value to their careers. Again, she has a point. One of the reasons players major in physical education or human performance (what is that, exactly?) is that they are less demanding than other degree programs—less likely to threaten the time or eligibility of certain players. There is an NCAA rule that limits football practice hours to twenty a week—but it gets stretched by everybody. Players spend lots of time watching tape by themselves, which is not technically considered "practice time."

SEC football fans tend to idealize the sport—and do not take kindly to critics like Bensel-Meyers. Indeed, on UT football Internet chat boards, fans absolutely excoriated the English professor. She was villified, insulted, called a traitor and a nut case. Some fans suggested that she was calling attention to the Vol tutoring program because she wanted a promotion! Few fans acknowledged that *maybe, just maybe*, Bensel Meyers had raised a couple of issues at least worthy of serious discussion. Nobody wondered aloud why the UTAD—and just about every other SEC athletic department—*insists* on running what is an *academic* program. Truth be told, there isn't much scrutiny of the academic side of collegiate football. You will rarely see a local newspaper investigate the local football team. It's too politically sensitive. The reporter would soon be *persona non grata* around the athletic department. I've been reading the the *Knoxville News Sentinel* for years, and I've never seen a single comprehensive article on the academic performance of football players—not one. Maybe I missed it. Likewise, you're not apt to find stories in Gainesville questioning old recruiting customs such as Gator players taking impressionable recruits out for nights of heavy drinking. You don't read stories in Alabama about overzealous boosters.

The central issue is that in their neverending quest to stay competitive, win titles, sell luxury boxes, and make money, college football programs must still recruit a significant number of athletes who are borderline students. Inside major-college football, this is where the rubber meets the road. The fact that borderline students are accepted is not, per se, a problem. John Henderson was, by one measure, a borderline student. I don't know of anyone who deserves to be in college more than he does. It's the *number* of such kids who are recruited that raises questions. For every John Henderson who comes ready to crack the books, there is (I would estimate) one football signee who has only a passing interest in class work. In some cases these athletes must be dragged through school for four or more years. They need a lot of academic attention (tutoring)—which, incidentally, the rest of the student-body is not receiving. Tegano points out that many players are eager to learn their first two years in college—and then tend to slack off their studies when the prospect of a pro career begins to dawn.

Teaching "Life Skills"

Every major university athletic department now runs a *major* "life skills" center for its athletes—they have for many years. These centers employ scores of tutors—and are increasingly engaged in providing a range of testing and counseling services for athletes—for substance-abuse, anger-management, career, and family issues. Those are social services—of a type that might be employed by a state agency. Athletic administrators speak of their academic/life-skill centers with pride, and well they should: they are well-run, do very good things, provide tangible help to the players. But they also beg the question: Why are they needed in the first place? And why do they keep getting bigger—to the point where they've begun to resemble little subsidiary schools/social agencies for the athletes?

The answer, again, is obvious: a significant number of major-college football players struggled to graduate from public high schools. Many come from poor families and single-parent homes, where education was not emphasized. They are good kids, but many have what Gerry DiNardo, the former LSU coach, calls "issues." Hence the booming business in "life skills" training. Without it, many of the better athletes in the SEC would disappear in a year or two.

Some still do, despite the considerable attention they receive. Tennessee recruited Onterrio Smith out of California two years ago. He is a very gifted running back—but he had "issues." Though unmarried, he's got a child. He was arrested a few months ago for assaulting the mother. On top of that, he reportedly flunked "multiple" drug tests at Tennessee. He was kicked off the team. Is the university, or the football coach, to be blamed for accepting him in the first place? Maybe. Some SEC teams—Alabama chief among them—now routinely sign thirty or more prospects annually—even though only twenty-five can receive athletic scholarships. Reason: the school knows that half a dozen players, typically, will not get into school.

There are more than a few kids like Smith in the system. Some buckle down and prosper; others do not. Who knows who'll succeed and who will fail? Certainly, colleges aren't to blame for those who fall by the wayside. Social problems start early in life. Coaches and recruiters will tell you that they are working hard to weed out bad apples, scrutinize recruits, find players who want to learn.

But make no mistake: coaches get paid to win. That is the bottom line. To do that, they must recruit the best players—and the better the athlete, the more likely he is to have academic or behavioral problems. Teams still recruit bad apples because they know the Darwinian fact: if they don't grab them and take a chance, a rival will. That's the system. Tegano and his SEC counterparts review the backgrounds of prospects that their coaches are recruiting. If there are warning signs—say, poor attendance in high school—they alert the coaches, and perhaps even suggest that the team back away from the prospect. Do the coaches comply? As Tegano acknowledges, it depends on how good the prospect is. "I'll be honest with you," he says. "If it's a great player, I'm not going to win the battle. If a player has the potential to be a problem, and he's Jamal Lewis, the coaches will continue to recruit him." That fact explains why a small number of players get into trouble. "Family background is important,"says Tegano. "If a kid comes from a two-parent family that values education, he doesn't have any problem."

The most disturbing thing I learned while researching this book is that SEC presidents are, in fact, not very powerful—not compared to their athletic departments, anyway. They are paid far less than the football coaches. What could be more symbolic of their place in the pecking order? Many do not stay in their jobs very long, partly because they get tired of clanking swords with the atavistic football factions at their school—the old-timers (most conspicuous at Alabama, but they are everywhere) who believe that everything with the football team would be fine if only those pointy-headed, bicycle-riding, long-haired, liberal *academic* types would stop carping about the importance of *ed-u-ca-tion*. Bear Bryant once said that "nobody ever rallied around a math class." But maybe that's because we don't have enough people in America talking about the importance of math.

Having said all this, I don't view major-college football like many critics do—those from privileged backgrounds, particularly. They view the sport as essentially evil—as corrupt, as exploitative, as something that cries out to be reined in. They hew to a high-minded university ideal which, by and large, does not really exist. Below the elite-university level, and in most parts of the country, "college" is a very practical undertaking for both the students and the institutions themselves. Students go to college if they have the money, if they have the motivation, if they have the grades, and if they don't have pressing family problems. The institutions themselves must make compromises to attract students and stay financially viable. The college graduation rate in America is only about 50 to 55 percent.

There are a lot of good things about college football. The kids benefit from the discipline imposed on them. They must learn to manage themselves and their time. Those who aren't motivated, who don't mature, don't last. There are many admirable people in the business—athletes, coaches, administrators. One doesn't hear much about the good—that Darwin Walker, a Tennessee defensive tackle, got a degree in engineering and opted *not* to leave early for the pros; that Billy Ratliff played through numerous injuries and still found time to hobble into hospitals and boys' clubs to cheer up patients and kids from troubled families. That Steve Spurrier helps raise money for ex-Gator athletes; that Ole Miss still takes time to tell its new players about the contributions of those who have passed through its football program before—like Chucky Mullins, who injured his spinal cord during a game, was paralyzed, and later died. One doesn't hear much about Phillip Fulmer taking his team to church or giving speeches to the Boy Scouts; one doesn't hear about David Cutcliffe and Lou Holtz setting high ethical standards for their players.

BRAGGING RIGHTS

"Providing Opportunities Is Our Business"

The real issue, I think, is proportion. How many risky students can you take—should you take? Whom do you recruit? That's the heart of the matter. Raynoch Thompson, the former Tennessee All-America linebacker, grew up in the New Orleans projects, without a father. He has a brother in jail (a not uncommon thing among football players). Did Thompson, who was a partial qualifier, who spent four years at Tennessee but did not graduate, belong in college? Did he benefit from college? I say yes to both questions. For while one could argue that Thompson was more athlete than student, he did in fact make significant progress toward a degree—and did so while, in effect, holding down a second job, football.

Had he not gone to college, Thompson might very well be hanging out on the mean streets, or worse. Having completed four years at UT, he is within striking distance of his degree—and the school will try to get him back on campus, as it should, to earn it. If he does, he was scholarship money well spent. If not, well, he was not such a good investment. Universities are not social agencies, to be sure, but as Bo Bahnsen, the compliance coordinator at LSU, puts it, "Providing opportunities is our business." Adds Pat Culbertson, LSU's faculty representative to the NCAA and chairman of the university's athletic council: "If we only recruited student athletes whom we were certain would graduate, we wouldn't be competitive on the football field, and we wouldn't be fulfilling our mission (as a state land-grant university) to the sons and daughters of Louisiana. We need to take risks for both reasons."

That said, Culbertson would like to see football schools "pay more attention to academics." Who wouldn't? One of the problems with major-college football is that the athletes are thrown into a very intense football culture as soon as they set foot on campus. They have little or no time to adjust to the academic and social challenges of college life. They start practice every year two or three weeks before school begins—and then, on top of that, September and October are the most frenetic months on the football calendar.

The players are told to study, urged to keep their wits about them. But that can be hard for youngsters to do when half their college life is devoted to football—and when everybody in the community is going loco about the huge game coming up on Saturday. How can one *not* get caught up in the large noisy parade that is big-time college football? As Thompson put it, "There are distractions." Lots of distractions. A Tibetan monk would have trouble keeping his focus in such an environment.

Some freshman footballers get a head start by taking a summer-school course before the official start of their freshman year. But typically the students must pay for such courses themselves. Says Culbertson: "One of the things we have pushed for at LSU, in terms of national legislation, would be to place our student-athletes on athletic aid during the summer before their official entrance. That would give them a jump academically, in terms of knowing what is expected of them. It could be very beneficial to their academic experience and the graduation rate. College is quite an adjustment for young people, some of whom have never been out of Carencro, Louisiana."

Or why not go back to the old rule of making all freshman athletes *ineligible* for varsity sports? Most partial qualifiers certainly seem to benefit from the first-year pause in their football career. Like Henderson, it gives them precious time to get their feet on the ground, to learn how to study. Athletic administrators say that idea is impractical because the scholarship limit of eighty-five is too low. Were freshmen ineligible, there wouldn't be enough players. Then why not expand the scholarship limit by, say, five or ten?

Beyond that, I believe that the NCAA should ratchet up initial eligibility standards a notch or two. Right now, they are quite low and considerably below the university entrance requirements for regular students. While the test-score issue is explosive, Culbertson says the core-curriculum requirements could be boosted. "I would like to see the NCAA have more academic units figured into the computation of [high school] grade point average. Right now, only thirteen units are applied. That says that academic preparation can be minimal," says Culbertson, "and I think that it's a mistake. I'd like to see us get more toward fifteen or sixteen units. We ought to require better and broader preparation for college."

Officials at Vanderbilt, where the vast majority of the football players graduate, believe their program should be the model for college football—or at least SEC football. They believe that universities should be held accountable for their high rates of attrition and sometimes low rates of graduation. One Vandy idea: take scholarships away from universities whose attrition and graduation rates fall below a certain threshold. I like that idea, but Vandy, a small private school, will have great trouble leading the big horses to water. "Schools legislate in their self-interest," says Bud Ford, Tennessee's media-relations director, implying that what is good for Vandy is not necessarily of benefit to larger schools.

"A Good Thing"

Jeremy Foley, the Florida athletic director, is a graduate of Hobart College—one of those small, northern liberal arts colleges where they must *hate* major-college football. He has been at Florida for twenty-three years. He's seen the downside of Florida football—years of losing and two NCAA sanctions. More recently, he's bathed in the glow of a football program that won ten games six straight years during the 1990s. Foley is bright and articulate—and an impassioned defender of SEC football, which has been good to him. I asked him, Is SEC football exessive? "Noooooo," came the quick reply. "Obviously I'm prejudiced, but I hear that complaint all the time. 'It's too big, it's a business, it's excessive.' If we lose sight of our main responsibility—which is to produce student-athletes and focus on academics, focus on making the players better citizens, and all we cared about was winning championships—if we lose that, then, yeah, it would be excessive. That's where people like myself, along with coaches and administrators and fans, have got to recognize that we need to keep it all in perspective. I've been here when the program wasn't run well and we had NCAA problems that were detrimental to the university. But if the program is about the right things and has some success, it can be beneficial to the entire university. It generates esprit de corps, makes alums want to come back. It makes people feel good about the university. And whether people like it or not, the exposure college sports gets is phenomenal. If you're on TV, people are talking about the university—not just the football team but the university. It raises the awarness of your university. So, no, I don't think it's excessive. I think it's a good thing."

Foley goes on: "Certainly, we have our share of problems. Every business does. Certainly, there are things we can do better. Every individual, every corporation, can do better. There are gambling issues, agent issues, academic issues, citizenship isues. When we have an athlete who strays, it's headline news. That's the world we live in. You wish bad things didn't happen. You can either throw your hands up and say, 'What are we going to do?' Or you can say, 'Hey, these things exist; let's fight through them and continue to educate peope about what we should and should not be doing. And let's focus on all the good things that are happening.'

"It's a common theme right now to want to beat up on the NCAA. Fine, we have some issues we need to deal with. We need to get better, and we will get better. But the NCAA as an organization does a lot of good things for intercollegiate athletics. It's the governing body. There are a lot of good things happening out there, all right? I'm not bewailing the fact that the good isn't reported. I just think that as administrators, we need to focus on the good, fight the challenges we need to fight, and when all is said and done we can produce a product that nine out of ten people will see as good. There will always be naysayers out there, and I understand that."

College football is a panorama—a great game with flaws. It once seemed a simple sport. It is now a complex enterprise serving many constituencies—the players, who occupy center stage; the coaches, whose jobs depend on player

A Summing Up

talent and player performance; the university alums, whose donations often ebb and flow in accordance with win-loss records; the fans, who attach great importance to winning; and the administrators, who must try to balance the players' interests with those of the school and the state and the fans.

On autumn Saturdays, leaves fall and the warts fade from view. The crowds boisterously emerge, the bands (loud and iridescent) strike up, the young men (rugged and confident) take the field. There is a great clatter in Oxford and Tuscaloosa, in Auburn and Columbia, in Knoxville and Gainesville, in Starkville and Athens, in Lexington and Baton Rouge, in Fayetteville and Nashville. Away from the roar of the stadiums, life slows in quiet anticipation. People know: a game is at hand. For four hours, all else is put aside. Southern passions—deep and primal—quietly surge. Life is reduced to blocking and tackling, throwing and catching. The game then becomes simple; the competitive fires, eternal. Bragging rights are on the line. It's time to play the game.

TWENTY-FOUR

FAVORITE THINGS

I spent months visiting SEC schools—not all of them, but most—watching games, eating, drinking, talking to fans, soaking up the football culture. Here are my (highly subjective) picks for . . .

Best School Colors:

1. **Ole Miss:** cardinal red and navy blue
2. **(Tie) Georgia:** red and black is a fine pairing with those well-known silver britches.

    LSU: purple and gold

Best Overall Saturday Football Experience:

1. **Neyland Stadium, Knoxville:** The total package—an impressive stadium, nice location (on the Tennessee river), a noisy crowd. And we do like the distinctive checkerboard end zones.
2. **Ben Hill Griffin Stadium, Gainesville:** A band box, but it's electric on a big-game Saturday night.

Best Social (Party) School

1. **Georgia:** Can't beat the downtown Athens music scene. About forty bars—with names like High Hat and Tasty World—and nearly that many bands on weekends. What other college town has a spot, World Bar, that sells hundreds of international beers and an excellent selection of single-malt scotch? It's for the professors!
2. **Florida:** Whew! Let's just say they are not bashful on football weekends. The Purple Porpoise and the Swamp are the places to be on University Avenue. And the downtown scene ain't bad, either.

Favorite Things

Prettiest Campus:
1. **Auburn:** Who knew? It's nice, and so much *brick*. The town is manageable, except for the traffic on Saturdays.
2. **(Tie) Ole Miss:** Small and stately—Oxford drips with tradition. Makes me wish I'd worn Oxford shirts, joined a fraternity, and dated a beauty queen in college. They still choose them at Mississippi. And both William Faulkner and John Grisham have lived in the town.

   Alabama: Large and stately. The president's mansion (six Ionic columns) is a grand historic site, full of American antiques. The Yankees wanted to burn it down, but were sweet-talked out of it by the university president's wife.

Best Academics:
Vanderbilt

Wittiest Coach:
Lou Holtz, South Carolina

Dimwittiest Coach
Ummm . . . : *You* choose!

Best Student Football Traditions:
1. **Toomer's Corner, Auburn:** Everybody's got a "walk" nowadays. At Auburn, they roll a street corner in toilet paper after victories. Now *that's* original.
2. **Hand prints at the Bell Tower, Alabama:** Football captains through the years literally leave their mark.
3. **Ringing the chapel bell, Georgia**

Best Alumni Tradition
The Grove, Ole Miss: Bloody Marys, succulent food—and, if you're polite, Archie Manning just might talk a little football with you.

Best Food:
1. **Dreamland, Tuscaloosa:** White bread, iced tea, and ribs, ribs, ribs. The real deal. Sweet home, Alabama.
2. **(Tie) Cajun cuisine, LSU:** Po'boys, jambalaya, and crayfish—my goodness.

   Varsity Inn, Athens: A fast-food mecca for football fans.
3. **Waysider, Tuscaloosa:** Grits, biscuits, and Daniel Moore paintings under a crimson roof.

BRAGGING RIGHTS

Strangest SEC sight, 1999:
A Hare Krishna band outside Ben Hill Griffin Stadium in Gainesville.

Most dramatic moment, 1999 season:
After Tennessee has scored a touchdown to take a 21-7 fourth-quarter lead over Alabama, the Tennessee defense is woofing on the sidelines while awaiting the kickoff. Spencer Riley, the Vol center, stokes the passions of the defensive unit by screaming: "Blood makes the grass grow! Blood makes the grass grow!"

Best Mascot:
1. **Georgia:** Uga, the white English bulldog, is thick-bodied, pugnacious—and wears a letterman's shirt.
2. **LSU:** In Baton Rouge, they drive a caged, 520-pound Bengal tiger named Mike around the field, with cheerleaders sitting happily on top. It's a sight, but as mascots go perhaps a bit *much*.

Prettiest Women
C'mon, there is no way to pick this one! Everyone's a winner here.

Best southern ditty:
"Song to Grits," by Roy Blount, Jr.

> When my mind's unsettled,
> When I don't feel spruce,
> When my nerves get frazzled,
> When my flesh gets loose,
> What knits me back together's
> Grits.
>
> Grits, grits, it's grits I sing,
> Grits fit in with anything.
>
> True grits, more grits,
> Fish, grits and collards,
> Life is good when grits are swallered.
> Grits sits right.
>
> Grits with gravy,
> Grits with cheese,
> Grits with bacon,
> Grits with peas,
> Grits with a minimum
> of two over-medium mixed in 'em: Um!
> Grits fit in with anything.

Favorite Things

Rich and poor,
black and white,
Lutheran and Campbell,
Jews and Southern Jesuits
All acknowledge buttered grits.

Give me two hands,
Give me my wits,
Give me fifty pounds of grits.

Grits at taps,
Grits at reveille,
I'm into grits real heavily.

BRAGGING RIGHTS

How Many College Students Does It Take to Change a Lightbulb in the South?

At **Vanderbilt**, it takes two. One to change the bulb, and one more to explain how they did it every bit as well as any Ivy Leaguer.

At **Georgia**, it takes three. One to change the bulb, and two to phone a friend at Georgia Tech and get instructions.

At **Florida**, it takes four. One to screw in the bulb, and three to figure out how to get high off the old one.

At **Alabama**, it takes five. One to change it, two to talk about how Bear Bryant would have done it, and two to throw the old bulb at Auburn students.

At **Ole Miss**, it takes six. One to change it, two to mix the drinks, and three to find the perfect J. Crew outfit to wear for the occasion.

At **LSU**, it takes seven—and each one gets credit for four semester hours.

At **Kentucky**, it takes eight. One to screw it in, and seven to discuss how much brighter it shines during basketball season.

At **Tennessee**, it takes ten. Two to figure out how to screw it in, two to buy an orange lampshade, and six to phone a radio call-in show and talk about how Phillip Fulmer is too stupid to do it.

At **Mississippi State**, it takes fifteen. One to screw in the bulb, two to buy the Skoal, and twelve to shout, "GO TO HELL, OLE MISS, GO TO HELL!!!"

At **Auburn**, it takes 100. One to change it, forty-nine to talk about how they do it better than Bama, and fifty who realize it's all a lie.

At **South Carolina**, it takes 80,000. One to screw it in, and 79,999 to discuss how this will finally be the year they have a good football team.

At **Arkansas**, it takes none. There is no electricity in Arkansas.